EVERYTHING ORIGA

Everything Origami is written for everyone who wants to fold paper. For beginners and experienced folders alike, there is always something new to learn. The secret to learning is to be patient, so everytime you do origami, don't rush, find your own pace, and take time to share it with everyone you can.

Matthew Gardiner, photographed by Christian Alexander.

THE AUTHOR

Matthew Gardiner

Matthew is an artist whose love of origami and technology is exemplified in Oribotics, a hybrid of robotics and origami (see www.matthewgardiner.net/art/Oribotics_origin). He is devoted to fostering origami in Australia, and for that reason he studied the subtle art of origami diagramming, and convention organisation with the Japanese Origami Academic Society.

THE CONTRIBUTORS

My Trinh Gardiner, graphic designer.

My Trinh (born My Trinh Ha) brings her German design aesthetic and logic to the origami diagrams in this book. Her love for origami has blossomed through her visits to Japanese origami conventions. The origami world knows her best for her design work on the Folding Australia convention books.

Darren Scott, origami artist.

Darren has been known to make off-the-cuff suggestions that result in ludicrously large origami projects like a walk-in-able house built from paper bricks, complete with origami laptop, a couch, sushi on a tray, and a penguin.

Jonathan Baxter, origami artist.

Jonathan Baxter has spent nearly 30 years exploring the origami world on journeys that have taken him around the world. From full-size dinosaurs, to city-wide festivals, to live action origami performances he has enjoyed stretching people's imaginations with what is possible with the paper-folding medium.

Steven Casey, origami artist.

Steven's innovative origami style has been cultivated for over 30 years, pursuing the ultimate echidna design from a single sheet. His work is highly regarded by the British, Japanese, USA, and other, international origami societies.

About Origami

What is origami?

Origami is a curious sounding word because it is not English, but Japanese in origin. Ori, from the root verb oru, means 'to fold' and kami is one of the many terms for paper. In the purest renditions, origami creates an intended shape from a single sheet of paper with no cutting, glueing, taping or any other fastening device allowed. To create less rigid versions one may make small cuts as in kirigami (cut paper) or long slits as in senbazuru – where a single sheet is effectively divided into a number of smaller, still connected squares. This book focuses on the action of folding paper and the manifestations from this action, although an occasional design requires cutting.

The origin of origami

No-one really knows when origami was invented. We do know that paper had to be invented first, so we can safely say that it is less than 2000 years old, but an exact date, even to the nearest century, cannot be authentically established. Despite its Japanese name, some claim that it is Chinese in origin; this cannot be entirely discounted since many art forms now claimed by others can be traced back to mainland China. We will accept that this art activity has been around for a long time.

One reason for origami's hazy history is that for many centuries there was almost no documentation on how to do it. The oldest book known to contain origami-like instructions, the Kanamodo, is from the 17th century, yet older woodblock prints show paper folding. The oldest origami book for amusement in the world is the *Hiden Senbazuru Orikata* from 1797. The title roughly translated means the secret technique of folding one thousand cranes. There are around one hundred designs known as 'traditional origami', that were passed from hand to hand in Japanese culture: typically a mother showing a child, or children sharing among themselves. In fact, until the middle of the 20th century, origami was thought of as something that women did as decorations for weddings, funerals and other ceremonial occasions, or something that young children did as a recreational pursuit.

Frederick Wilhelm August Froebel

Frederick Wilhelm August Froebel (1782 - 1852), a German who pioneered the concept of kindergartens or pre-schools, recognised the advantages of early education. He saw the potential of paper folding in assisting young minds to grasp the mathematical concepts of proportion, ratio and symmetry through simple origami models and related activities such as tanagrams. In and after his work origami was used primarily with young people as a way to improve listening, as well as improve cognitive and dexterity skills; it does not seem to have been used as a tool for teaching curriculum subjects. Nor was it followed up with further exercises at the elementary or high school level, not even in Germany or Japan. There is T. Sundara Rowe's 1893 book *Geometric Exercises in Paper Folding*, but there is no evidence of its material being used in any maths-based curriculum.

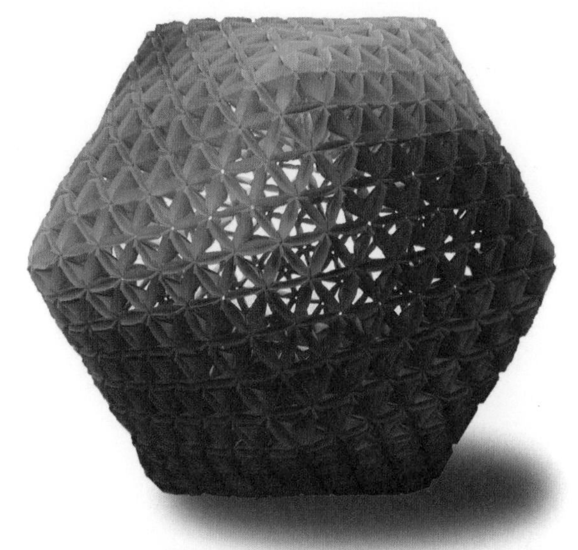

Miyuki Kawamura, Geosphere, Japan.
Miyuki Kawamura's amazing origami is possible because of her love of folding, art and mathematics.

Travel of origami

So origami, for the most part, stays in the background as an obscure, whimsical diversion until after the Second World War, when people from around the world started to visit Japan in greater numbers, and Japanese citizens increased their travel to other countries. Unwittingly, this seemingly innocent pastime started to spread around the world, especially with exchange students – those young ambassadors of Japanese culture. The intrepid exchange students might not be conversant in the language of their hosts, yet they could communicate through origami as their fingers did the talking. A finished model could be given as a gift, cementing a friendship through paper folding.

The gift of an origami crane brings peace and friendship around the world.

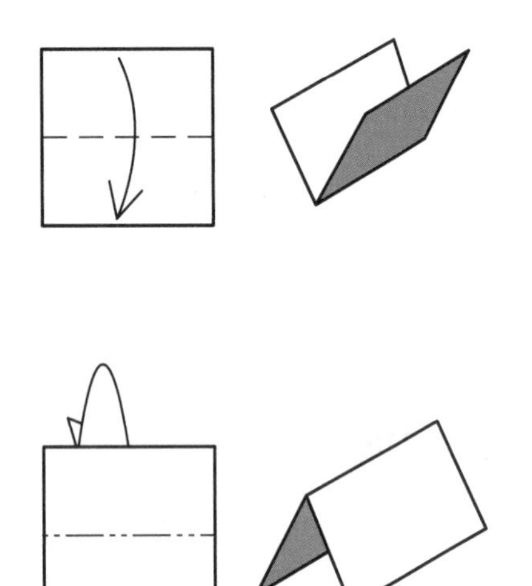

Origami notation, or symbols; the keys to understanding origami. The most basic folds, valley and mountain folds, are described by dashed, and dashed and dotted lines respectively.

Creation of Diagrams

Another important development in the post World War II era was the creation of the standard notation to explain the steps to fold a design. This accomplishment is attributed to two pioneers of the contemporary origami movement, Akira Yoshizawa of Japan and Samuel Randlett of the United States of America. Their ingenious efforts mean that a paper folder in one country using this standard form of notation can share the instructions for making their designs with a paper folder from another country without either understanding the language of the other. You will find a list of these notations at the end if this chapter and at the beginning of many books on origami. Please study them carefully – they really are the key to fully understanding the instructions throughout the manual.

David Brill, Horse, diagrams published in 'Brilliant Origami'.

Birth of Contemporary Origami

As exchange students moved on, leaving behind warm memories and basic folding skills, experimentation began to take place and new designs began to emerge. As a contemporary collection of designs evolved, new methods for folding the paper were discovered, new approaches for extracting the desired shape from the paper were developed, and the field of fine art origami began to mature.

At the dawn of this contemporary age of origami new creations often came from varying those already in existence. Many came from what we know as 'base folds' because they are the start of traditional models – many, including the Fish, Frog, Bird and Water-bomb bases, are named after these traditional models. A number of these have been included at the end of this chapter and again I urge you to study these carefully, as many of the models featured in the manual are derived from them. Traditional base folds had limitations for subject matter with many appendages, such as insects or octopi. So new base folds evolved that divided paper in the proportions required, along with new techniques for collapsing paper into these shapes. Some designers, notably Robert Lang, have even used mathematical theory and computer programs to design bases with the desired proportions and number of appendages. Experimentation produced different specialties and preferences for both the starting and ending configurations. Dollar bill folding starts with a rectangle instead of a square and modular origami starts with many pieces of paper instead of a single one. Paper airplanes and action models end with a model that is not static, but should fly or move.

Satoshi Kamiya's Ryujin 3.5, from a single sheet of paper. The inclusion of 3.5 in the title indicates the version; like software, origami design can be updated.

Robert Lang's Samurai Helmet Beetle, a masterwork of origami insect design.

Origami Artist Jonathan Baxter folded a series of massive scale dinosaur skeletons in the USA – this one eighth scale model is 3m (10ft) from nose to tail. The full scale version was 30m (100ft) in length.

In the '50s and early '60s we start to see a handful of origami books printed in English containing international designs. In the '70s and '80s this increases to several dozen, and in the early years of the 21st century hundreds of publications in the English language contain unique origami designs. Now there are more than 30,000 documented designs with hundreds of new designs being invented each year. Some of these designs place several hundred creases in a single square of paper to create the desired shape, while others may make a few folds in many pieces of paper and connect them together to create elaborate geometric shapes.

Evidence of the renaissance: 'The Lord of the Rings' "Three hunters", Gimli, Aragorn, Legolas, by a little folder from a Paris suburb, Eric Joisel.

When reflecting on the history of origami, with the accelerated pace of new designs, and understanding of its potential, we can safely say that the late 20th and early 21st century is origami's renaissance period. I know of no other art form as ancient as origami that can make this claim. Why should a venerable, ancient art form from one culture flourish best when exposed to the outside world? While there are many leading Japanese in contemporary origami there can be no doubt that outside influences from beyond its cultural roots have accelerated discoveries and developments in the origami of the 21st century.

East and West

One often-mentioned theory pertains to the different ways that eastern and western societies approach instruction in art. The eastern tradition is to master techniques exactly as shown by the teacher (sensei); mastering the art is performing with a perfection comparable to that of the instructor. I recall, from a class given by Japan's legendary origami master, Akira Yoshizawa, one assignment of folding a simple sheep head. The sensei had provided the instructions, numbering no more than half a dozen steps, to an experienced class which had no trouble following them. But when the results were inspected, everyone had failed! In order to impress the sensei, each student had embellished the design with small details or nuances to make the ovine head more life-like! The big mistake was that we had not done what the sensei asked, but rather had created our own sheep heads from his design. Therein lies the difference between the two cultures. In the West we tend to de-construct, pull things apart, do our own thing, re-assemble them in different configurations. It is frowned upon in western art to reproduce the same image twice; how could that be creative? So in the West those origami paper gifts of birds and boxes, frogs and hats, were carefully taken apart, studied and re-assembled.

Paul Jackson, of the Israeli Origami Centre, is famous for his abstract origami forms. This work is 25cm high and is hand coloured with pastel.

Origami House by Melbourne Origami Group. A life-size origami house, complete with chairs, laptop, light switches, sushi and a penguin! All from folded paper.

Buddha, Takashi Hojyo, Tokyo, Japan
Takashi Hojyo is is renowned for his complex single sheet origami works that have a strong sculptural feel.

Along the way new methods and techniques for creating shapes from paper were discovered and, in the spirit that has traditionally emanated from the art of paper folding, these were shared with others through informal gatherings and later at national and international conventions.

Japan will always be looked upon as the world centre of origami. Although substantial innovations and discoveries have occurred elsewhere in the world, it must now truly be considered an international art form. One can find origami books written in English, French, Spanish, German, Russian, Italian, Hebrew, and a host of other languages. Just as Swiss cheese need no longer be Swiss, Russian eggs be Russian, or French water colour painting be French, so too do we come to accept that origami need no longer be Japanese.

Increasing status of origami

Even though developments have accelerated in recent decades, the level of understanding that we have today did not happen overnight. It has taken tens of thousands of hours of patient experimentation to reach the standards of today's modern designs. When making a design, recording the steps in origami notation, and unfolding the result (that western deconstruction habit), the origami designer begins to see the placement and layout of creases and their relationship to each other.

The trained origami eye can read the crease lines on a sheet of paper, interpret their significance, and collapse the paper into the shape its designer intended. You can see the creases in the paper as being the messages, or encoded instructions the folder seeks to transfer to the paper in order to extract the desired shape. No amount of yelling, wishing or coaxing can change the shape of the paper, but with the right messages through creasing the paper it becomes like clay in the hands of an origami artist. In fact, an ever-growing number of designs exist only as crease pattern designs, due to their complexity and use of techniques that defy standard notation. One literally places all the creases needed to complete the model (or at least the base), on the paper first before collapsing it down into the specified shape. It is not uncommon for several hundred pre-creases to be placed in the paper before collapsing.

Devil and Fractal Pyramid, Jun Maekawa, Tokyo, Japan.
Jun Maekawa's famous sell-out book "Viva Origami", published in 1983, introduced the world to complex origami.

Pleurotes de l'olivier - Omphalotus olearius
Vincent Floderer from France continually evolves his own crumpling technique to create very natural origami works.

HOW TO FOLD

BY: MATTHEW GARDINER

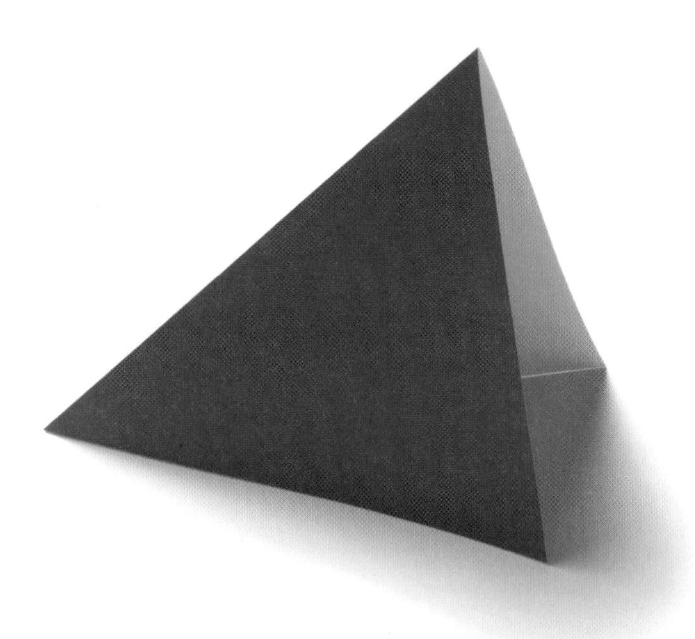

The art of origami begins with simple folds. Many beginners rush through their first folds, not paying attention to accuracy. The key to high quality origami is the quality of each fold. There are many kinds of folds, but the principles described below can be applied to most folds. Origami paper has a coloured side and a white side. When diagrams refer to the coloured side, it is to indicate which colour will be the dominant colour in the final model.

Good origami is patient origami.

1

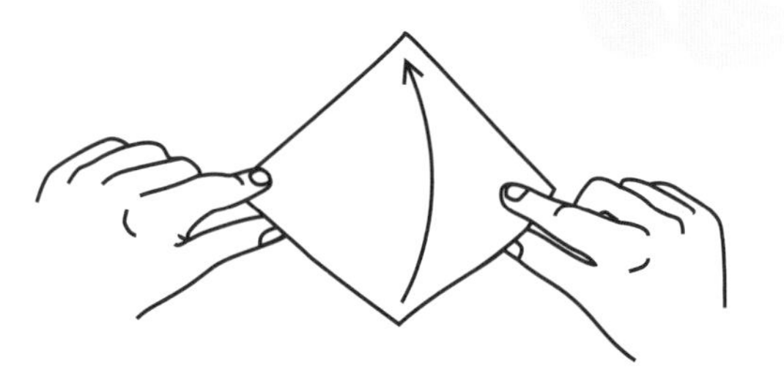

Gently lift the bottom corner to the top corner. Don't crease yet, just hold the paper in position.

2

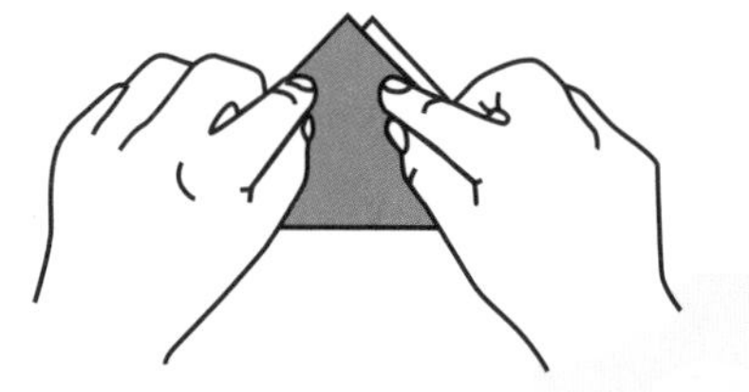

Line up the corners exactly. The image above is not aligned correctly.

3

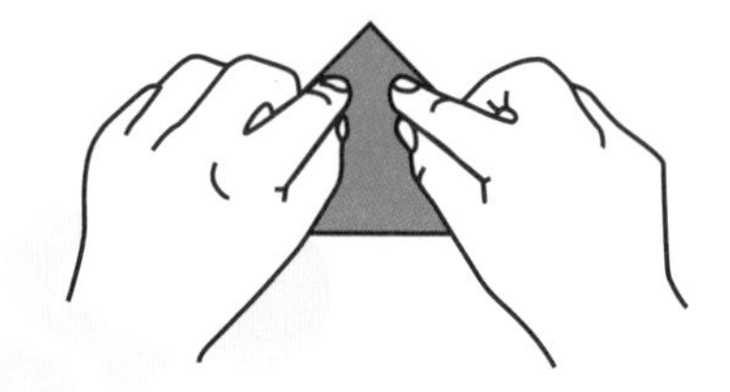

The corners are exactly aligned; there is no visible difference.

4

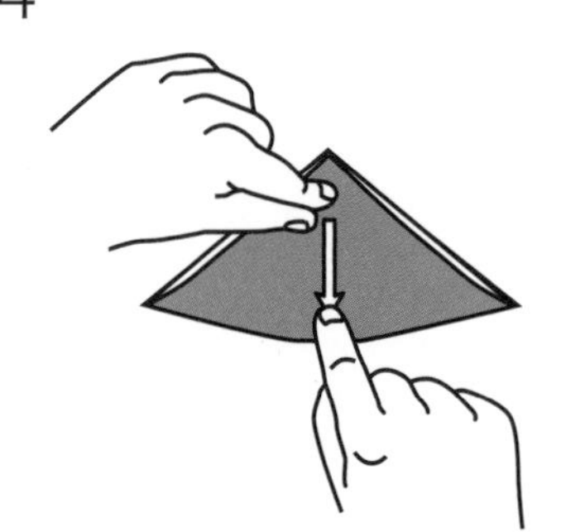

Hold the corner with one hand, and slide the forefinger of the other hand down to the bottom.

5

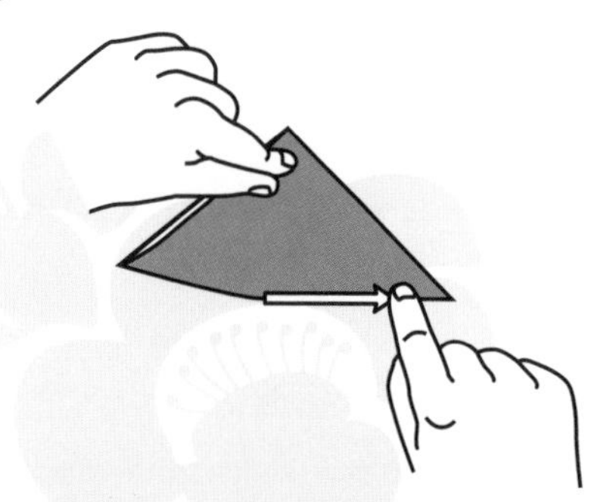

Crease from the centre to the edge. Check that the crease goes exactly through the corner.

6

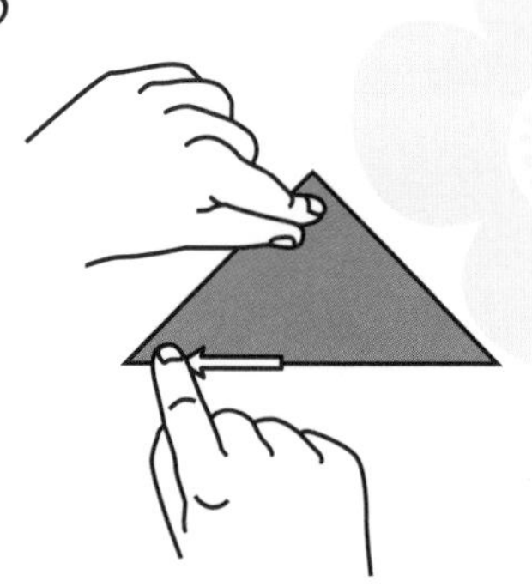

Crease from the centre to the edge on the other side to complete the fold.

Like the diagonal fold the book fold is very simple. The best way to make both folds is to check twice (or more) and fold once. In origami, to check is to use other parts of the paper as references to make sure your crease is accurate. In these two introductory folds, the edges and corners are the references. In origami you will use existing creases, corners, edges, intersections of creases, and points to help make sure your fold is accurate.

Good origami is accurate origami.

1

Lift the bottom edge to the top edge.

2

Align the corners and then align the edges and the edges on one side.

3

Align the opposite corner and edges so that both sides are perfectly aligned.

4

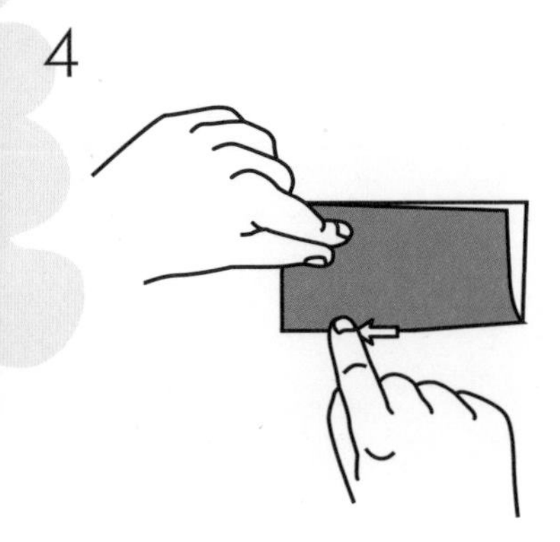

Hold one corner and crease from the centre to the edge.

5

Crease from the centre to the other edge to complete the fold. All corners and edges should be aligned.

SYMBOLS

BY: MATTHEW GARDINER

LINES

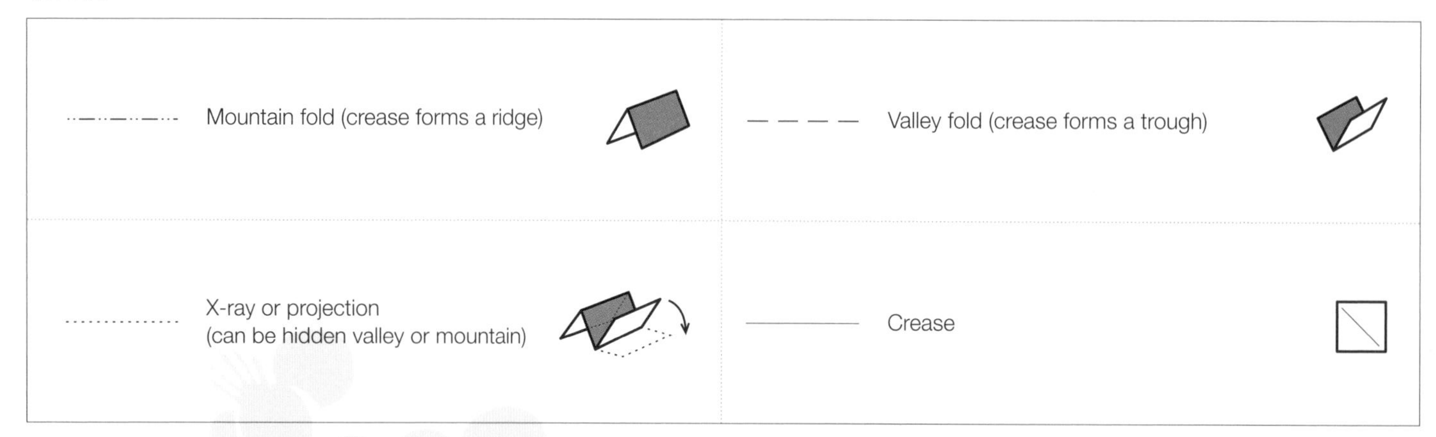

ARROWS

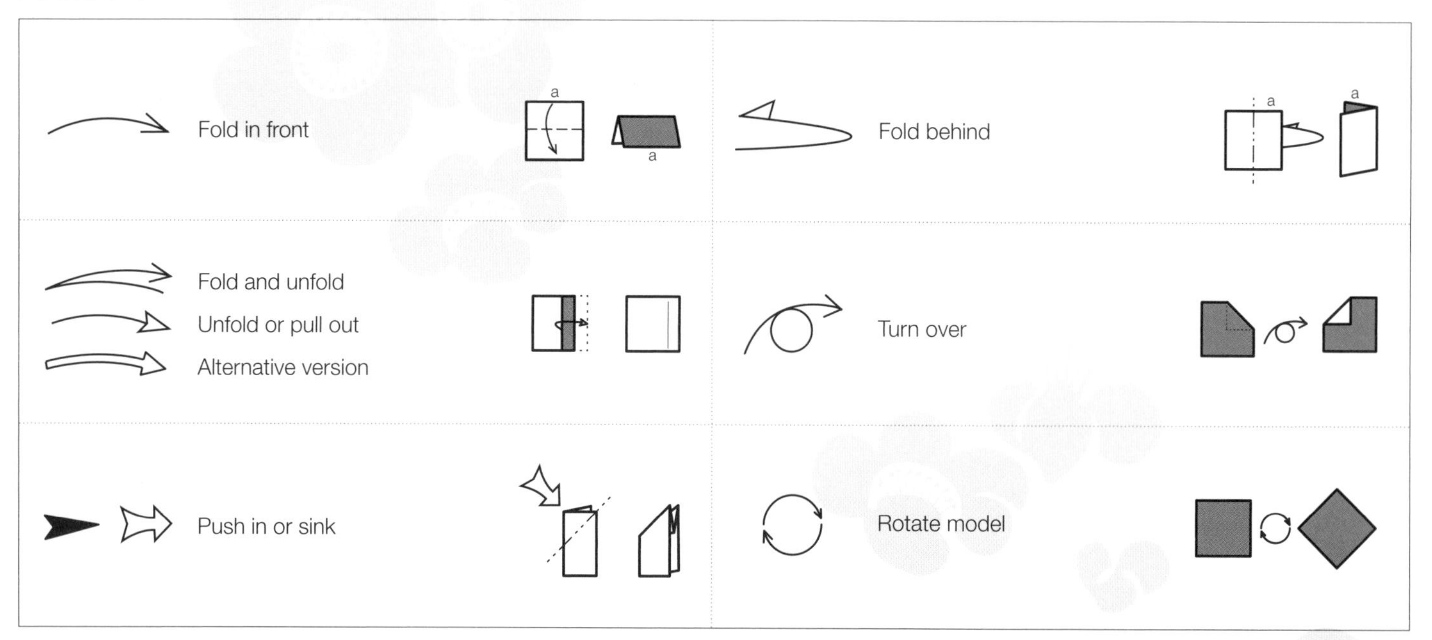

EXTRAS

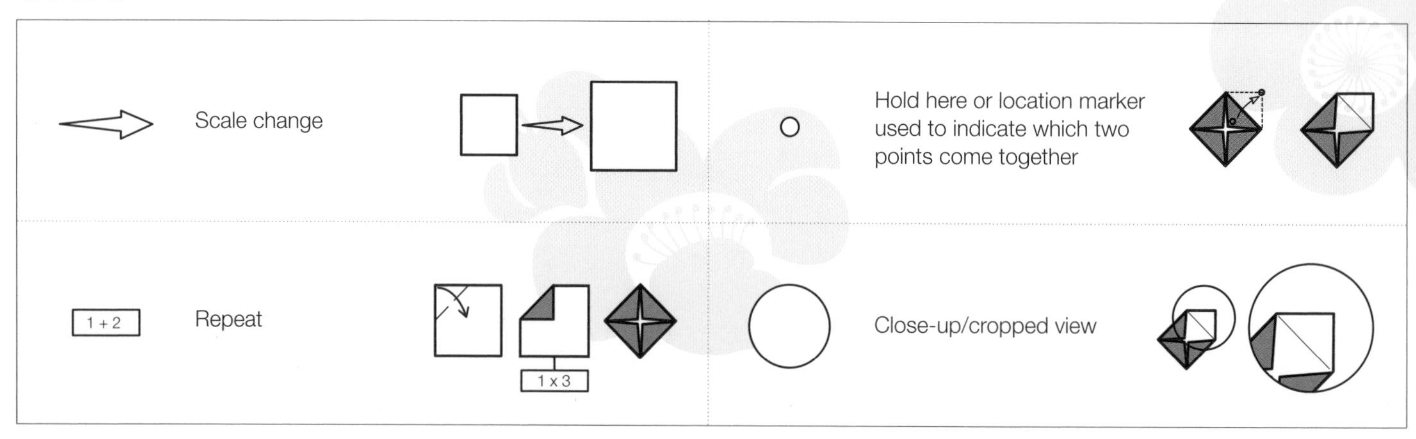

Types of Folds

BY: Matthew Gardiner

Book fold

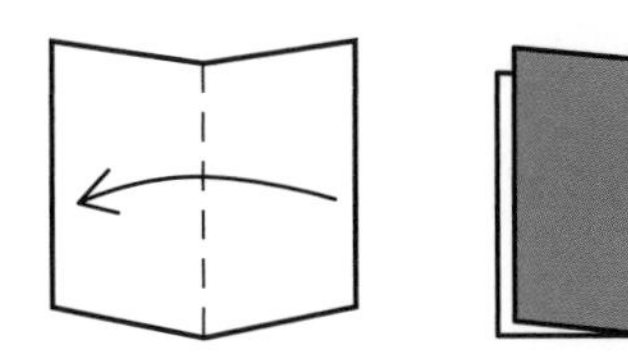

Valley fold one edge to another, like closing a book.

Cupboard fold

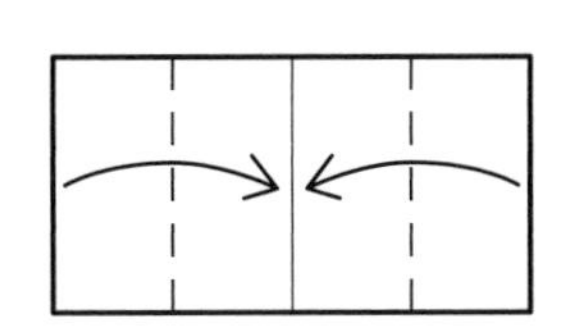

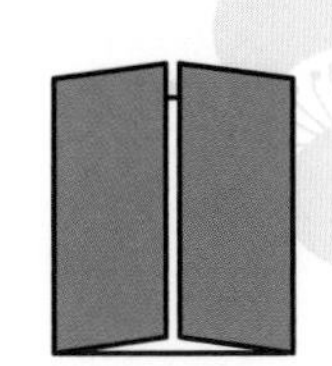

Fold both edges to the middle crease, like closing two cupboard doors.

Blintz

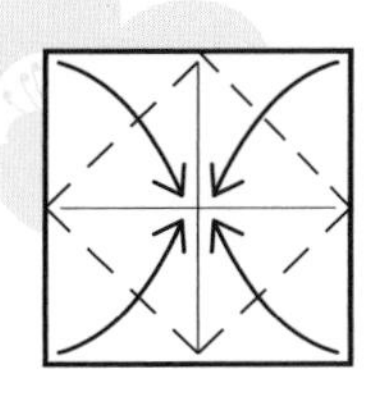

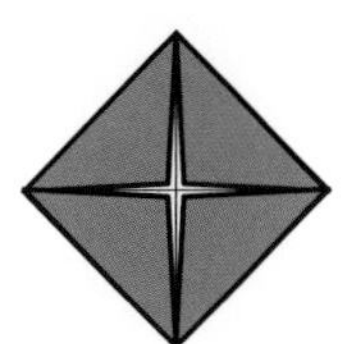

Fold all corners to the middle. This was named after a style of pastry called a blintz.

Pleat

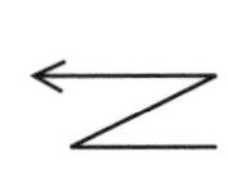

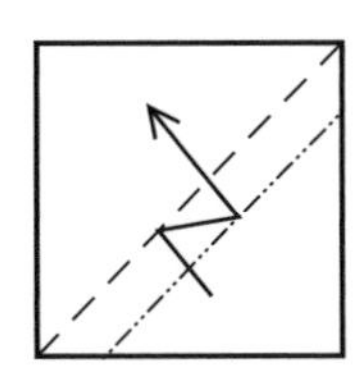

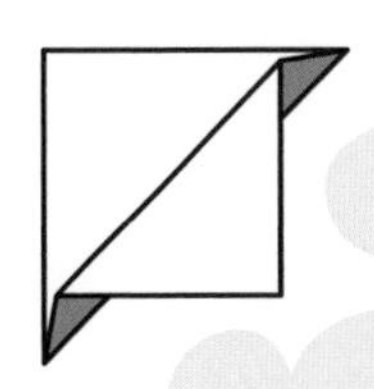

A mountain and valley fold combination.

Bisect - Divide a point in two

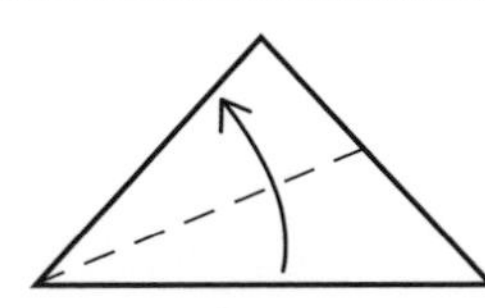

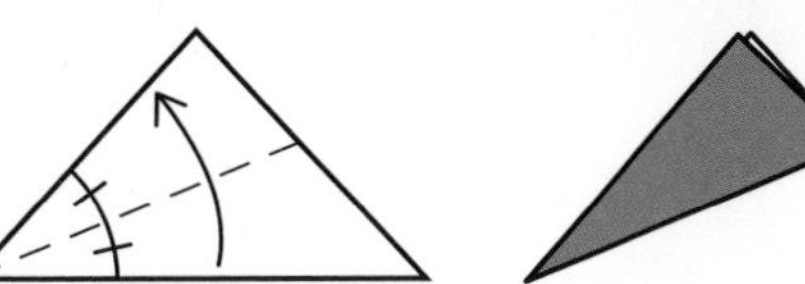

Many folds use a corner and two edges to position the fold line. The most common is a bisection, or division of an angle in two.

Fold one edge to meet the other, making sure the crease goes through the corner.

Inside reverse fold

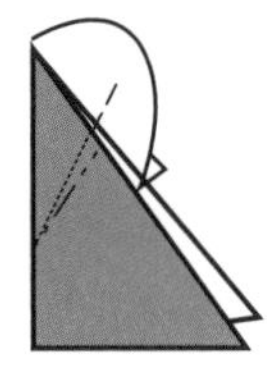
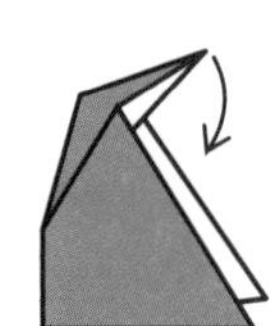

The spine of the existing fold is reversed and pushed inside.

Outside reverse fold

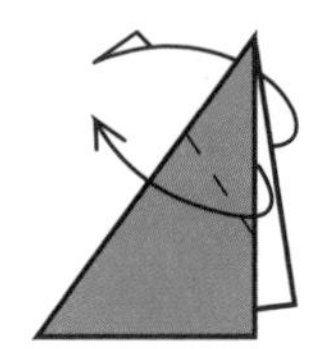
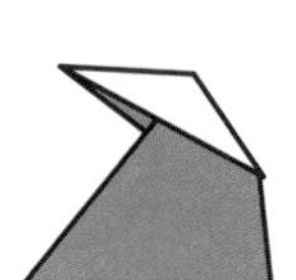

The spine of the existing fold is reversed and wrapped outside.

Double Reverse

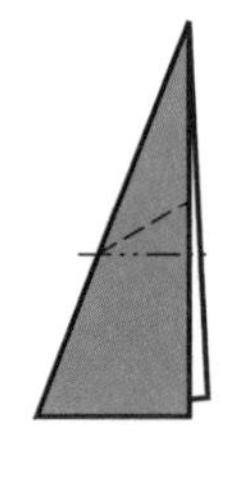
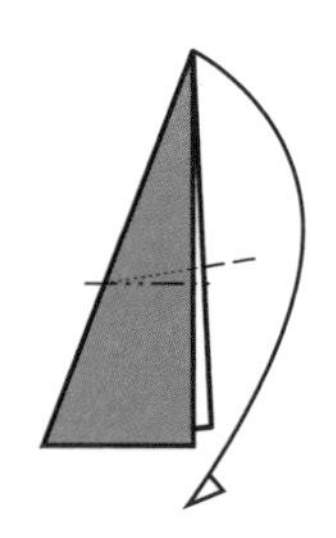
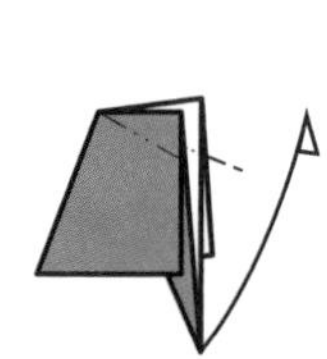

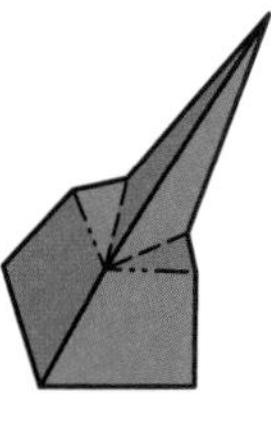

A double reverse fold is two reverse folds made in sequence on the same point.

The last diagram shows the paper slightly unfolded, to illustrate the folds that are made.

Inside Crimp

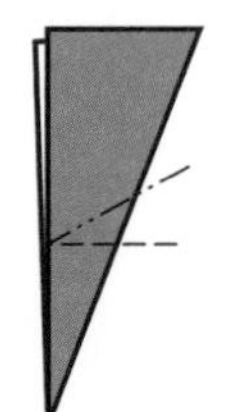

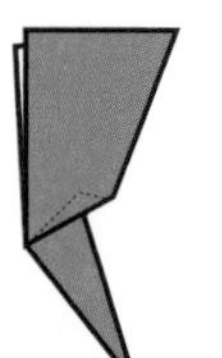

Outside Crimp

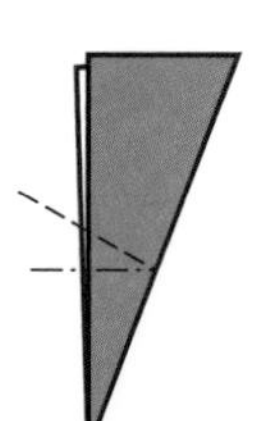
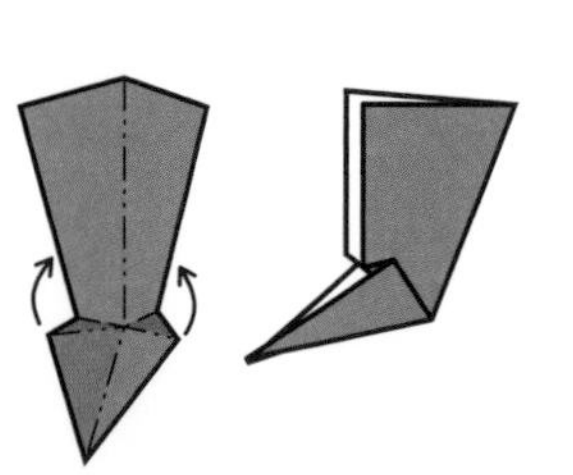

Crimps are often used for making feet or shaping legs. They can be thought of as a pleat mirrored on both sides of the point.

An inside crimp tucks the pleat on the inside of the point.

An outside crimp wraps the pleat over the outside of the point.

Petal fold

The petal fold is found in the bird and lily base.

1

Fold top layer to the centre crease.

2

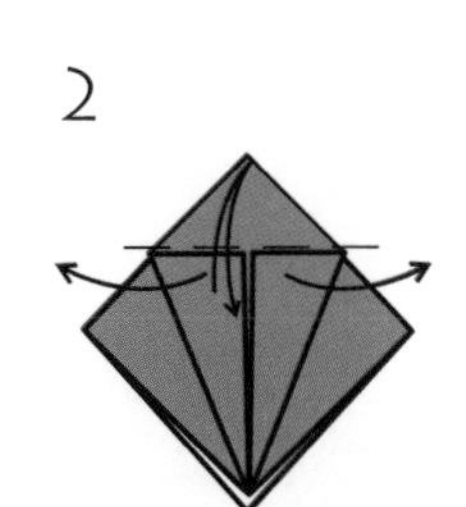

Fold and unfold the top triangle down. Unfold flaps.

3

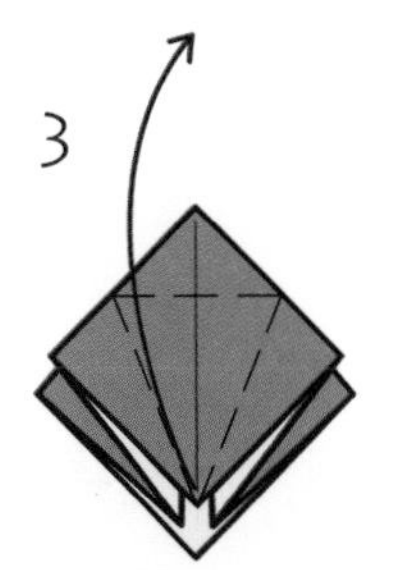

Lift the top layer upwards.

4

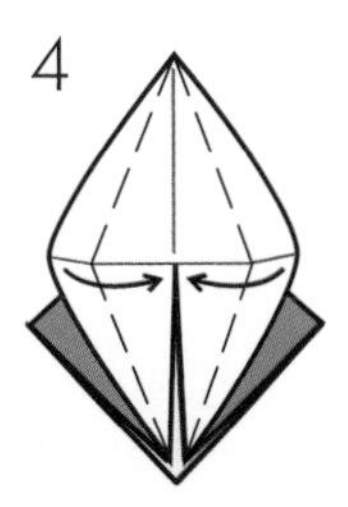

Step 3 in progress, the model is 3D. Fold the top layer inwards on existing creases.

5

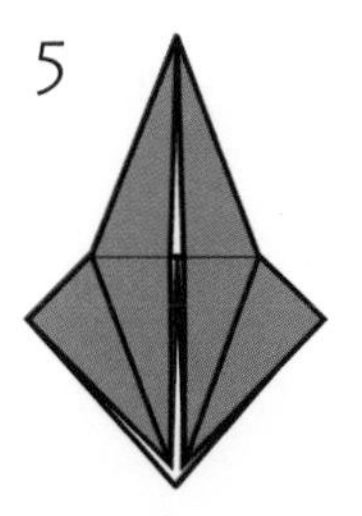

Completed petal fold.

Squash

A squash fold is the symmetrical flattening of a point. The flattening movement is known as squashing the point.

1

Pre-crease on the line for the squash fold.

2

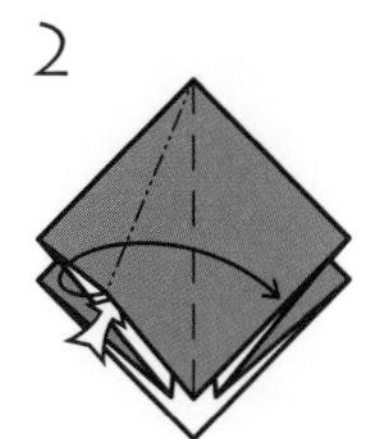

Open up the paper by inserting your finger. Fold the paper across.

3

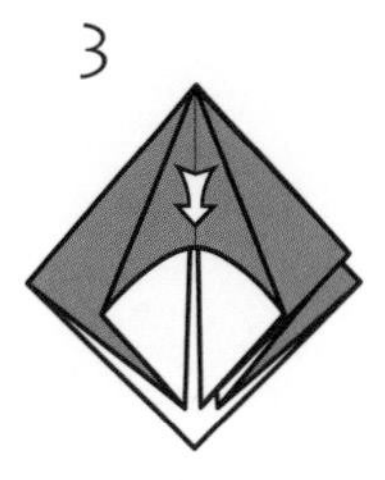

As you put the paper in place, gently squash the point into a symmetrical shape.

4

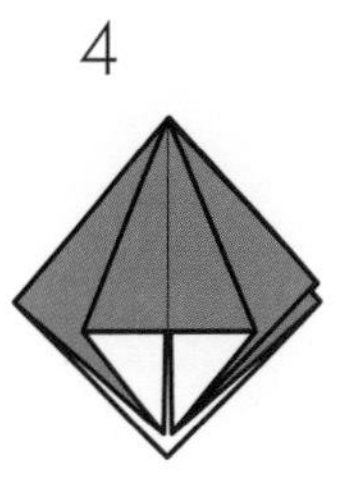

Completed squash fold.

Open sink

1

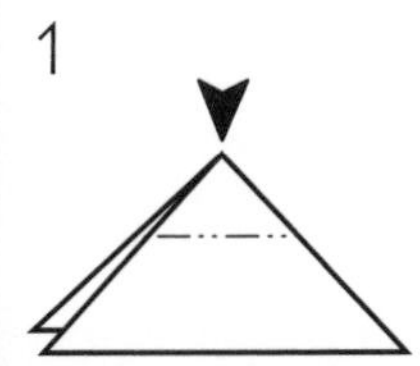

Pre-crease through all layers along the sink line. It's best to make a mountain and a valley fold on this line.

2

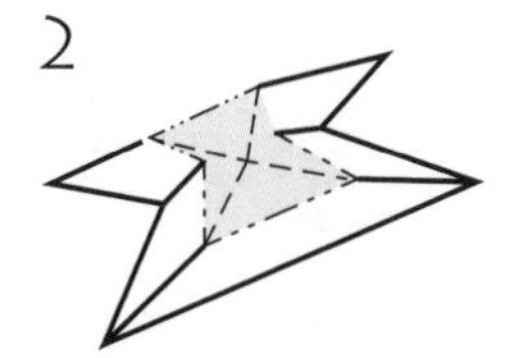

Open out the point, and push the point into the paper. Take care to reverse folds as shown. The sink should squash flat.

3

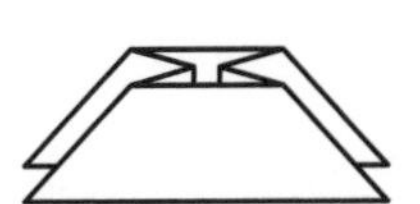

Completed sink.

RABBIT EAR

The rabbit ear fold is named after a most useful shape – that of a rabbit ear. It is used to make a new point.

1

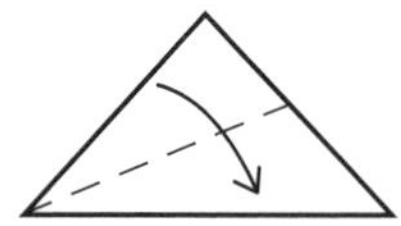

2

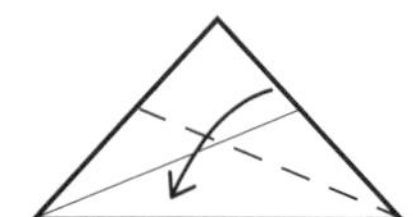

3

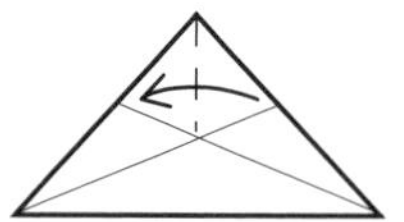

1- 3. Divide each corner of the triangle with valley folds.

4

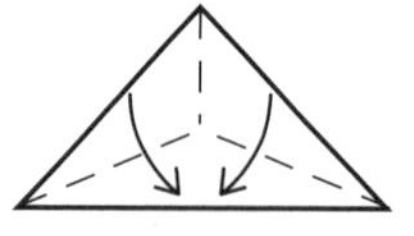

Fold top edges to the bottom, the middle crease will form a point.

5

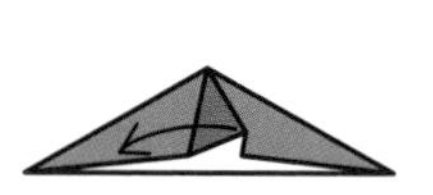

Fold the point to one side.

6

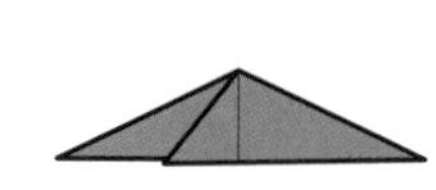

Completed rabbit ear.

DOUBLE RABBIT EAR

The double rabbit ear is a rabbit ear fold that is mirrored on both sides of the point.

1

Make a rabbit ear fold on the point.

2

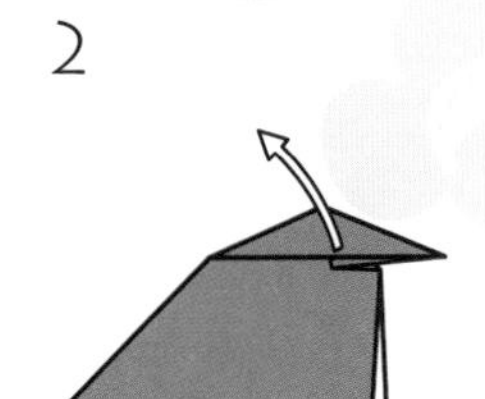

Unfold the rabbit ear.

3

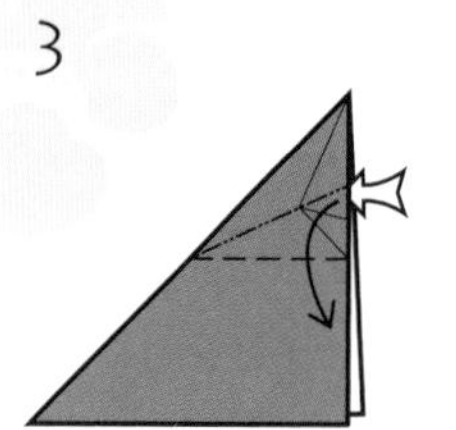

Squash fold the point.

4

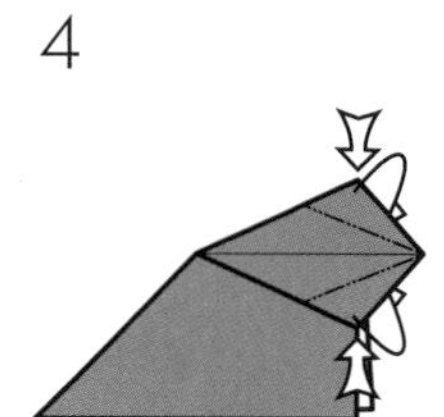

Inside reverse fold the two points.

5

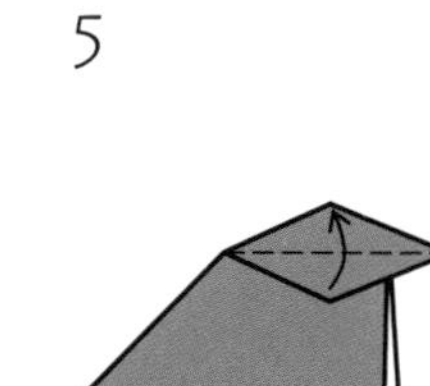

Valley fold point upwards.

6

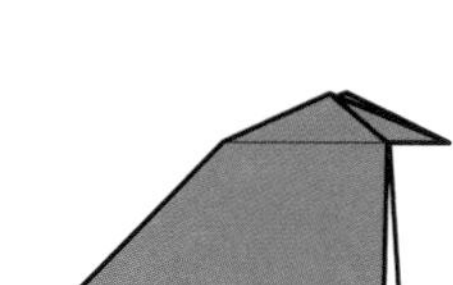

Completed double rabbit ear.

SWIVEL FOLD

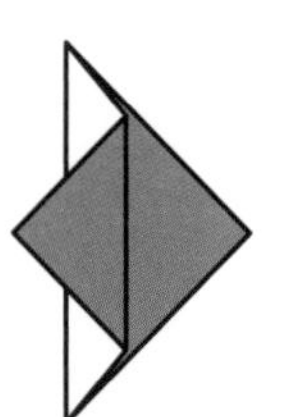

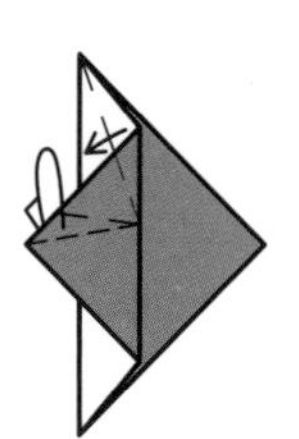

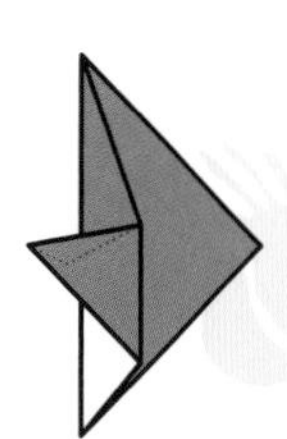

A swivel fold is often made on a pleat. It narrows its two points, and the excess paper swivels under one of the points.

WATERBOMB BASE

BY: MATTHEW GARDINER

Origami has standard shapes often repeated because they are very useful. The original use of this base form was to make the waterbomb model, but its five points make a versatile shape for many designs.

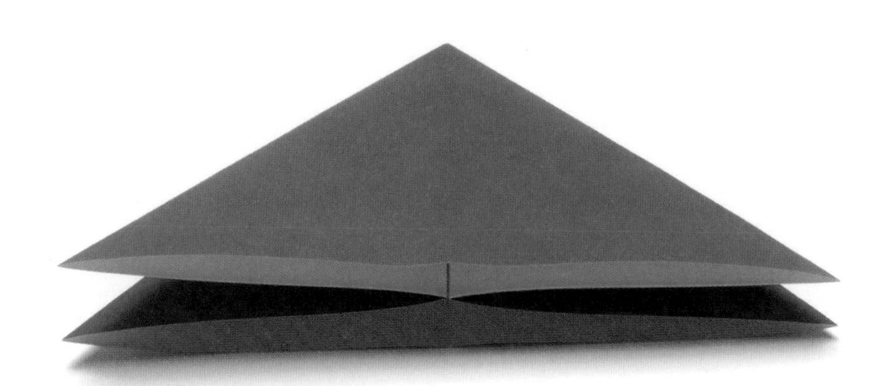

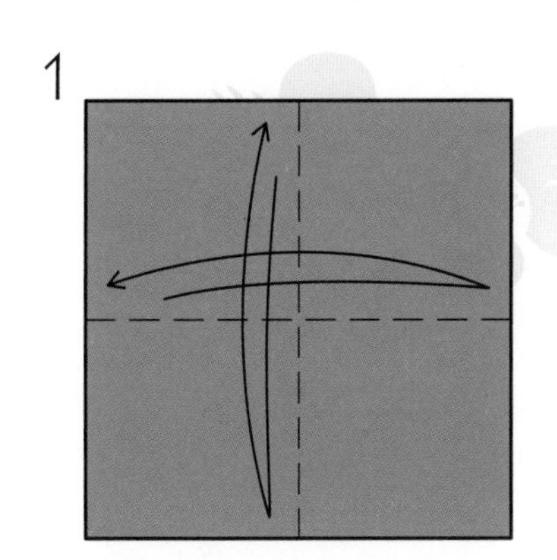

1

Begin coloured side up.
Book fold and unfold. Turn over.

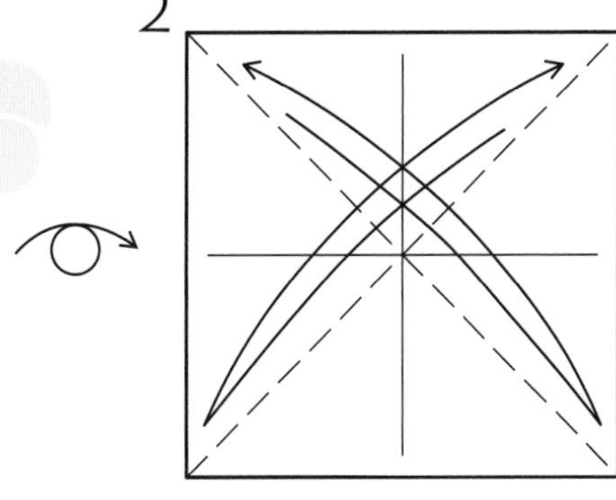

2

Fold and unfold diagonals.

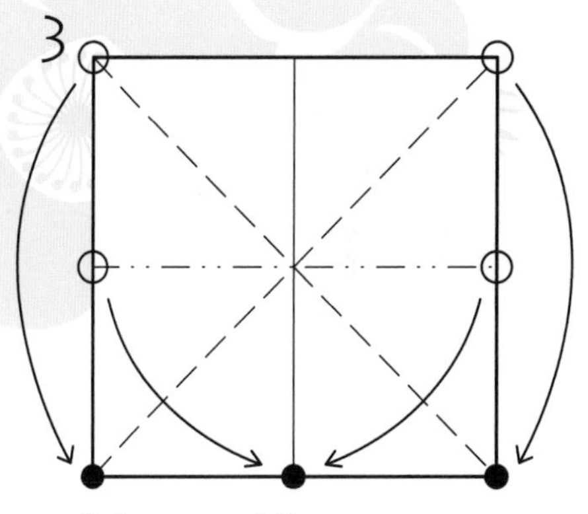

3

Collapse on existing creases.

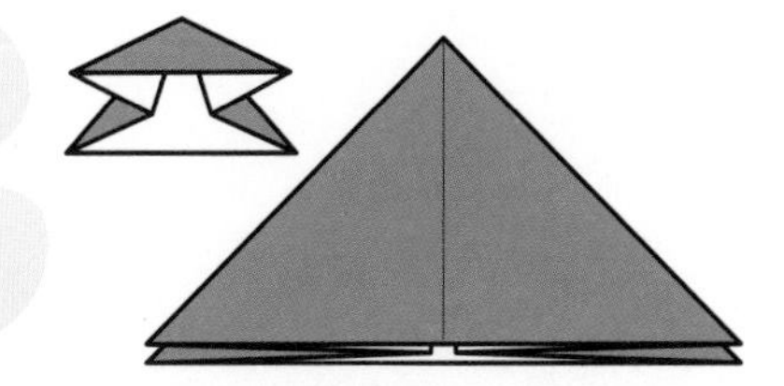

4

Completed waterbomb base.

PRELIMINARY BASE

BY: MATTHEW GARDINER

The preliminary base is the starting point for the bird base and the frog/lily base. It is a very common origami base. Interestingly, the preliminary base is an inside-out waterbomb base. Try making a waterbomb base using the same creases in the preliminary base. Hint: unfold the base and turn the paper over.

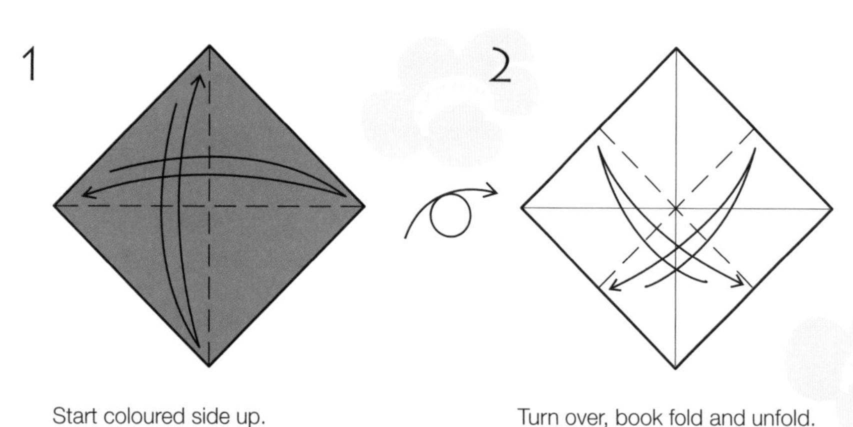

1. Start coloured side up. Fold and unfold diagonals.

2. Turn over, book fold and unfold.

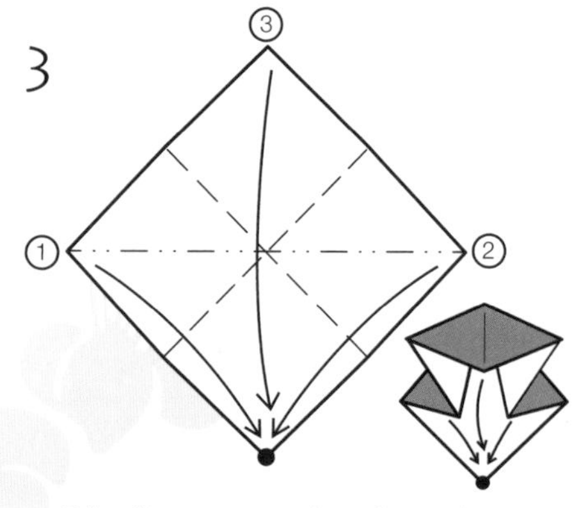

3. Bring three corners down to meet bottom corner. Start with corners 1 and 2 together followed by corner 3.

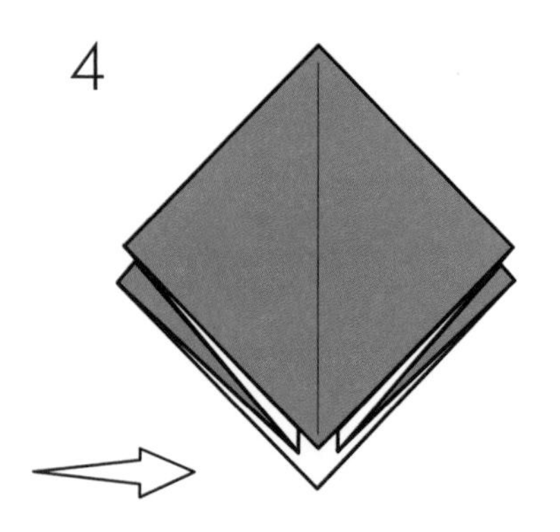

4. Completed preliminary base.

Frog/Lily Base

BY: Matthew Gardiner

The frog base is also called lily base, because of its use in both the traditional lily and frog. It begins with a preliminary base.

1

Start from the preliminary base. Rotate 180°.

2

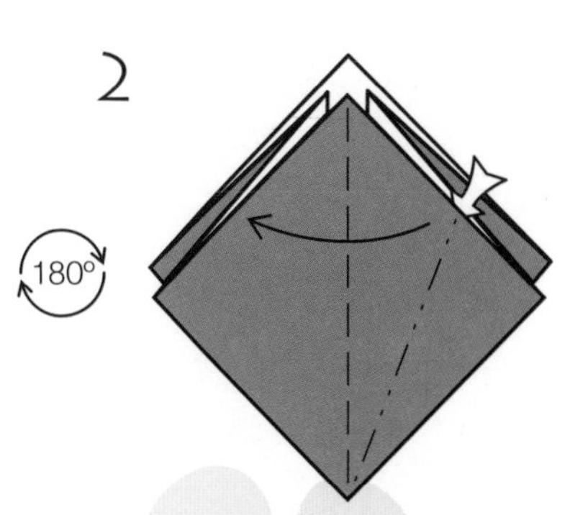

Check that the open points are at the top. Pre-crease then squash fold the top layer on one side.

3

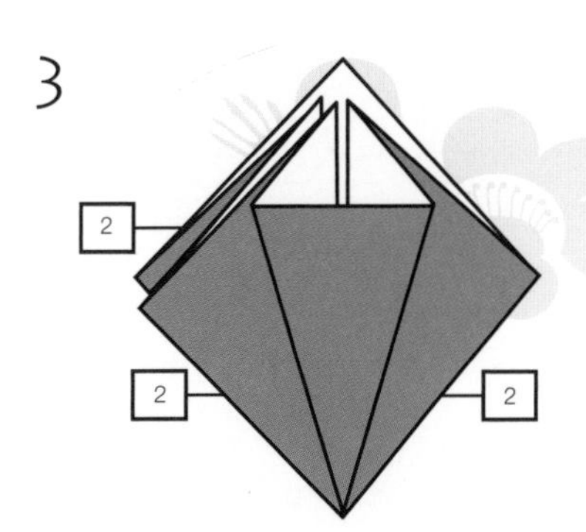

Repeat step 2 on the other three points.

4

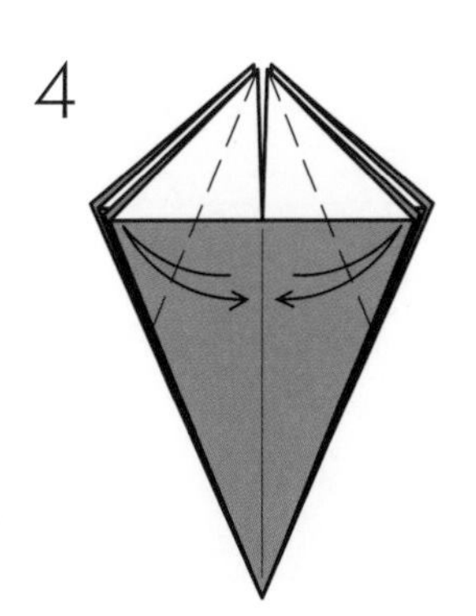

Fold the top layer only to the centre crease.

5

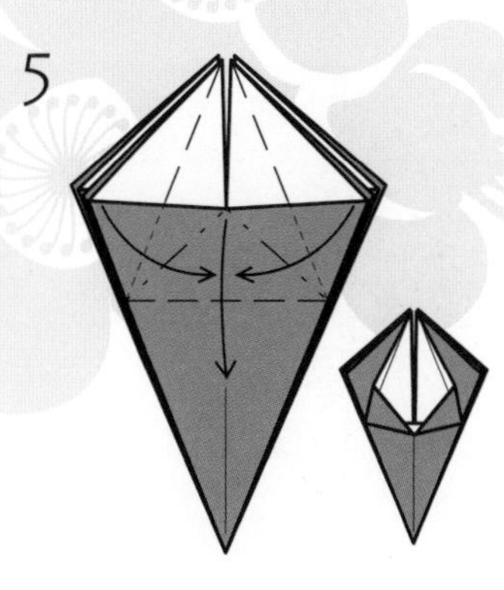

Petal fold: pull down the top layer, and fold the sides to the middle. Lastly make the mountain folds.

6

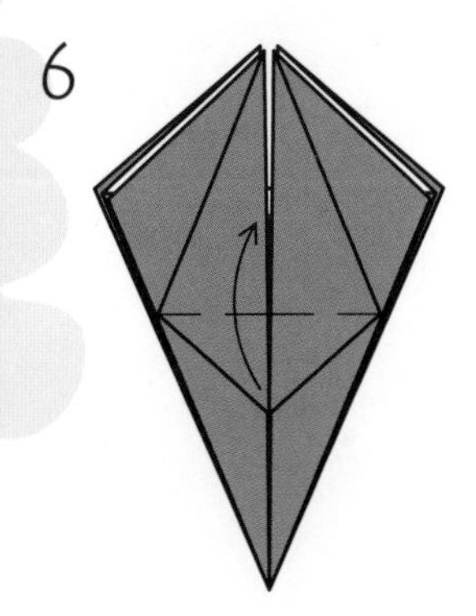

Completed petal fold. Valley fold the triangle flap upwards.

7

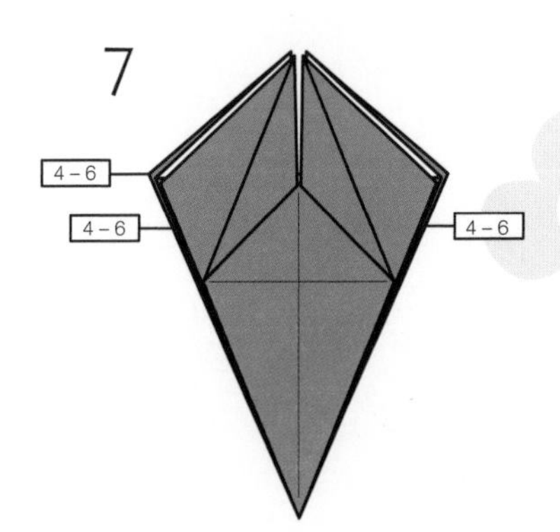

Repeat steps 4 to 6 on the three remaining sides.

8

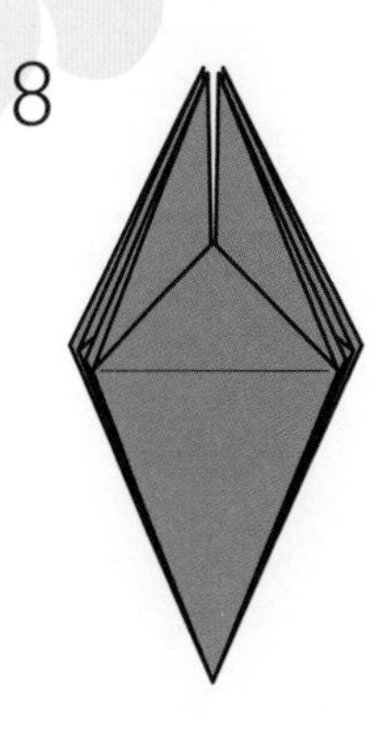

Completed frog/lily base.

Bird Base

By: Matthew Gardiner

The bird base is the start of the classic origami crane. It is also useful for creating a wide variety of birds and other animals.

1

Start from the preliminary base.

2

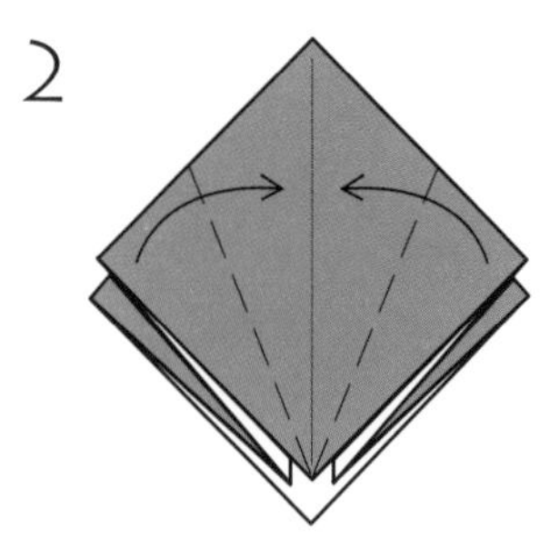

Fold top layer to the centre crease.

3

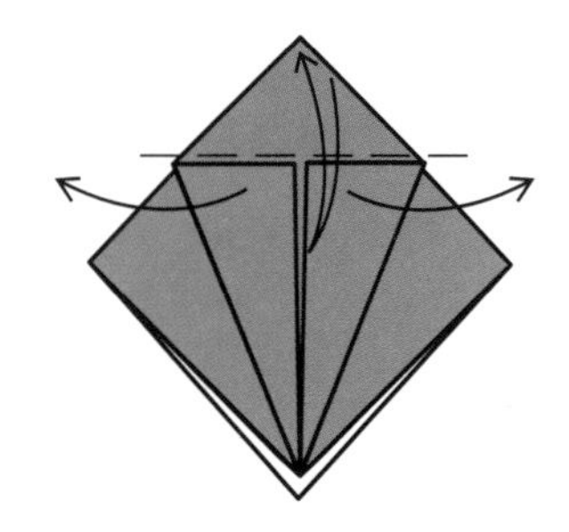

Fold and unfold the top triangle down. Unfold flaps.

4

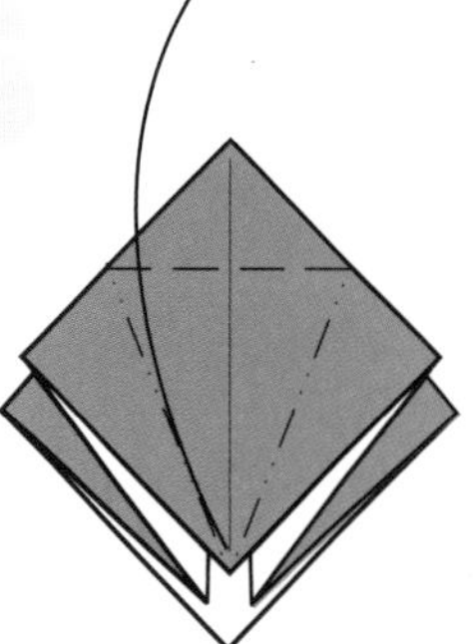

Lift the top layer upwards.

5

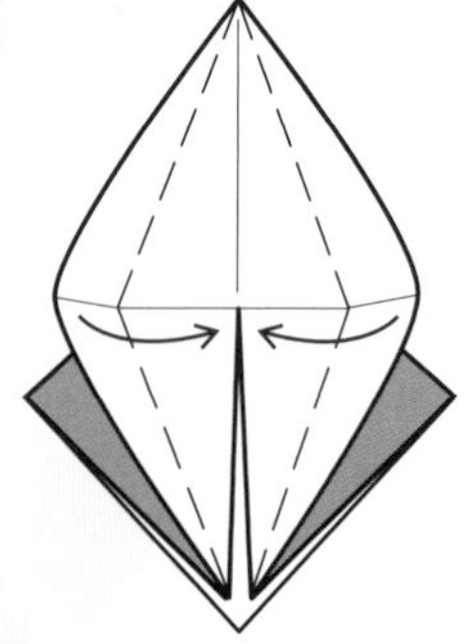

Step 4 in progress, the model is 3D. Fold the top layer inwards on existing creases.

6

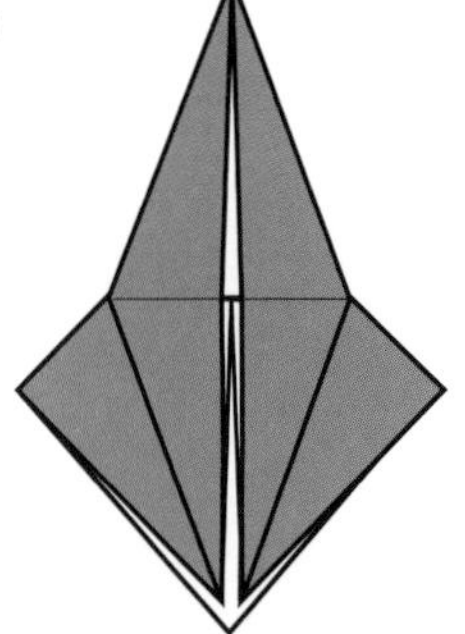

Step 4 completed, the model will be flat. Turn over.

7

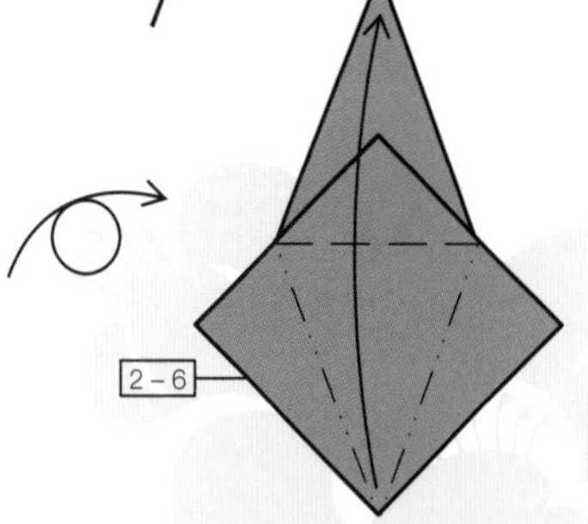

Repeat steps 2 – 6 on this side.

8

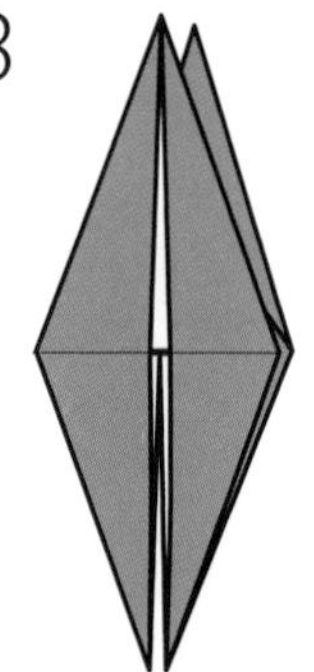

Completed bird base.

Fish Base

BY: Matthew Gardiner

The fish base is used to make the traditional fish, but can also be used as a starting point for more complex models.

1

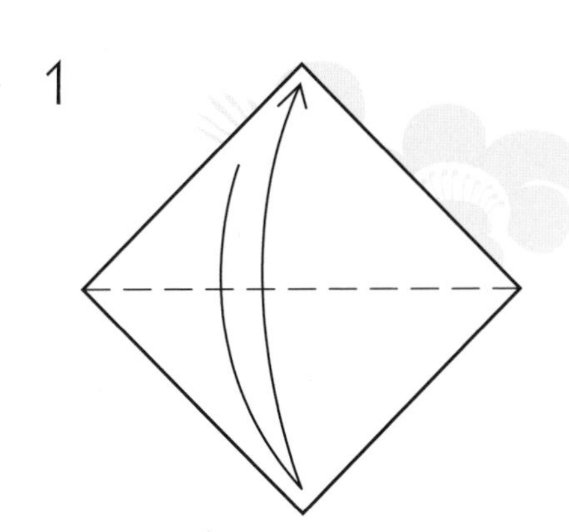

Start with white side up. Fold and unfold diagonal.

2

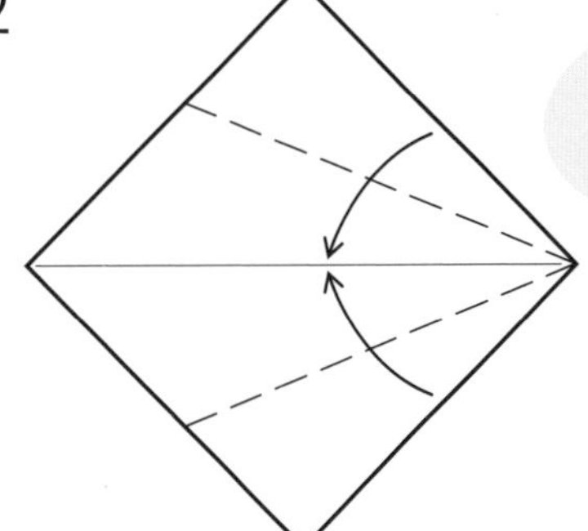

Fold both sides to the middle.

3

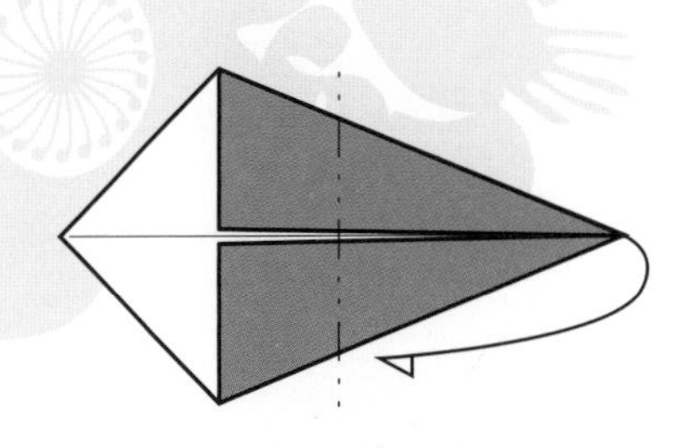

Mountain fold in half behind.

4

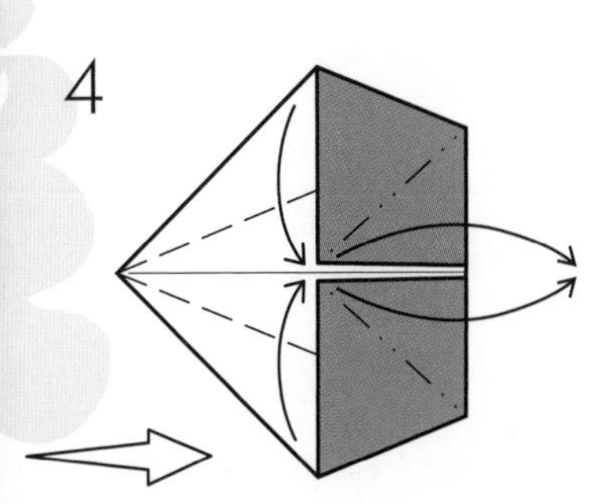

Squash fold both sides.

5

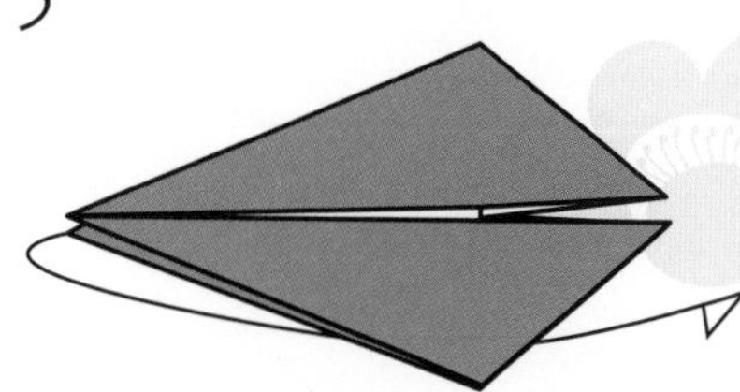

Mountain fold the back layer behind.

6

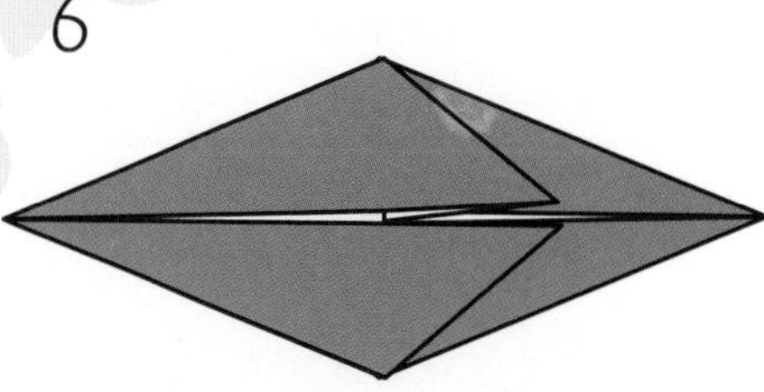

Completed fish base.

ORIGAMI PAPERS

BY: MATTHEW GARDINER

The origami artist can fold any kind of paper they can get their hands on, and experience tells them the best choice for a particular model. The following is a guide to types of papers for origami.

Kami - Origami Squares

The highest quality origami papers originate in Japan. Manufacturers such as Kurosawa and Toyo produce high quality squares of origami papers in a wide variety of colours and patterns. Kami, as it is often called by origami artists, has its best use in teaching or learning origami models, because it is coloured on both sides of the paper.

Kinder Squares

Unfortunately, many people start with this low quality paper. It is prone to tearing during the most critical moment in an origami model. While it looks like great paper, it is often not square and the inks used in colouring them will fade more rapidly when exposed to sunlight. This paper is good for very quick sketching, and work with young children, but not for quality origami.

Washi Paper

Washi paper is traditional Japanese paper. Wa meaning Japanese, and shi meaning paper. It is a term for a specific type of Japanese handmade paper. In Japan handmade paper is used for all official documents, a policy which keeps the art of paper-making alive and well. The strength and thinness of many kinds of washi make it ideal for origami.

Chiyogami

Chiyogami is patterned washi paper originating from Japan. The attractiveness of the paper is unsurpassed. When folding take care not to fold a model that is too complex, as the patterned inks often form a thick layer over the paper, making complex creases difficult. Chiyogami is a fine choice for traditional cranes, decorative models and patterns for geometric models.

Art papers

With the many choices of paper in art stores today, you are spoilt for choice. High quality acid-free water colour paper can be painted and folded. Art papers are often used with a technique called 'wet folding', whereby the origami paper is dampened before folding. Try out new paper stocks, and after a while you will get a 'feel' for the kinds of papers that will suit a particular model.

Foil and laminated papers

Paper made with foil can be easily sculpted, as the metal in the foil has a stronger and more flexible shape memory than paper. Many origami artists require colours and textures not available together in commercial stocks. Papers can be joined together in the studio with methyl cellulose or spray adhesives.

MORE ORIGAMI

Origami is flourishing all around the world in an open sharing way, thanks to countless numbers of volunteers and not-for-profit organisations. Below are the website addresses of a number of origami societies. This list is by no means complete, however the information on these pages will introduce you to the world of origami meetings and conventions, to where most of the world's origami knowledge is stored; in the minds of passionate folders as memorised instructions. So get out there and attend an origami convention, attend local meetings and learn from the best teachers in the world: the people who love it!

AUSTRALIA
Melbourne Origami Group, Folding Australia.
http://www.papercrane.org

FRANCE
Mouvement Français des Plieurs de Papier (MFPP)
http://mfpp.free.fr/

GERMANY
Origami Deutschland
http://www.papierfalten.de

ISRAEL
Israeli Origami Centre
http://www.origami.co.il/

ITALY
Centro Diffusione Origami
http://www.origami-cdo.it/

JAPAN
Japan Origami Academic Society (JOAS)
http://www.origami.gr.jp

JAPAN
Nippon Origami Association (NOA)
http://www.origami-noa.com

KOREA
Korea Jongie Jupgi Association
http://www.origami.or.kr

NETHERLANDS
Origami Sociteit Nederland
http://www.origami-osn.nl/

SPAIN
La Asociación Española de Papiroflexia
http://www.pajarita.org/

UNITED KINGDOM
British Origami Society (BOS)
http://www.britishorigami.info

UNITED STATES
Origami USA (OUSA)
http://www.origami-usa.org

PAPER CRANE

MODEL: TRADITIONAL, JAPAN
DIAGRAM: MATTHEW GARDINER

The traditional Japanese paper crane or *orizuru* is famous throughout the world. It is a symbol of origami and a symbol of peace. An ancient Japanese legend says that whoever folds 1000 cranes will be granted a wish.

Today, in Hiroshima, stands the peace memorial of Sadako Sasaki built by her classmates in her memory to inspire peace around the world. Sadako was a victim of atom-bomb disease and she folded cranes until she died. She never gave up on her wish to be well.

1

2

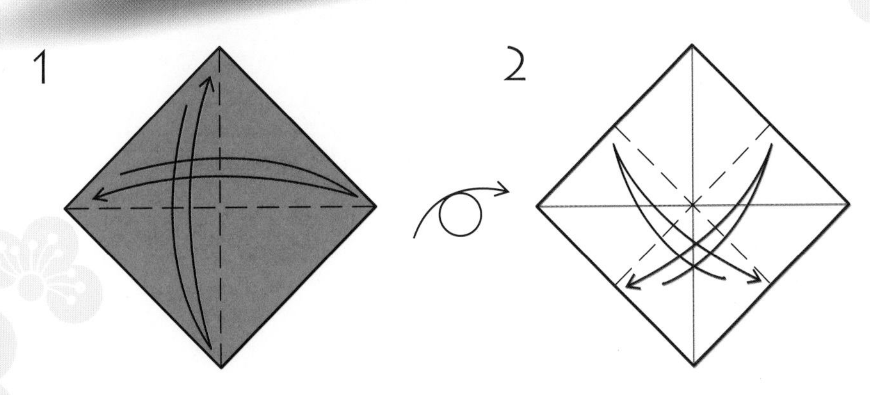

Start coloured side up.
Fold and unfold diagonals. Turn over.

Book fold and unfold.

3

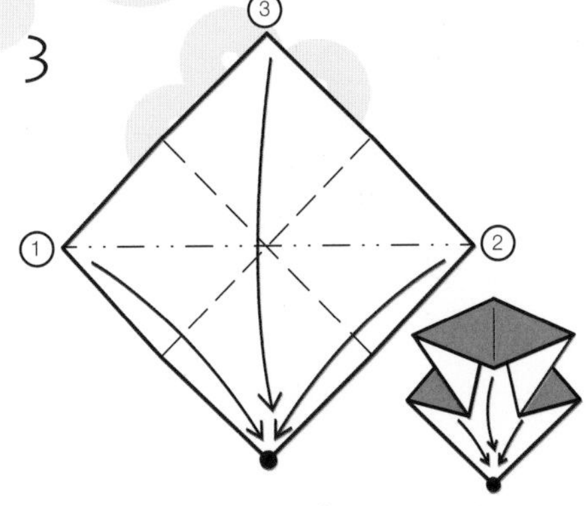

Bring three corners down to meet bottom corner. Start with corners 1 and 2 together followed by corner 3.

4

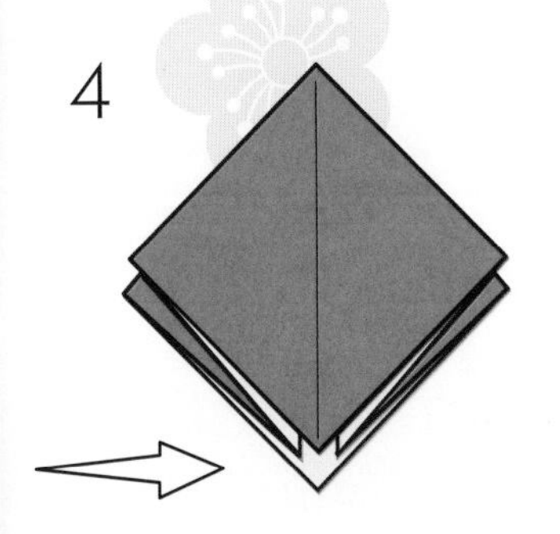

Completed preliminary base.

5

Fold top layer to the centre crease.

6

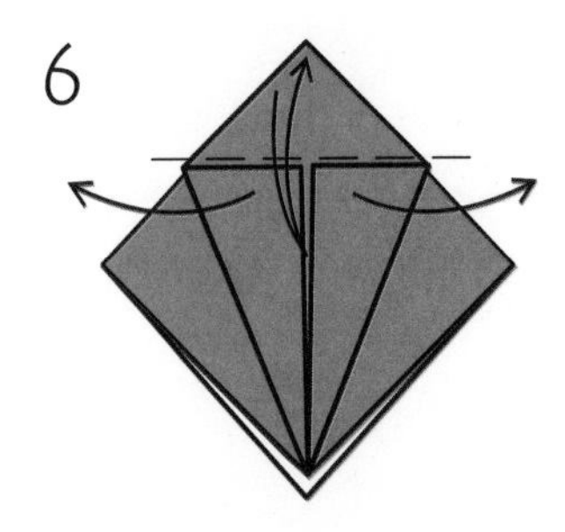

Fold and unfold the top triangle down.
Unfold flaps.

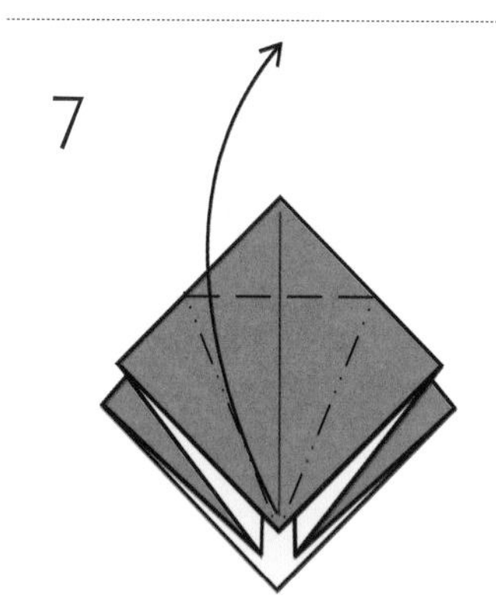

Lift the top layer upwards.

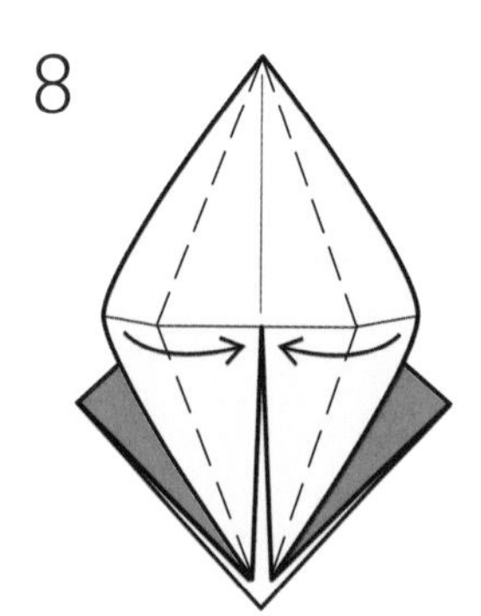

Step 7 in progress, the model is 3D. Fold the top layer inwards on existing creases.

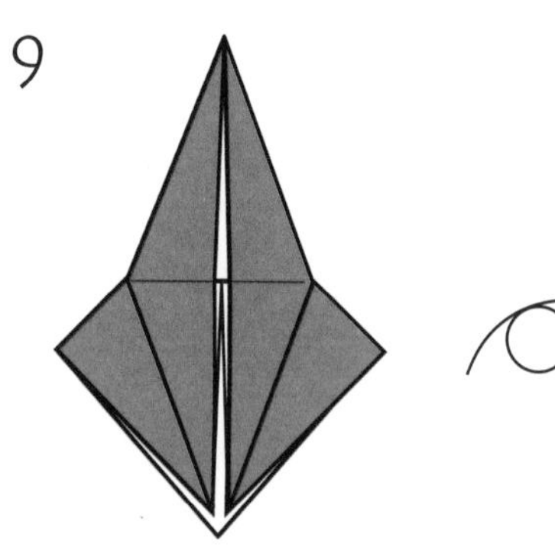

Step 7 completed, the model will be flat. Turn over.

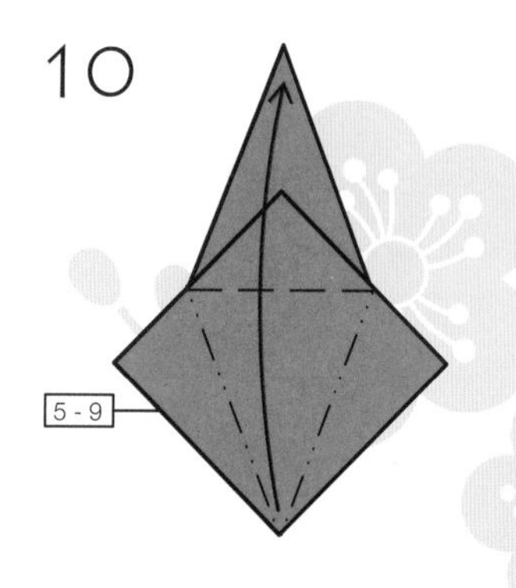

Repeat steps 5-9 on this side.

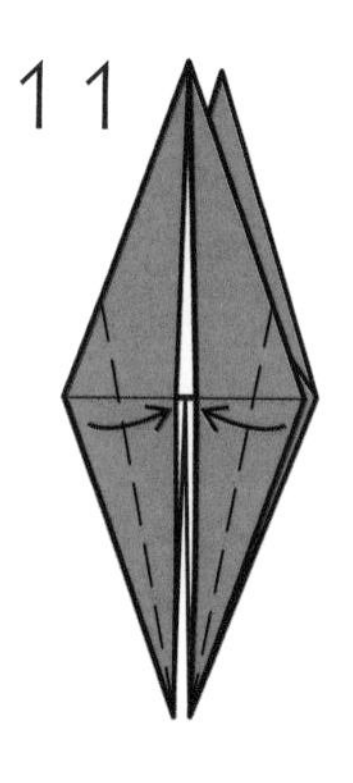

Narrow the bottom points on the top layer only. Repeat behind.

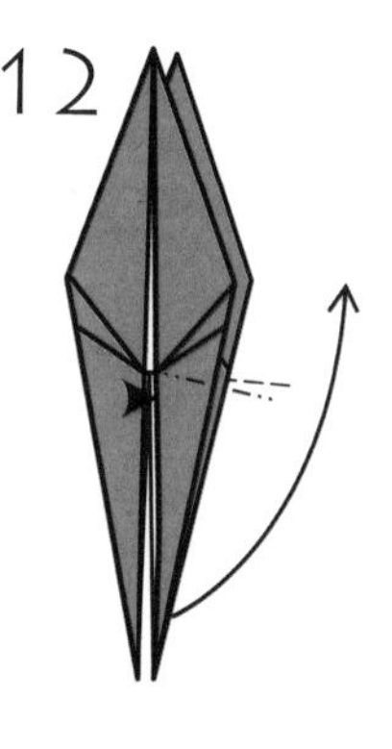

Reverse fold the bottom point upwards.

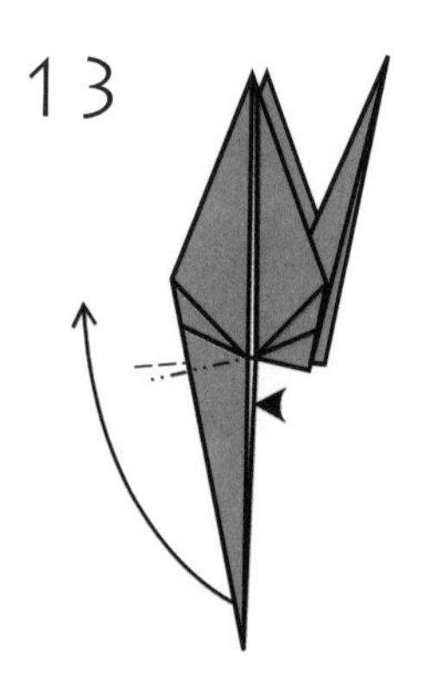

Your model should look like this. Repeat on the other side.

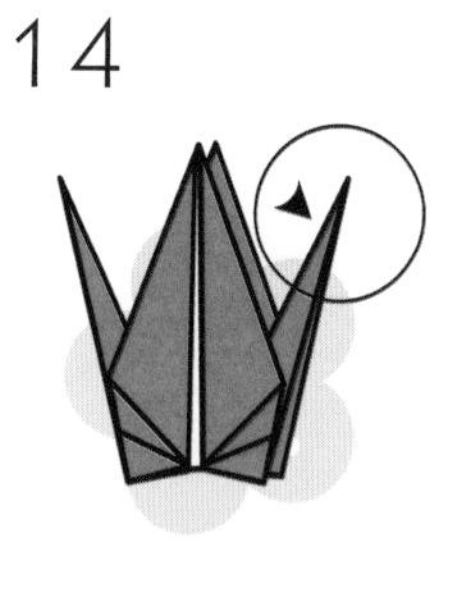

Completed body. The next steps focus on the head.

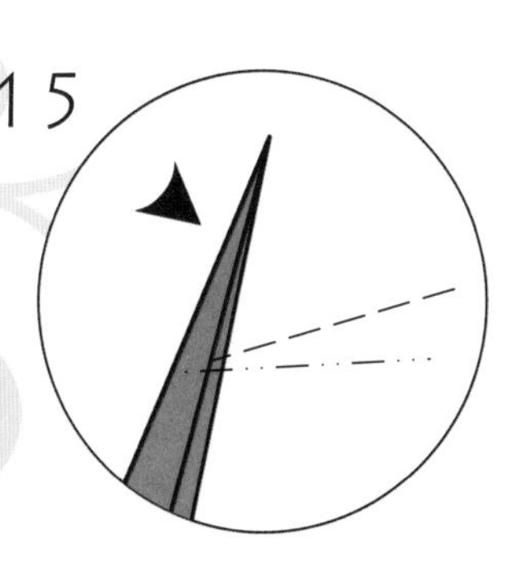

Reverse fold the point to create the head.

16

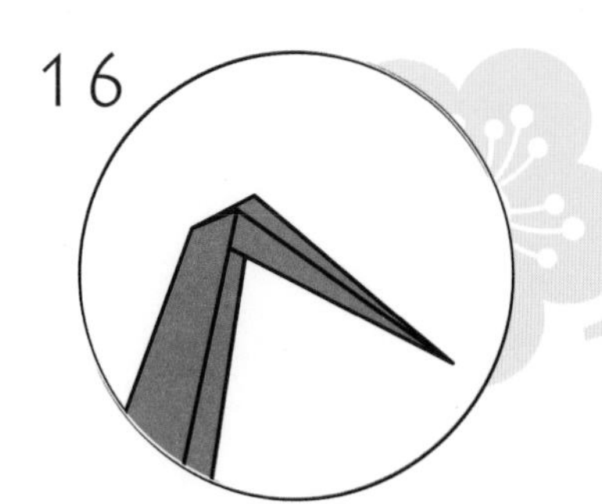

Head completed.

17

Fold wings down.

18

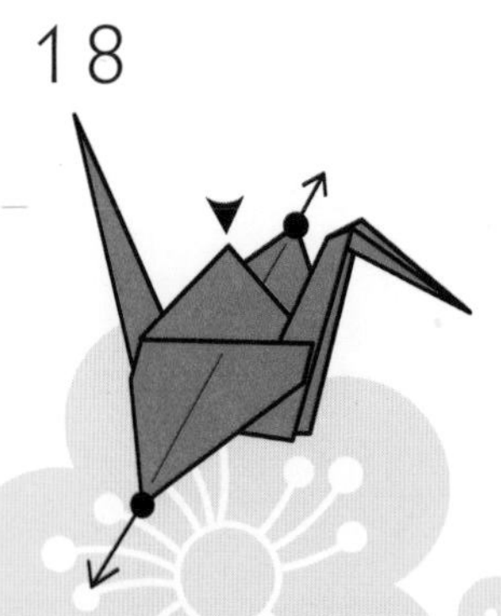

Pull the wings gently to shape the body.

19

Completed paper crane – repeat 1000 times for a wish.

Senbazuru

Model: Traditional, Japan
Diagram: Matthew Gardiner

Senbazuru is a Japanese word that literally means 1000 cranes. One of the world's oldest known origami books, *Hiden Senbazuru Orikata*, reveals the secrets of folding senbazuru origami. This technique requires specific cuts in the paper, that create multiple squares that are joined by small areas of paper. This technique requires a high degree of patience and skill, so take your time when folding, and be prepared to make many attempts.

A special note.

These diagrams differ to the other diagrams in this book; in that you are not shown every step of the way. You are encouraged to discover your own way.

First learn how to fold a paper crane from memory, and then become familiar with the parts of the crane; the wings, the tail and the head. Study where these parts originate on the unfolded sheet.

Once you have this familiarity, the folding of the cranes in the correct location will not be too difficult.

The difficult part is not tearing the paper connections while you are folding. More paper between the cuts will provide additional strength, so leave more paper rather than less when cutting, and then refine the cuts when the model is folded.

These diagrams have two special symbols.

The location of cuts as red lines.

The location of the head of each crane is marked as a small circle.

1A

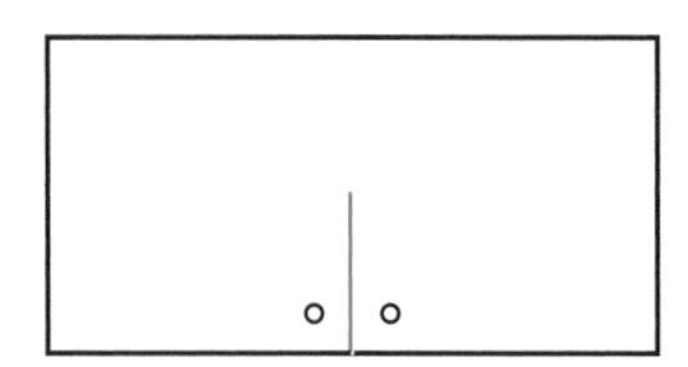

Joined at the wing. 2:1 rectangle.

1B

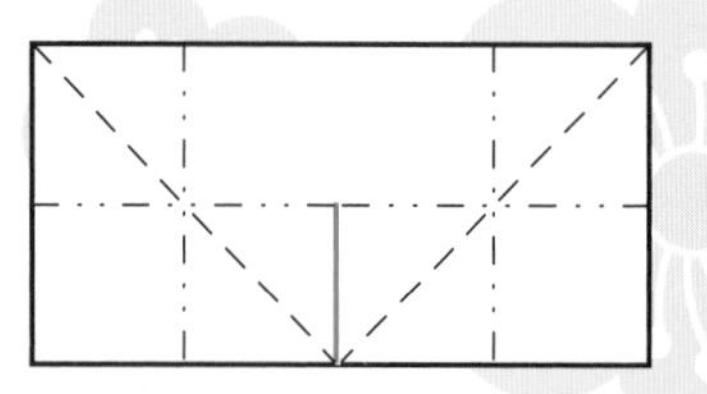

Place these creases, then cut on red line.

1C

Joined at the wing.

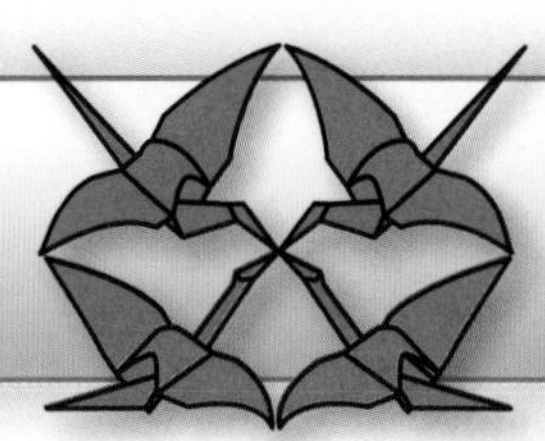

2A

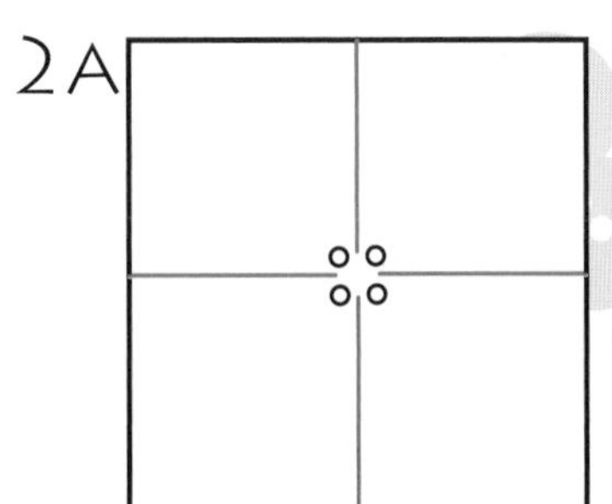

4 Kissing cranes.
1:1 square.

2B

Fold into quarters, make the creases as shown, then cut on red lines.

2C

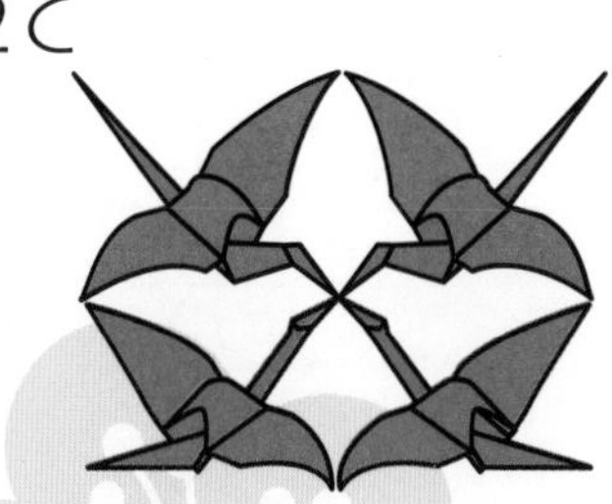

Fold carefully to keep the cranes still kissing.

3A

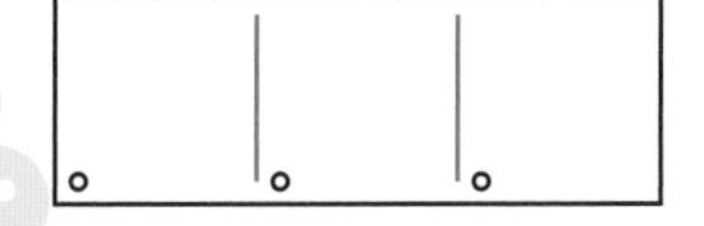

3 in a row.
3:1 rectangle.

3B

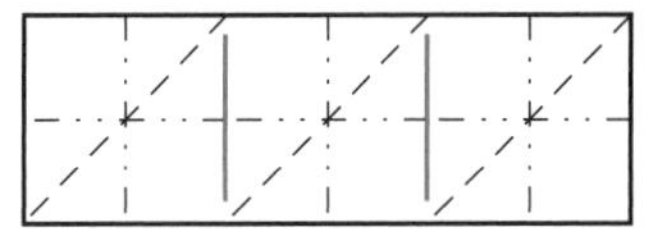

Fold into thirds, make creases as shown, then cut on red lines.

3C

These cranes are joined tail to wing. Can you make a longer chain?

4A

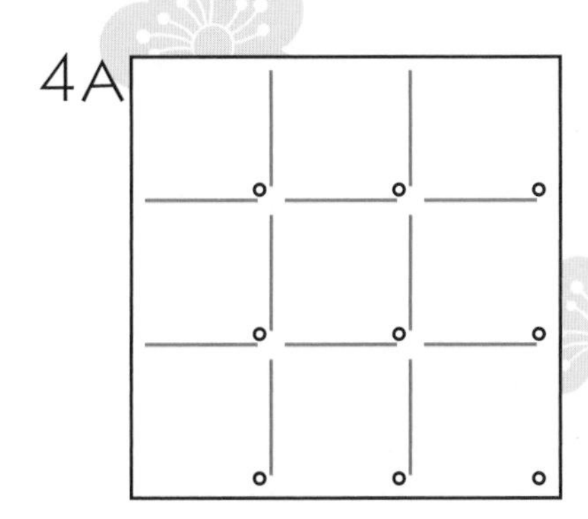

3 squared.
1:1 Square.

4B

Fold into thirds. make creases as shown, then cut on red lines.

4C

This beautiful model is worth the time it takes to master.

BUTTERFLY

MODEL: TRADITIONAL, JAPAN
DIAGRAM: MATTHEW GARDINER

Butterflies capture the imagination of children and adults alike. Their delicate shape is perfect for hanging decorations. Try using a patterned sheet of origami paper.

This butterfly is a traditional fold from Japan.

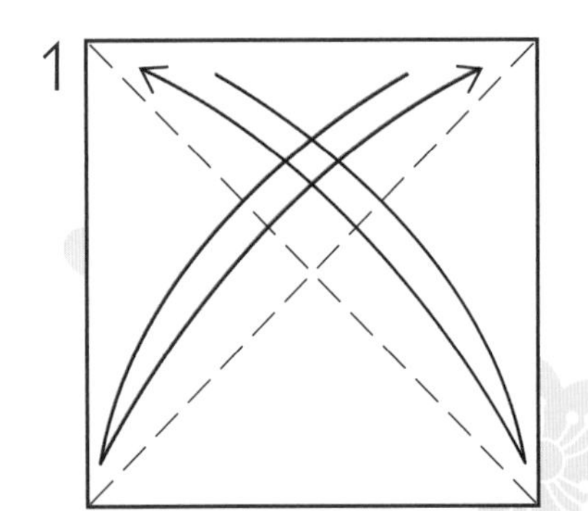

Fold and unfold diagonals.

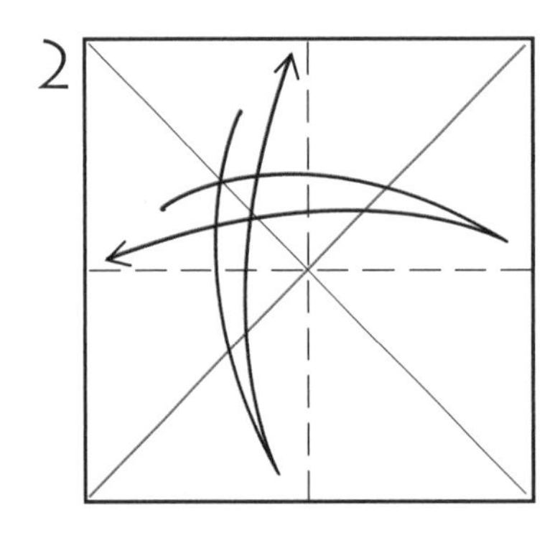

Book fold.

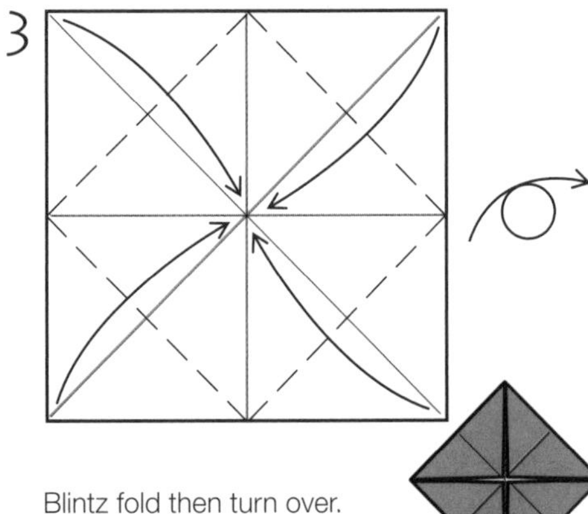

Blintz fold then turn over.

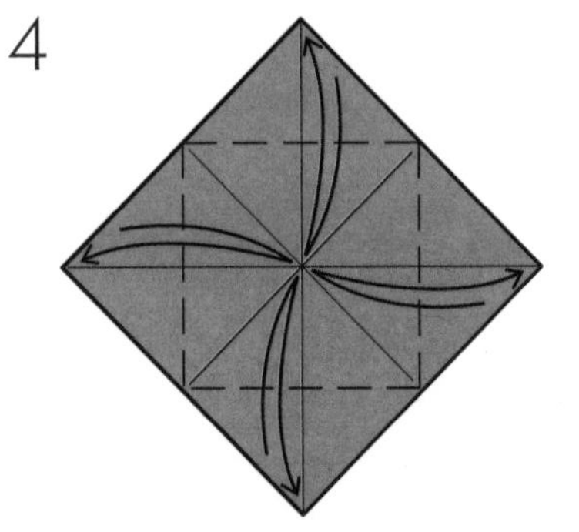

Blintz fold then turn over.

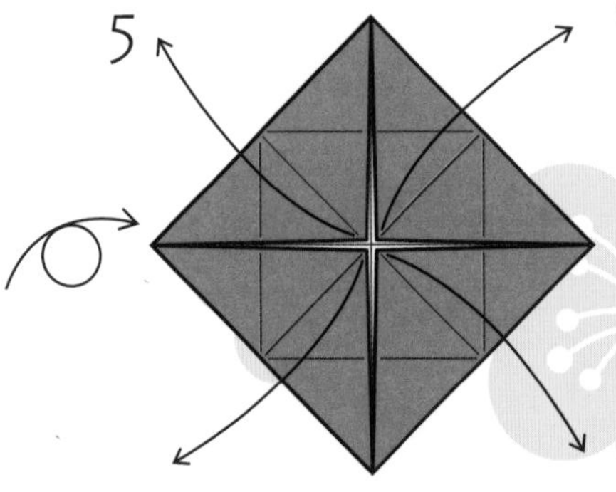

Completely unfold out to a flat sheet.

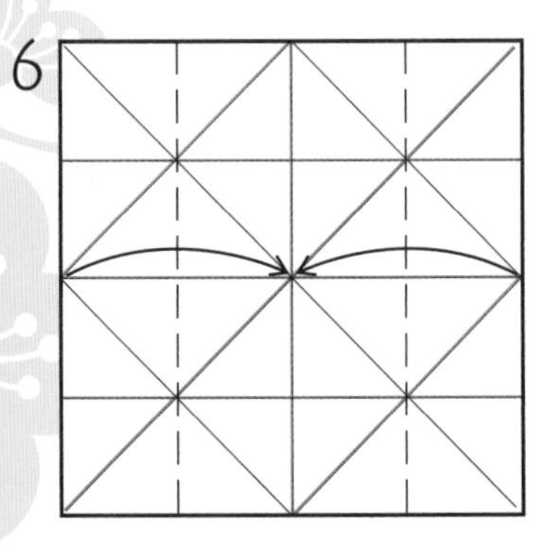

Fold sides to the middle.

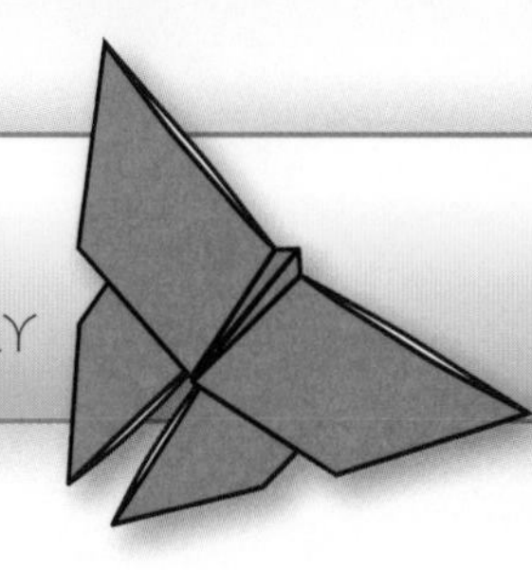

7

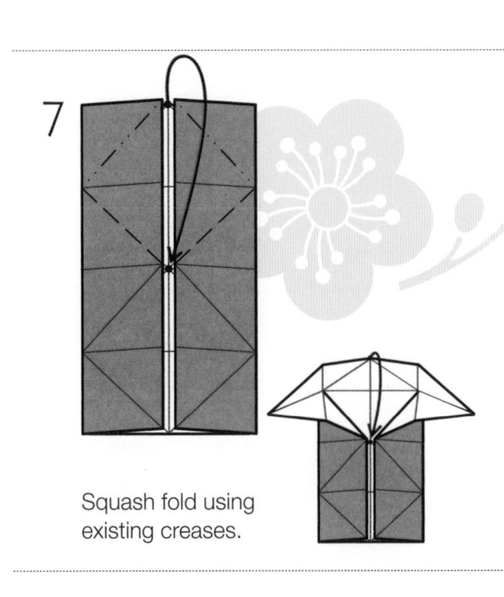

Squash fold using existing creases.

8

Repeat step 7 on the bottom.

9

Mountain fold in half.

10

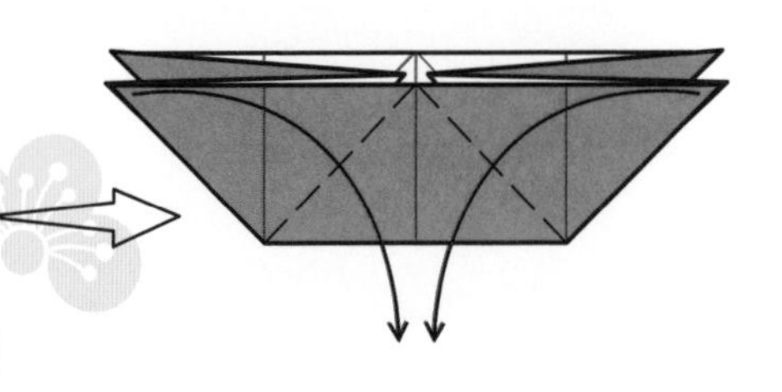

Fold points on the top layer down.

11

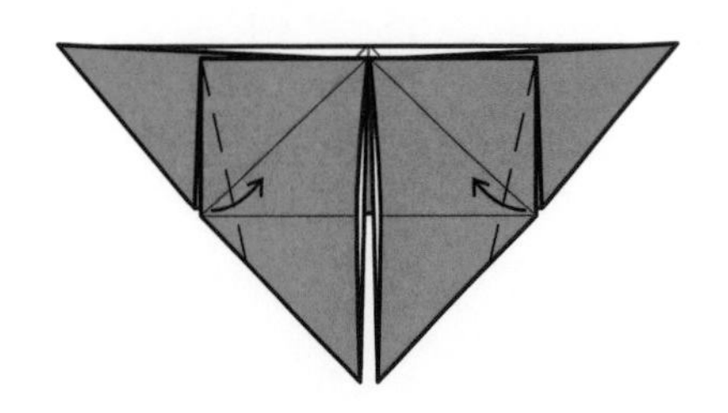

Fold sides in.

12

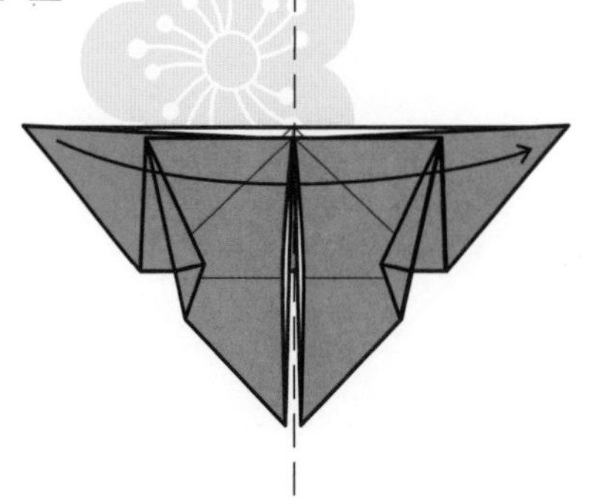

Fold in half.

13

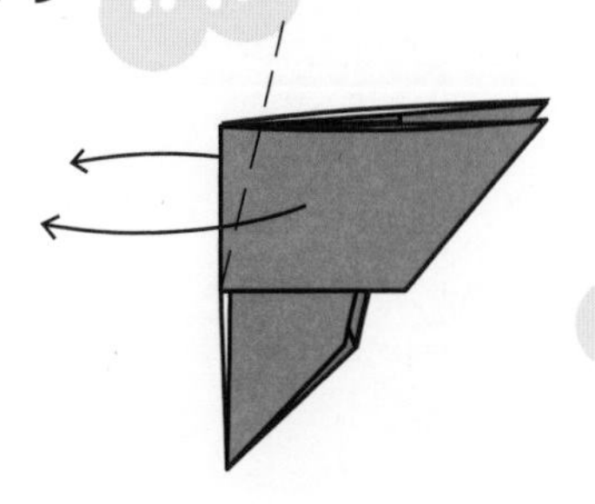

Fold both wings.

14

Fold one wing back.

15

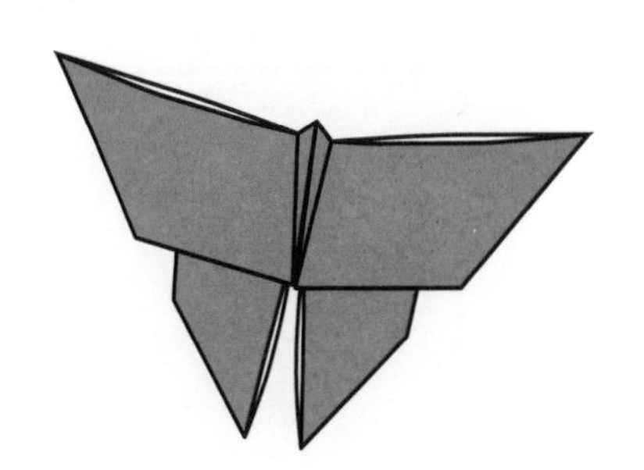

Completed butterfly.

YAKKO-SAN

MODEL: TRADITIONAL, JAPAN
DIAGRAM: MATTHEW GARDINER

Yakko-san is a very old, very well-known traditional origami form. It originates from the era of the samurai. Yakko-san comes from the word *Yatsuko* meaning servant. Yakko-san was the man carrying the baggage for his master. In contemporary Japanese society, Yakko-san has come to mean "young man".

Yakko-san is a popular design in Japanese kimono prints.

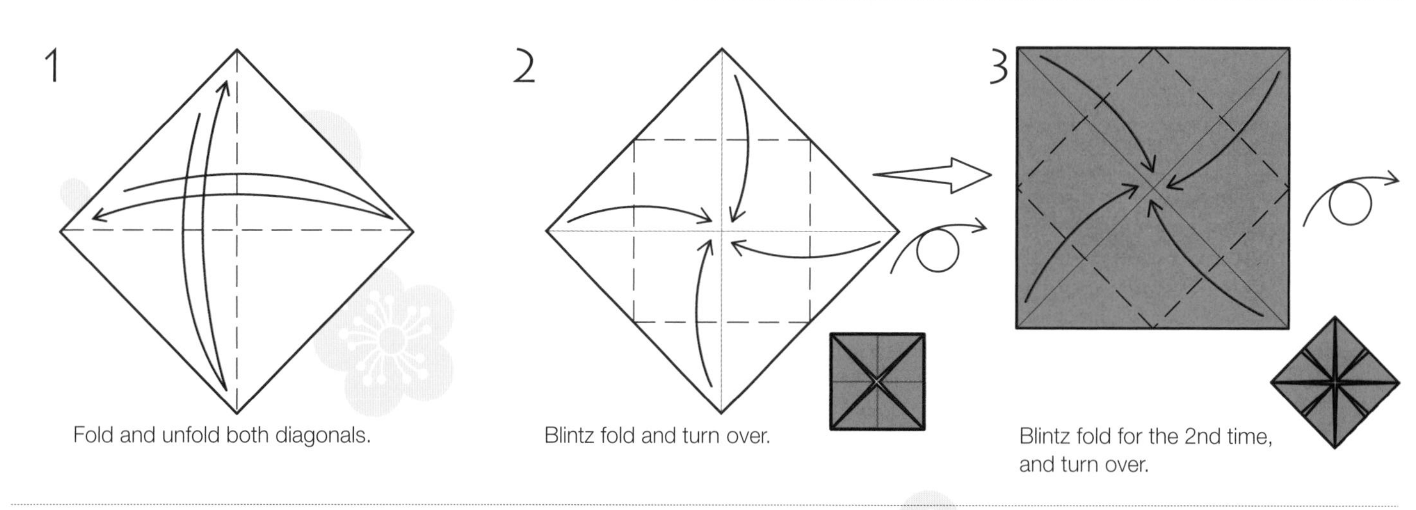

1 Fold and unfold both diagonals.

2 Blintz fold and turn over.

3 Blintz fold for the 2nd time, and turn over.

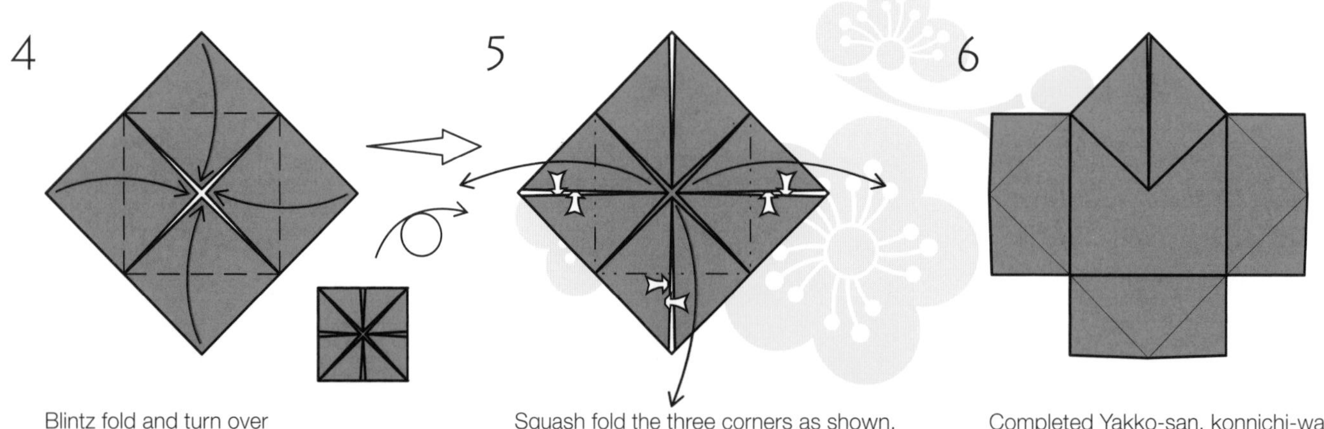

4 Blintz fold and turn over for the 3rd time.

5 Squash fold the three corners as shown. The corners will open outwards and form the square arms and feet.

6 Completed Yakko-san, konnichi-wa.

Samurai Helmet

Model: Traditional, Japan
Diagram: Matthew Gardiner

The samurai helmet, or *kabuto* can be made from a large square of paper and be worn as a paper warrior's hat.

1

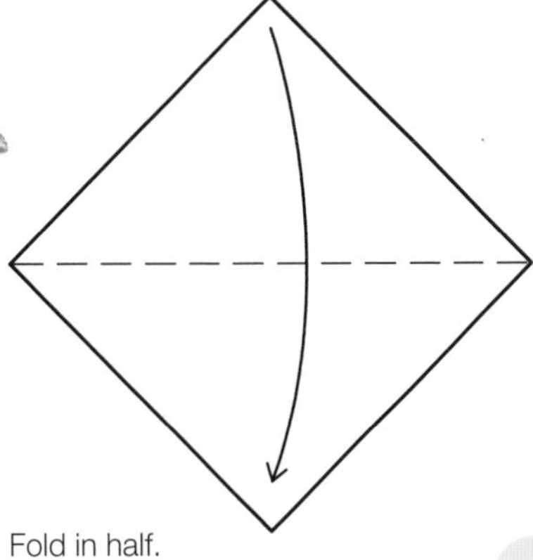

Fold in half.

2

Fold corners down.

3

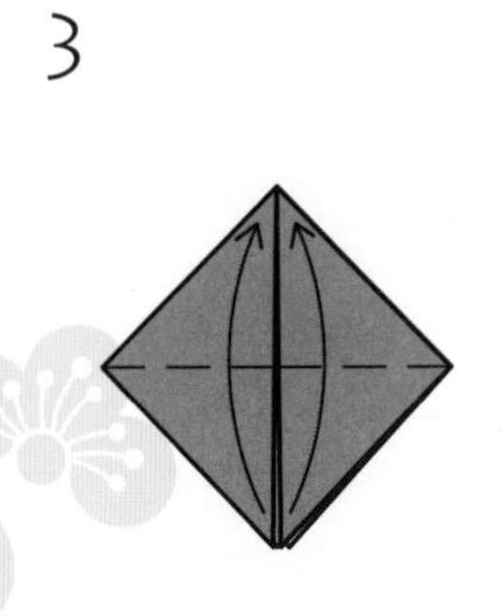

Fold flaps up.

4

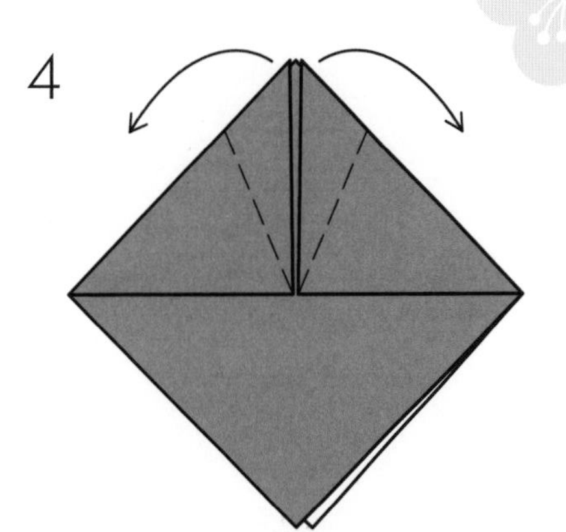

Fold top corners outwards.

5

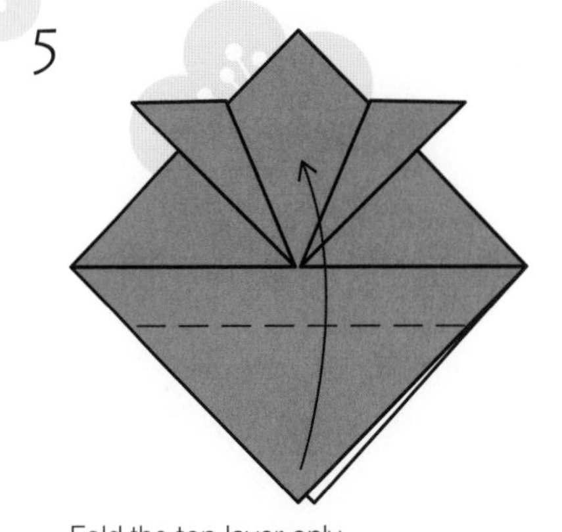

Fold the top layer only.

6

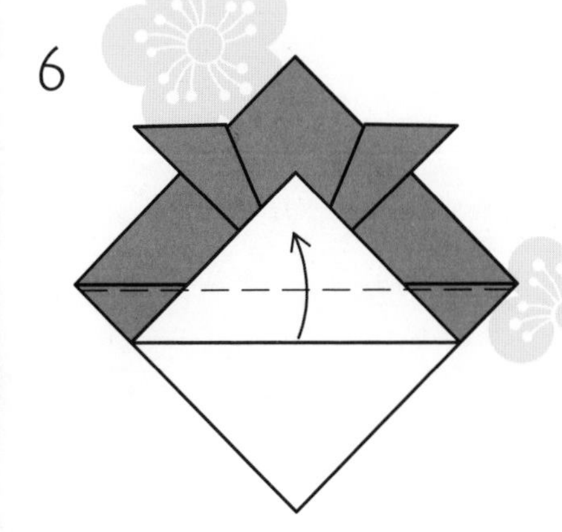

Fold up.

7

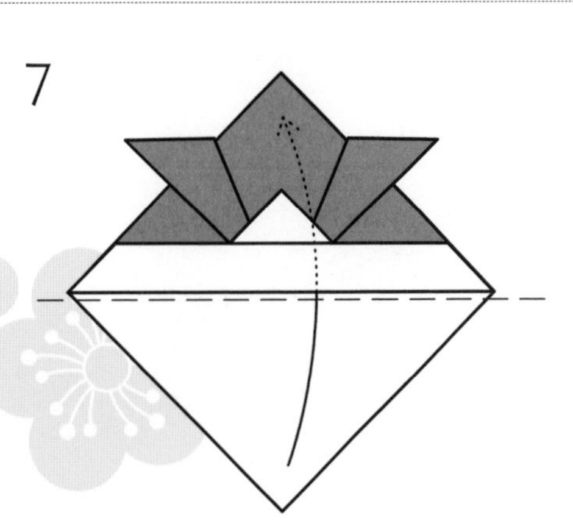

Fold up, then tuck in inside the helmet.

8

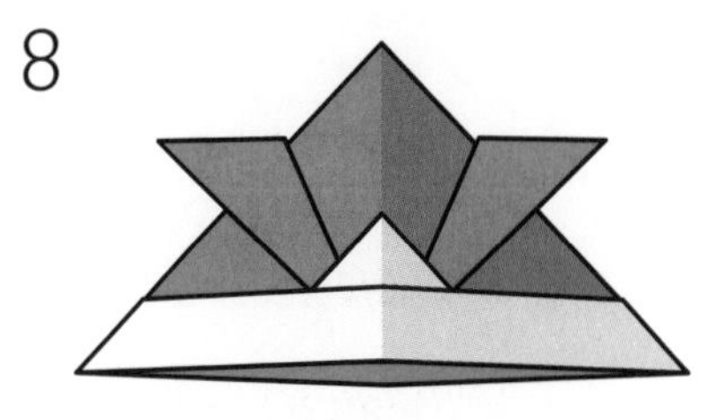

The finished Samurai helmet.

FISH

MODEL: TRADITIONAL, JAPAN
DIAGRAM: MATTHEW GARDINER

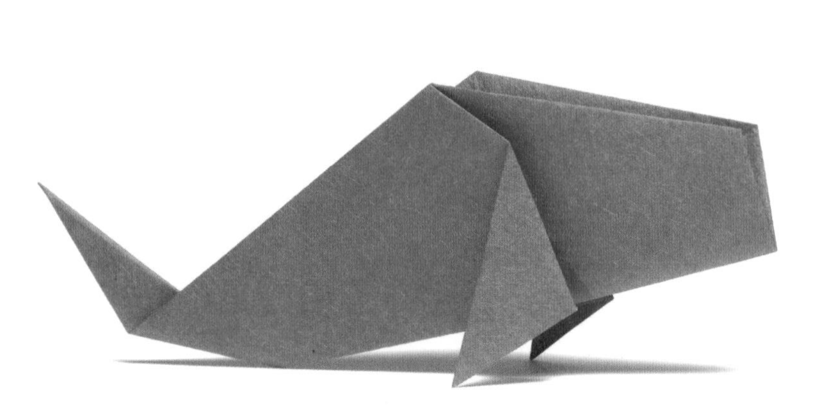

Fish are adored by the Japanese, both as a food and as a symbol of health, vitality and energy. A Japanese annual festival for boys uses the highly spirited carp (koi) as a symbol for energy and power. Look above the rooftops in late April to early May in Japan and you will see paper and cloth fish flying high. One fish per boy in the household is flown. Use a bright colour for this origami fish.

1

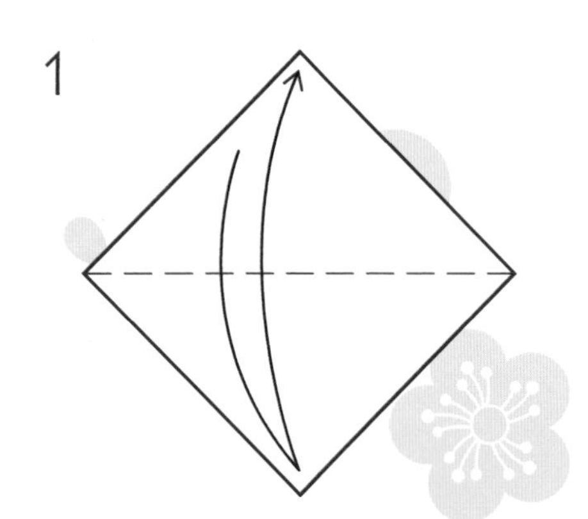

Start with white side up. Fold and unfold diagonal.

2

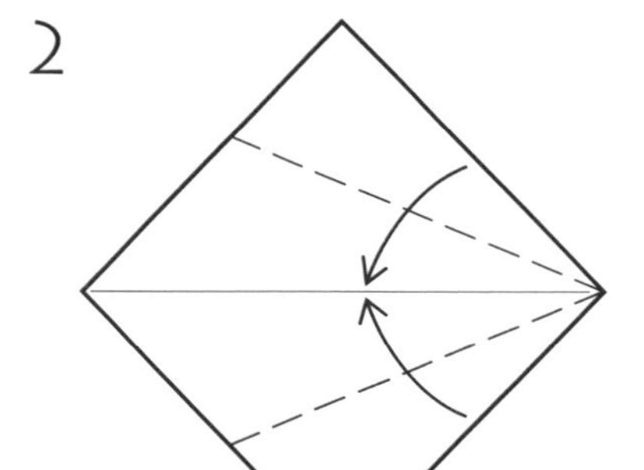

Fold both sides to the middle.

3

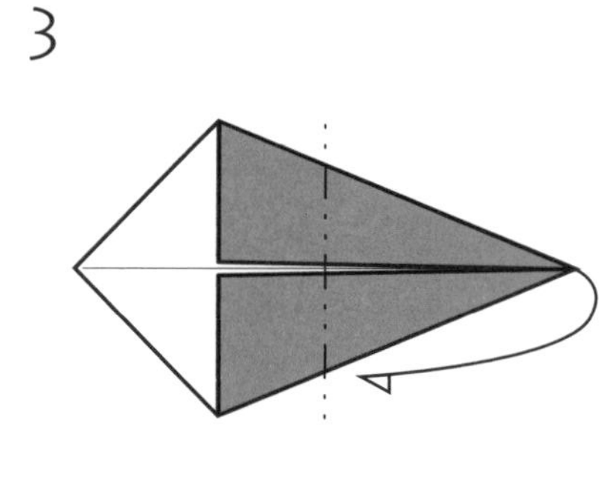

Mountain fold in half behind.

4

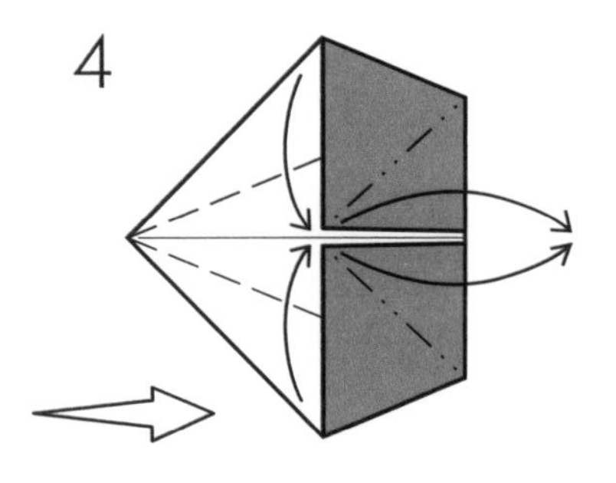

Squash fold both sides.

5

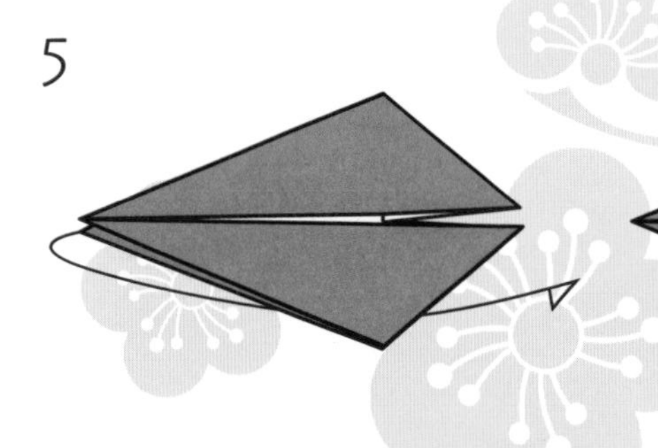

Mountain fold the back layer behind.

6

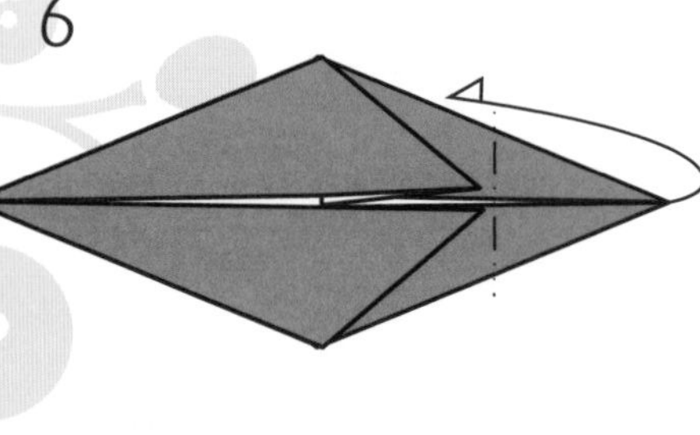

This is known as the fish base.
Mountain fold the point.

7

Mountain fold in half behind.

8

Fold the fins down on both sides.

9

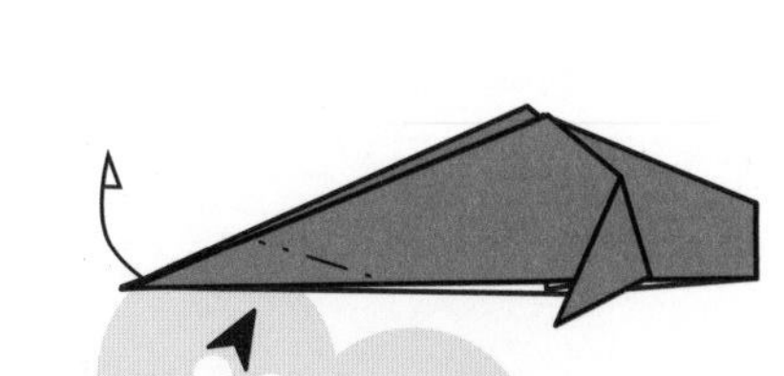

Inside reverse fold the tail.

Completed fish.

KIMONO

MODEL: TRADITIONAL, JAPAN
DIAGRAM: MATTHEW GARDINER

Kimono actually means ki (wearing) and mono (thing), however in modern Japan it now describes a particular kind of customary Japanese clothing. Worn by both men and women, kimonos are nowadays mostly worn during formal events, such as marriage. The fabric of a kimono is often expensive beyond reckoning due to the intricate designs sewn with silken threads. Choose a fine patterned sheet of chiyogami or yuzen for this traditional model.

This design can be used to make a kimono for a paper doll.

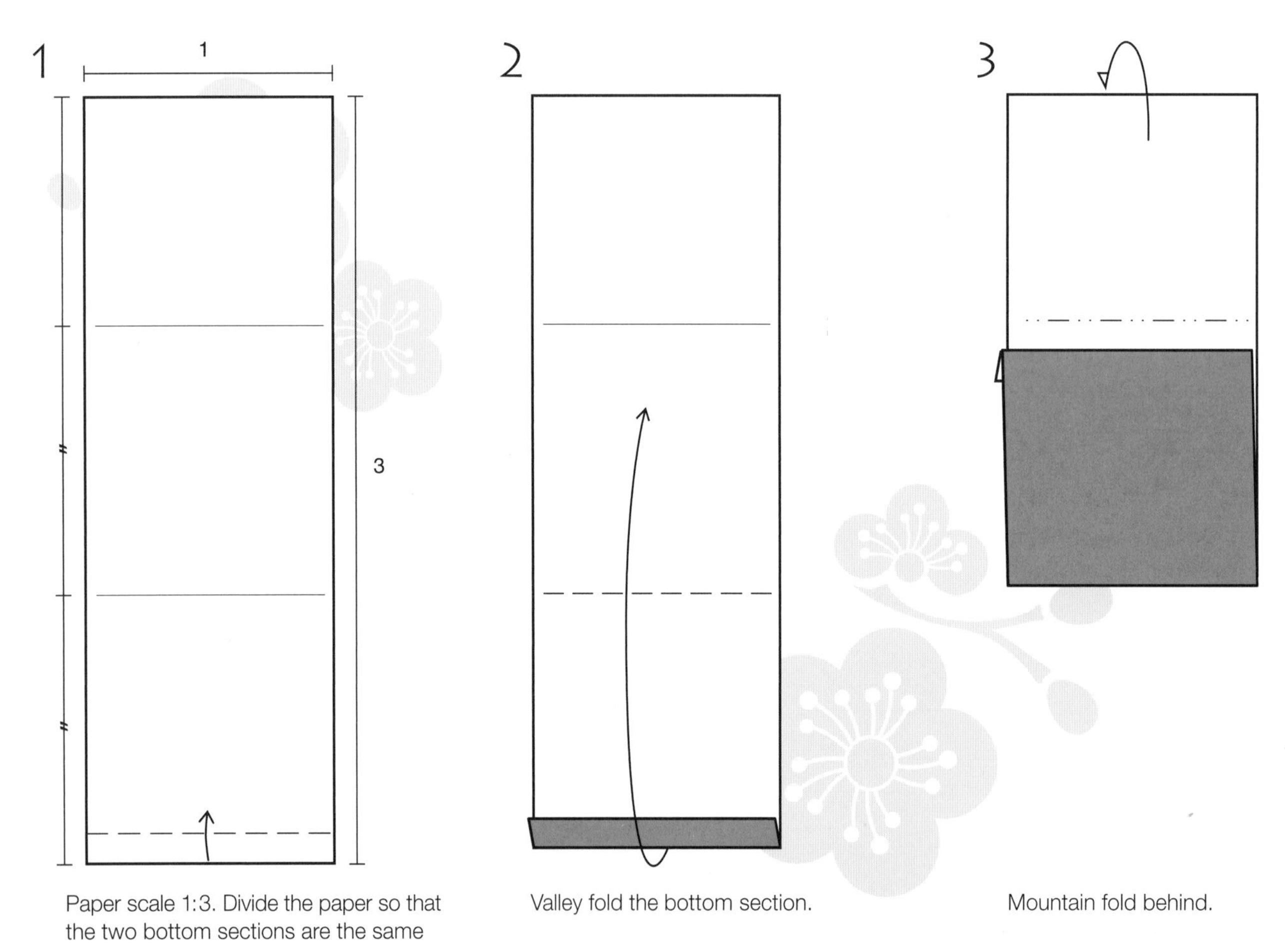

Paper scale 1:3. Divide the paper so that the two bottom sections are the same height and the top section is smaller. Valley fold a small flap at the bottom.

Valley fold the bottom section.

Mountain fold behind.

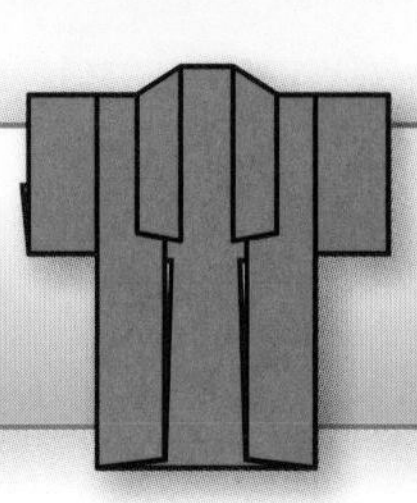

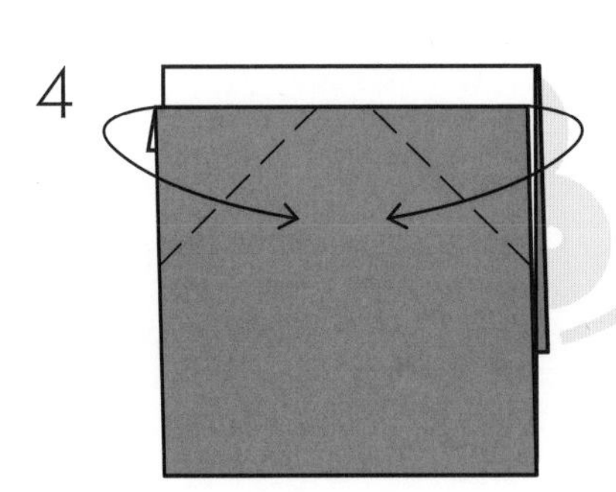

Fold the two top corners inwards.

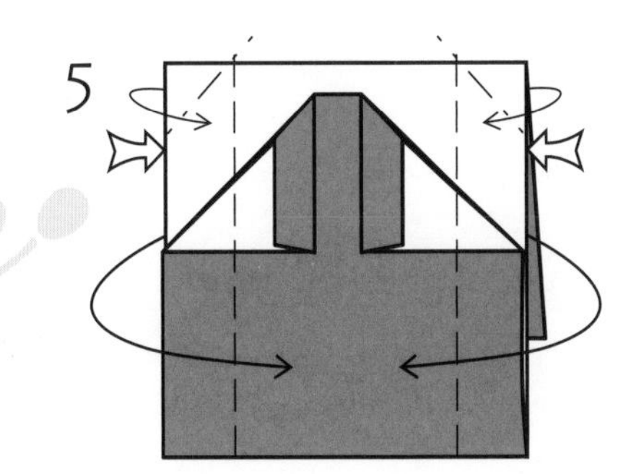

Squash fold both sides, through the top layers.

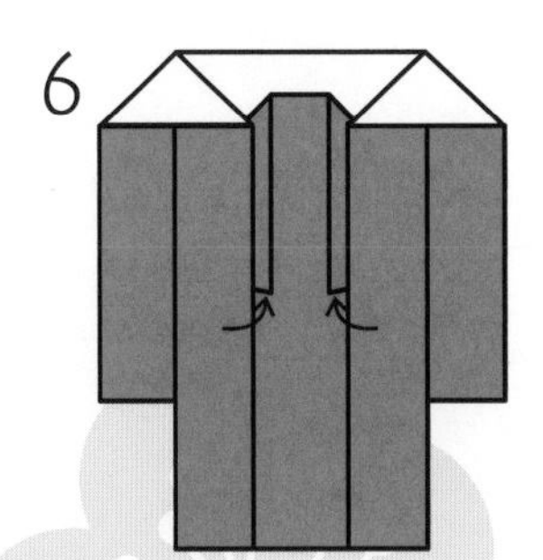

Tuck the front layer underneath the lower layer.

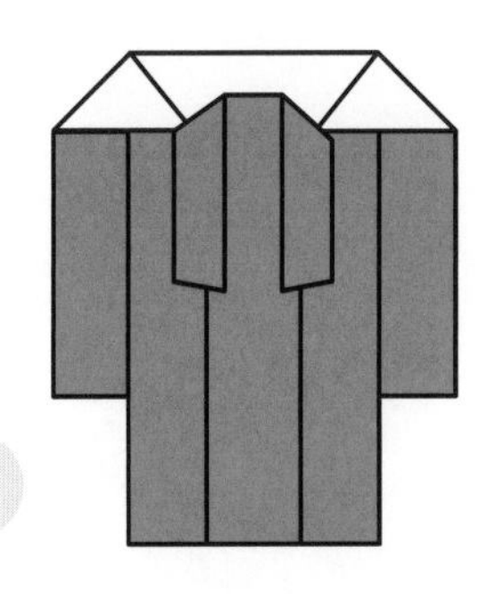

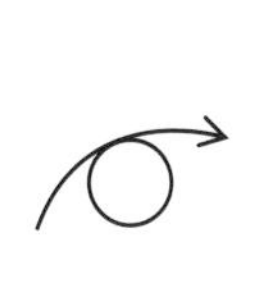

Your model should look like this.
Turn over.

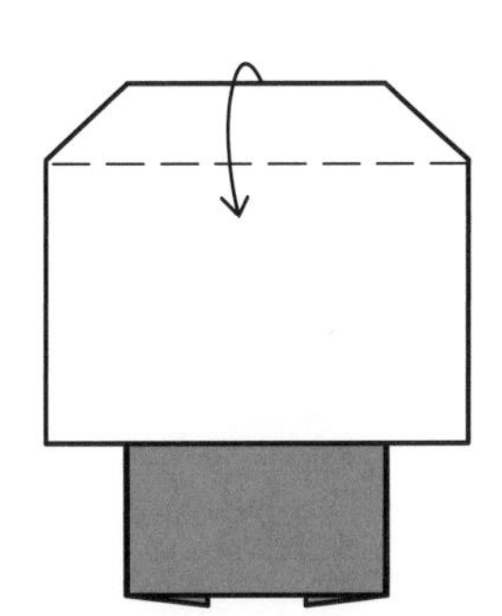

Fold down.

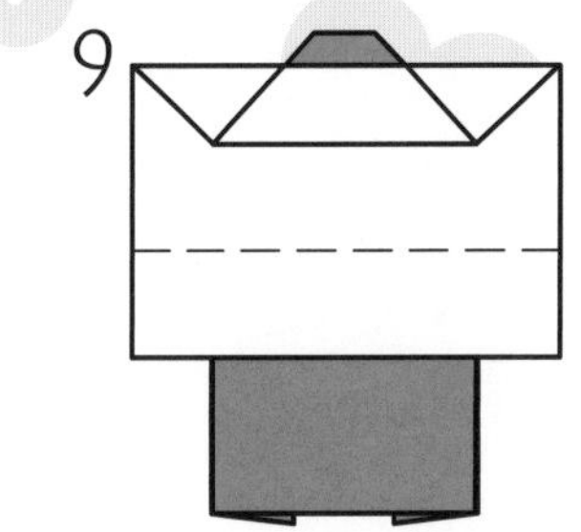

Fold upwards, creating the height of the kimono sleeves.

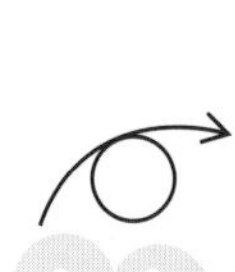

Your model should look like this.
Turn over.

Completed kimono.

TATO

MODEL: TRADITIONAL, JAPAN
DIAGRAM: MATTHEW GARDINER

The tato is a form of paper purse or puzzle in Japan. Tatogami is a folded paper that is used to store expensive kimonos, however this tato design is for smaller objects. Origami masters Shuzo Fujimoto and Michio Uchiyama are renowned for their innovation in expanding tato designs. The primary method involves dividing the square radially, in this case into eight segments, that fold inward over each other.

Tato can be folded from fabric, or two laminated sheets of paper for maximum durability and effect.

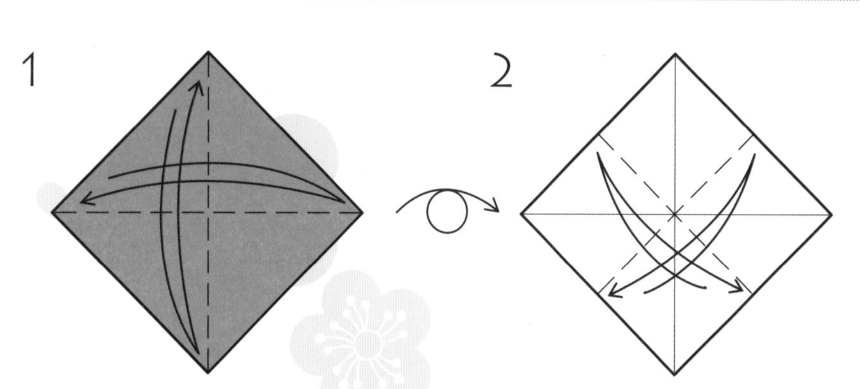

1 Start coloured side up.
Fold and unfold diagonals. Turn over.

2 Book fold and unfold.

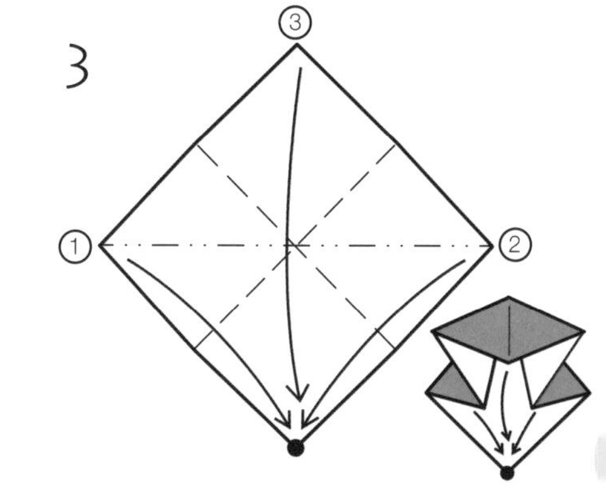

3 Collapse into the preliminary base.

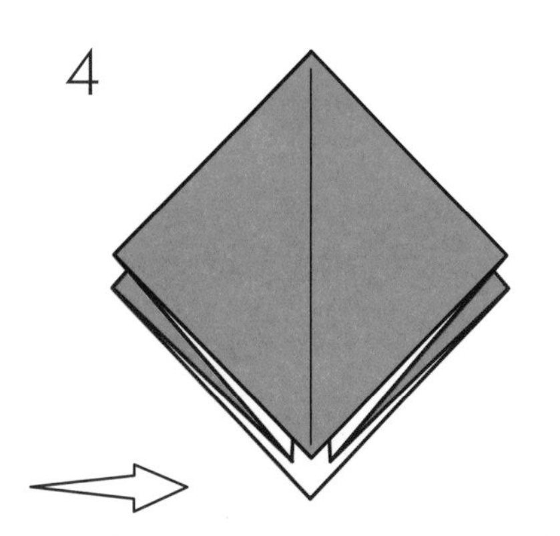

4 The preliminary base.

5 Fold edges of top layer to the centre.

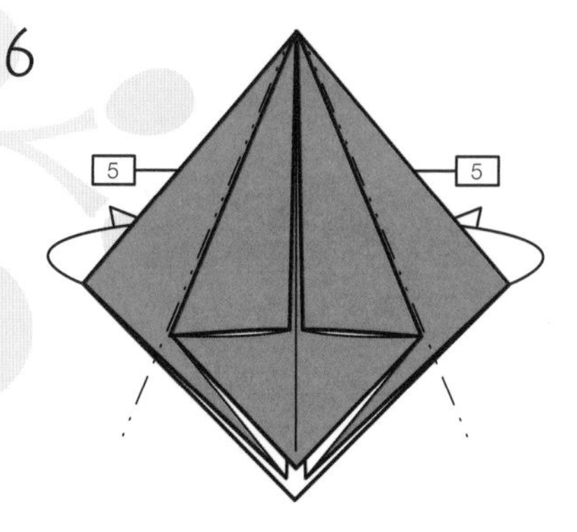

6 Repeat step 5 on the other side.

7

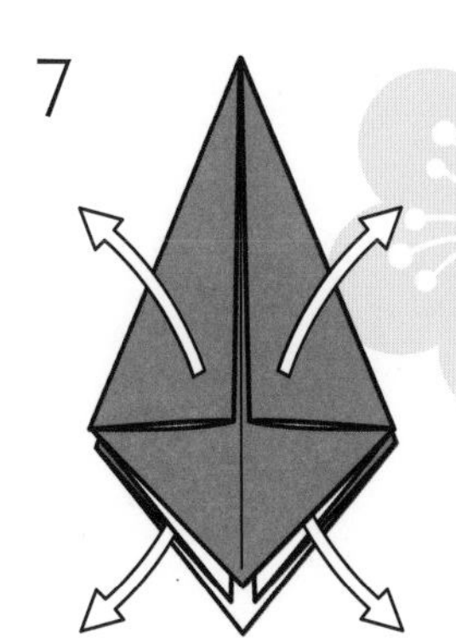

Unfold to a flat sheet.

8

Fold corners in at the intersection of existing creases. This makes a perfect octagon.

9

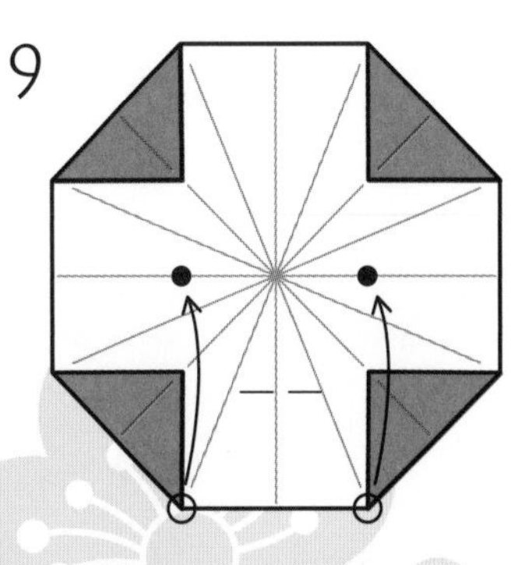

Fold the edge to the middle. Be careful to only crease as shown.

10

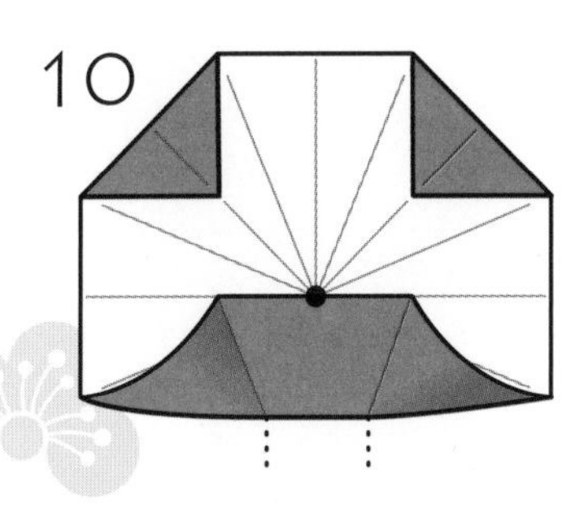

Step 9 in process. Only crease between the dotted lines.

11

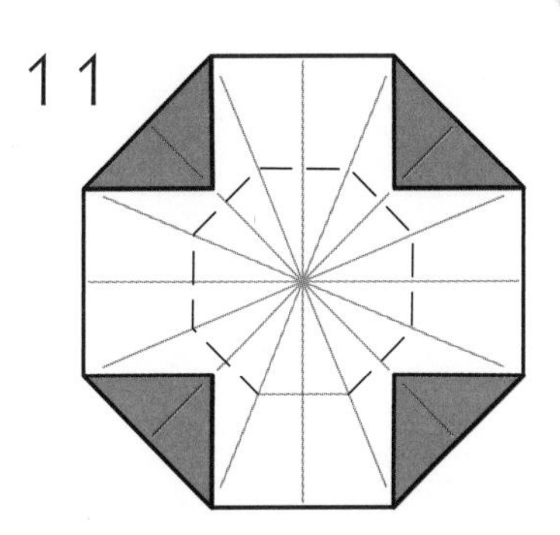

Repeat step 9 all around the octagon.

12

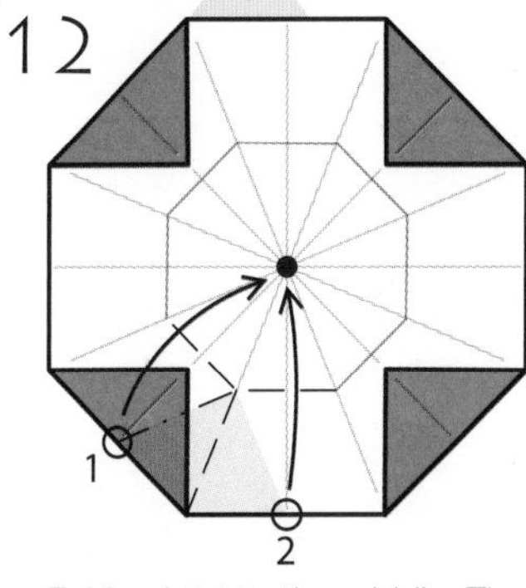

Fold point 1 to the middle. Then fold point 2. This will create a point with the greyed-out paper. Fold this point to the left. Look ahead to step 13, to see the result.

13

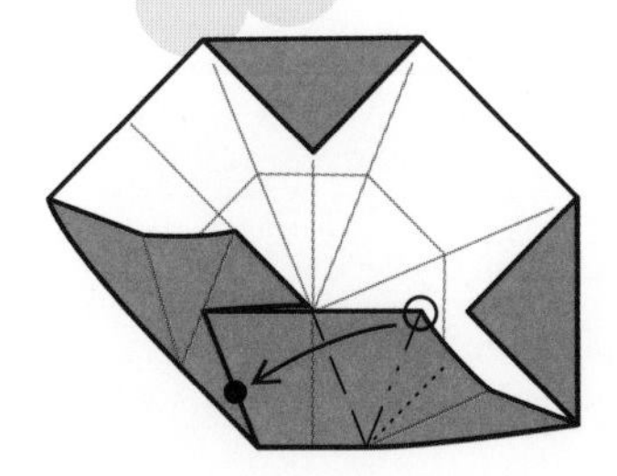

Fold the point marked by the circle to the point marked by the dot.

14

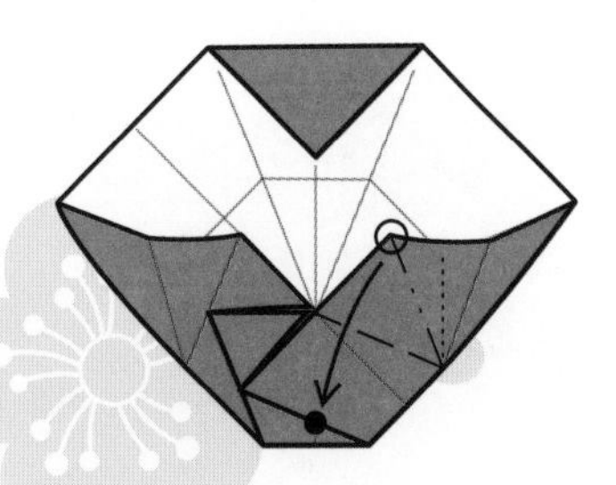

Repeat step 13 on the remaining points. The last point needs to be tucked under the first point.

15

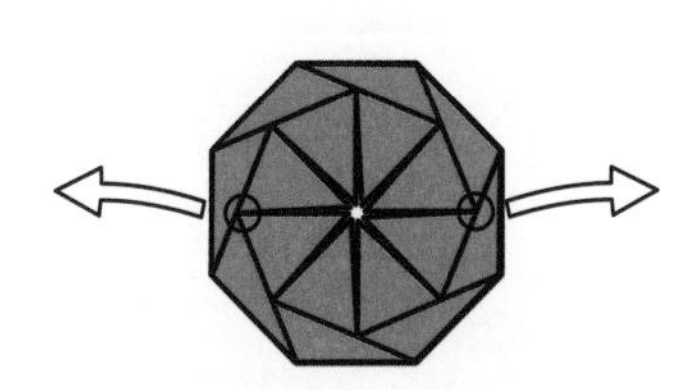

The finished tato. To open the purse gently pull on two opposite points.

WINDMILL

MODEL: TRADITIONAL, JAPAN
DIAGRAM: MATTHEW GARDINER

Windmills are iconic in the Netherlands where they harness the power of the wind for grinding grain and carving wood. This little windmill can harness the power of your breath when combined with a drawing pin and chopstick. A gentle breeze will have this model in a spin.

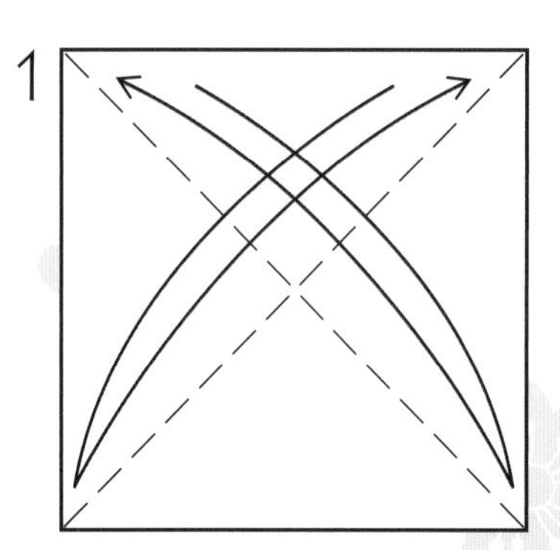

Fold and unfold diagonals.

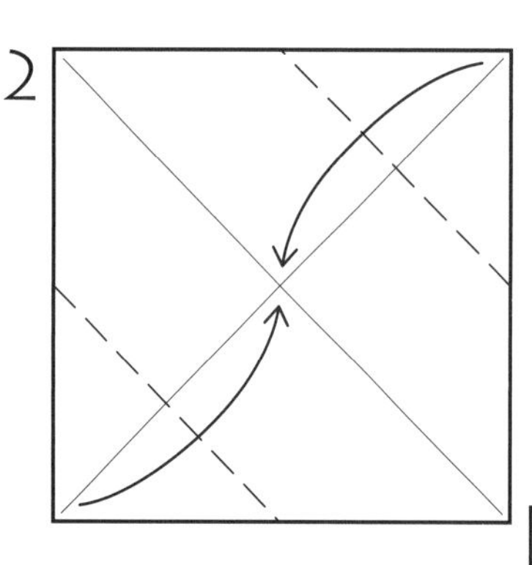

Half blintz fold and unfold. Turn over.

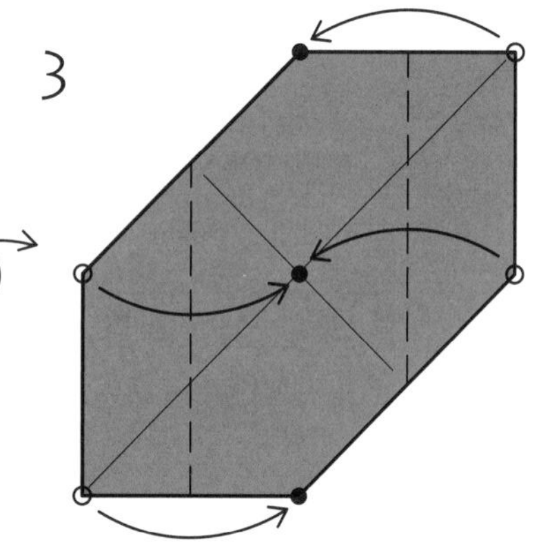

Fold and unfold in half.

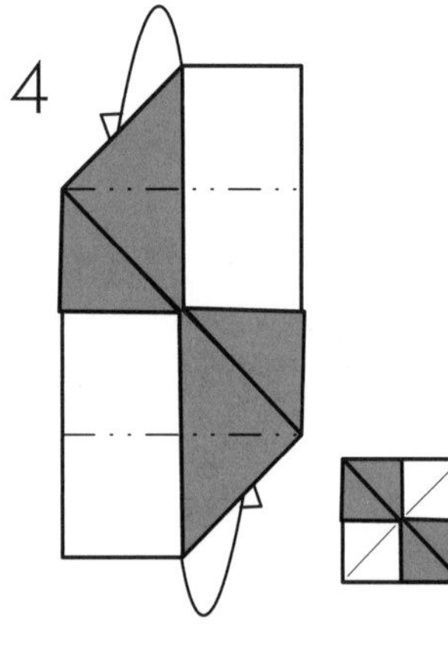

Mountain fold bottom and top edges to the centre. Turn over.

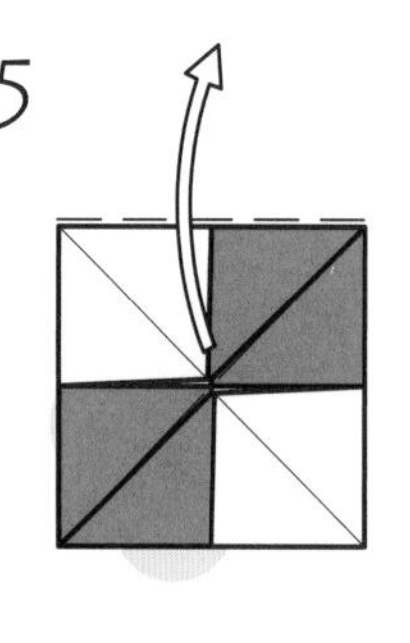

Pull out the paper from the middle.

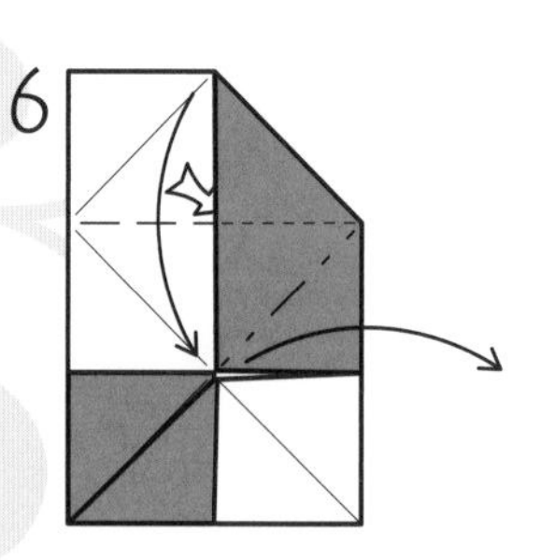

Squash fold, bringing the top centre corners outwards.

7

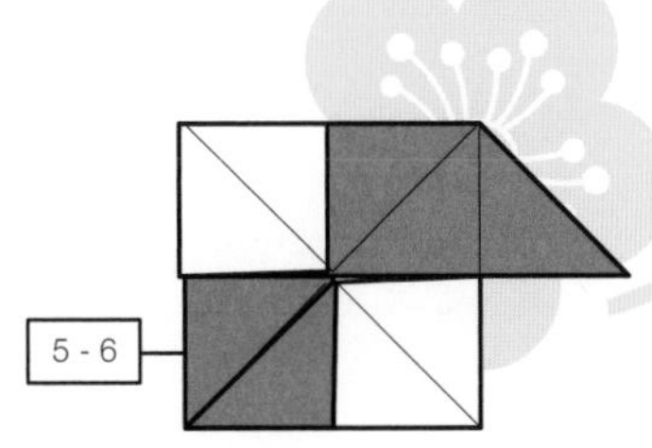

Repeat steps 5-6 on the bottom right corner.

8

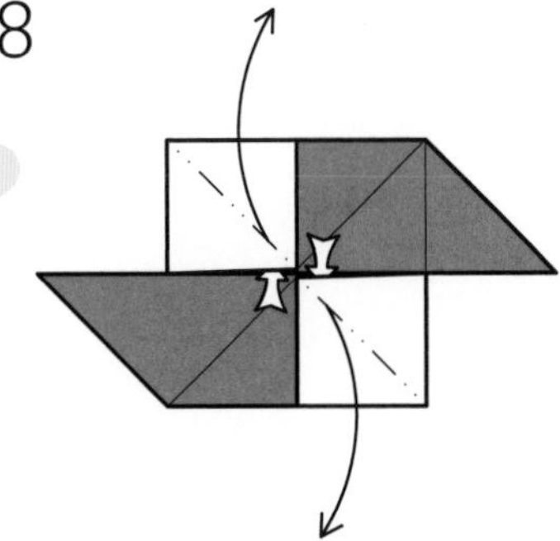

Squash fold the remaining corners outwards.

9

Completed windmill.

10

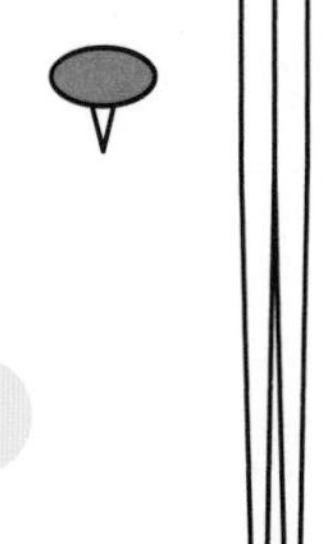

Take a drawing pin and wooden chopstick or pencil.

11

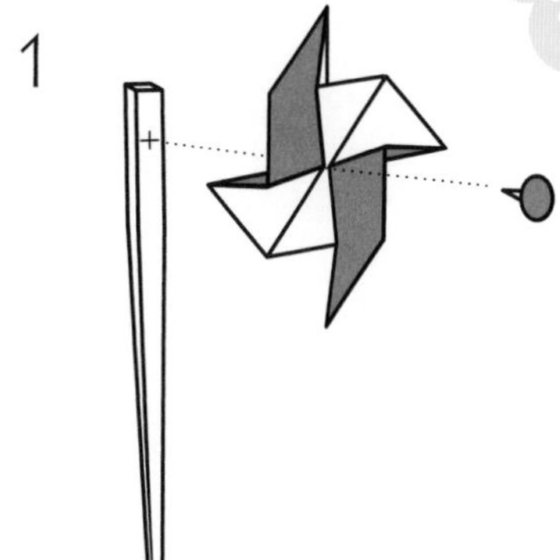

Push the pin through the centre of the windmill and into the chopstick.

12

Blow gently to make the windmill spin.

PAJARITO

MODEL: TRADITIONAL, SPAIN
DIAGRAM: MATTHEW GARDINER

Pajarito, or "Little Bird" is the most famous traditional design from Spain. Historically, Spanish origami was born from the geometric fascination of the Moors. The model requires a 3D transformation move at the end. Be careful when folding to make sure the mountain and valley folds are placed correctly. Then the final move will be almost "natural" for the paper.

The pajarito is the icon of Spanish origami. Papiroflexia is the Spanish way of saying paper folding.

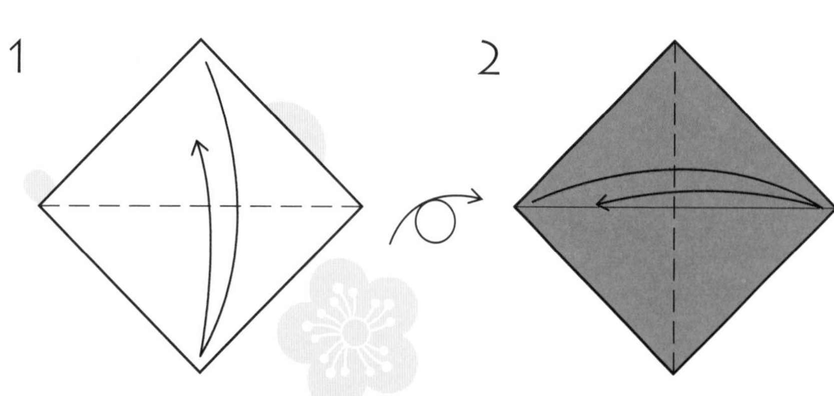

1. Begin white side up. Fold and unfold diagonal. Turn over.

2. Fold and unfold diagonal.

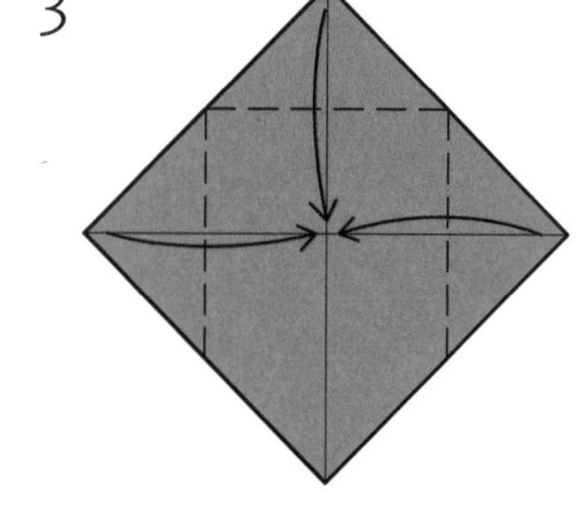

3. Fold three corners to the centre.

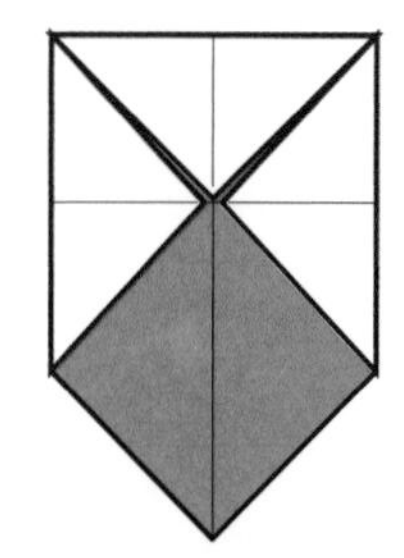

4. Completed step 3. Turn over.

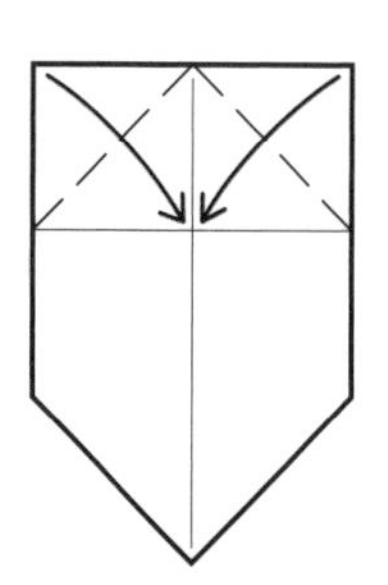

5. Fold top corners down to centre point.

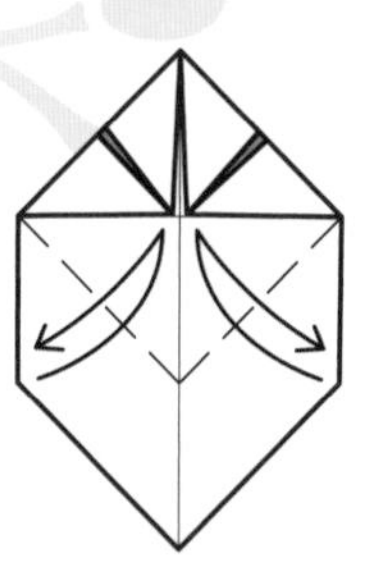

6. Fold and unfold, be careful to only crease as shown.

7

Unfold corners and side flaps.
Turn over.

8

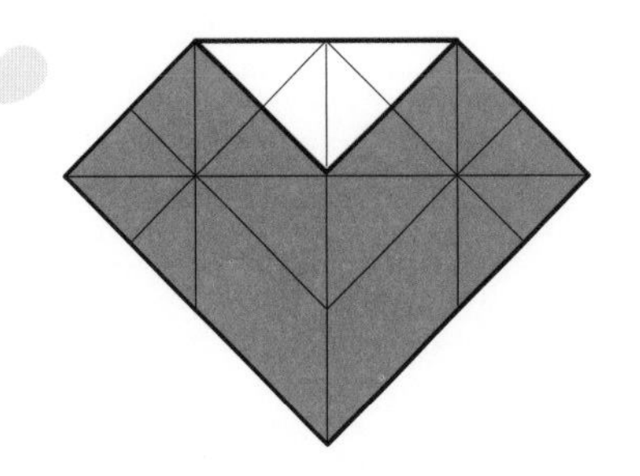

Your model should look like this.
Turn over.

9

Fold on existing creases. Pay attention to the mountain and valley folds.

10

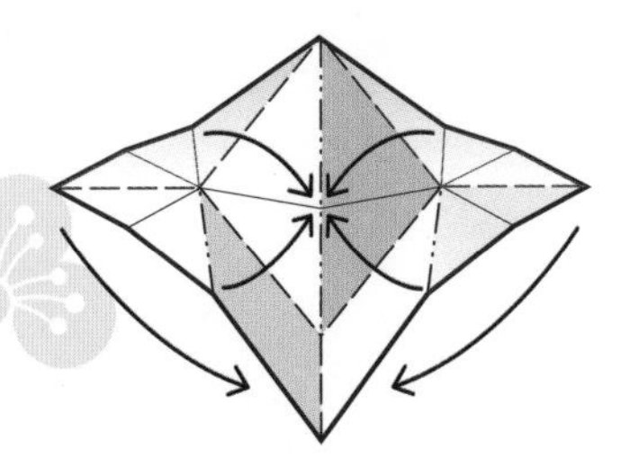

The 3D move in progress.

11

Completed pajarito.

Cup

MODEL: Traditional, Japan
DIAGRAM: Matthew Gardiner

The cup is a traditional model that actually works.

1

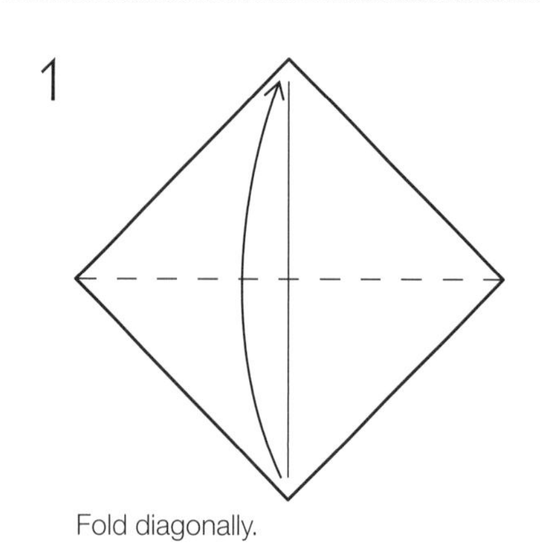

Fold diagonally.

2

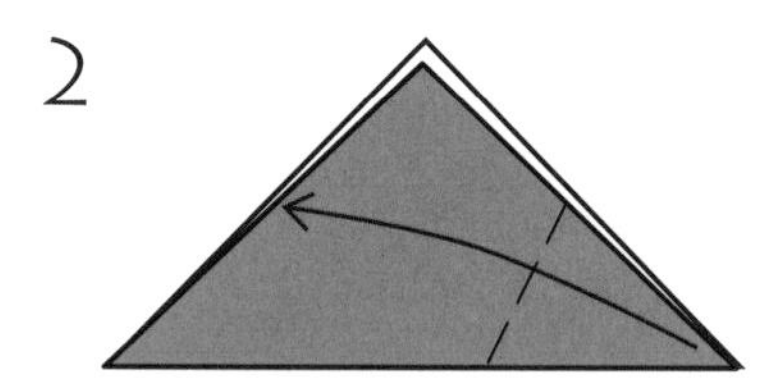

Fold corner to side. Notice that the top edge of the fold will end up parallel to the bottom edge.

3

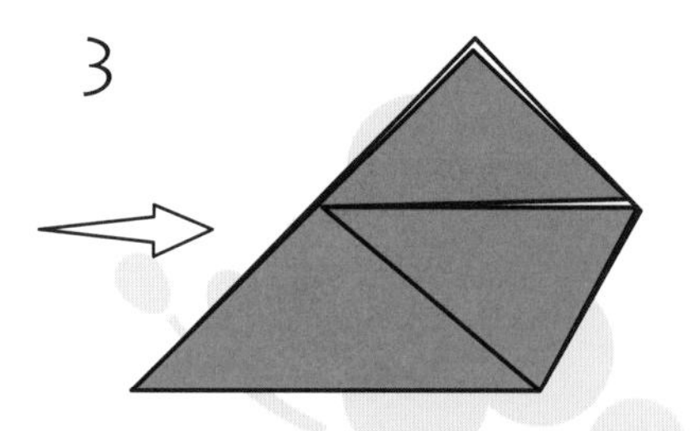

It should look like this. Turn over.

4

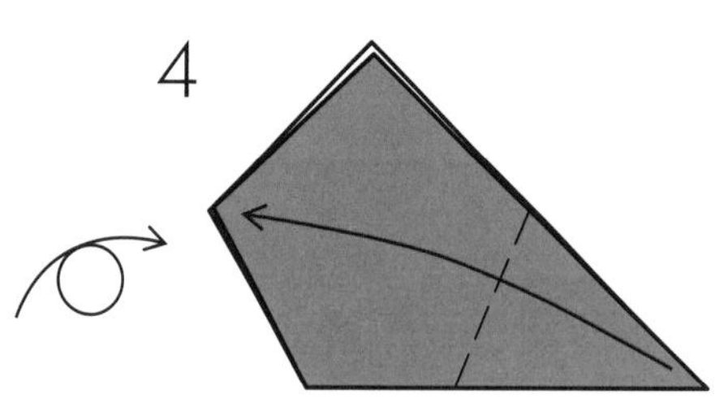

Repeat step 2 on the other side.

5

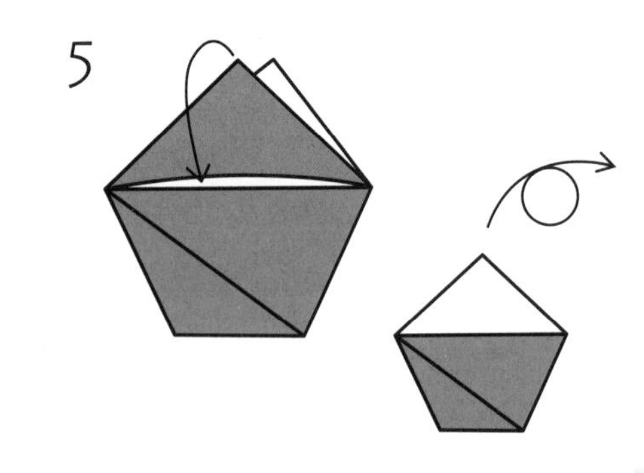

Slip top corner into pocket. Turn over.

6

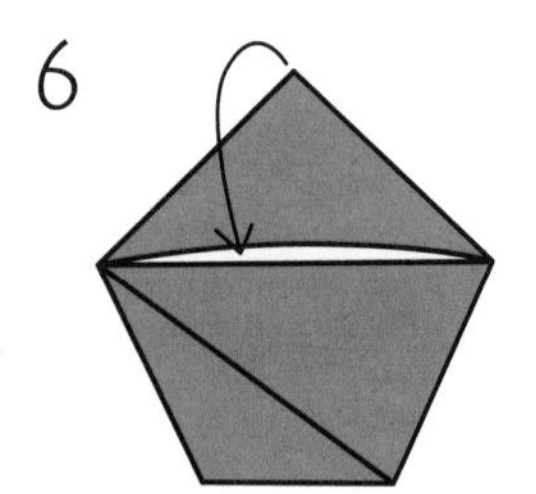

Repeat step 5 with the remaining point.

7

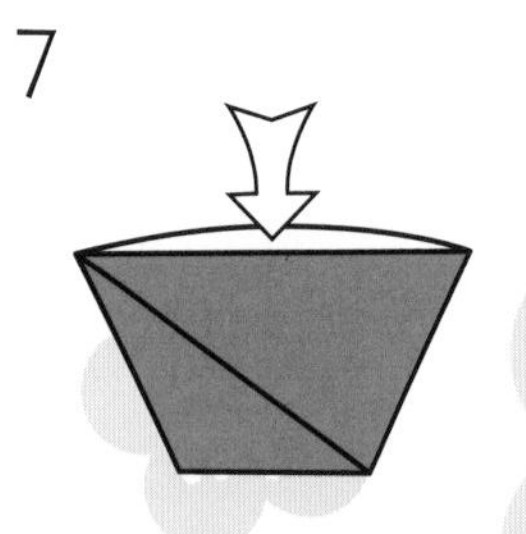

Open up pocket.

8

Completed cup.

SWAN

MODEL: TRADITIONAL, JAPAN
DIAGRAM: MATTHEW GARDINER

This simple origami swan expresses the form of this elegant bird swimming on the water of a lake.

1

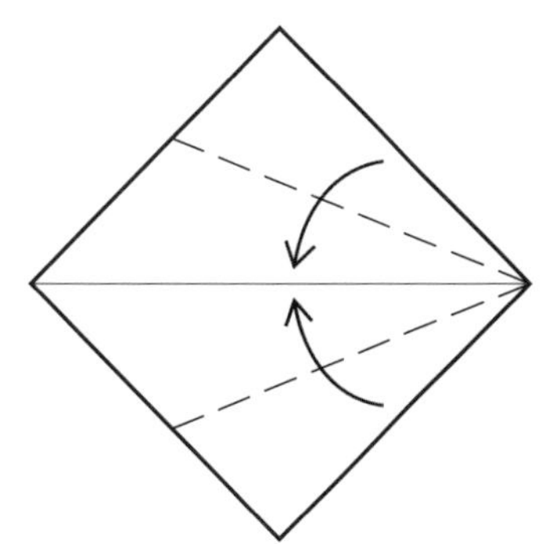

Pre-crease diagonal. Fold sides to the middle.

2

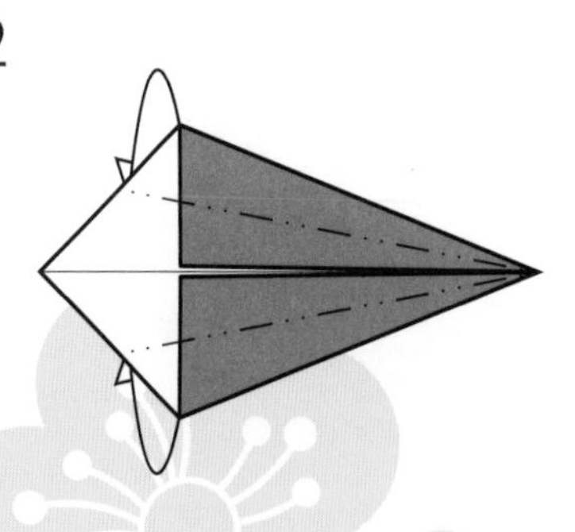

Mountain fold both sides to the middle.

3

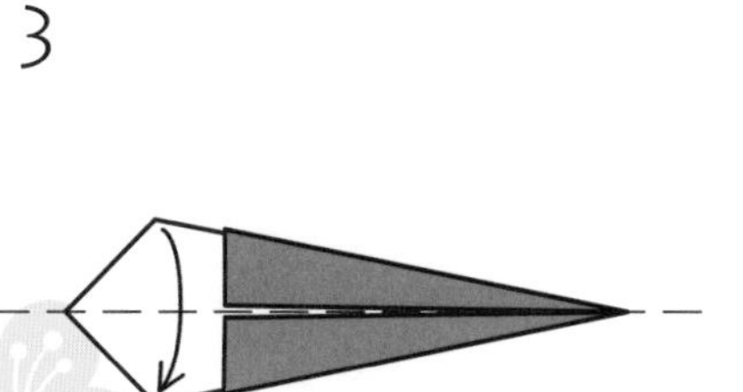

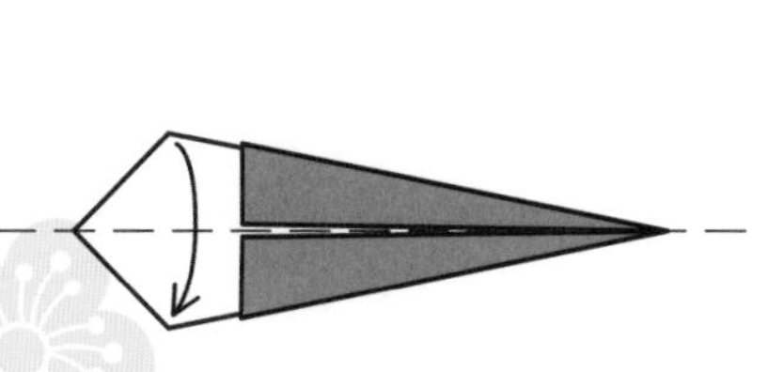

Fold in half.

4

5

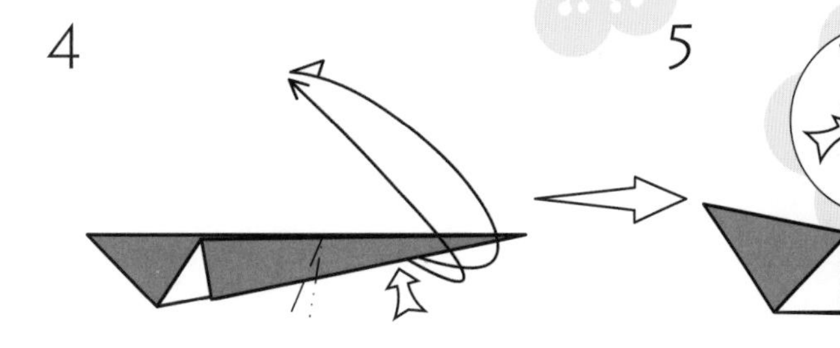

Outside reverse fold the neck.

Outside reverse fold the head.

6

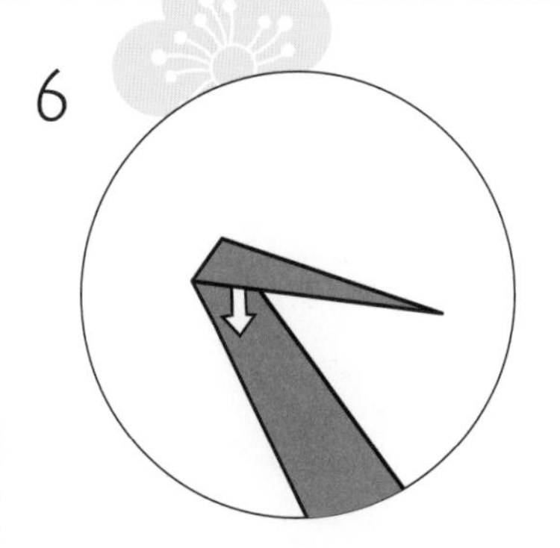

Pull out hidden paper on both sides of the head.

7

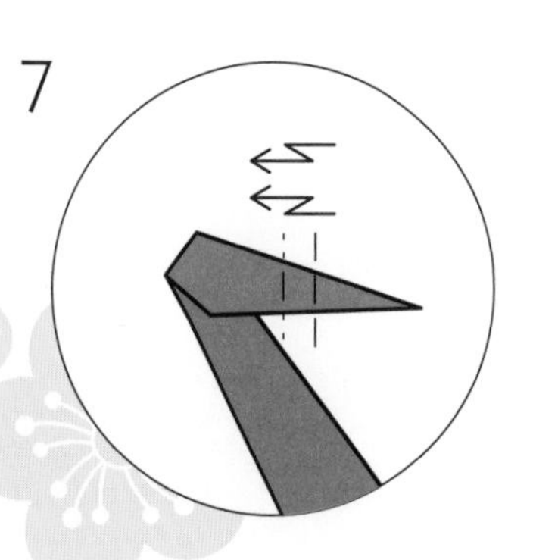

Pleat, then double reverse fold the head to form the beak.

8

Completed swan.

MENKO

MODEL: TRADITIONAL, JAPAN
DIAGRAM: MATTHEW GARDINER

Menko is a Japanese game that is played by two or more players with thick cards. A player's card is placed on a hardwood or concrete floor and the other player throws down their card, trying to flip the other player's card with a gust of wind or by striking their card against the other card. If they succeed, they take both cards. The player who collects the most cards wins.

This design can also be used in the household as a decorative coaster. Use chiyogami, and apply a coat or two of laquer to transform the menko into a useful item.

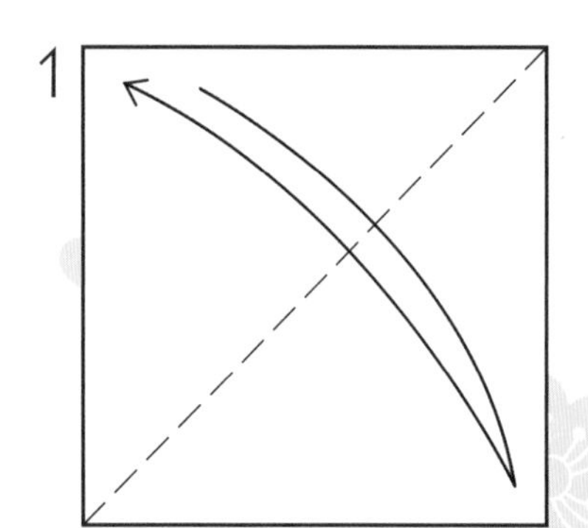

Fold diagonally then unfold.

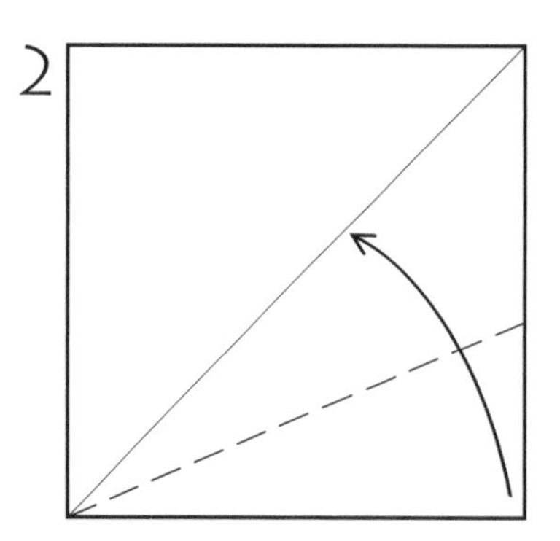

Fold bottom edge to diagonal crease.

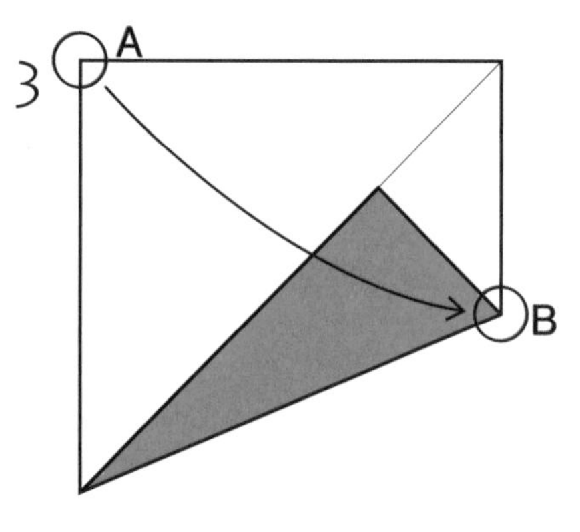

Fold point A to point B. Make a small crease at top.

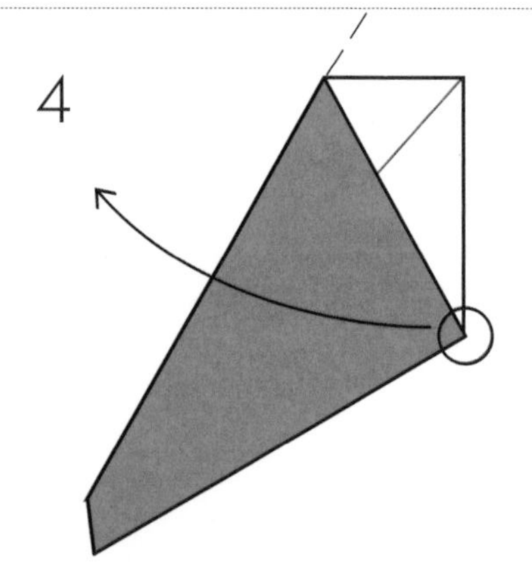

Where the crease touches the top edge is one third.

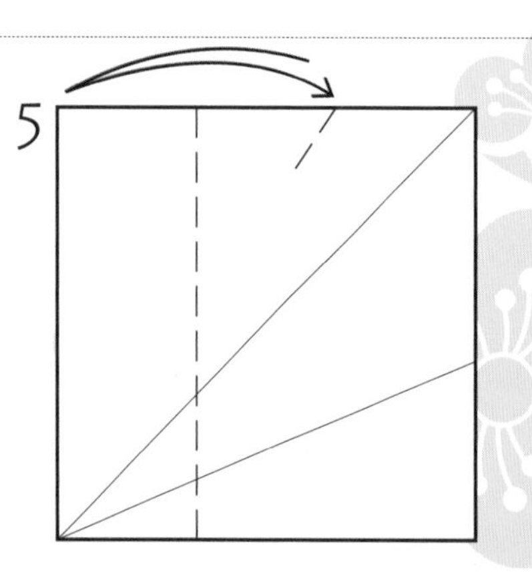

Fold and unfold the side edge to meet the third.

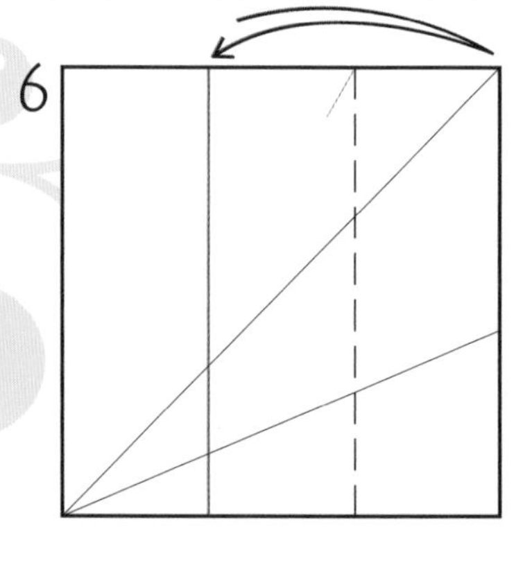

Fold the other edge to meet fold from step 5.

7

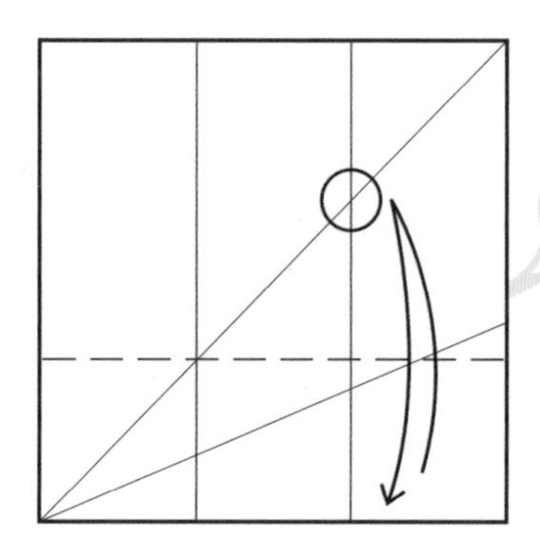

Fold the bottom edge to meet the marked intersection then unfold.

8

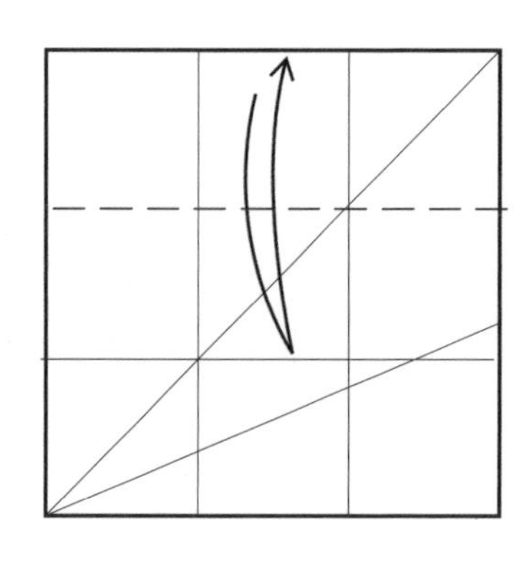

Fold and unfold top edge to meet fold from step 7.

9

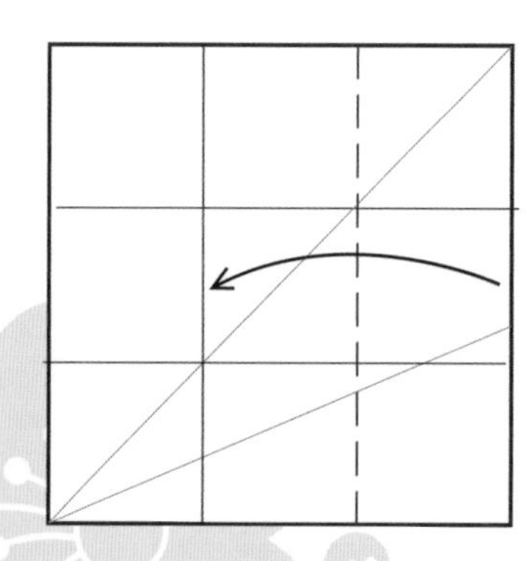

Fold in.

10

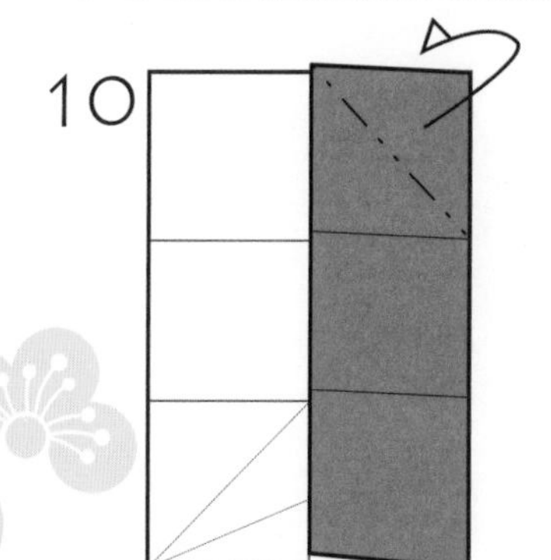

Mountain fold behind.

11

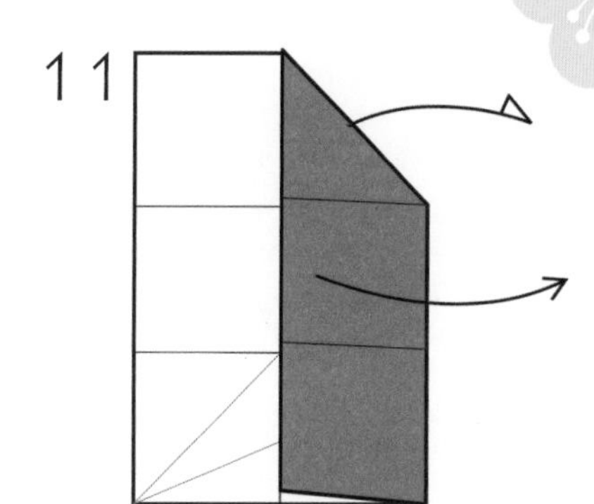

Unfold corner and open up the sheet.

12

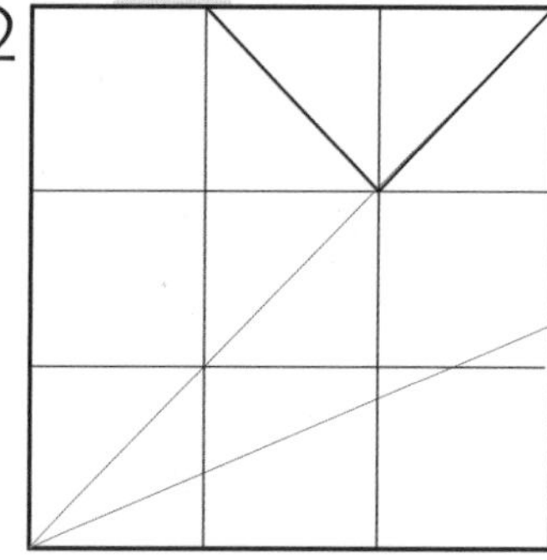

Completed steps 9-11.

13

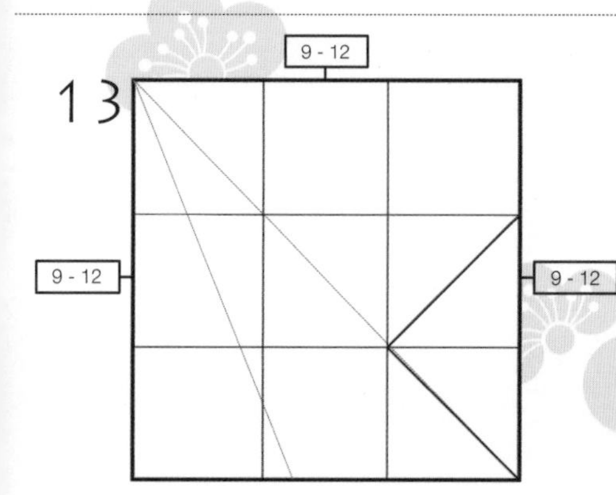

Turn the model 90°. Repeat steps 9-12 on the three remaining sides.

14

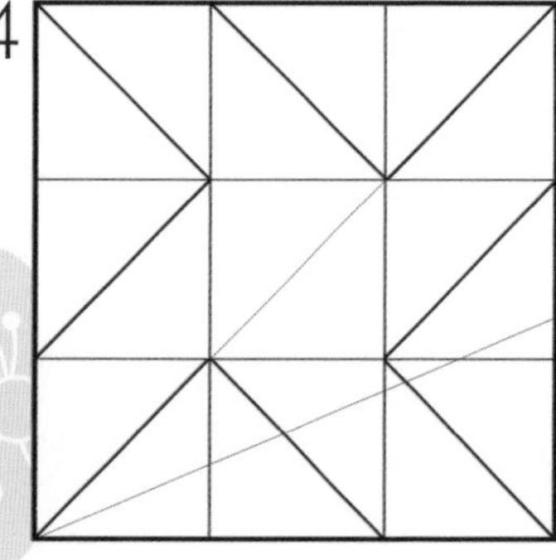

Completed crease pattern.

15

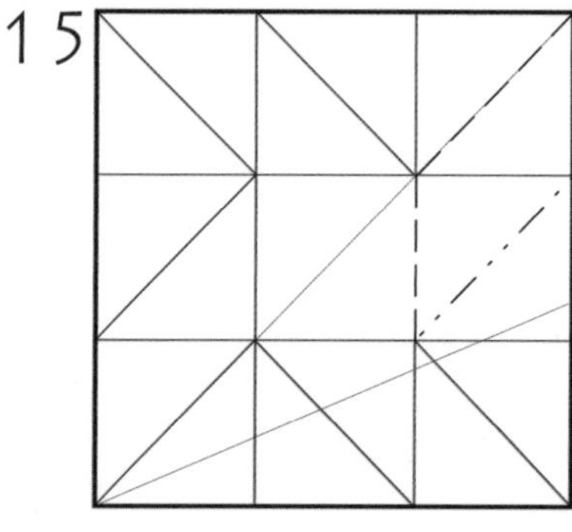

Assembly. Make the first folds as shown.

16

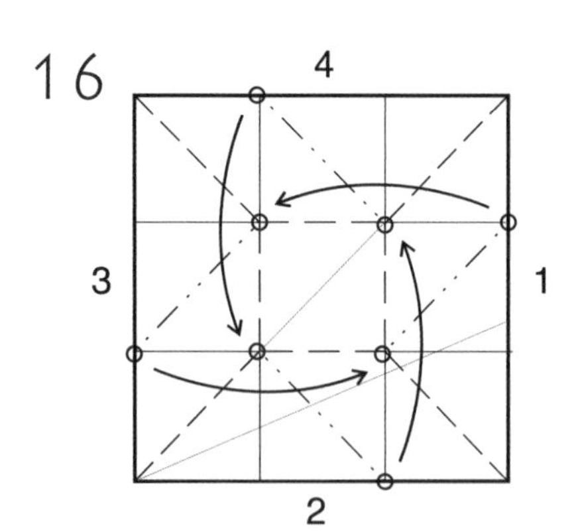

Repeat step 15 on side 2, then 3, then with 4. The last side needs to be woven to sit flat.

17

It will look like a pinwheel. Turn over.

18

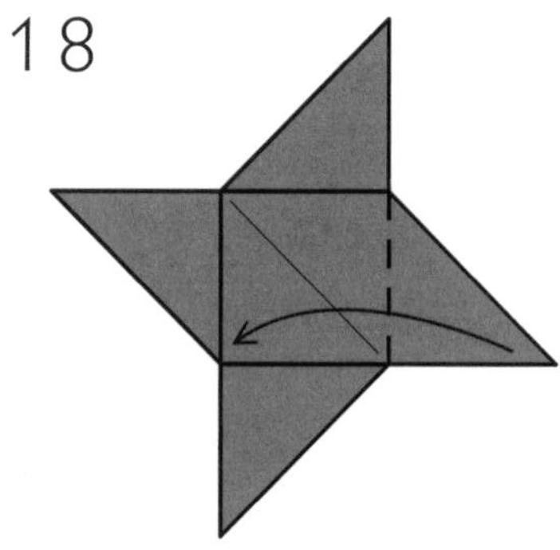

Fold point along existing crease.

19

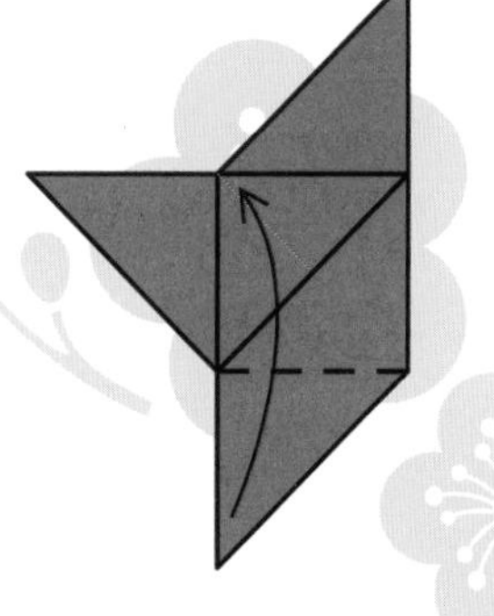

Fold the next point on top of the last.

20

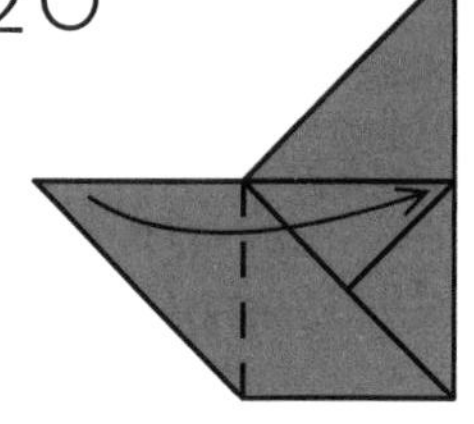

Again...

21

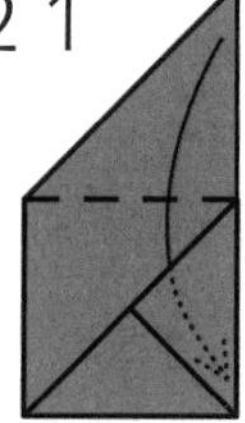

Fold the last point, then unfold and tuck it under the first point to lock the menko.

22

Completed menko.

Chopstick Duck

MODEL: MATTHEW GARDINER
DIAGRAM: MATTHEW GARDINER

The chopstick duck is a simple origami model made from a chopstick paper wrapping. This decorative little duck also becomes a rest for your chopsticks for the duration of your meal. You may find it necessary to trim your wrapper at the end, as wrappers come in different dimensions.

A chopstick rest in Japan is called a hashi-oki; they are usually made from ceramic.

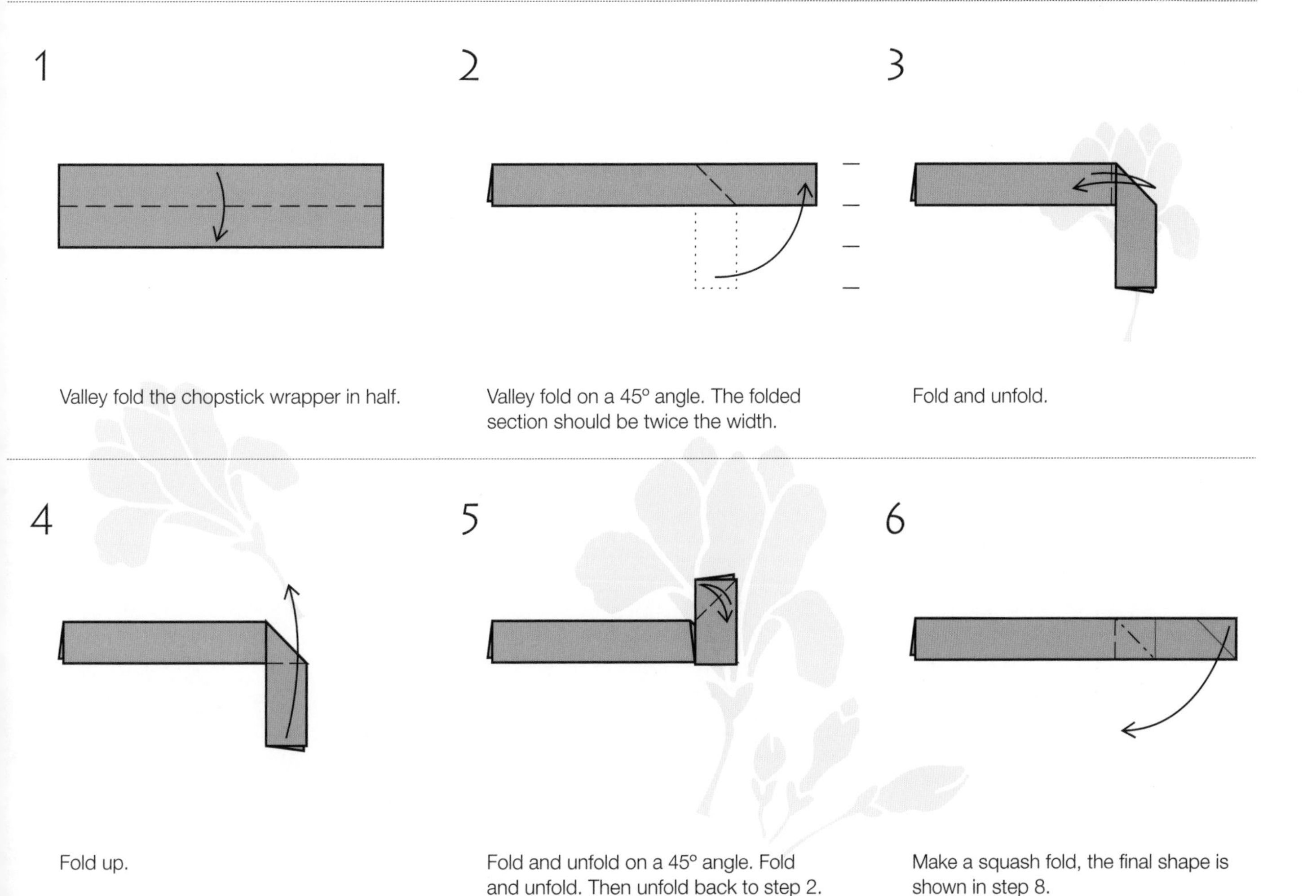

1. Valley fold the chopstick wrapper in half.

2. Valley fold on a 45° angle. The folded section should be twice the width.

3. Fold and unfold.

4. Fold up.

5. Fold and unfold on a 45° angle. Fold and unfold. Then unfold back to step 2.

6. Make a squash fold, the final shape is shown in step 8.

The Chopstick Duck

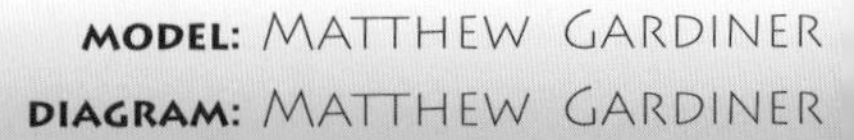

Model: Matthew Gardiner
Diagram: Matthew Gardiner

7

The squash fold in progress.

8

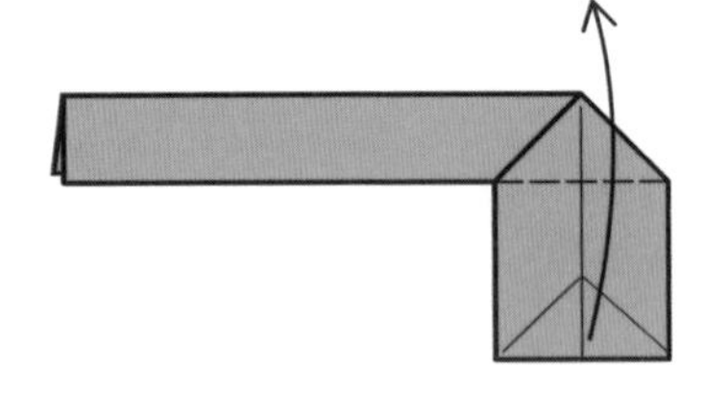

Fold up.

9

Fold to the side.

10

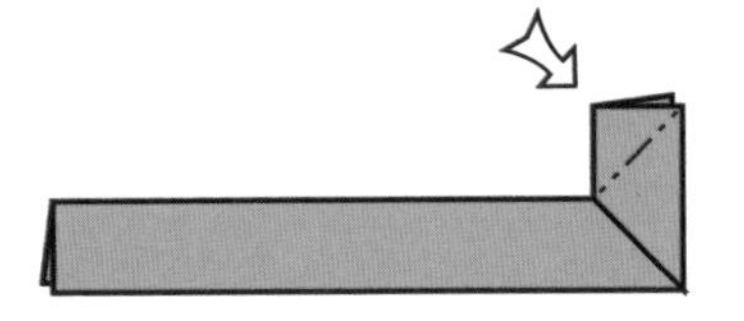

Make an inside reverse fold.

11

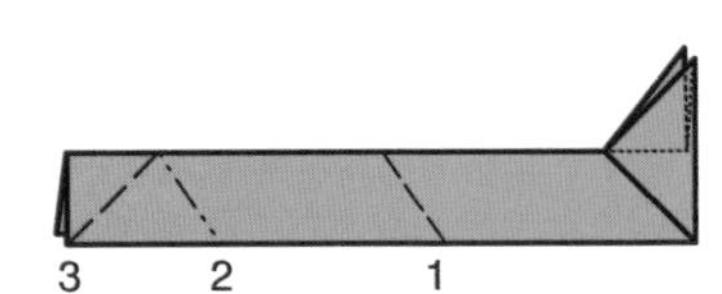

Completed inside reverse fold. Make three folds in order to shape the duck's neck and head.

12

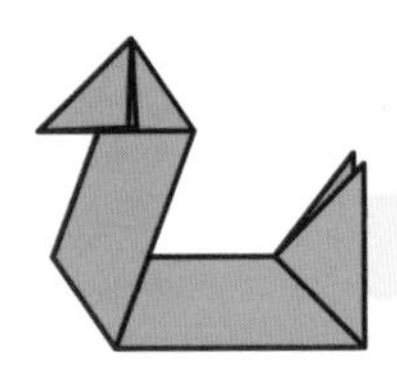

The shaped duck. Unfold back to previous step. If your paper is too long, this is the best time to trim it.

13

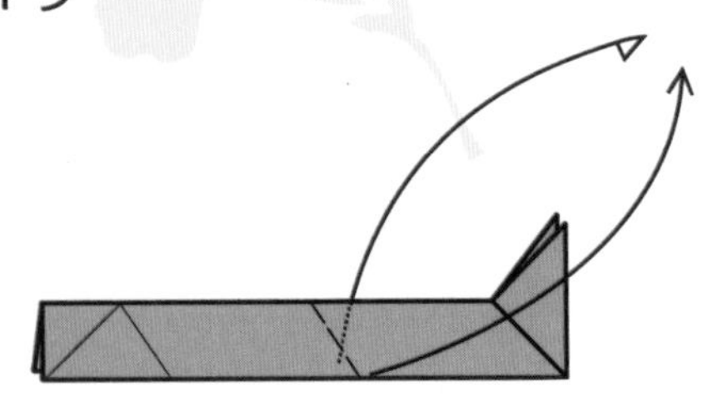

Make an outside reverse fold on the first fold.

14

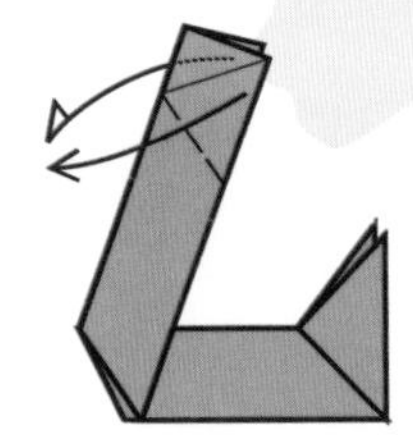

Make an outside reverse fold on the second fold.

15

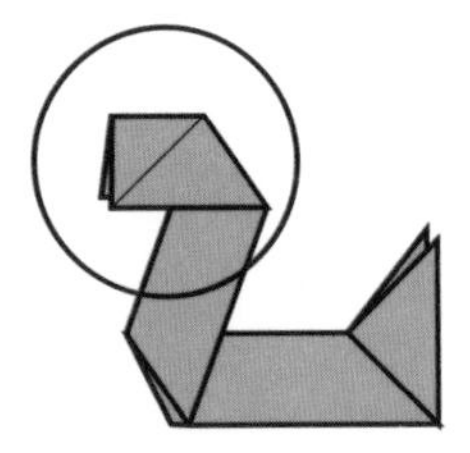

The model should look like this. The following steps are a close-up of the head.

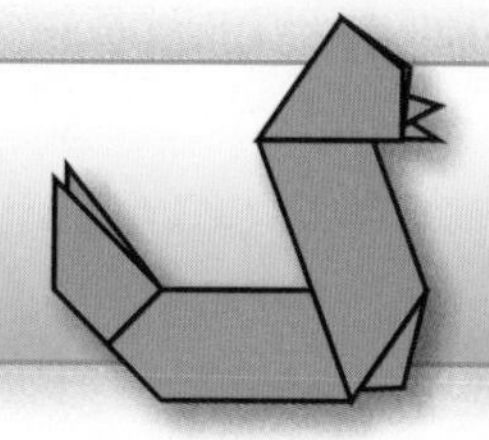

16

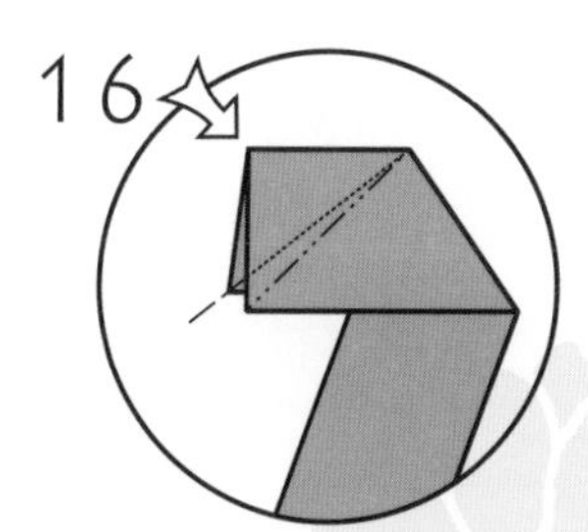

Make an inside reverse fold.

17

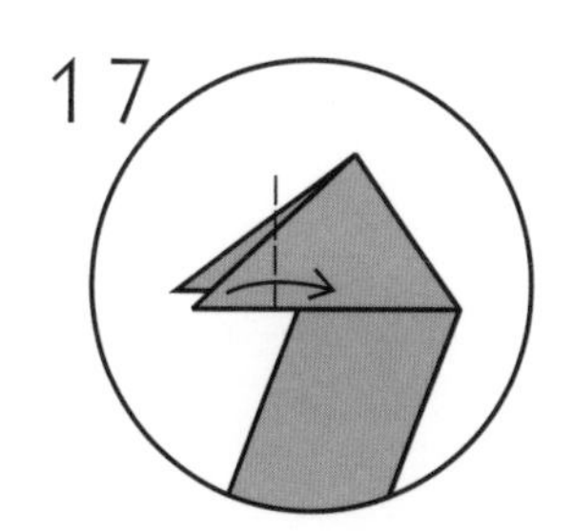

Valley fold both points of the beak.

18

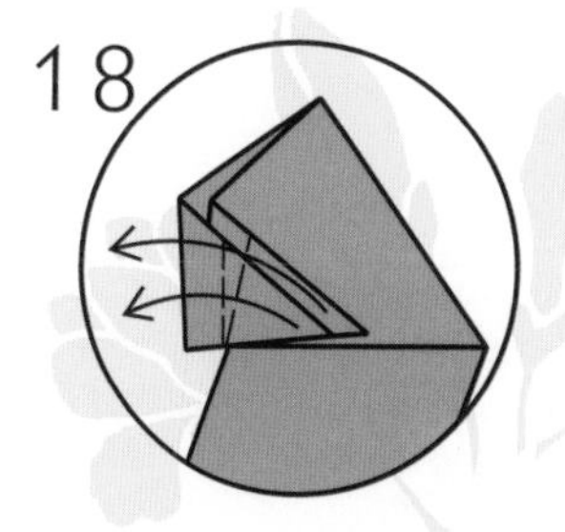

Valley fold the points of the beak, fold one higher than the other.

19

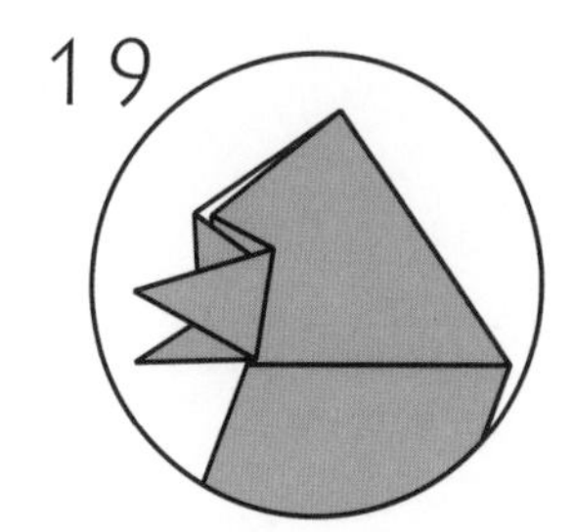

Completed step 18. Turn over.

20

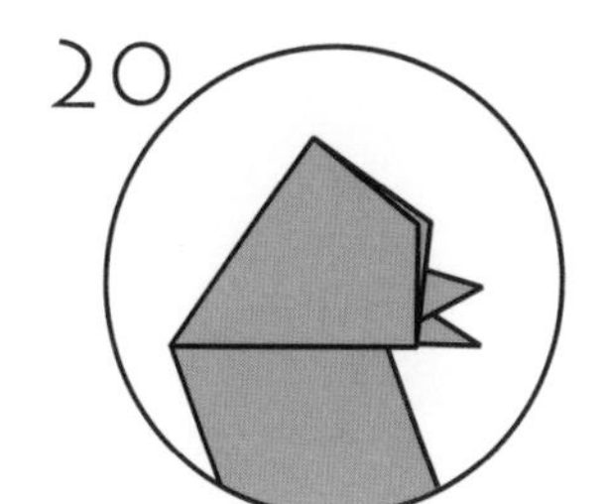

This is the duck's 'good side'.

21

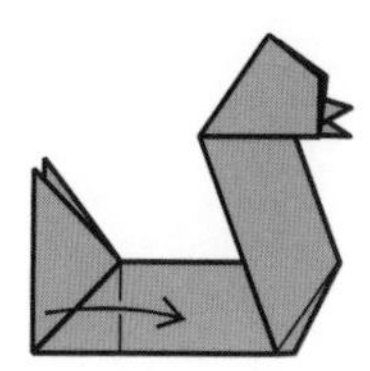

Open the tail on the crease shown.

22

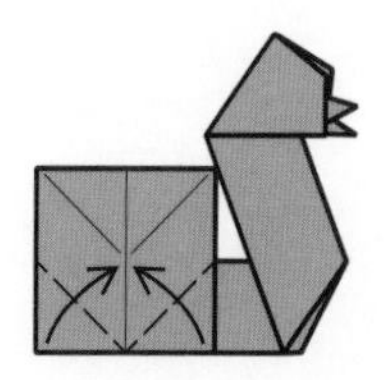

Fold corners to the middle.

23

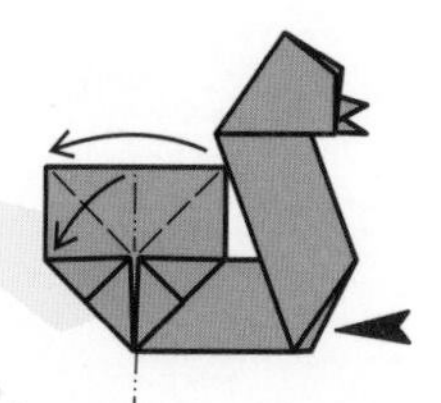

Fold back to original position. Open the front of the duck slightly with your finger.

24

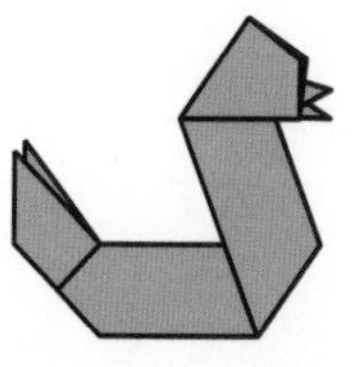

Completed chopstick duck.

Spanish Box

MODEL: Traditional, Spain
DIAGRAM: Matthew Gardiner

The traditional Spanish box was brought to the world origami stage by the British magician and origami expert Robert Harbin during his famous BBC television series. It's a practical decorative model, and if you use a 30cm (12in) sheet, or larger, of stiff card you can create a strong vessel for sweets and foods at parties.

The Spanish box is so named because of the decorative pleating on the rim of the box.

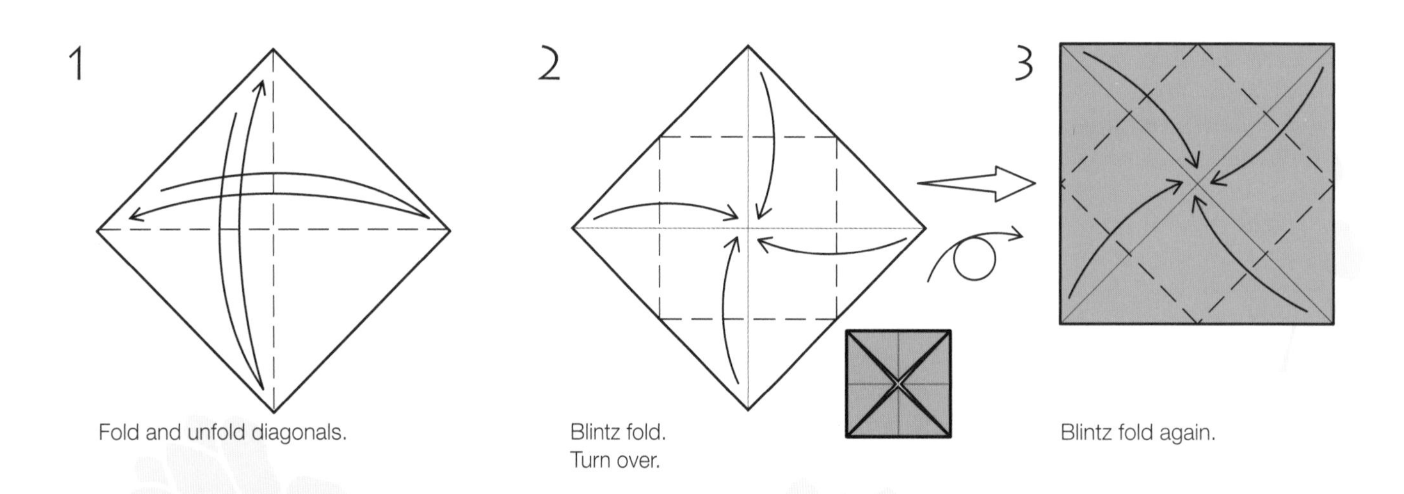

1. Fold and unfold diagonals.
2. Blintz fold. Turn over.
3. Blintz fold again.

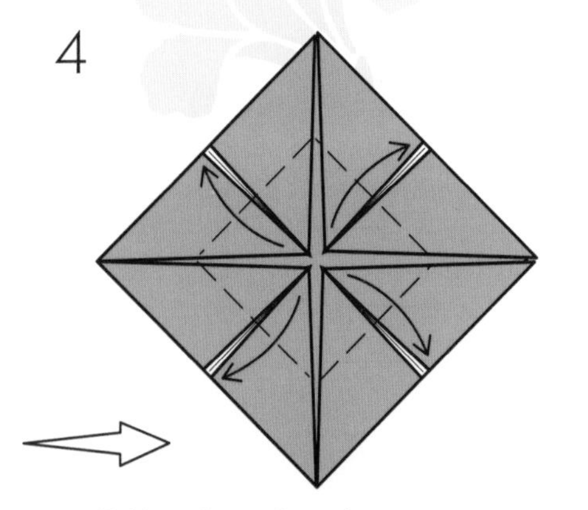

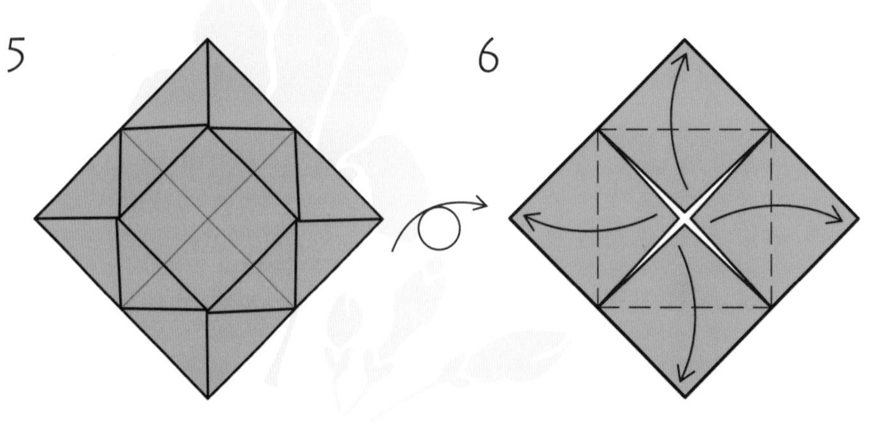

4. Fold top layers from the centre to corners.
5. Completed step 4. Turn over.
6. Fold top layers from the centre to corners.

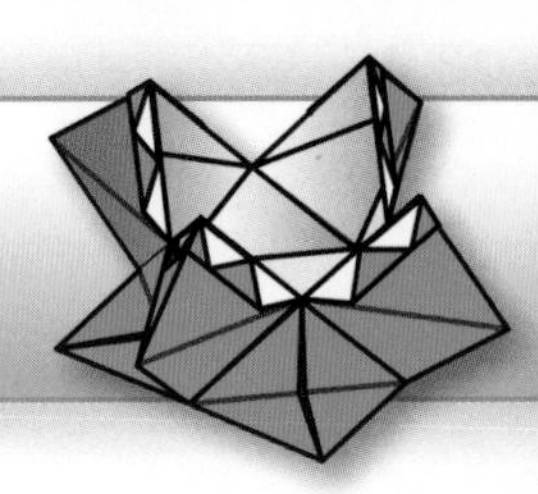

7

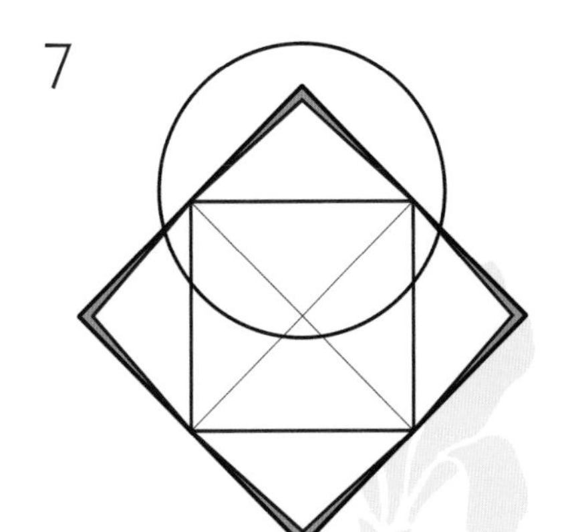

Detail of corner.

8

Fold over as shown.

9

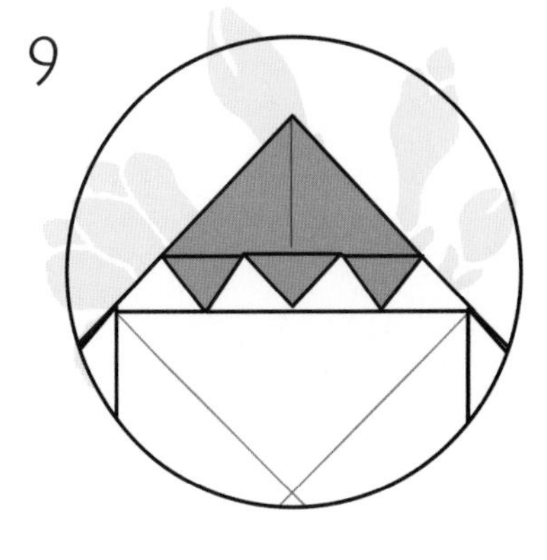

Completed step 8.

10

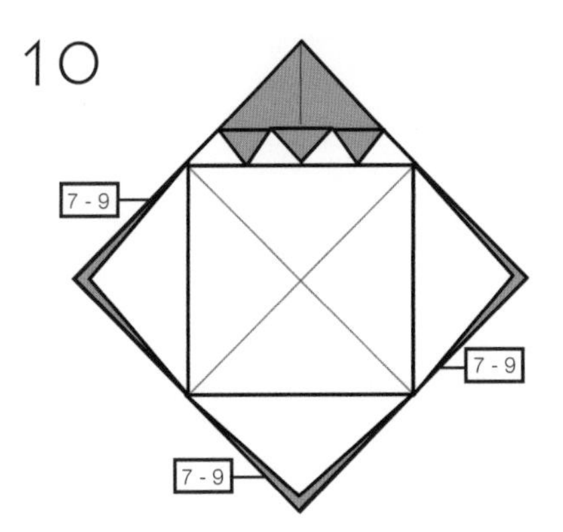

Repeat steps 7-9 on other three corners.

11

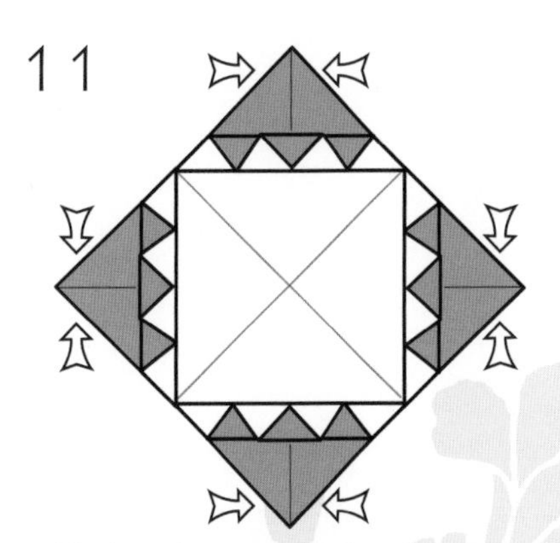

Pinch each corner as shown by the white arrows making the box 3D.

12

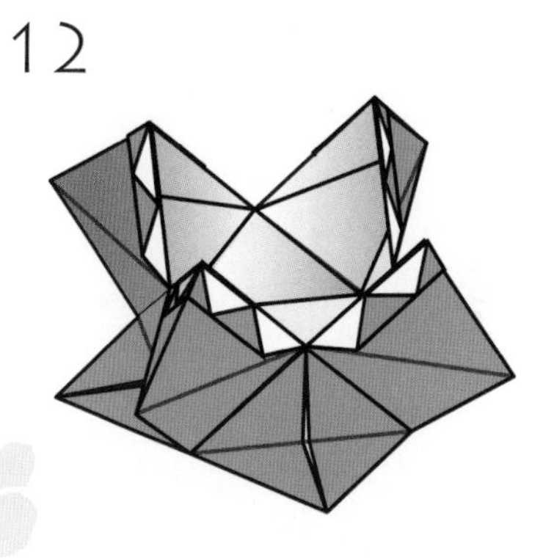

Completed Spanish box.

WENTWORTH DISH

MODEL: NICK ROBINSON
DIAGRAM: NICK ROBINSON

Nick Robinson has a penchant for creating simple paper dishes that have elegant forms and equally elegant paper locks. A paper lock is a sequence of folds that when completed is hard to open, hence the term 'lock'. The finished shape of his Wentworth dish has variations that can be achieved by altering the angle of one fold.

The dishes Nick Robinson is so fond of folding are inspired by the work of origami artist Philip Shen.

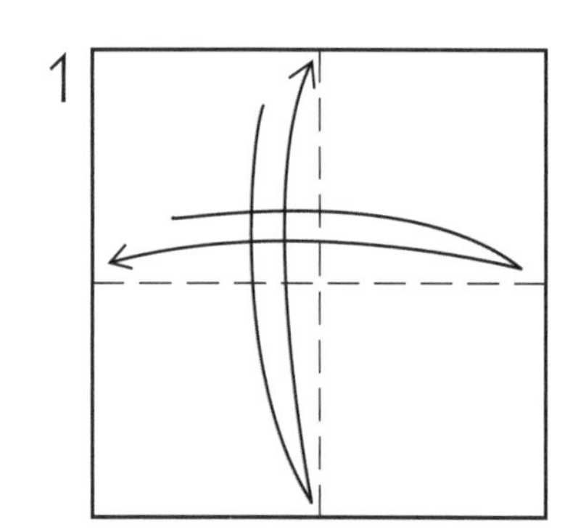

Fold and unfold.

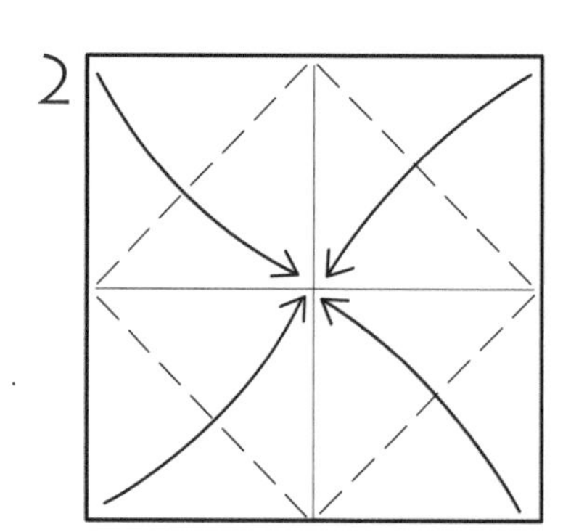

Blintz fold. Turn over.
Rotate the paper 45°.

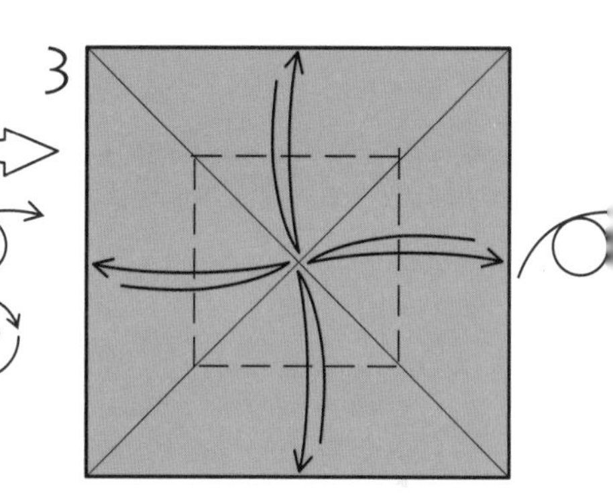

Fold and unfold edges to the centre as shown. Turn over.

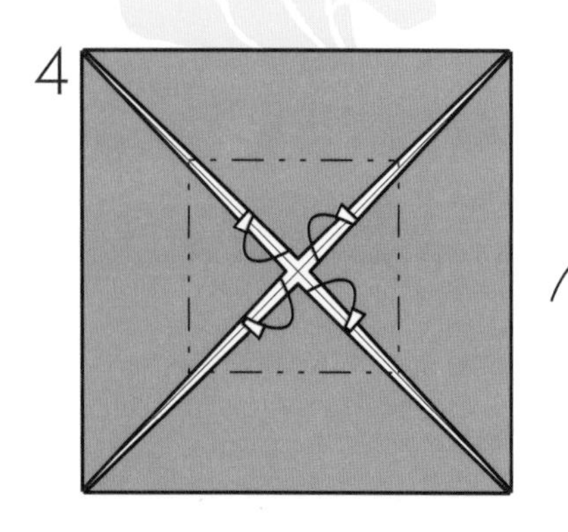

Fold corners inside.
Turn over again.

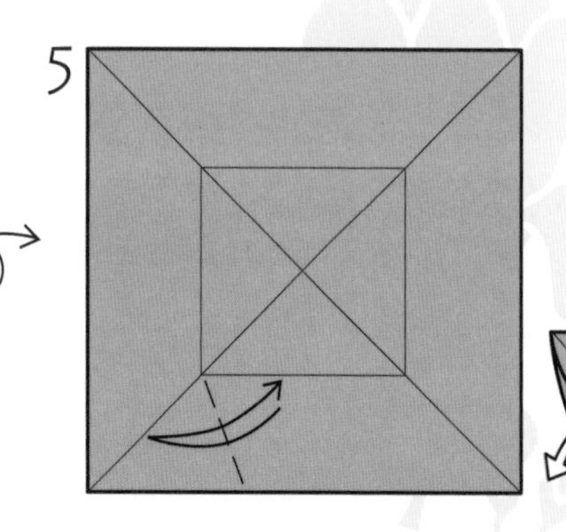

Fold and unfold.

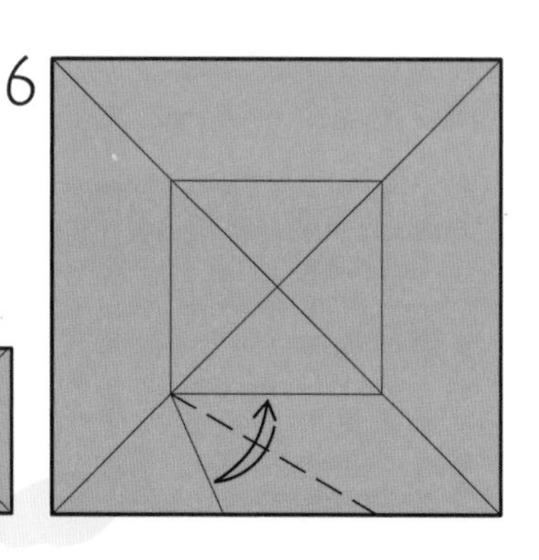

Fold and unfold.

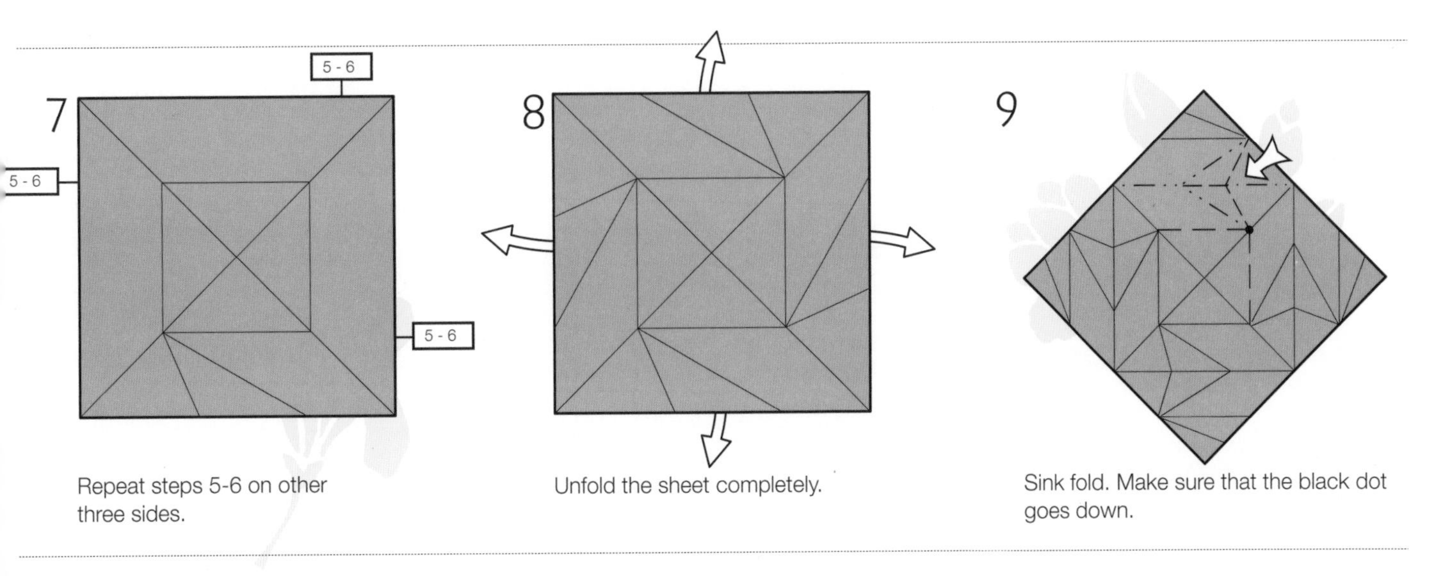

Repeat steps 5-6 on other three sides.

Unfold the sheet completely.

Sink fold. Make sure that the black dot goes down.

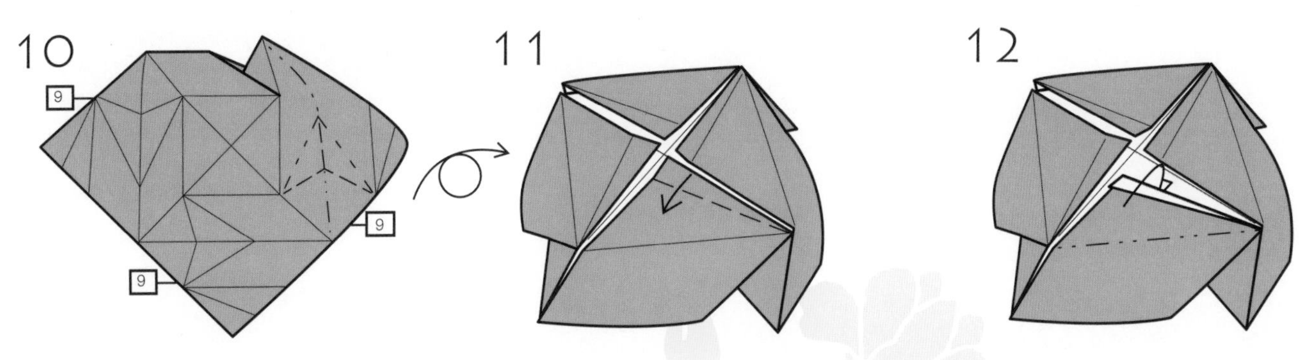

Repeat step 9 on the other three sides. Turn over.

To lock the bottom fold up.

Tuck flap inside for a white centre.

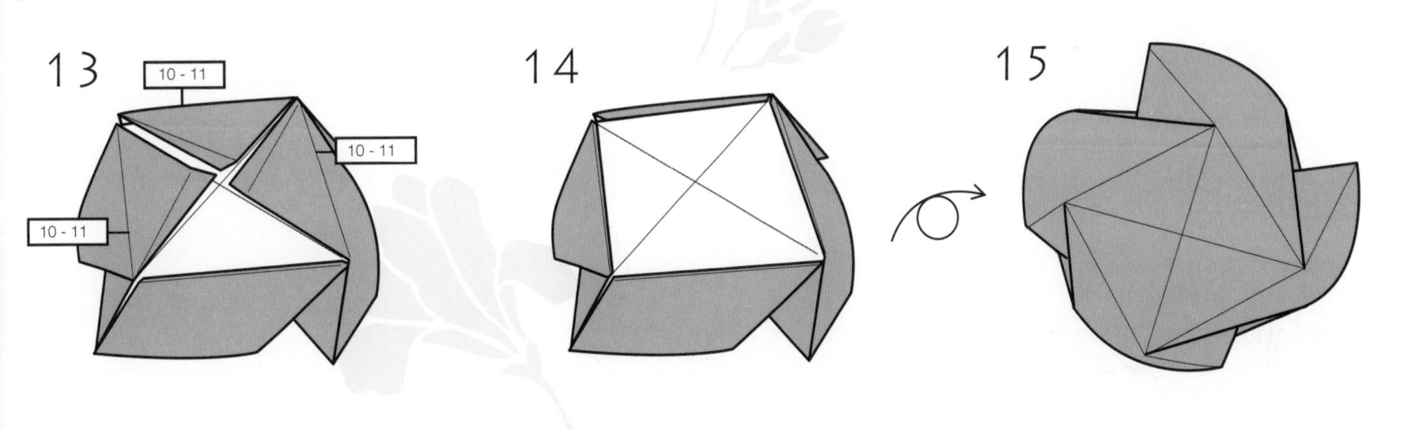

Repeat steps 10-11 on other three sides.

Completed back. Turn over.

Completed dish.

VARIATION 1

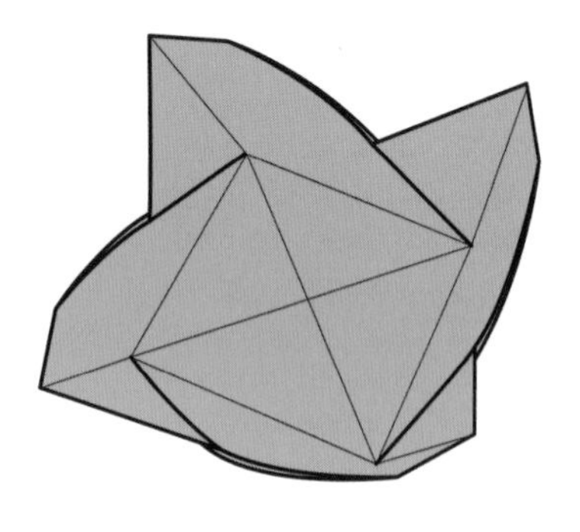

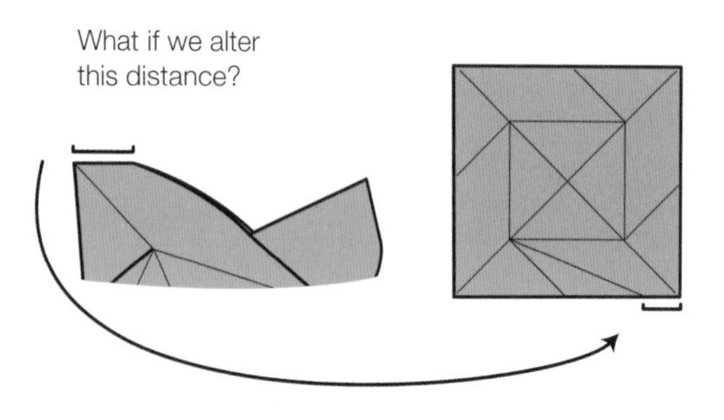

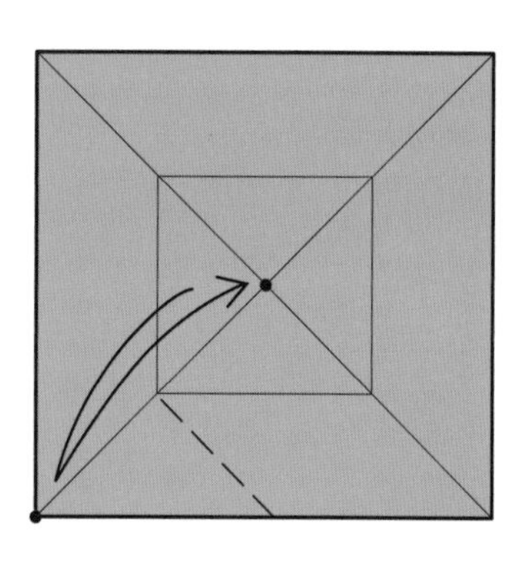

Start from step 6 of the completed dish diagram. Fold and unfold.

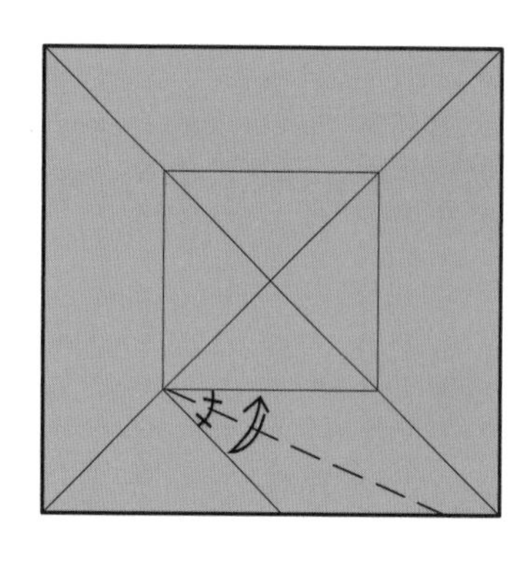

Fold and unfold, bisecting the angle.

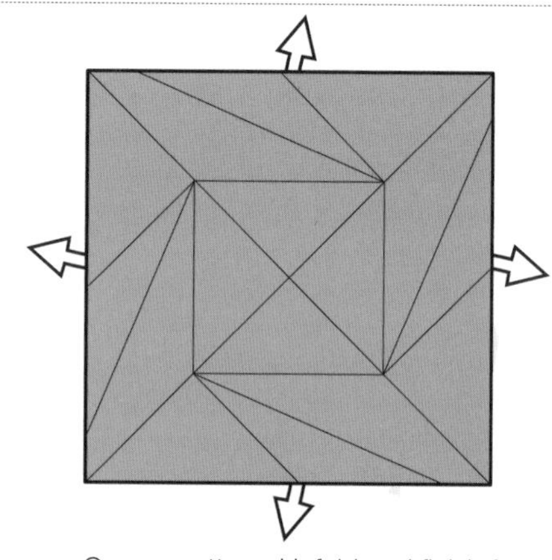

Crease pattern. Unfold and finish from step 9, following completed dish diagram.

VARIATION 2

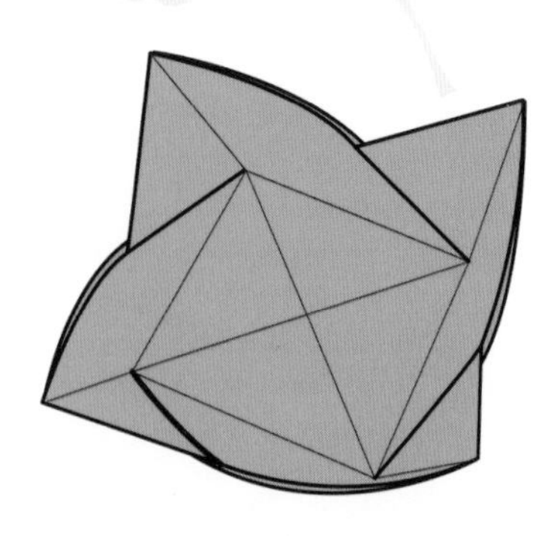

This variation is similar to the previous one, but note the angle of the crease in the second step.

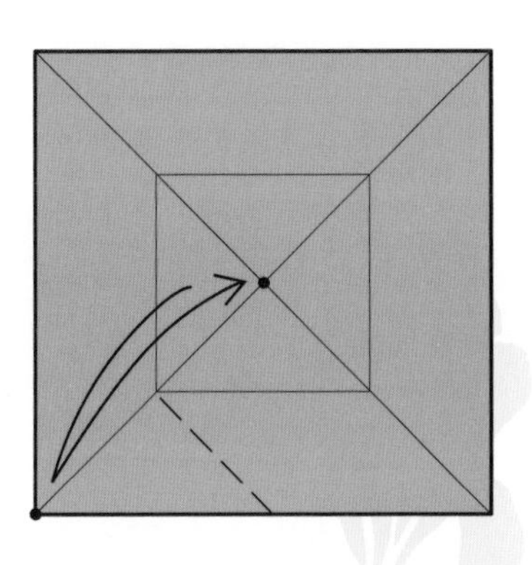

Start from step 6 of the completed dish diagram. Fold and unfold.

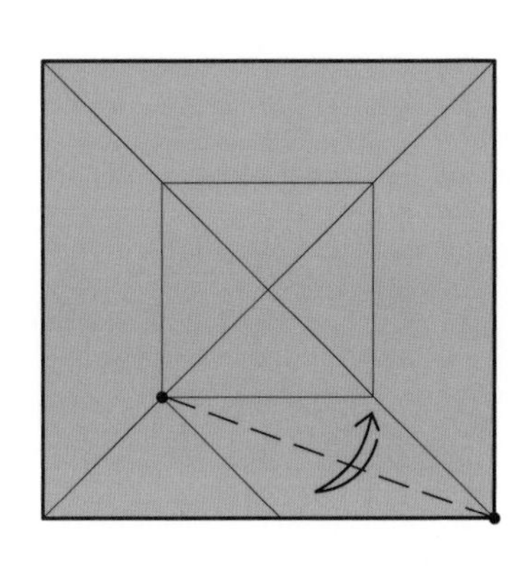

Fold and unfold, corner to corner.

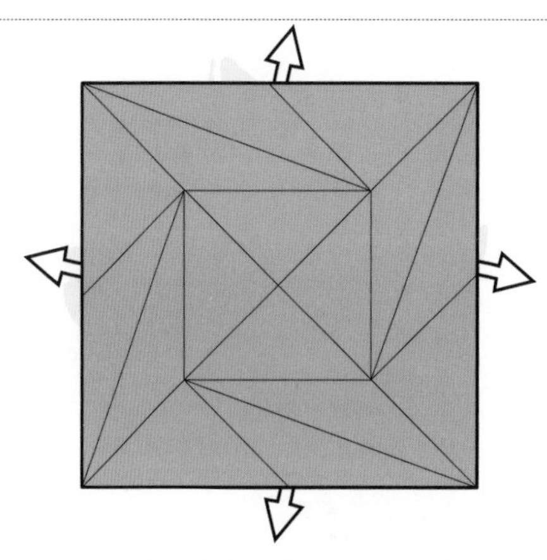

Unfold and finish from step 9 of the dish diagram.

VARIATION 3

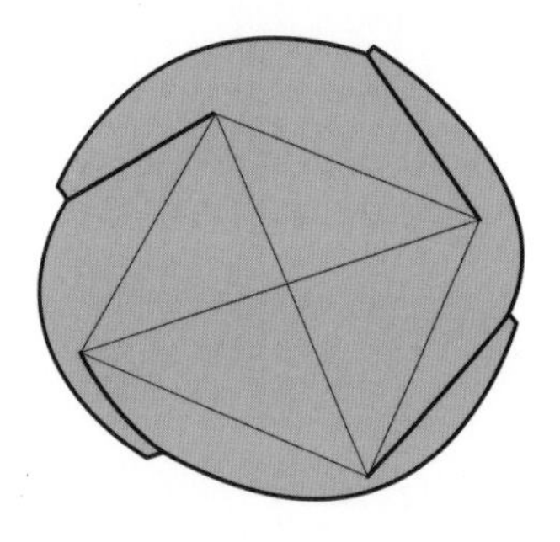

This variation produces a square side profile. The top of the dish can be curved as shown or made angular with strong creases.

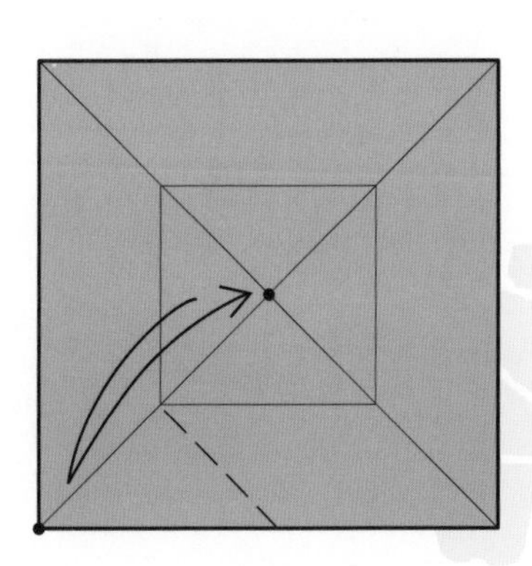

Start from step 6 of the completed dish diagram. Fold and unfold.

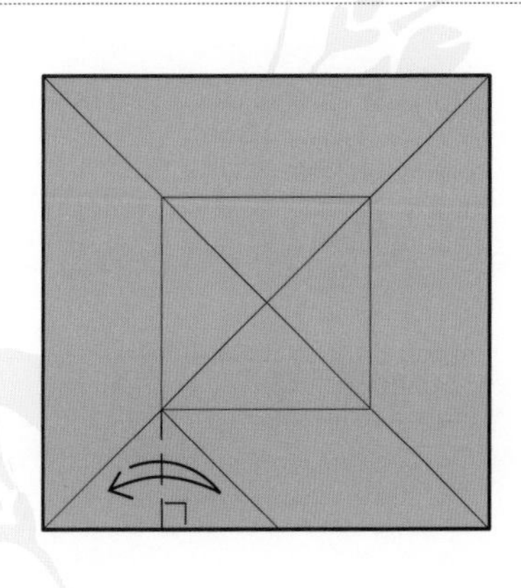

Fold and unfold.

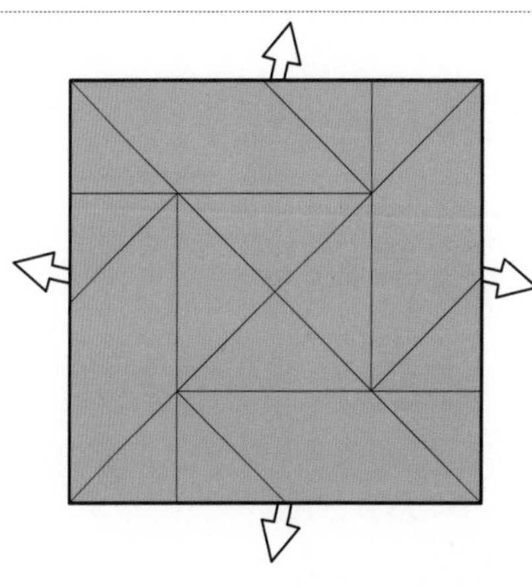

Crease pattern. Unfold and finish from step 9, following completed dish diagram.

Standing Fan

MODEL: Traditional, Japan
DIAGRAM: Matthew Gardiner

Table decoration is never complete without an origami inspired napkin fold. The best results are achieved with an ironed napkin. For large napkins, you may find more pleats in step 2 will make a more attractive fan.

The standing fan napkin fold looks elegant on any table setting.

1

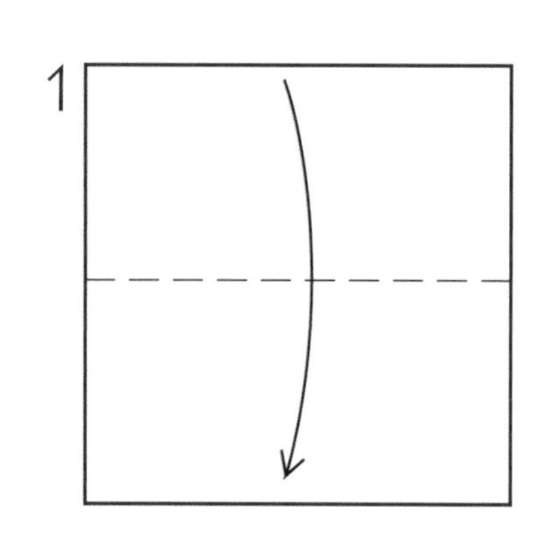

Fold in half.

2

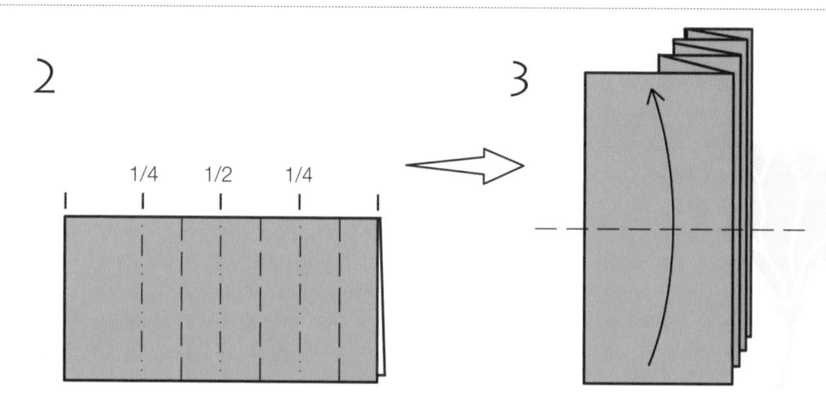

Accordion fold.

3

Fold up all layers.

4

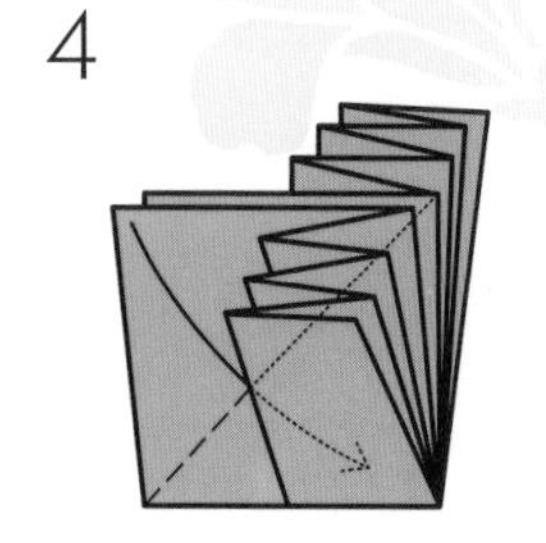

To make the stand fold corners of both layers diagonally, tucking them under the accordion folds.

5

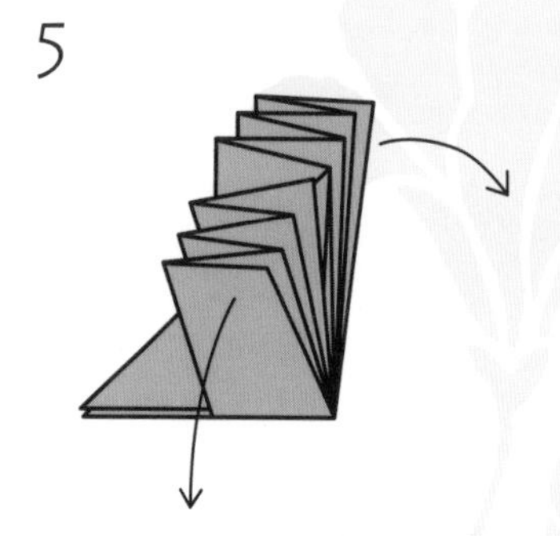

Push outwards.

6

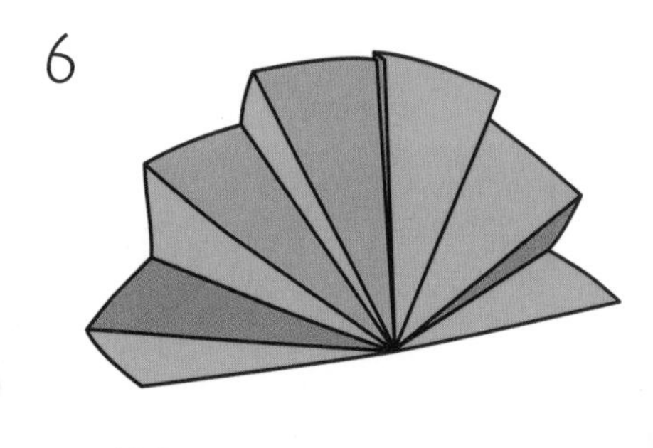

Completed standing fan napkin fold.

Water Lily

MODEL: Traditional, Japan
DIAGRAM: Matthew Gardiner

The water lily is a beautiful form, invoking the charm of the lily floating on the water.

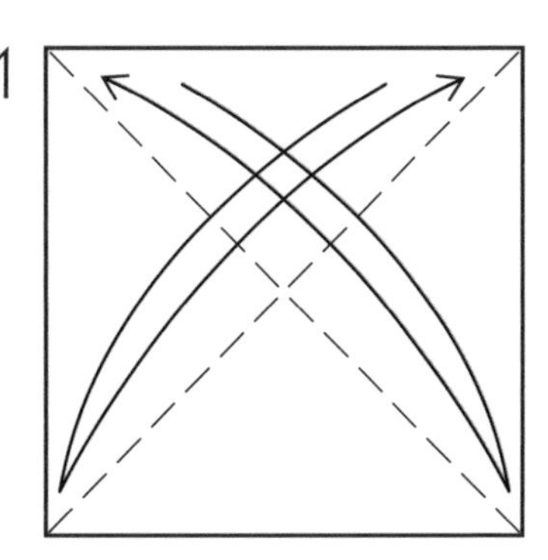

Fold and unfold diagonals.

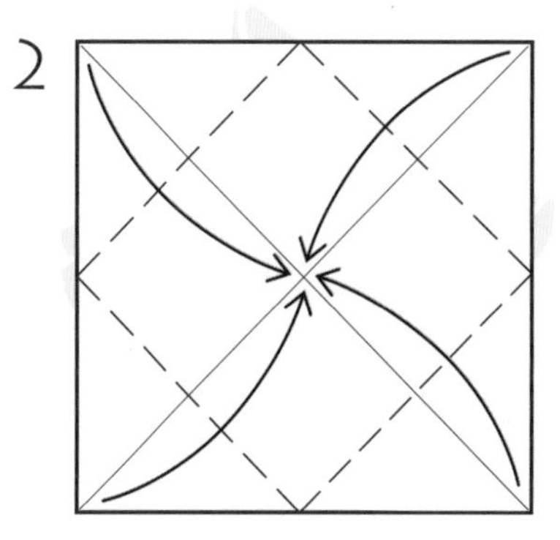

Fold corners to the centre.

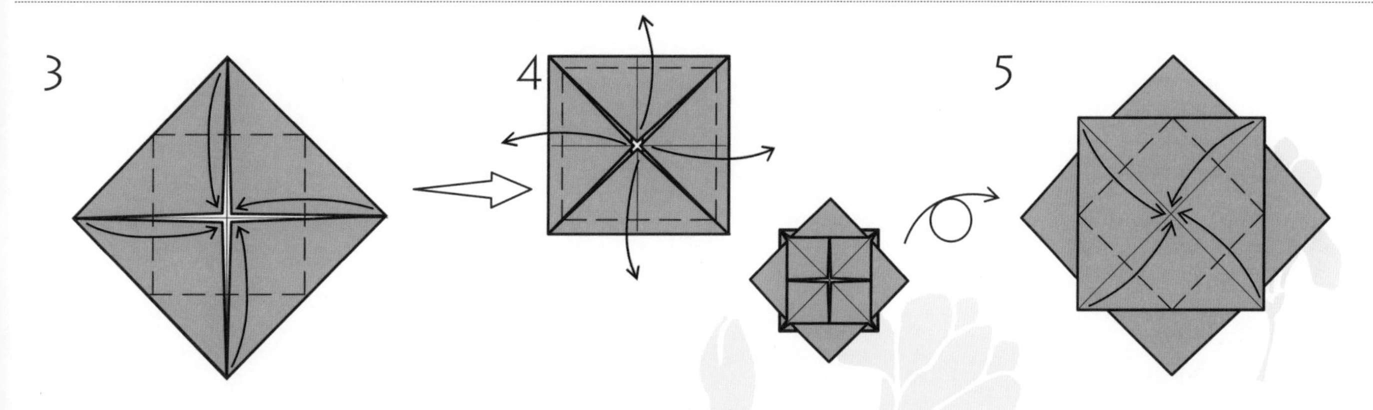

Fold corners to the centre again.

Fold indicated corners outwards leaving a small gap at the edges. Turn over.

While folding the indicated corners to the centre, the model will change into 3D.

Completed step 5. Turn over.

Fold indicated corners outside leaving a little gap at the edges. Turn over.

Completed water lily.

Iris

MODEL: Traditional, Japan
DIAGRAM: Matthew Gardiner

The iris takes its name from the Greek word for rainbow. Its name reflects the wide range of colours of the iris. This model looks best when folded from a blended or two-toned paper.

The iris is a popular symbol, appearing on the flag of Brussels, and in the fleur-de-lis, the symbol of Florence, Italy.

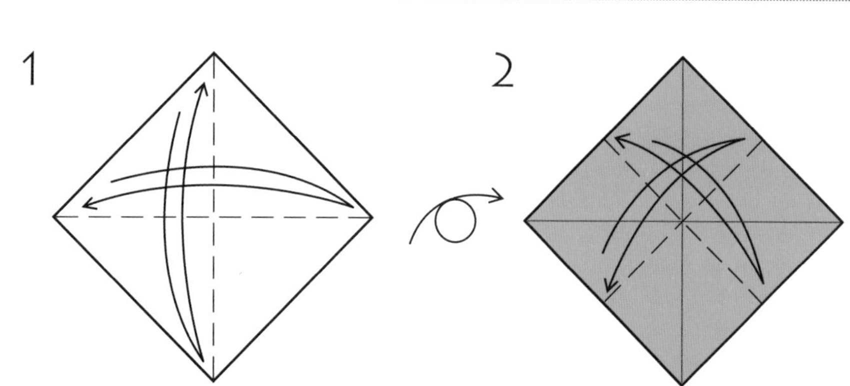

Fold and unfold diagonals. Turn over.

Book fold and unfold.

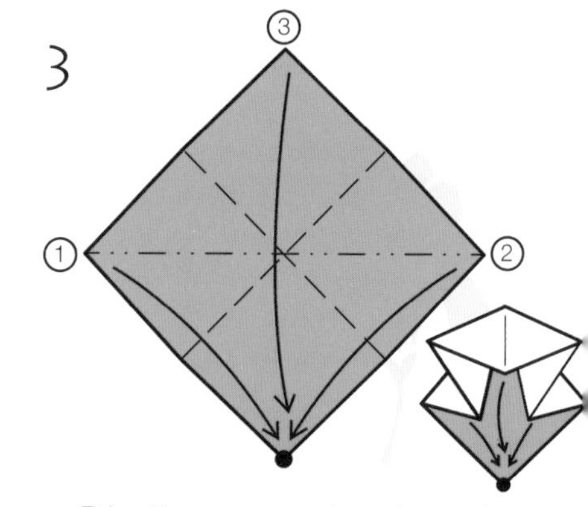

Bring three corners down to meet bottom corner. Start with corners 1 and 2 together followed by corner 3.

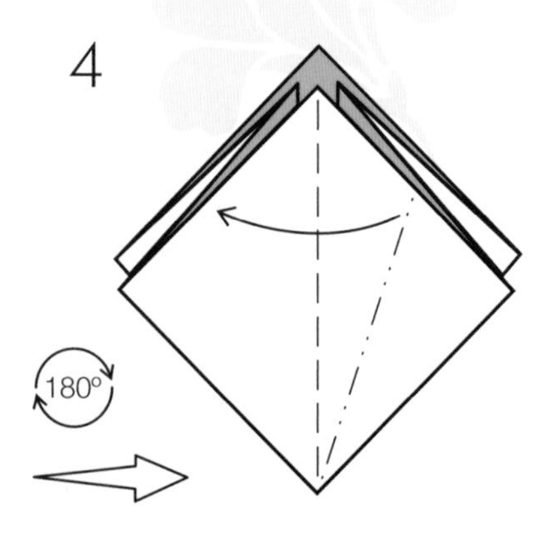

Pre-crease then squash fold.

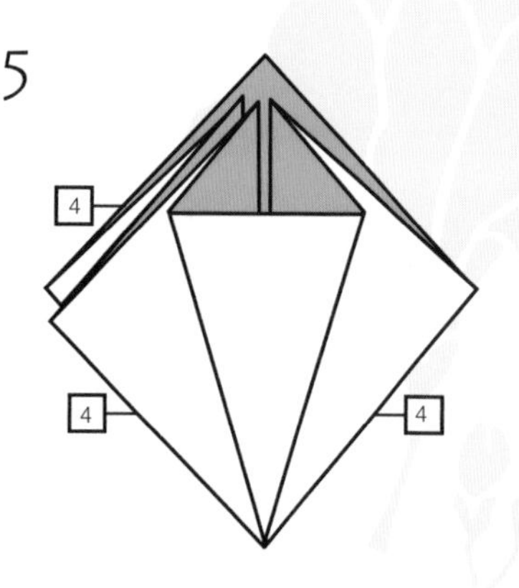

Repeat step 4 on the other three sides.

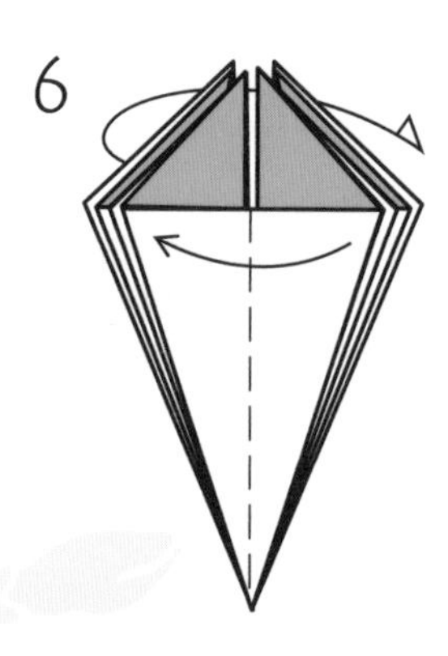

Turn top and back layer over.

7

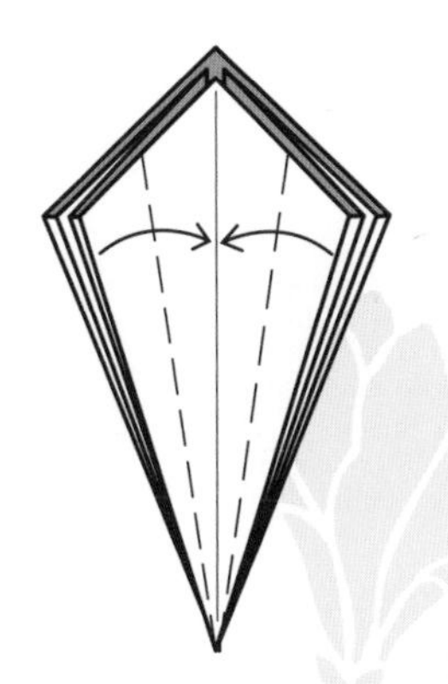

Fold top layer edges to meet the middle.

8

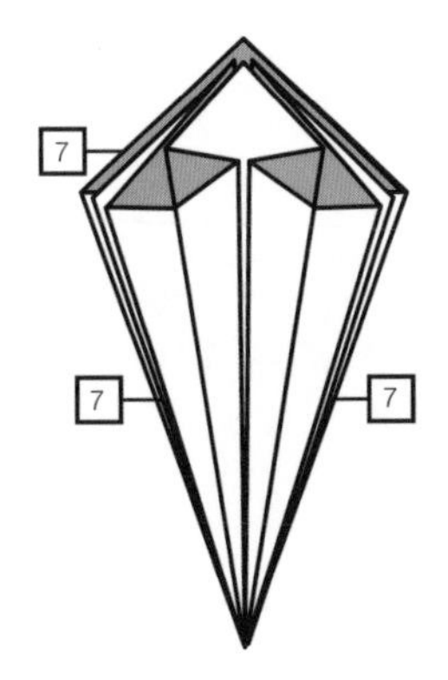

Repeat step 7 to both sides and behind.

9

Fold front petal down.

10

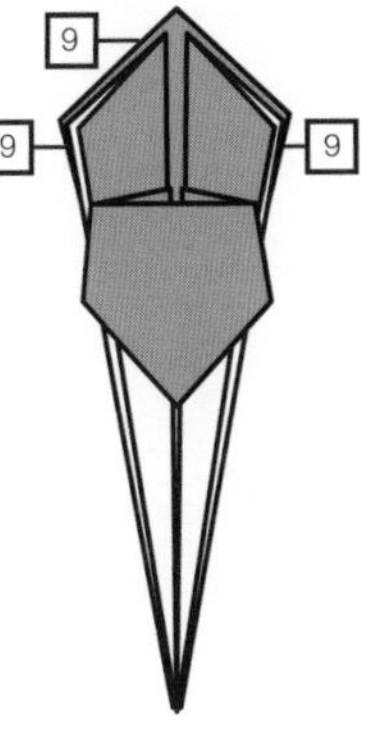

Repeat step 9 on all three sides making the model 3D. Start with both side petals followed by the back petal.

11

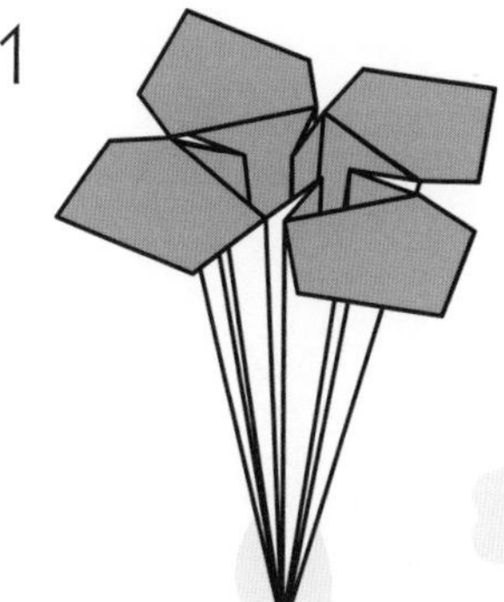

Completed iris.

LILY

MODEL: TRADITIONAL, JAPAN
DIAGRAM: MATTHEW GARDINER

Follow the instructions for the iris on the previous page up to step 7, but start with the coloured side up.

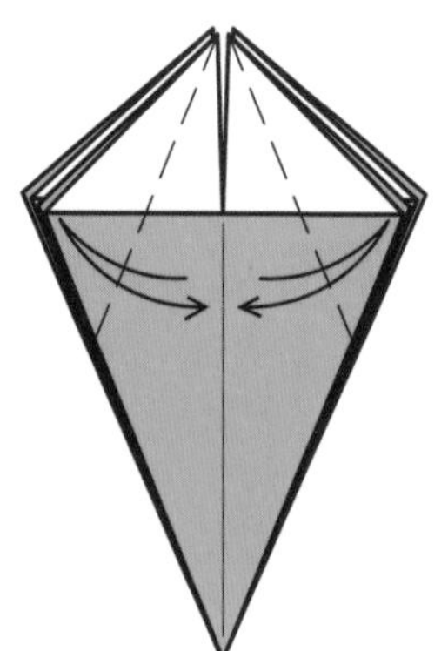

Start from step 7 of the iris. Fold the top layer only to the centre crease.

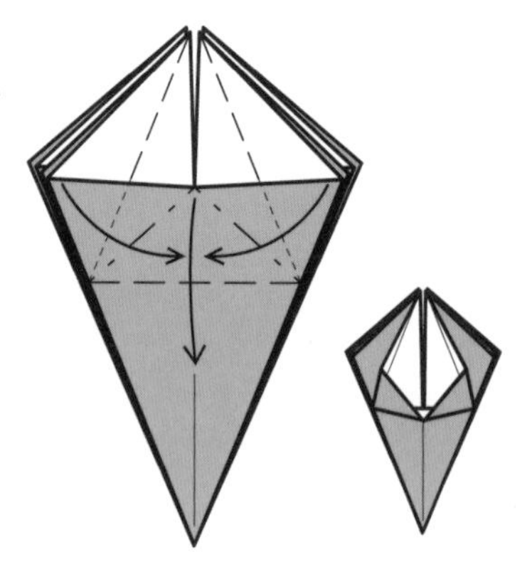

Petal fold; pull down the top layer, and fold the sides to the middle. Lastly, make the mountain folds.

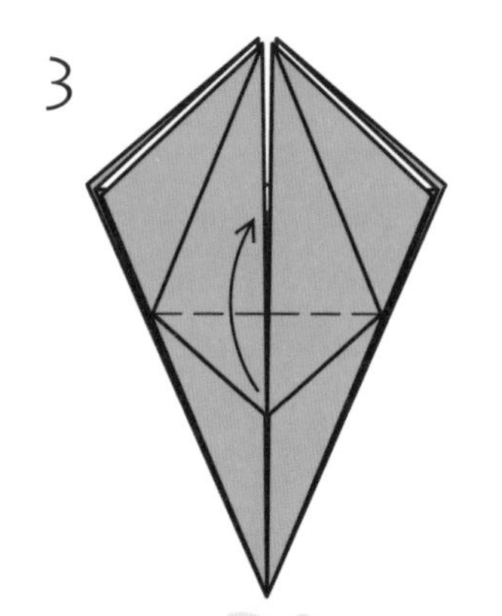

Completed petal fold.
Fold the triangle flap upwards.

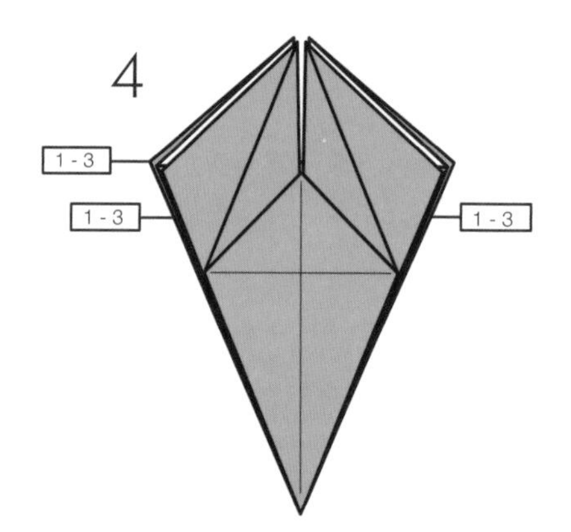

Repeat steps 1-3 on the three remaining sides.

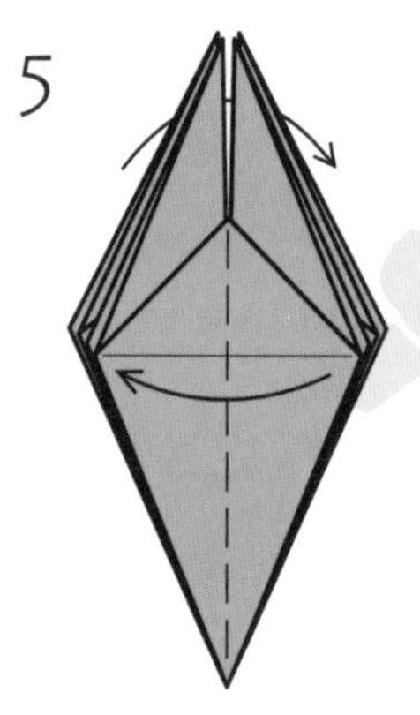

Fold one layer in front and behind.

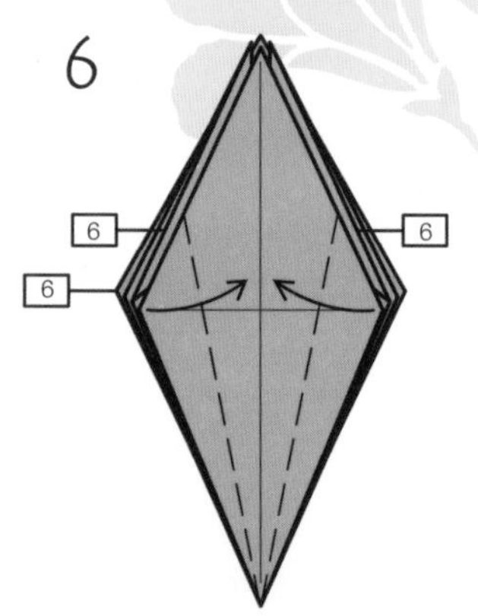

Fold edges to the middle, thinning the lily. Repeat on the other three sides.

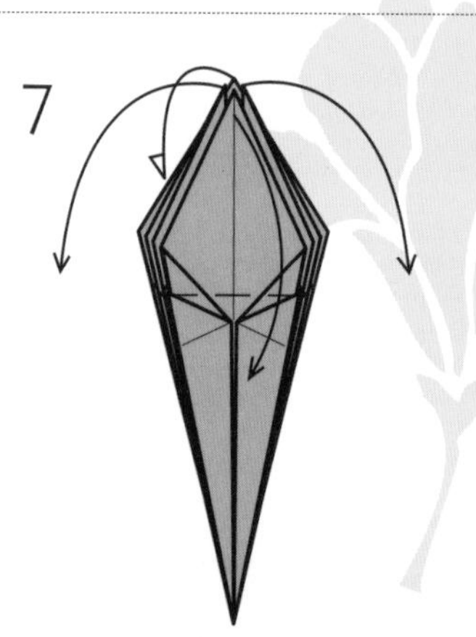

Make a soft, curved valley fold on all four sides to open out the lily.

Completed lily.

VERDI'S VASE

MODEL: TRADITIONAL, CHINA
DIAGRAM: MARK KENNEDY

This traditional Chinese vase was popularised in the United States by Verdi Adams, who taught it to a generation of paperfolders at The Origami Center of America. It is a fantastic model that produces a solid 3D form. Be careful when opening the model during the last steps so the paper doesn't crumple.

These diagrams were originally published in the OUSA Newsletter # 34, Fall 1989. They are reproduced here with permisson from Mark Kennedy.

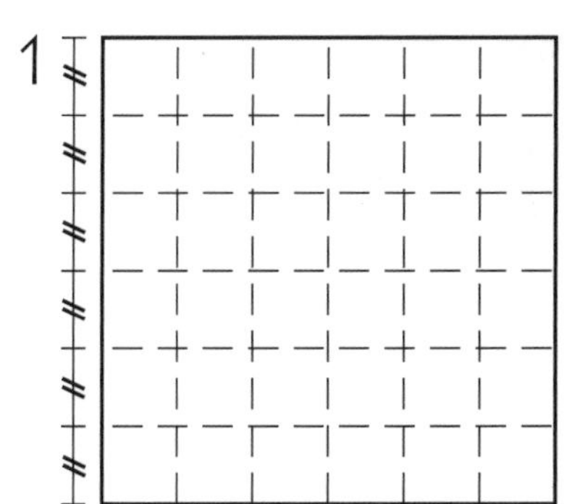

White side up. Crease into sixths in both directions.

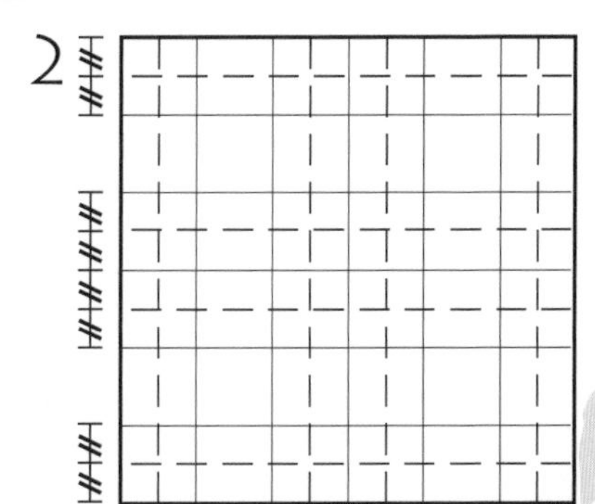

Crease in half the first, third, fourth and sixth 6ths in both directions.

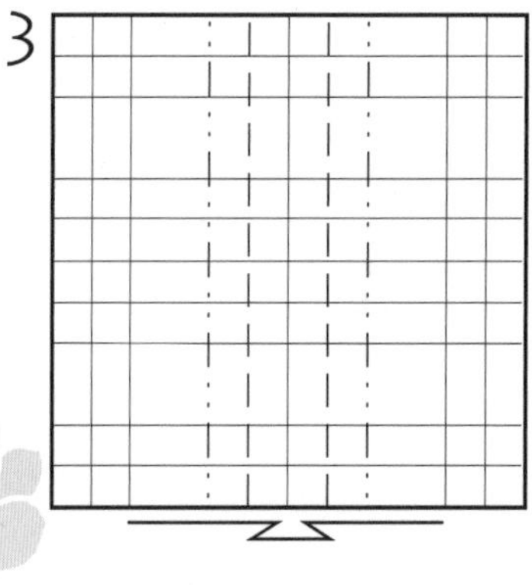

On existing creases, pleat to the centre line.

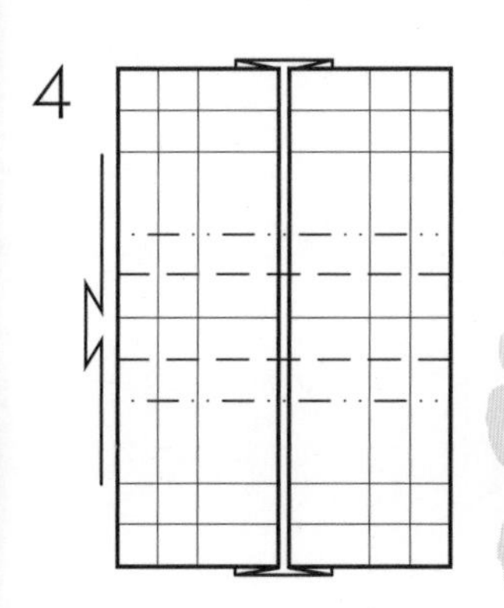

On existing creases, pleat to the centre line.

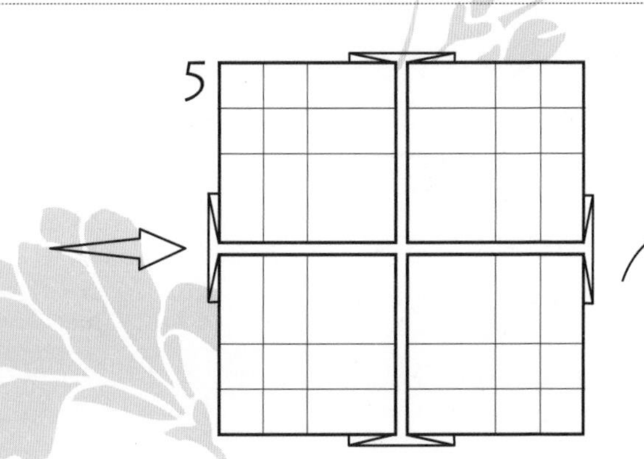

The model should look like this. Turn over.

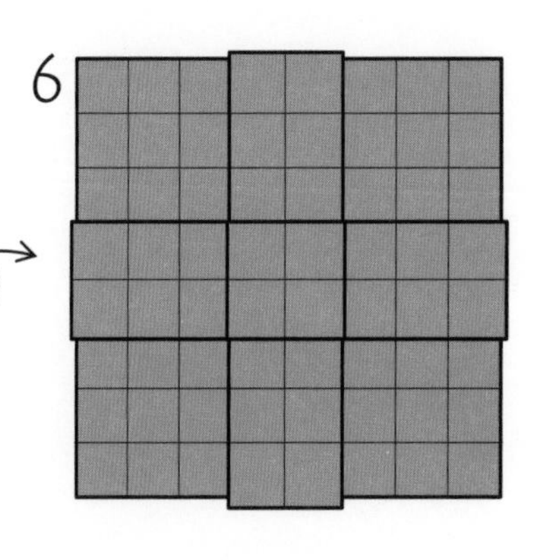

Completed step 5.

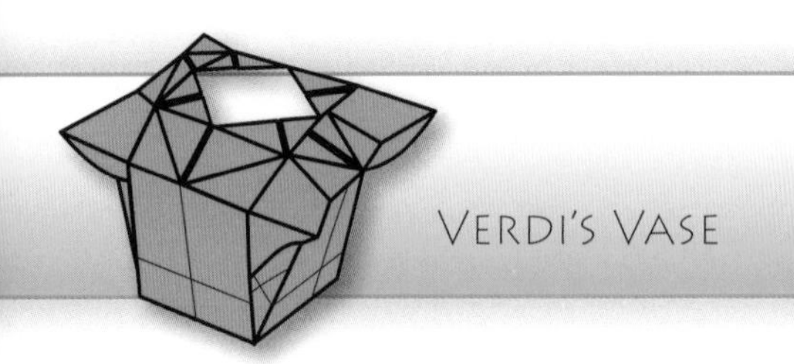

MODEL: TRADITIONAL
DIAGRAM: MARK KENNEDY

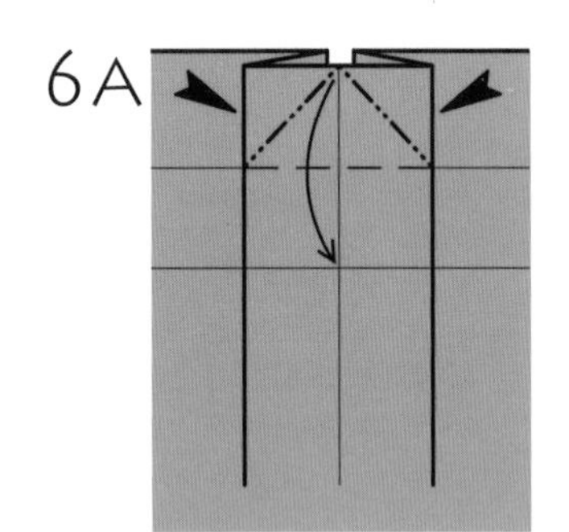

Pull down top layer while squashing in the sides.

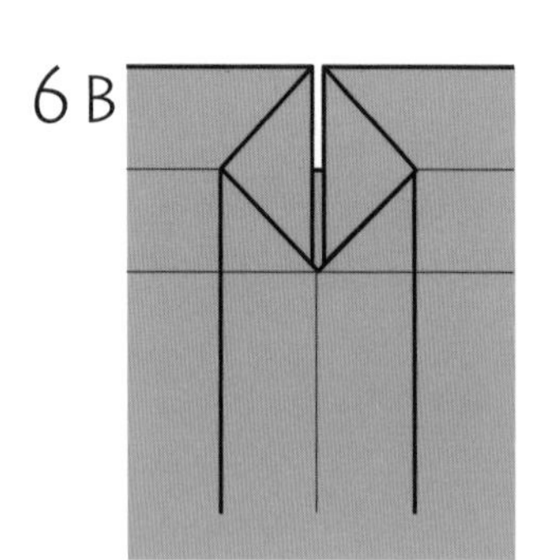

Squashes complete.

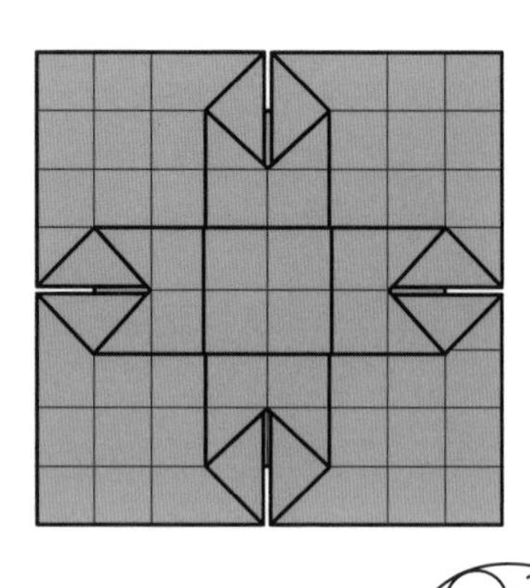

Moves completed on all four sides. Turn over.

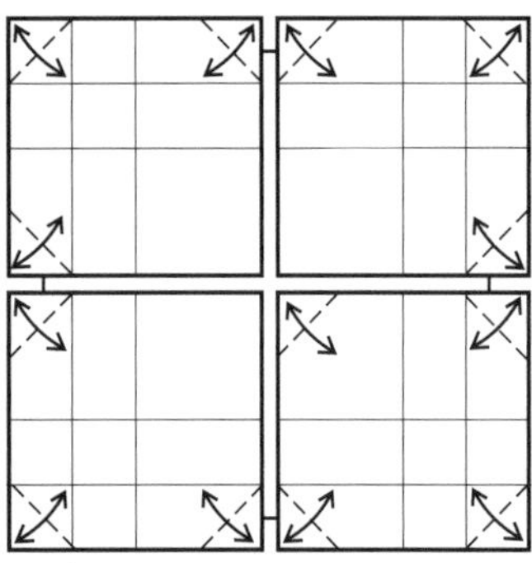

Pre-crease corners as shown to make step 11 easier.

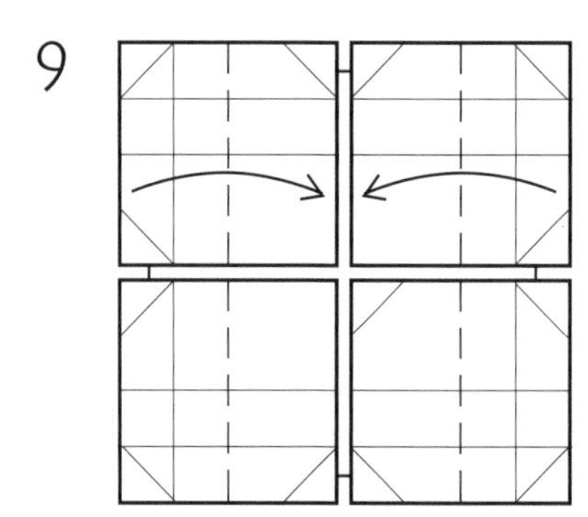

Cupboard door fold sides to the centre.

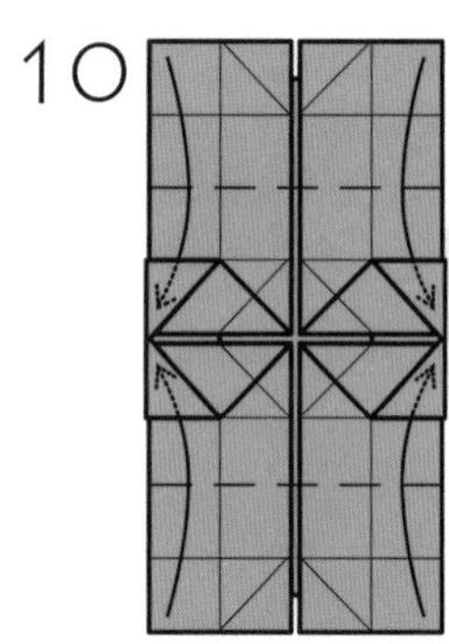

Cupboard door fold top and bottom to centre and tuck the corners into the pockets.

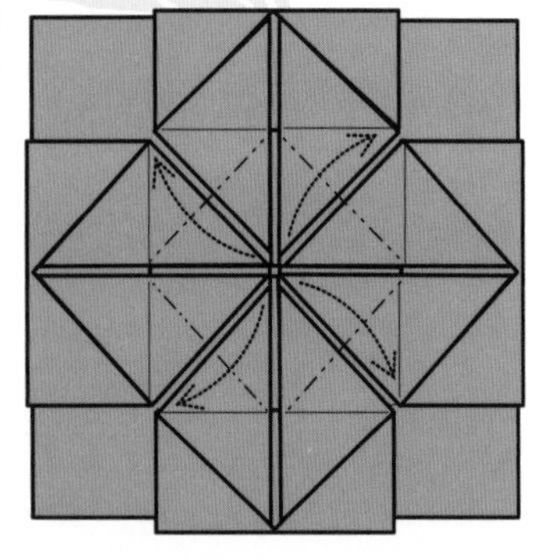

Cupboard door fold top and bottom to centre and tuck the corners into the pockets.

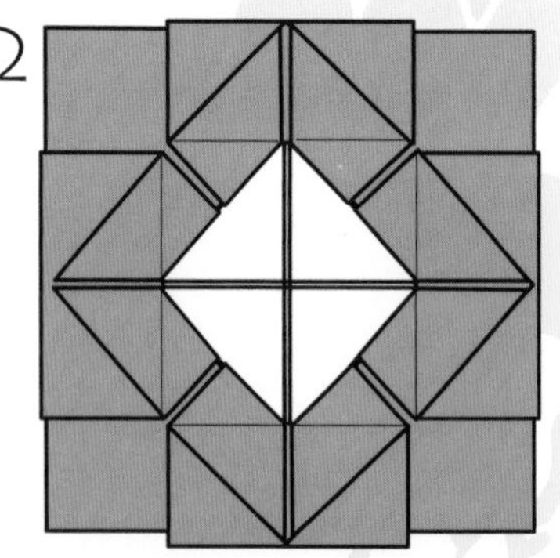

All folding is done. Turn over.

13

Start to open out vase by pulling out the extra layers along the sides. Be careful and work slowly.

14

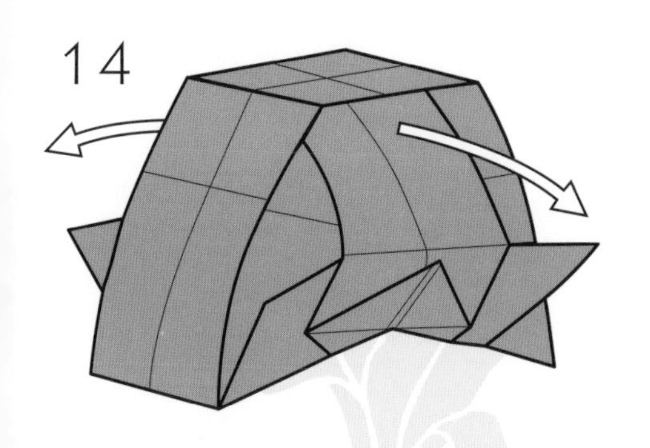

One pair of sides already pulled out. Pull out the other side.

15

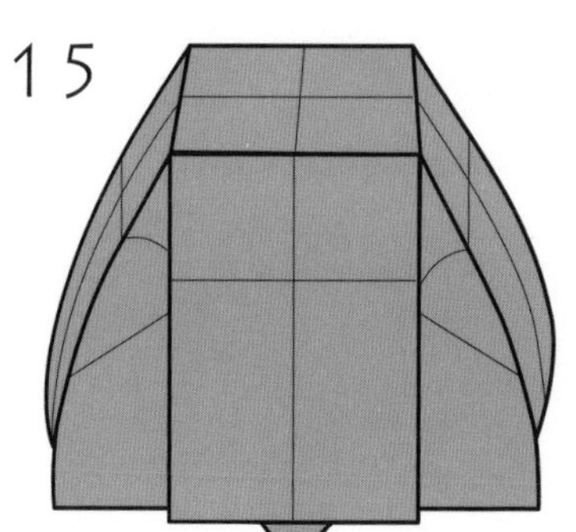

All sides are pulled out.

16

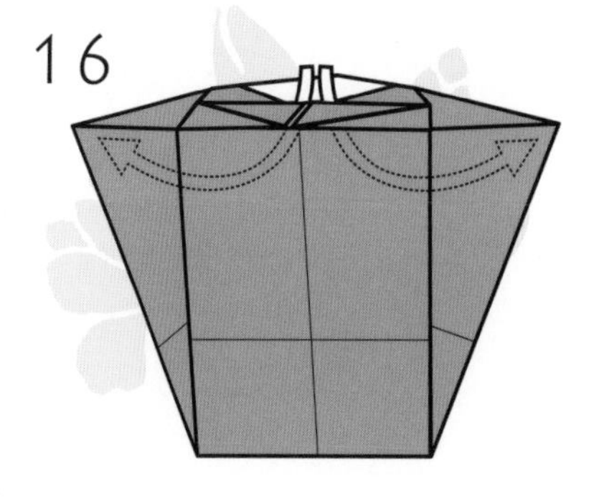

Turn over. Reach inside the top of the vase, poke out and round the corners.

17

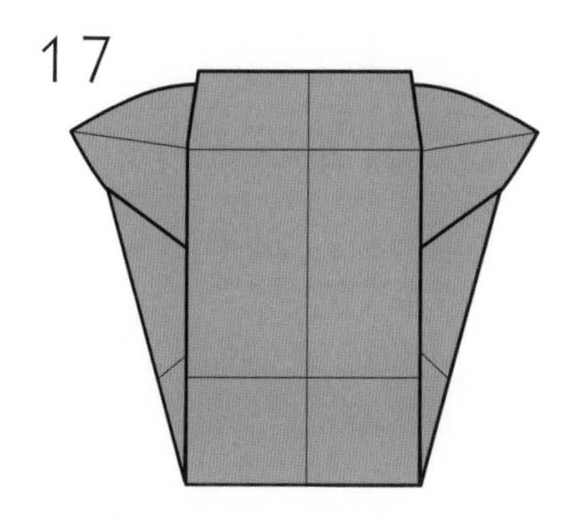

Completed vase – side view.

18

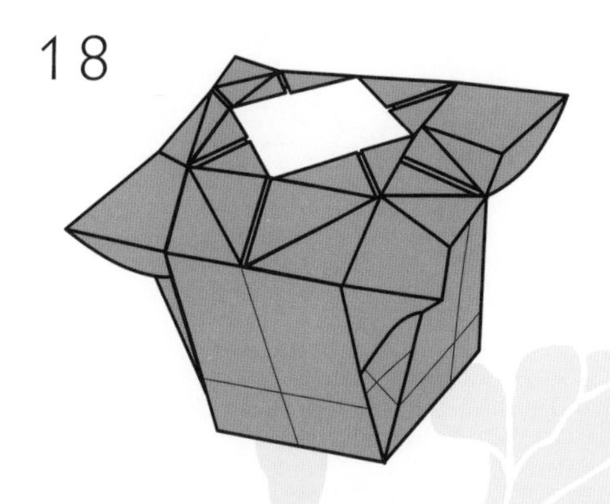

Completed vase – top view.

ALPINE LANDSCAPE

MODEL: GARETH LOUIS
DIAGRAM: GARETH LOUIS

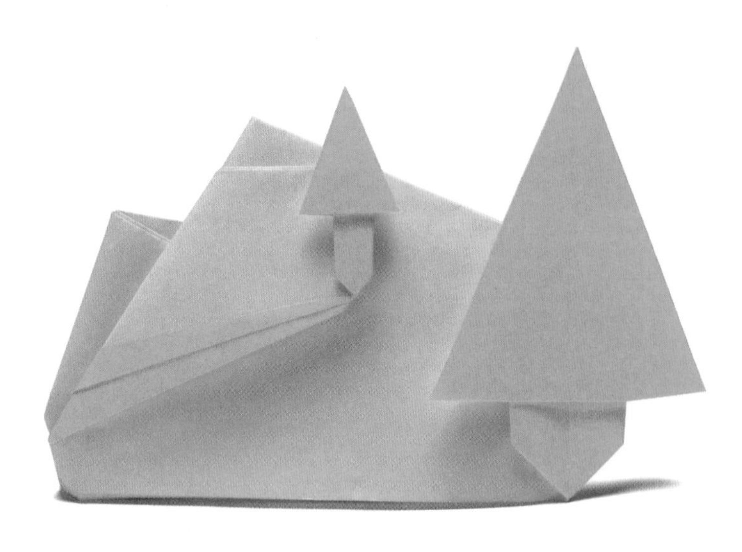

The Alpine landscape is an innovative decoration by artist Gareth Louis. The final form uses colour changes in the paper to show the shadow of a tree in perspective. This model will sit nicely on a desk or mantelpiece as a unique artwork.

Gareth Louis' origami often has a charming sense of humour, and high degree of practicality.

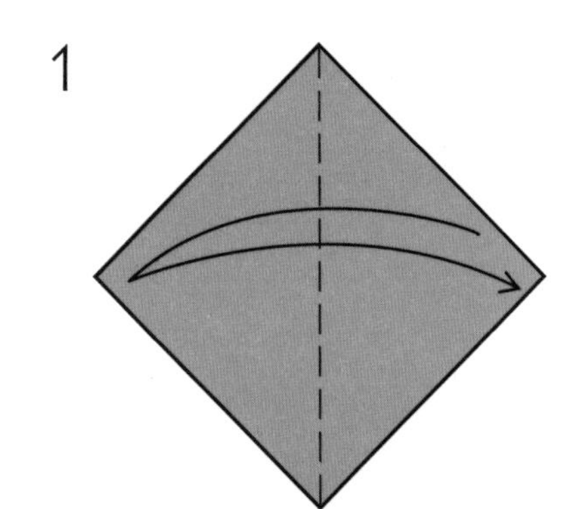

1 Coloured side up. Pre-crease.

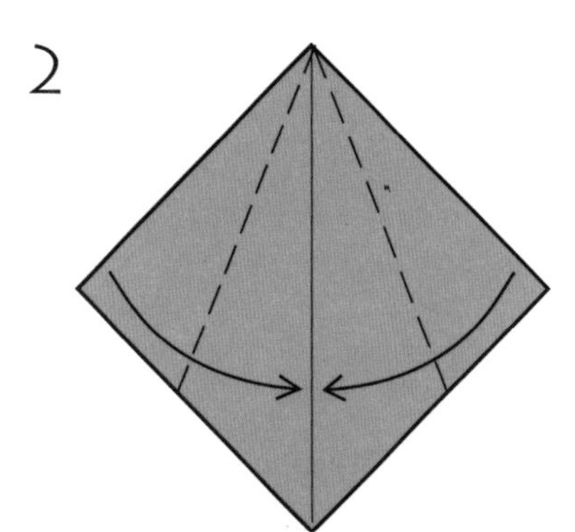

2 Valley fold raw edges to the centre crease.

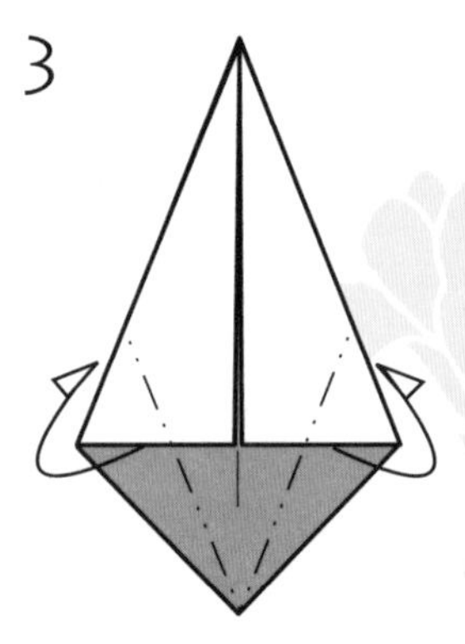

3 Mountain fold along angle bisectors.

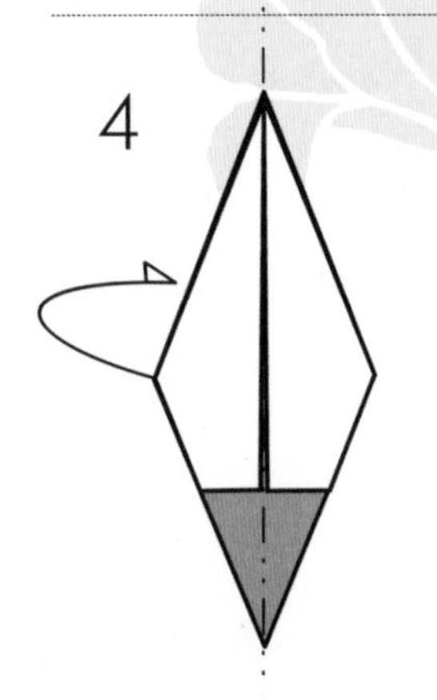

4 Mountain fold in half.

5 Reverse fold along angle bisectors of the coloured region.

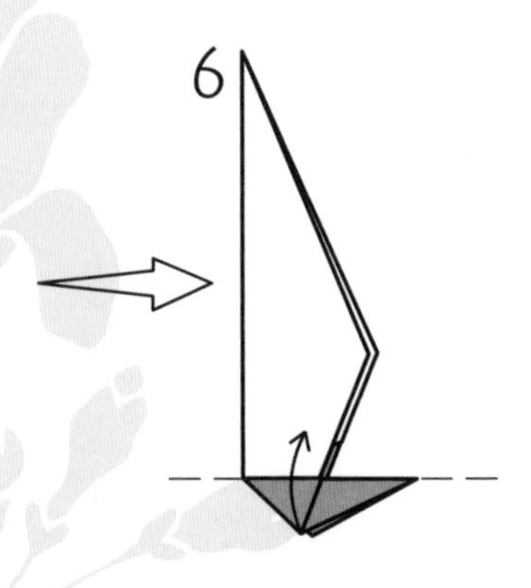

6 Open up a coloured flap.

7

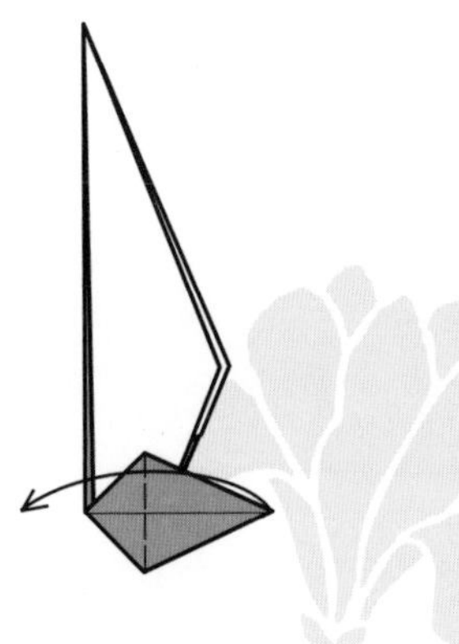

Valley fold.

8

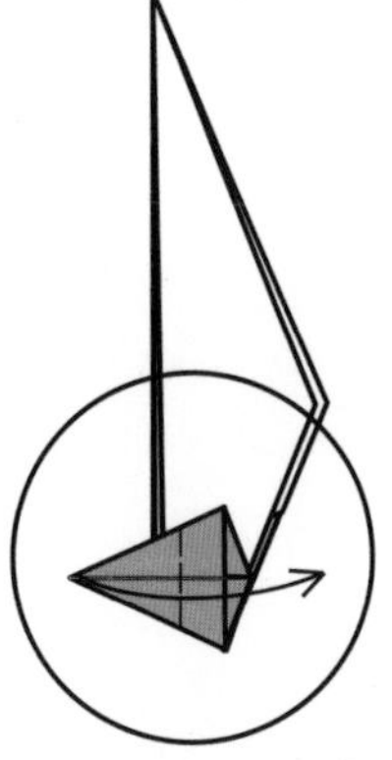

Valley fold arbitrarily.

9

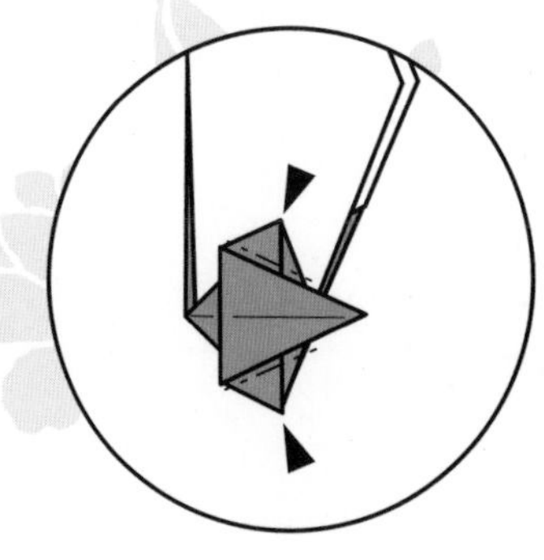

Enlargement. Pre-crease along edges then reverse the two tips.

10

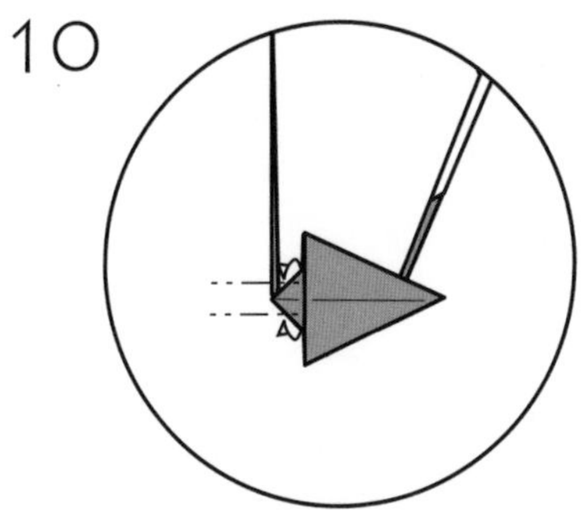

Mountain fold to narrow the stem.

11

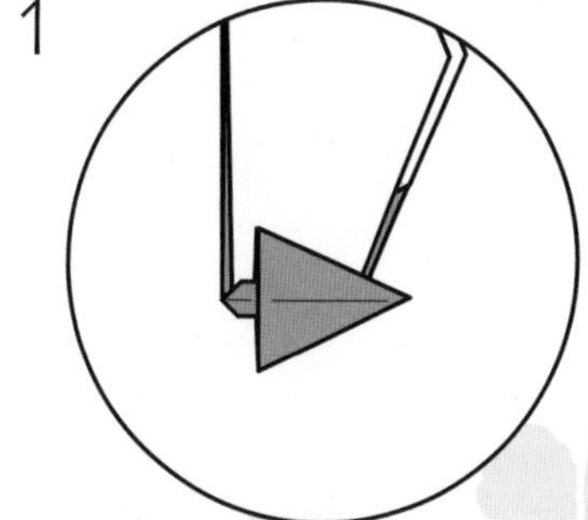

Completed timber.

12

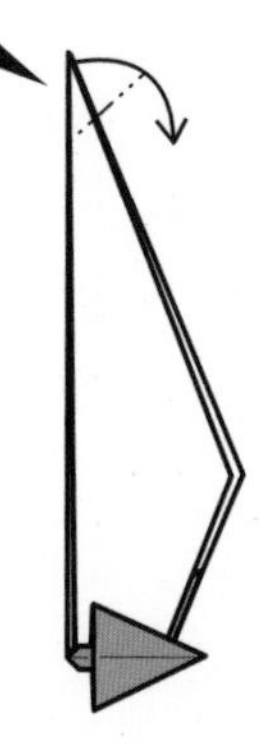

Normal view. Reverse the point arbitrarily.

13

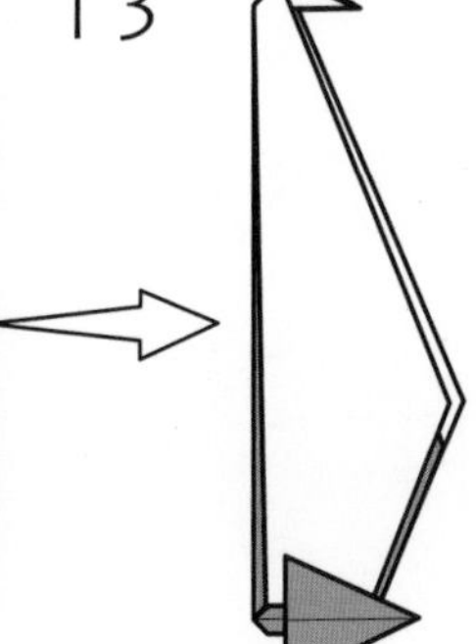

Completed step 12. Turn over.

14

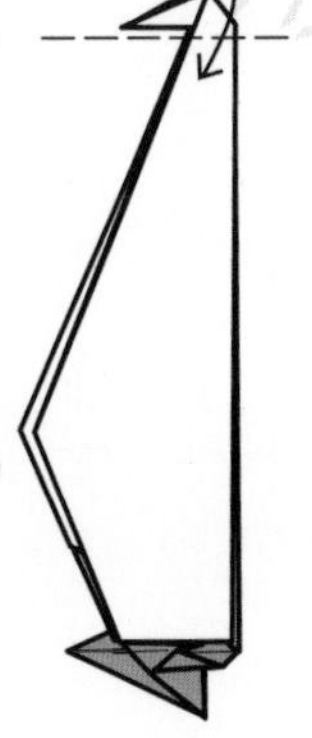

Unfold down.

15

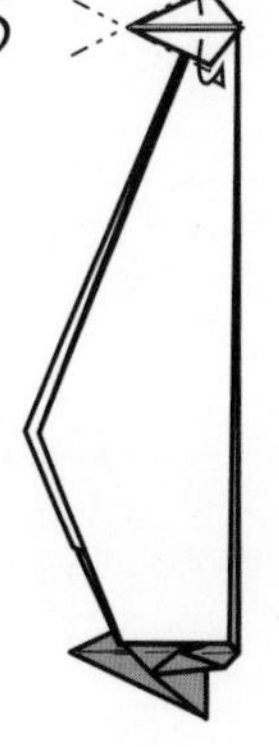

Wrap around a layer to reveal an alternate colour.

16

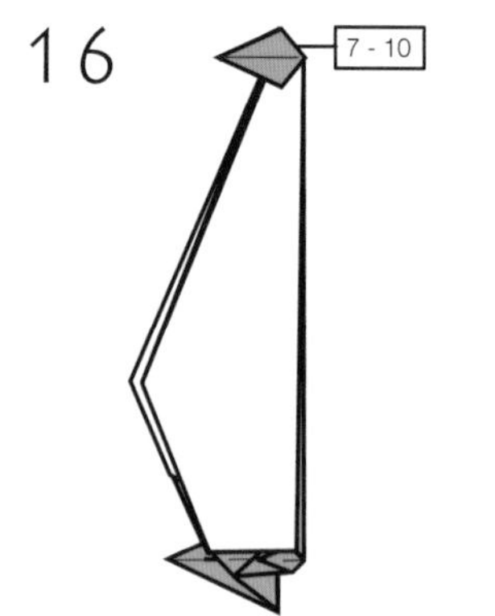

Repeat steps 7-10 on this coloured segment.

17

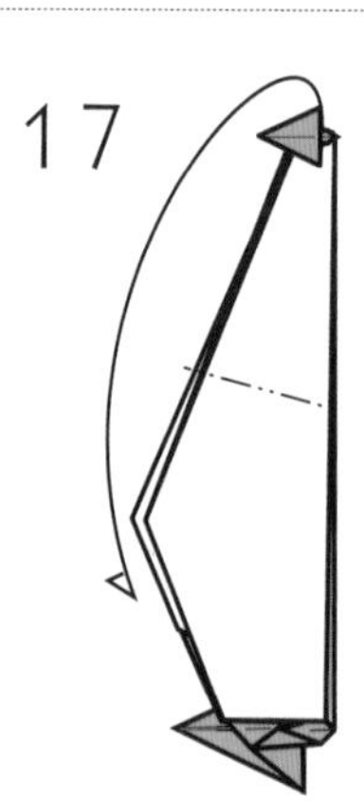

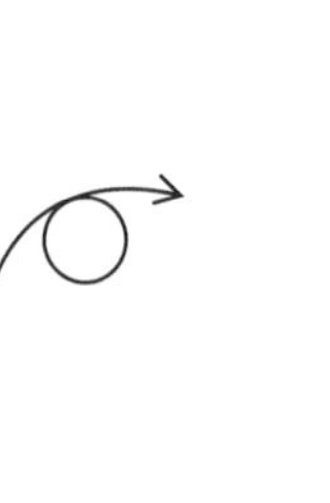

Mountain fold arbitrarily. Look at the next drawing for the correct position. Turn over.

18

Like this.

19

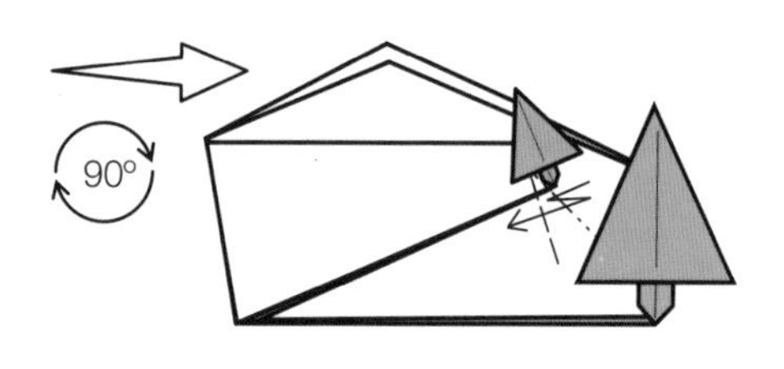

Rotate 90°. Pleat the small tree into position.

20

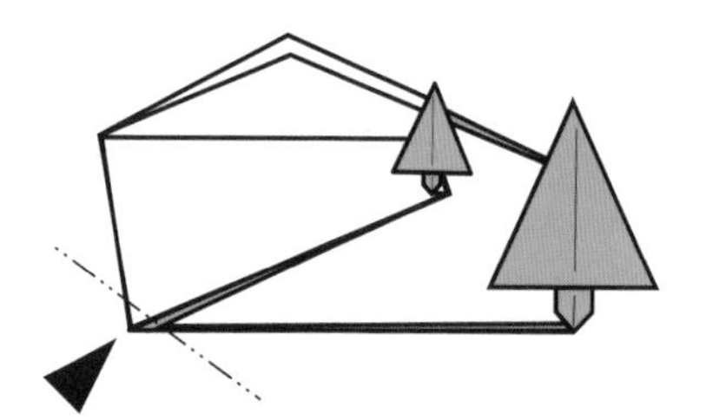

Reverse tip.

21

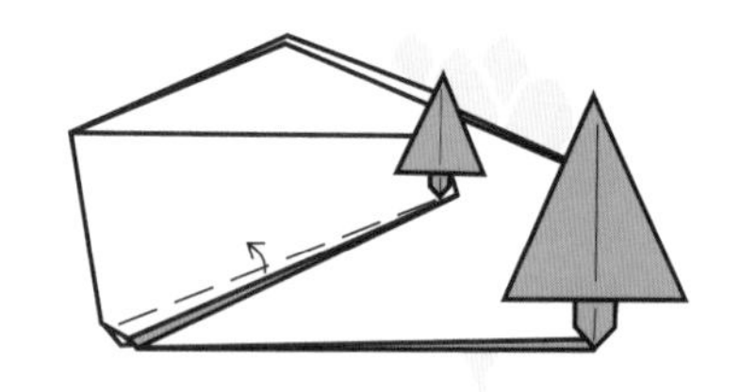

Make a tiny squash releasing a small portion of trapped paper. Now there is a little trail.

22

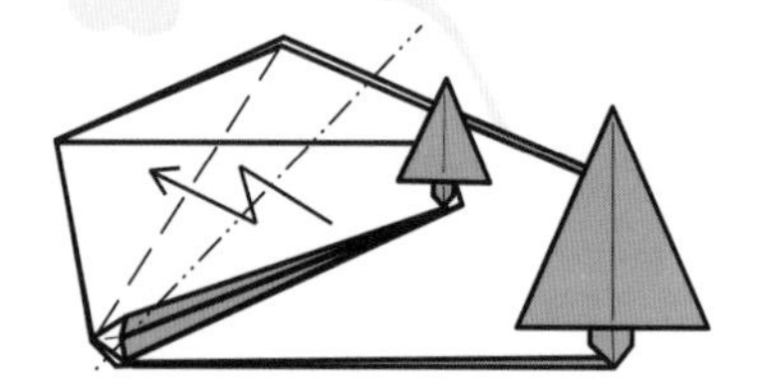

Pleat arbitrarily to form the hills.

23

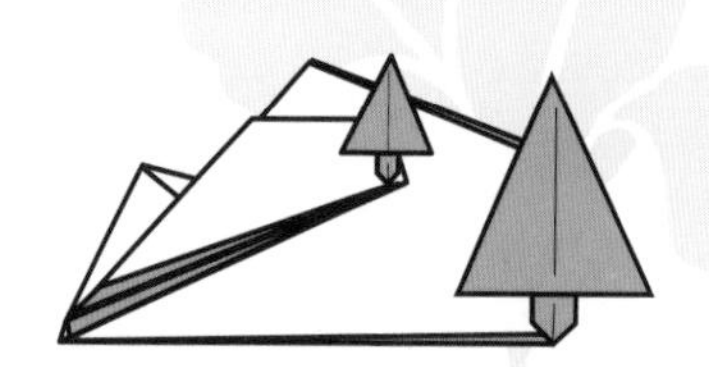

Completed step 22. Turn over.

24

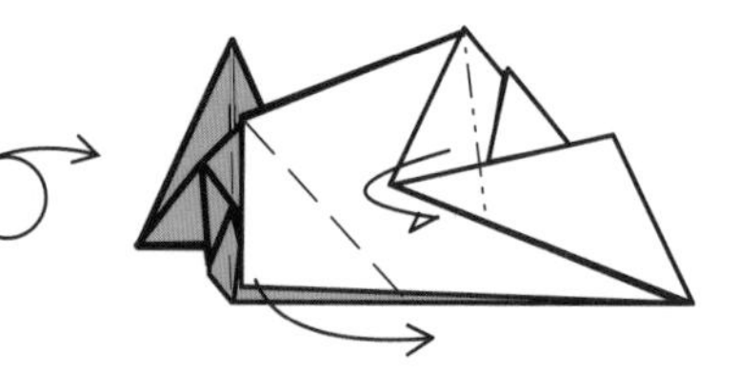

Mountain fold to lock the hills. Then valley fold outwards lightly...

25

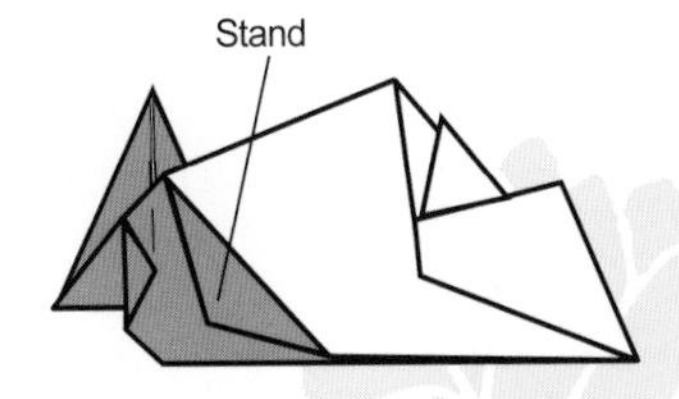

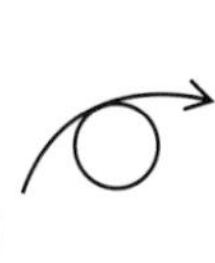

...and you will have a stand for the model. Turn over.

26

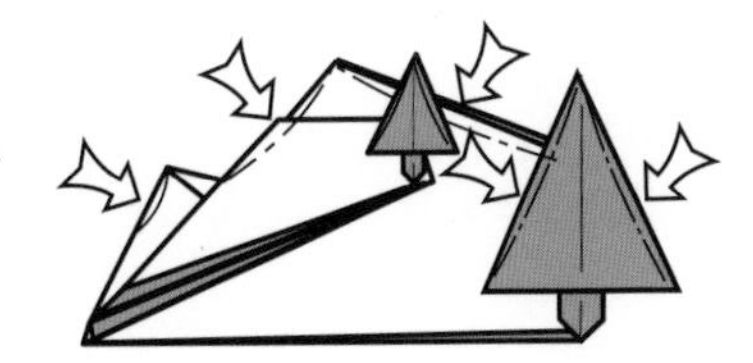

To reveal the landscape, shape off any area as you desire.

27

Completed alpine landscape.

PUFFY STAR

MODEL: TRADITIONAL
DIAGRAM: MATTHEW GARDINER

The puffy star is a traditional form popular in Asian countries. It is often made for new year celebrations for good luck. They can be strung together with a needle and thread to make hanging decorations. You will need strips of paper about 1.5cm x 30cm (0.6in x 12in).

Knotology, a term coined by Heinz Strobl, is the art of folding strips of paper. Many geometric forms can be made from making the pentagon as shown below.

1

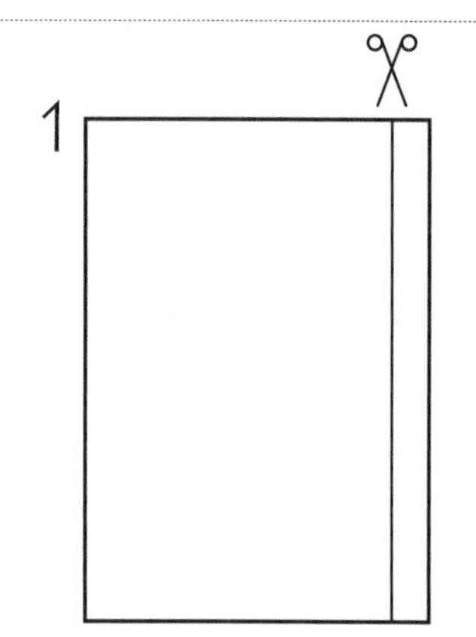

Cut 1.5cm (0.6in) from an A4 (8.5 x 11in) sheet of paper.

2

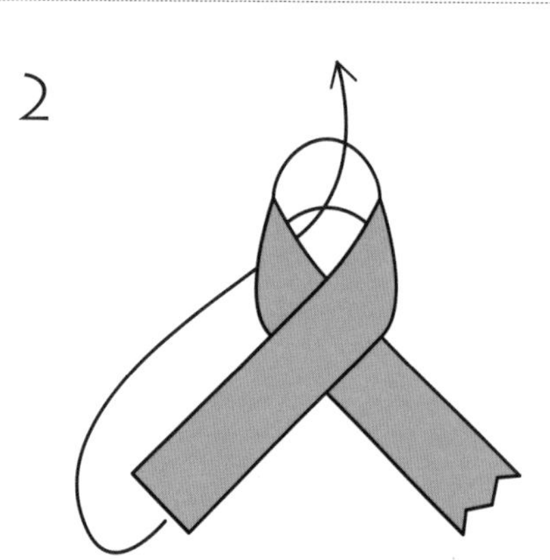

At one end of the strip, make a knot as shown.

3

Gently pull both ends until the pentagonal shape is clearly formed.

4

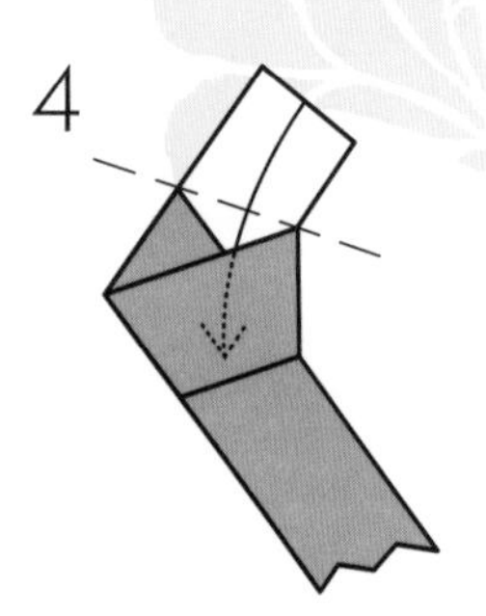

Fold the end of the strip over and tuck under the layer.

5

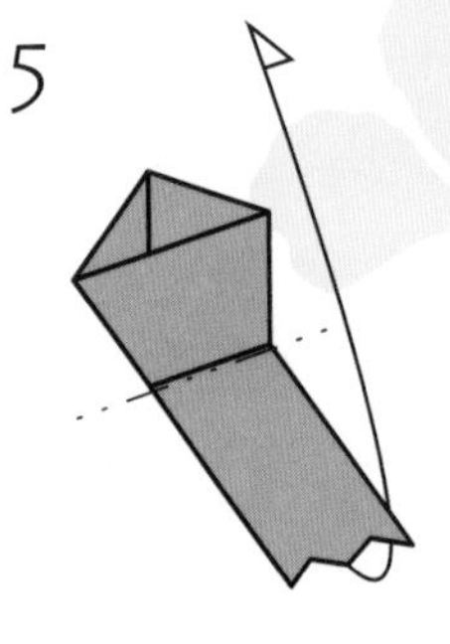

The next steps follow the pentagon shape, wrapping up the puffy star.

6

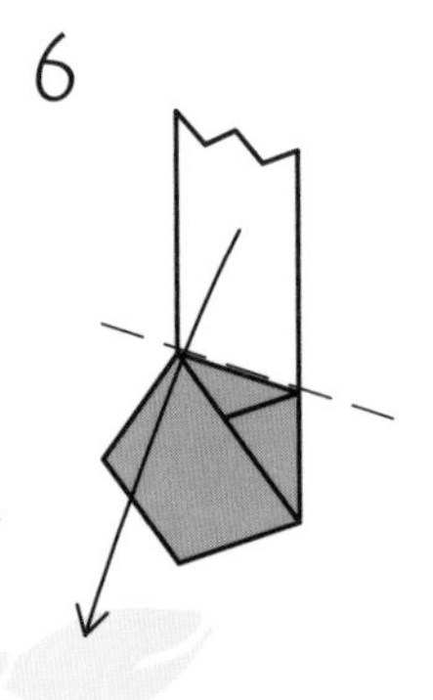

Valley fold.

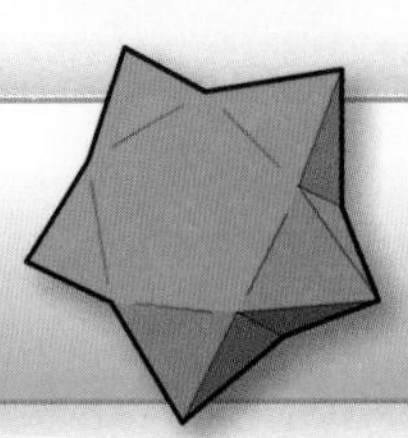

7

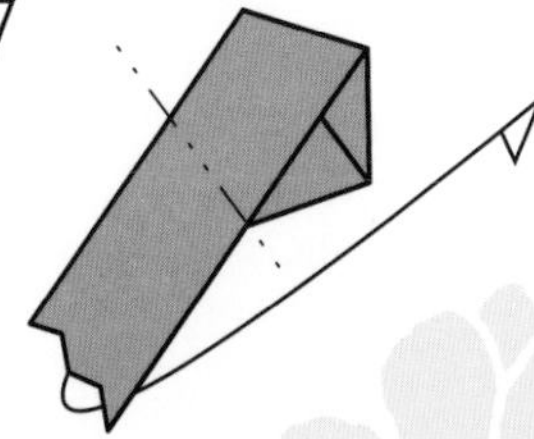

Mountain fold.

8

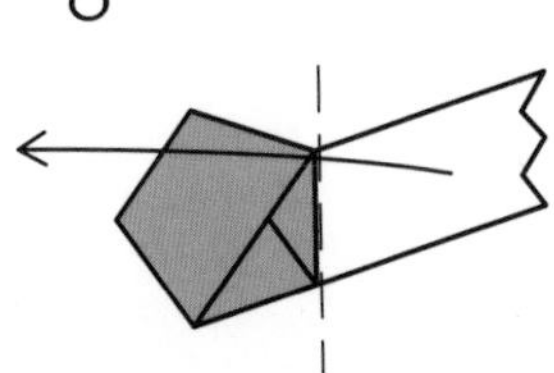

Valley fold.

9

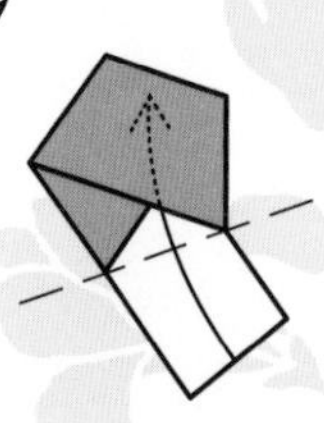

Keep wrapping until you end up with a small stub. Tuck the stub under the next layer.

10

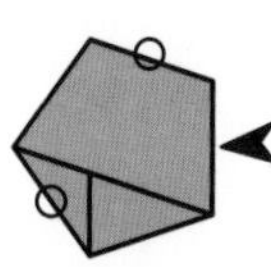

Hold at the circles and use the back of your nail to push in the side of the star.

11

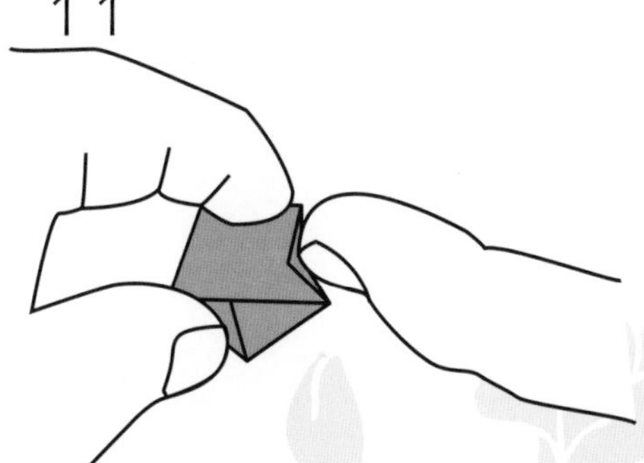

Step 10 completed.

12

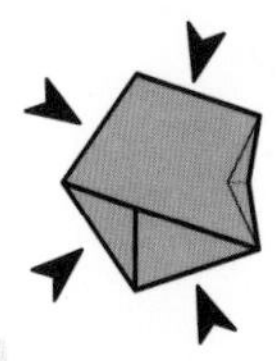

Push in the wall of the star on the remaining sides.

13

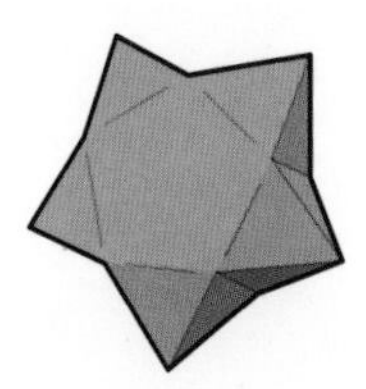

Completed puffy star.

HEART

MODEL: MATTHEW GARDINER
DIAGRAM: MATTHEW GARDINER

This heart can be a folded love letter, or as a decoration on the front of a card. Use A4 (8.5 x 11in) paper.

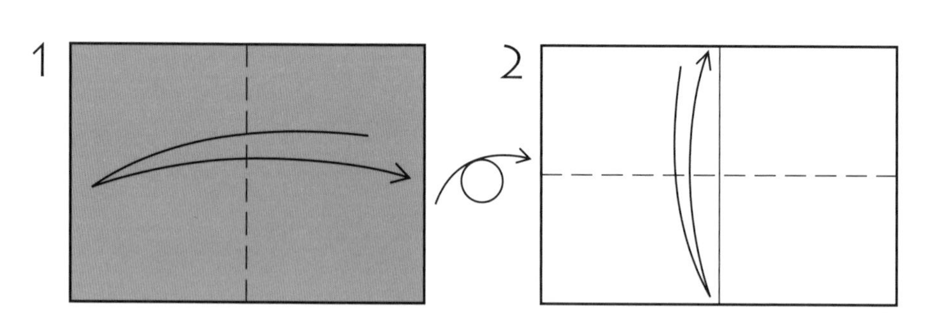

Book fold and unfold. Turn over.

Fold in half lengthways and unfold.

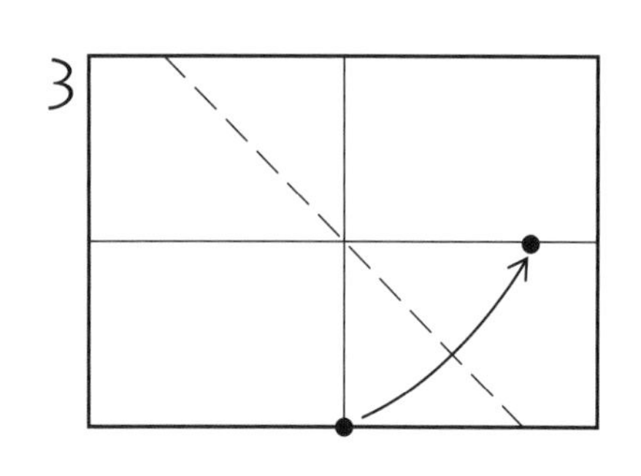

Valley fold a diagonal so that the vertical crease touches the horizontal crease.

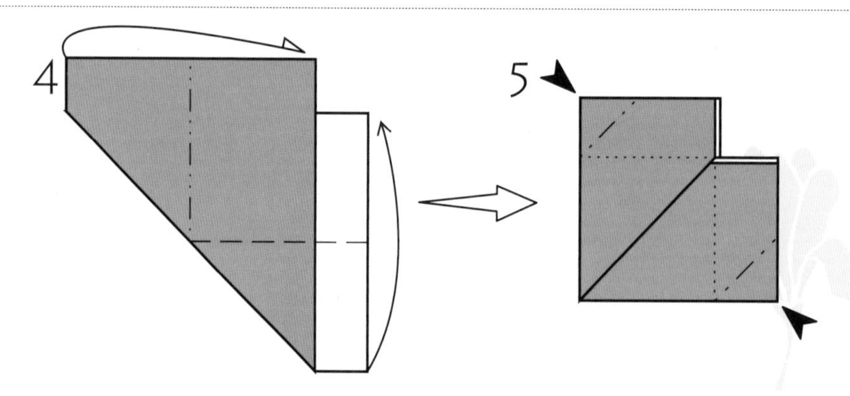

Fold the corners together, noting the mountain fold on the upper part and the valley fold on the lower part.

Inside reverse fold the points. The edge of the crease should match with the inner layer of the paper.

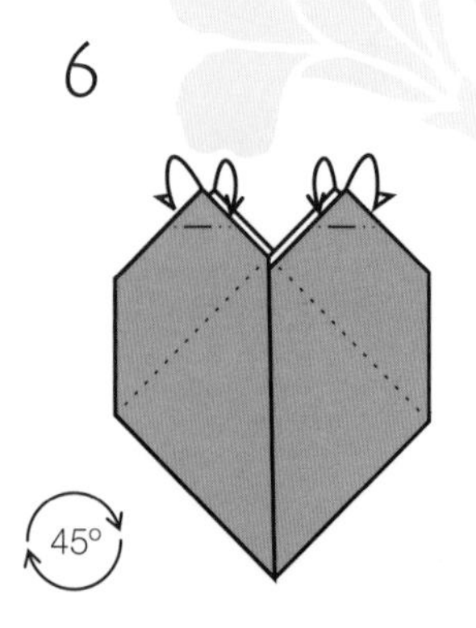

Fold the tips inside the heart.

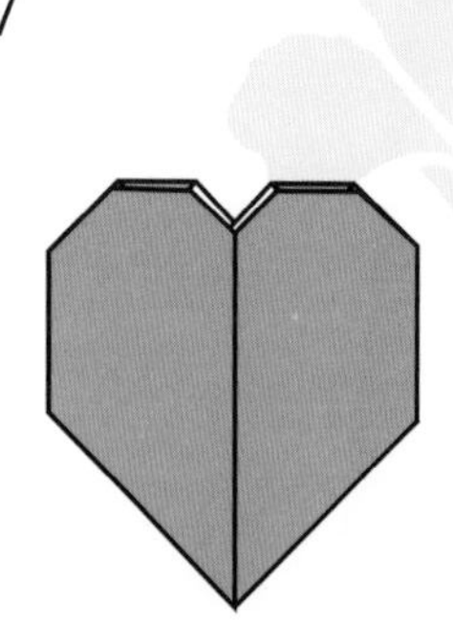

Completed heart.

FLAPPING BIRD

MODEL: TRADITIONAL, JAPAN
DIAGRAM: MATTHEW GARDINER

The flapping bird is a variation of the paper crane. This variation has a beautiful mechanism that pulls the paper of the wings, causing them to flap. There are a few varieties of flapping birds – this one is the original and a classic.

The smallest flapping bird in the world was folded by Akira Naito in Japan. His smallest ever model so far is a paper crane folded from a 0.1mm (0.0039in) square, using plastic film instead of paper, a microscope and special handmade micro origami tools.

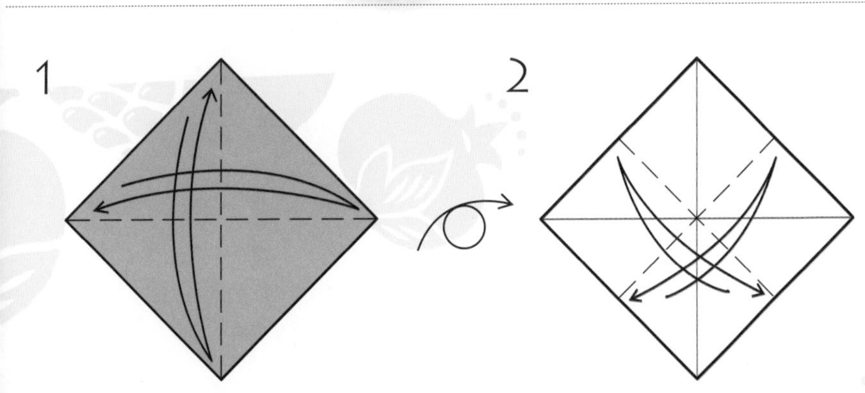

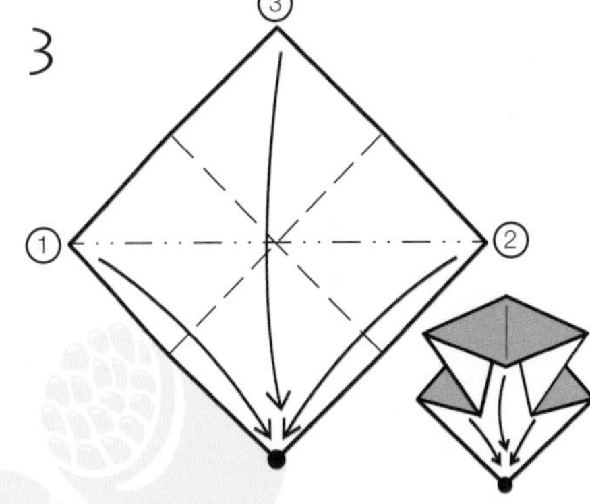

Start coloured side up.
Fold and unfold diagonals. Turn over.

Book fold and unfold.

Bring three corners down to meet bottom corner. Start with corners 1 and 2 together followed by corner 3.

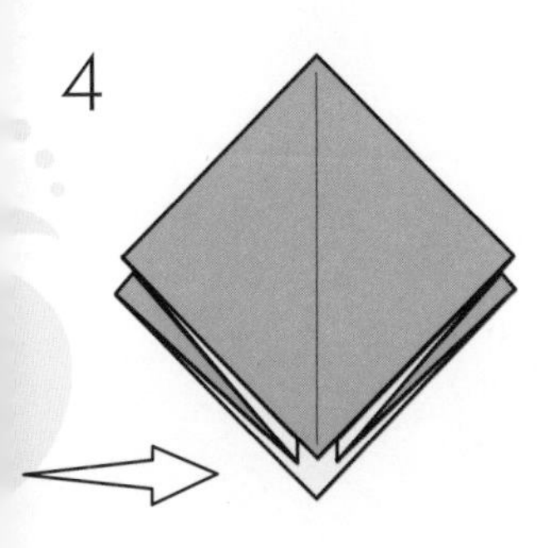

5

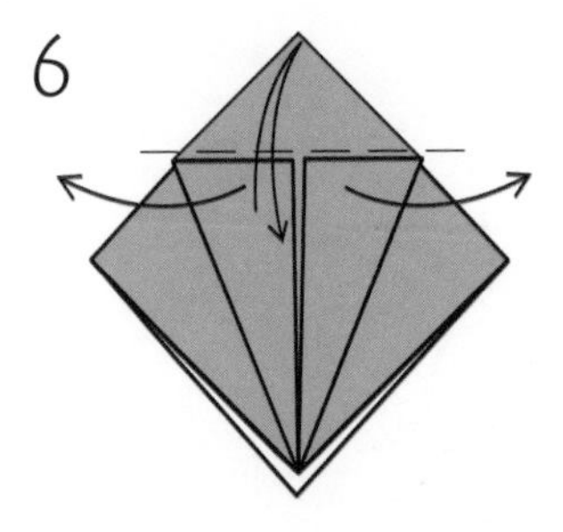

Completed preliminary base.

Fold top layer to the centre crease.

Fold the top triangle down and unfold.
Unfold flaps.

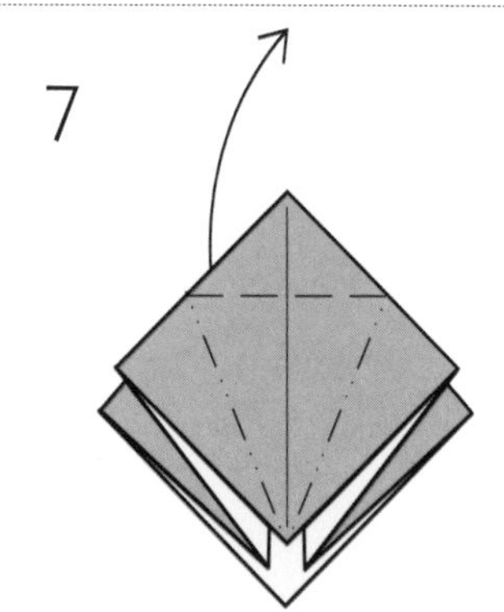

Lift the top layer upwards.

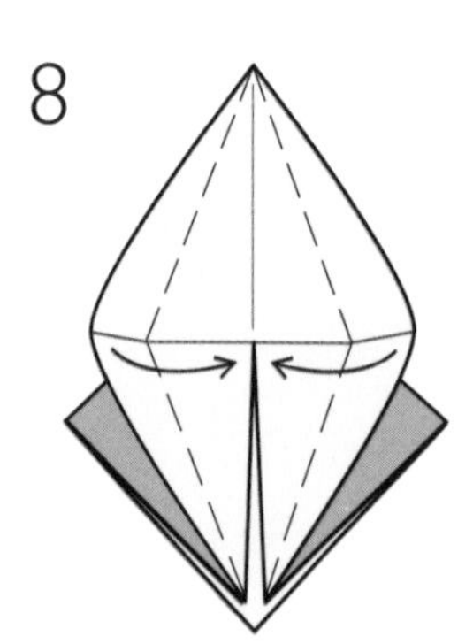

Step 7 in progress, the model is 3D. Fold the top layer inwards on existing creases.

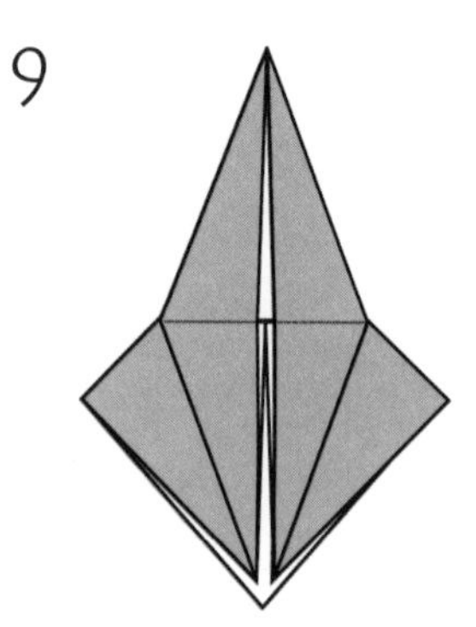

Step 7 completed, the model will be flat. Turn over.

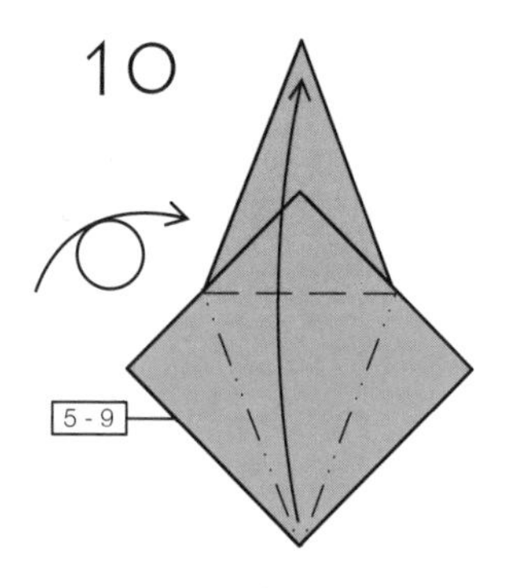

Repeat steps 5-9 on this side.

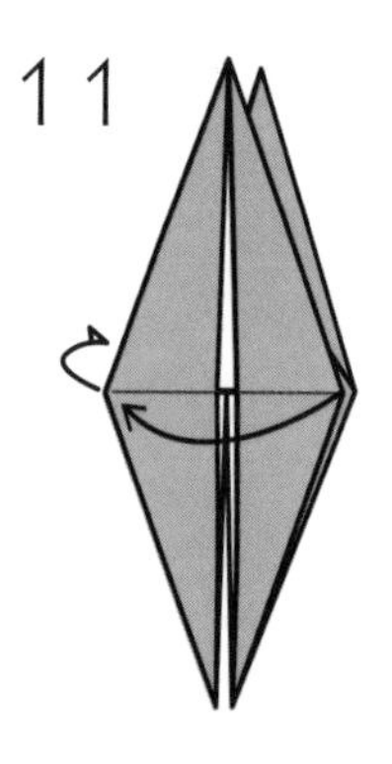

Turn front and back flap over.

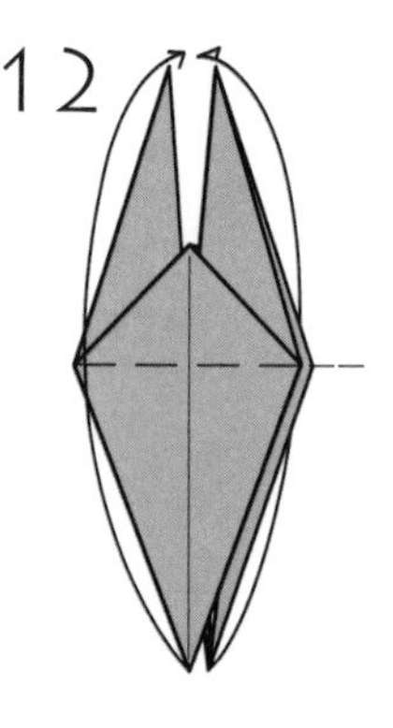

Fold flaps up.

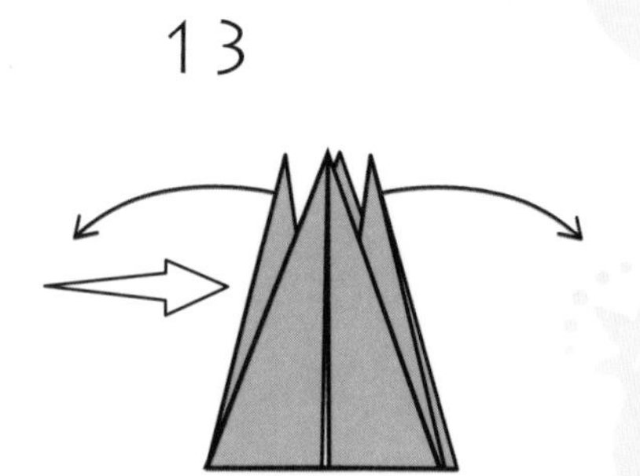

Swivel the two points outwards. These form the head and tail.

The next steps show details of forming the head.

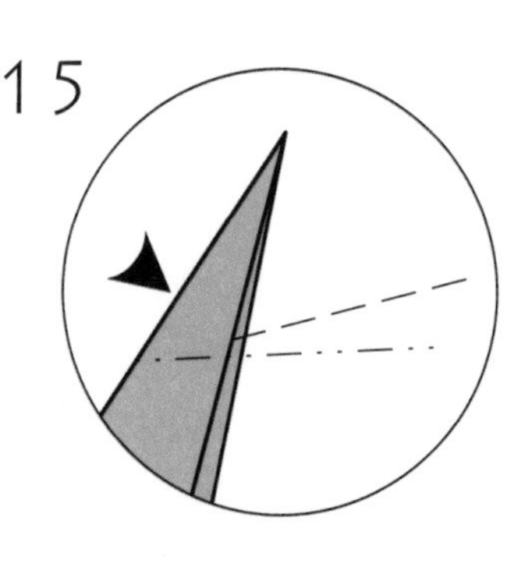

Reverse fold.

16

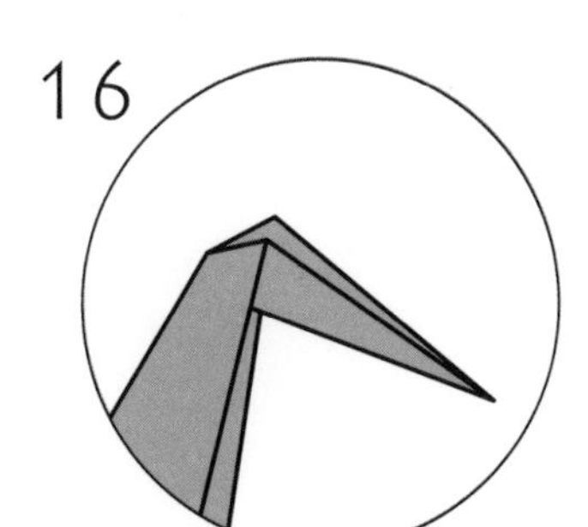

Step 15 completed.

17

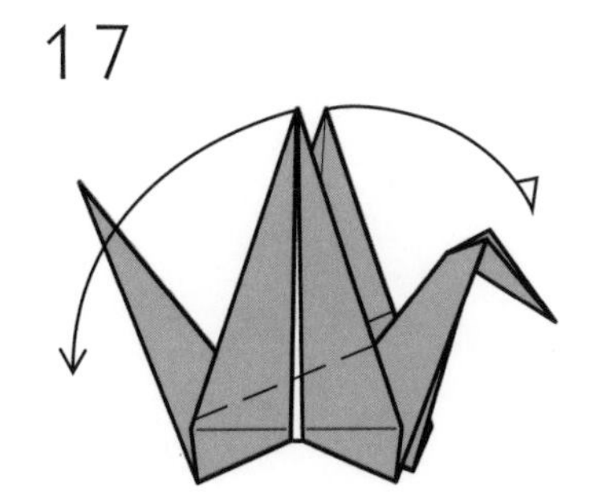

Fold down wings. Make soft folds.

18

Completed flapping bird.

19

To make the bird flap hold the model at the black dots. Gently pull on the tail and the wings will flap down. Gently release and the wings will go back up. Repeat.

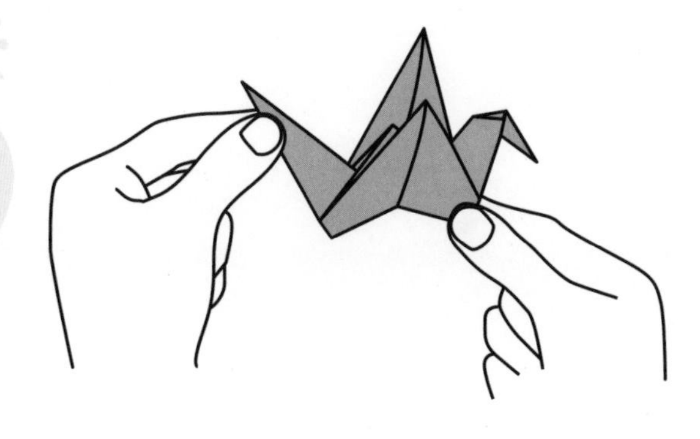

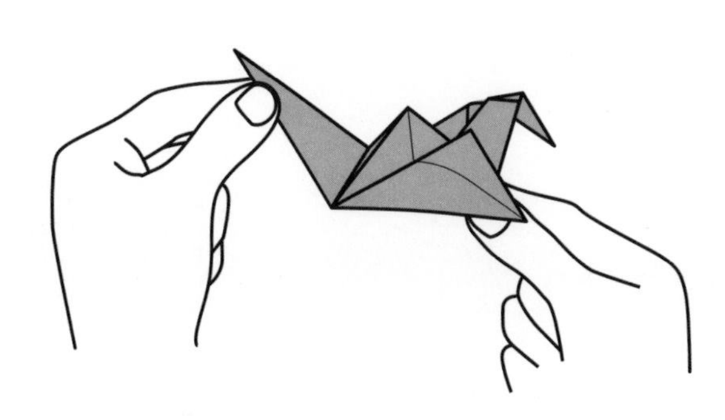

Drinking Bird

Model: Traditional
Diagram: Matthew Gardiner

The drinking bird is a well-known toy, a bird that drinks the water and keeps drinking by itself. This origami model is a little different – the bird does drink, but you have to help it.

The drinking bird has a pool, and a very interesting origami mechanism that pushes its head forwards as you push upwards.

1

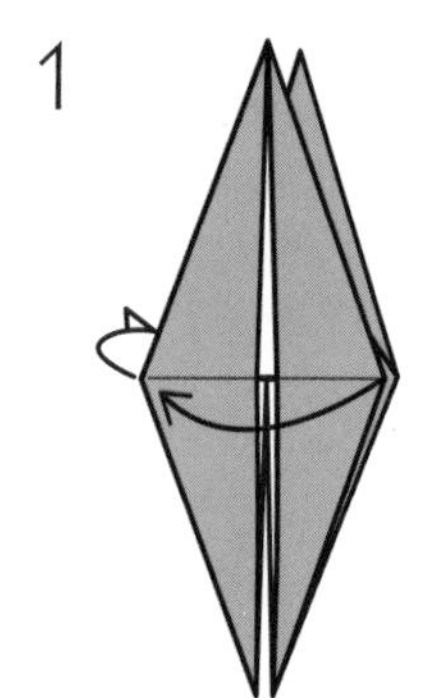

Start from the bird base (Step 11, on page 2). Turn front and back flap over.

2

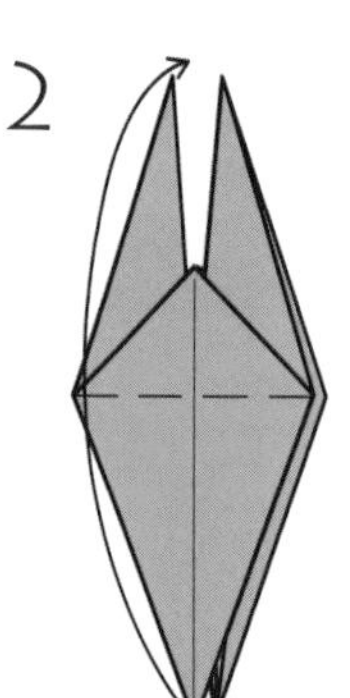

Move top layer up.

3

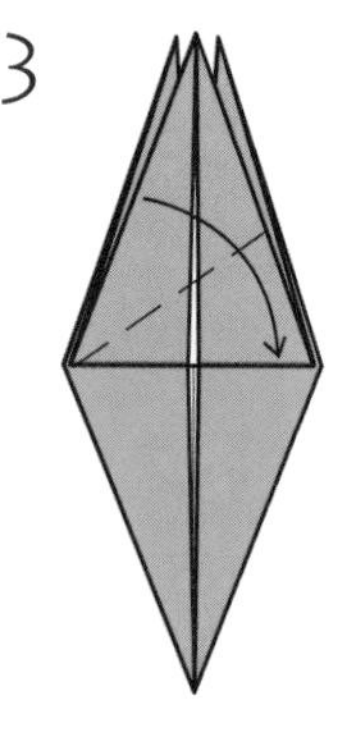

Fold down.

4

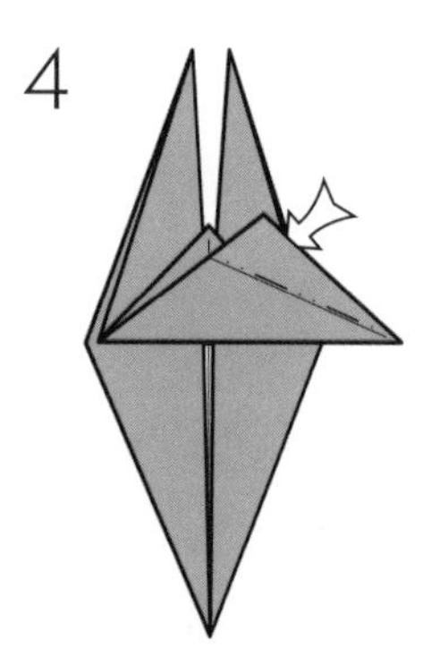

Reverse fold top layer. Steps 3-4 are a different way to make a rabbit ear fold.

5

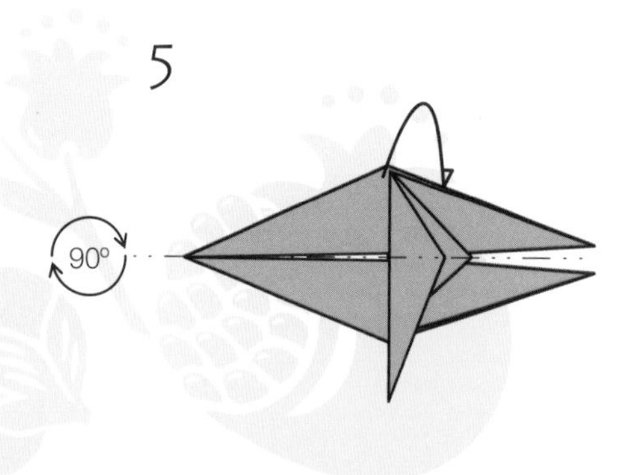

Rotate 90°. Mountain fold the model in half. Allow the top layer to flip up.

6

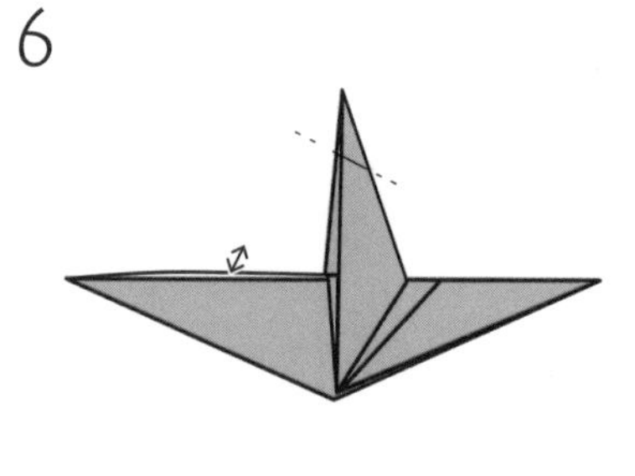

To form the head, inside reverse fold. Widen out drinking trough.

7

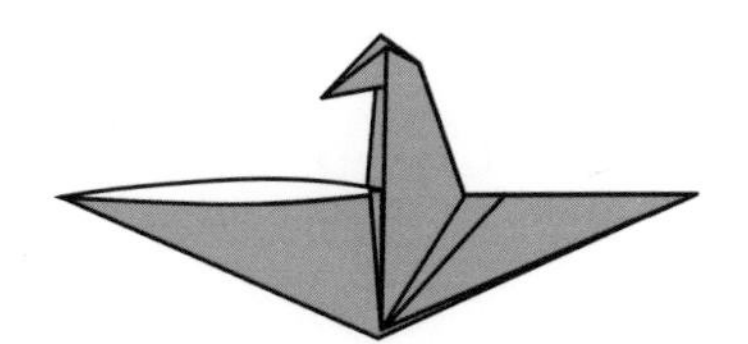

Completed drinking bird.

8

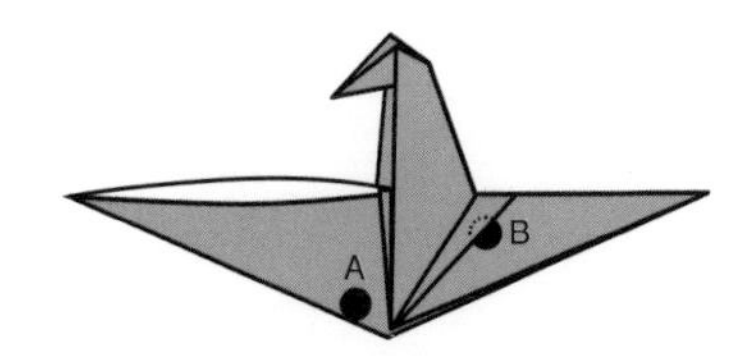

To make the bird drink hold the trough in one hand (at point A) and slip your fingers inside the pockets at point B and move your fingers up and down.

9

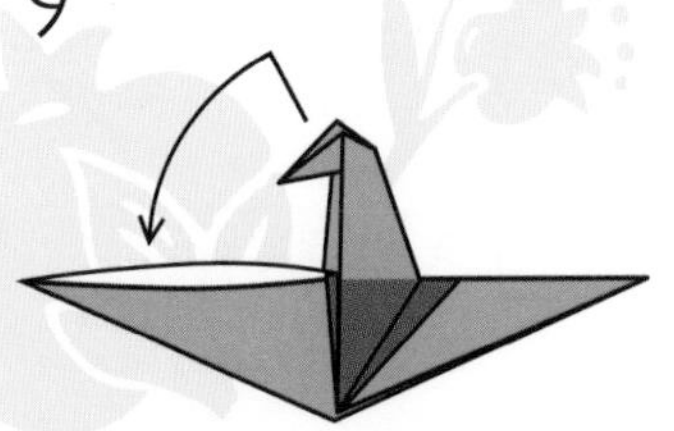

Allow the layers of paper under the neck, as shown by the darkened area, to become loose. As you push up, the bird's neck will dip forward and drink.

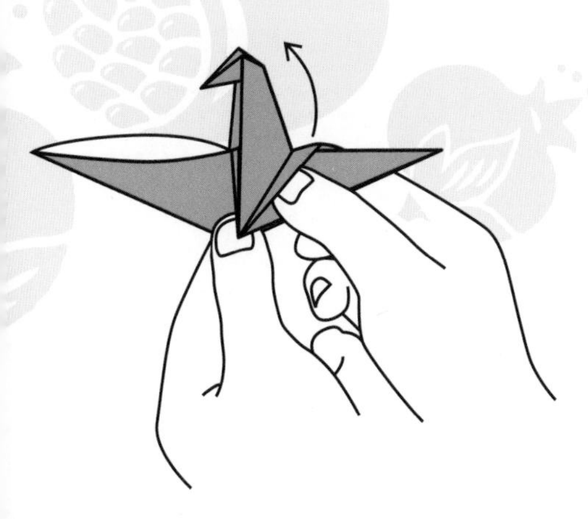

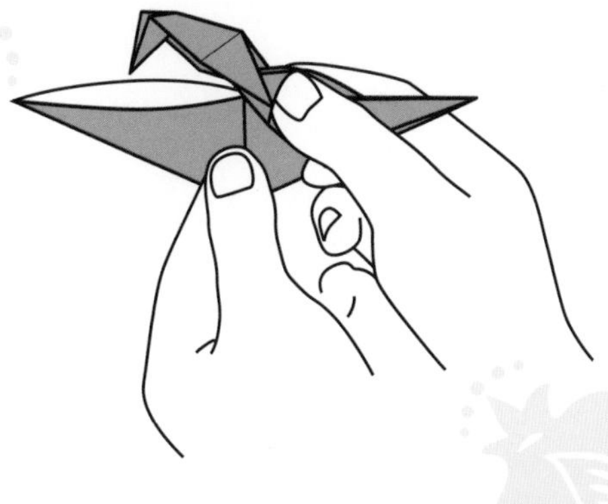

BOAT

MODEL: TRADITIONAL, JAPAN
DIAGRAM: MATTHEW GARDINER

The boat is a fantastic origami model. At step 9 the model forms a hat and by step 14 you have an origami model that actually floats. For longer floating time, use a greaseproof paper, or better yet, modern technology has produced synthetic paper that won't soak up water, so your boat won't sink.

A German artist named Frank Bölter has used this origami design, with special paper and lots of help, to actually sail down rivers in Europe!

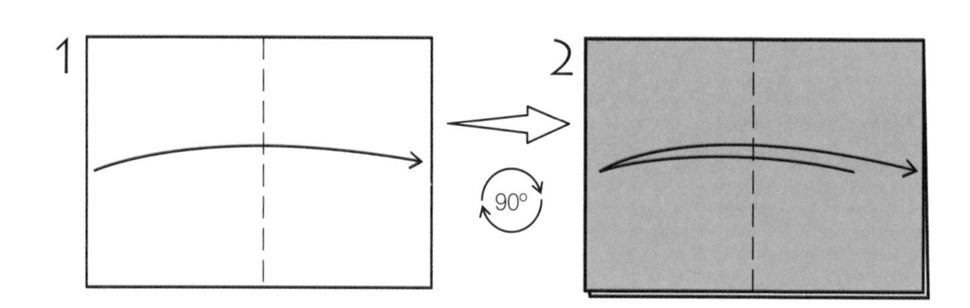

Start with a rectangle. A4 (8.5 x 11in) is a good size – use a sheet of newspaper for a wearable hat. Book fold.

Turn 90° and book fold and unfold again.

Fold corners down.

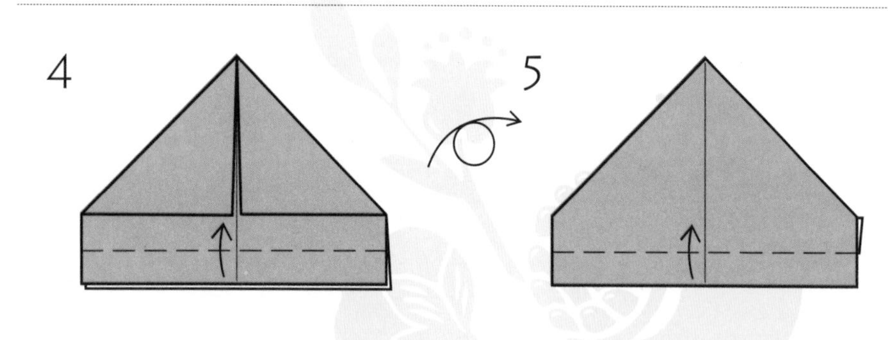

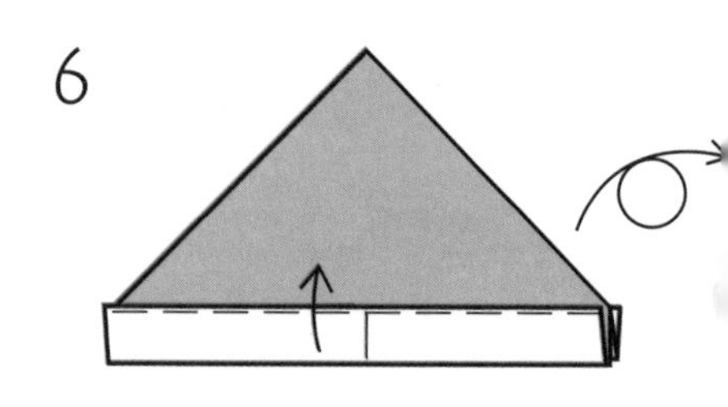

Fold up to the bottom of the triangles. Turn over.

Fold up to match the fold in step 4.

Fold up over the bottom of the triangle. Turn over.

7

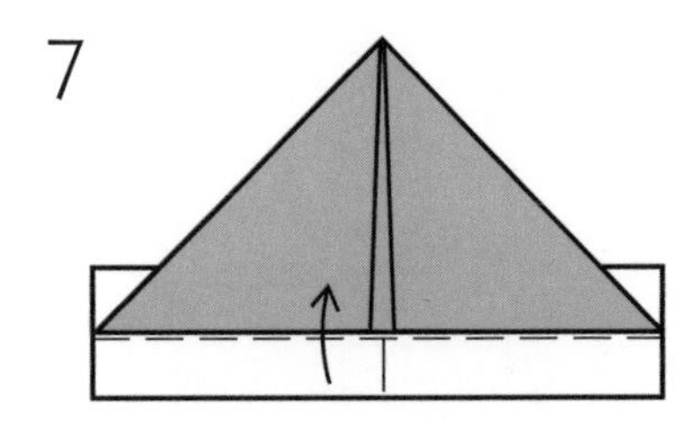

Repeat step 6.

8

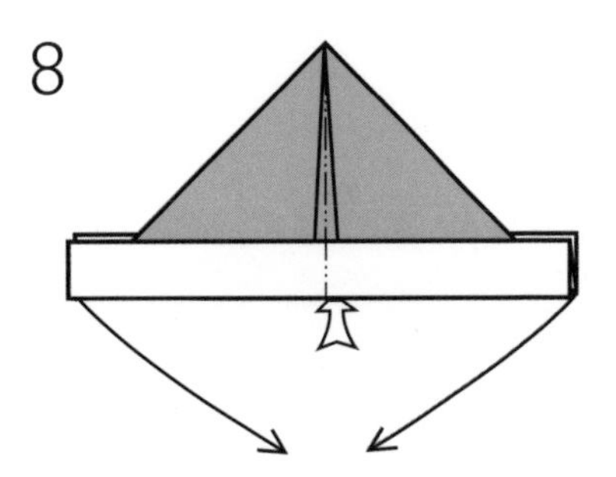

Lift the middle and push both points together, to make a squash fold.

9

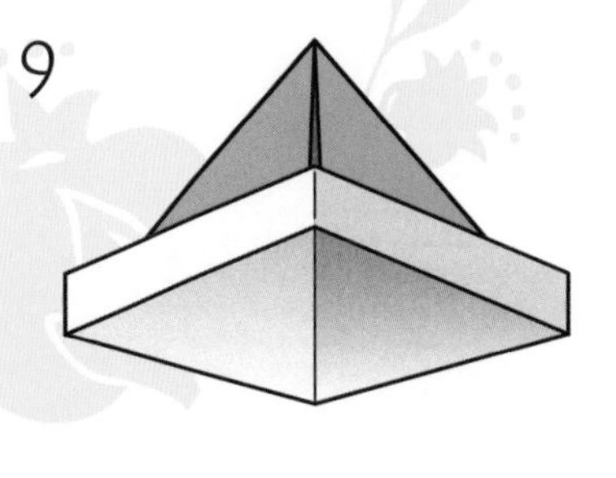

Squash fold in progress. This stage can also be used as a hat.

10

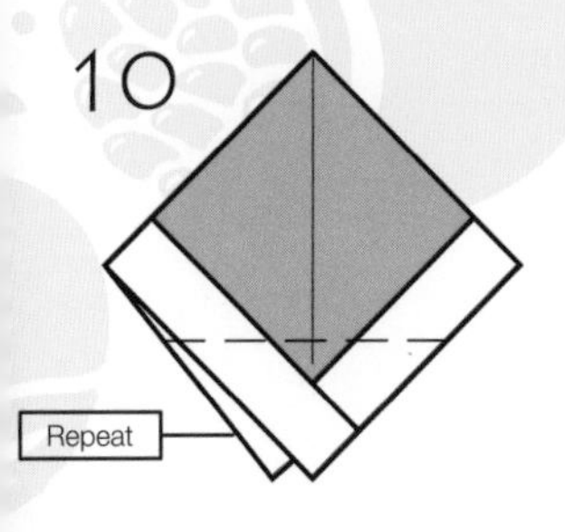

Fold bottom point about one third. Repeat behind.

11

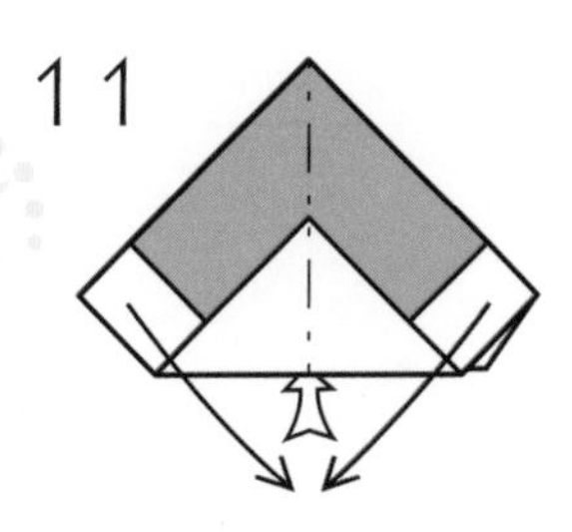

Squash fold, lifting the middle, similar to step 8.

12

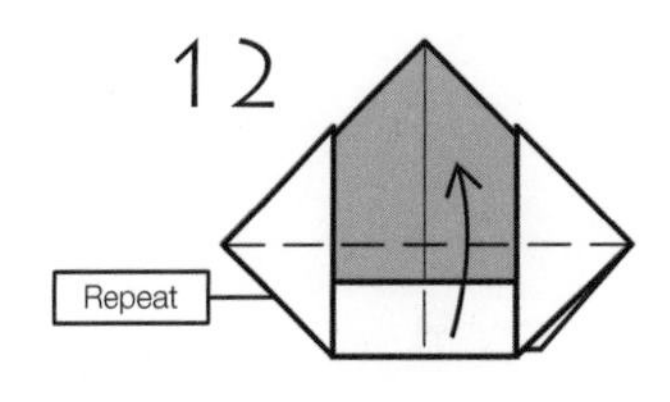

Fold up. Repeat behind.

13

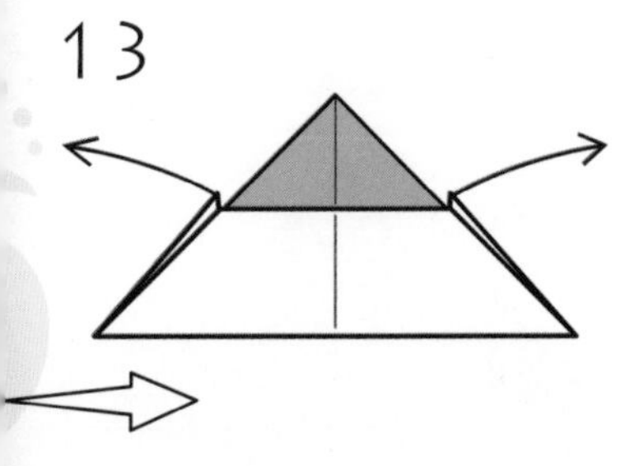

Pull the points out to shape the boat. The boat will become 3D.

14

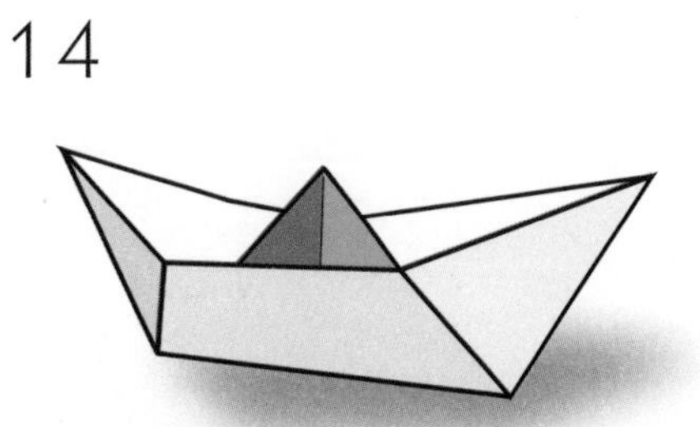

Completed boat.

WATER BOMB

MODEL: TRADITIONAL, JAPAN
DIAGRAM: MATTHEW GARDINER

The water bomb is a classic because in the last move you actually get to inflate it! The model forms a box that can hold a liquid. Ironically, the water bomb when made from paper, does not actually hold water for very long. Use plastic or greaseproof paper to keep the water a little longer.

Australian composer David Young wrote "16 Boxes", a musical piece for percussion with origami accompaniment. To perform this, the artist must fold 16 origami boxes (waterbombs) in 12 minutes: that's 45 seconds each.

1

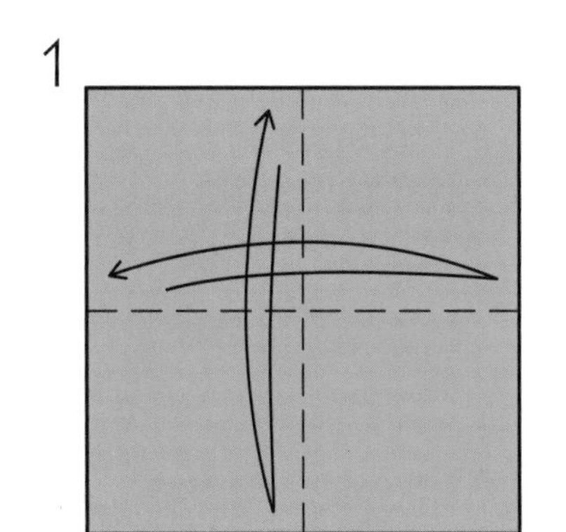

Begin coloured side up.
Book fold and unfold. Turn over.

2

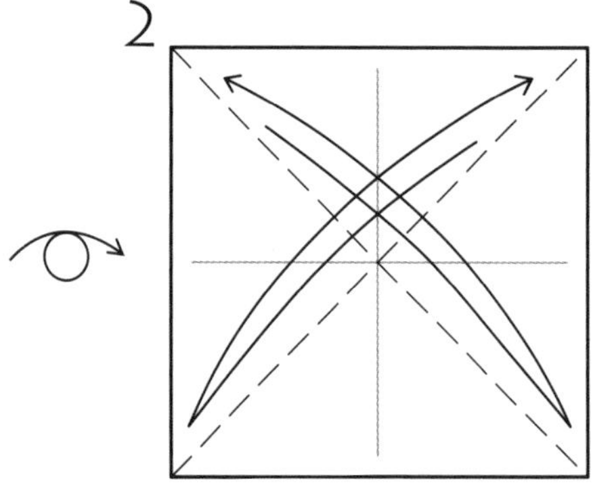

Fold and unfold diagonals.

3

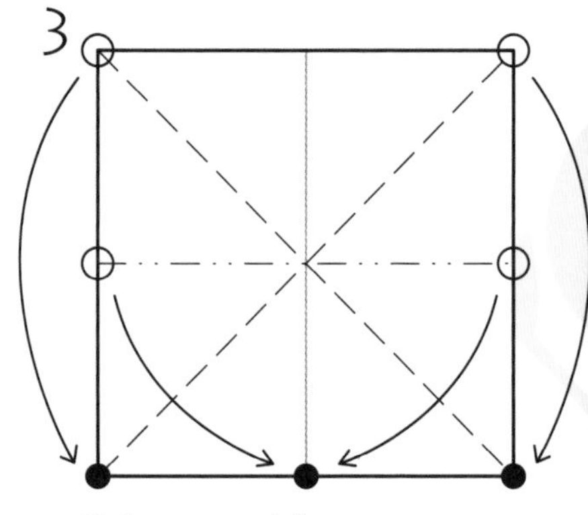

Collapse on existing creases.

4

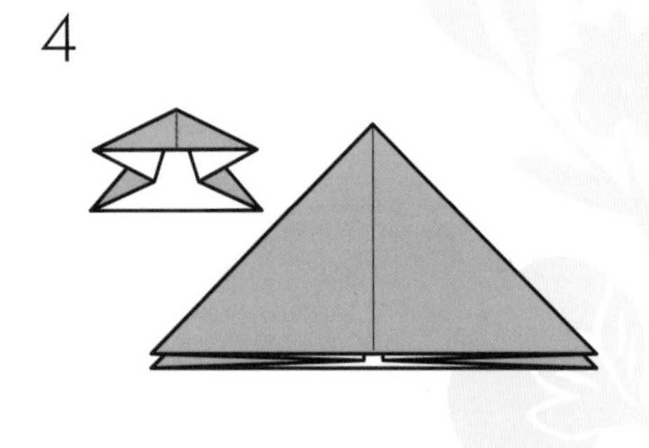

The waterbomb base.

5

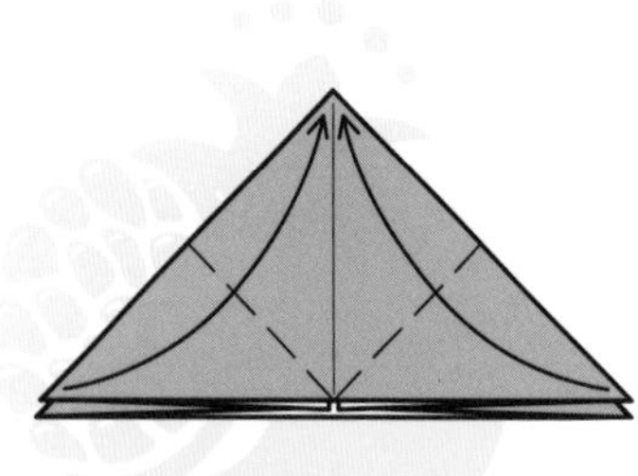

Fold corners up. Turn over.

6

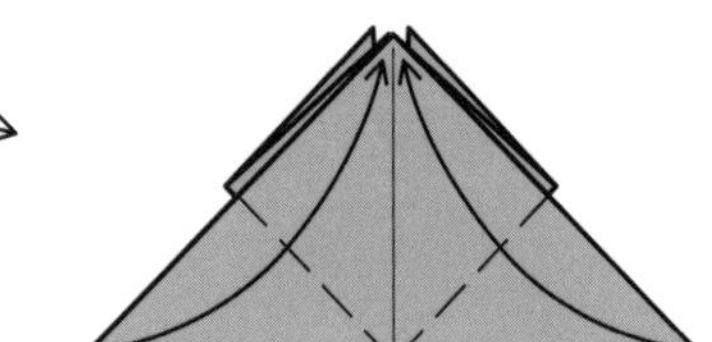

Repeat step 5.

7

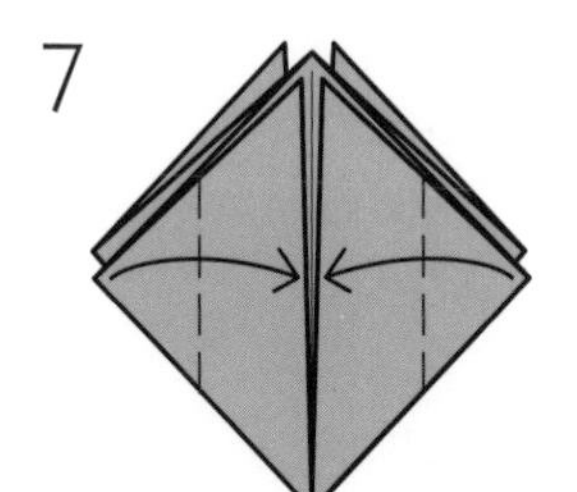

Fold corners of top layer to the middle.

8

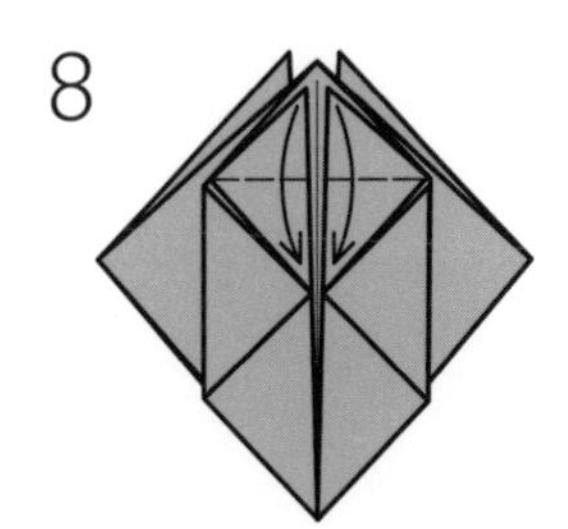

Fold top two flaps down.

9

Pre-crease the triangles, and then tuck them into the pockets.

10

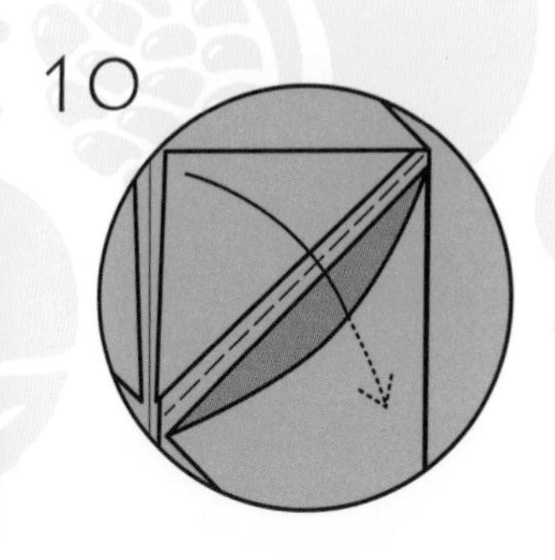

Detail of step 9, showing how to insert the triangle into the pocket.

11

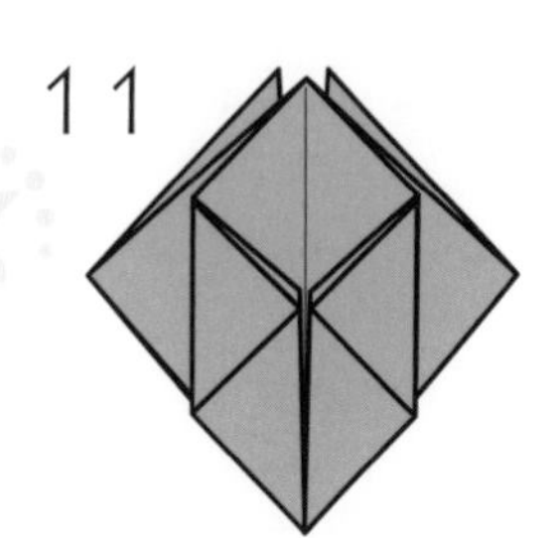

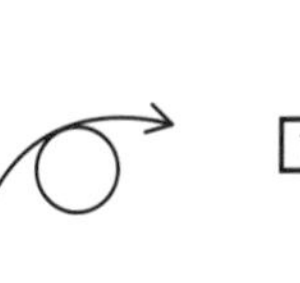

Step 9 completed. Turn over.

12

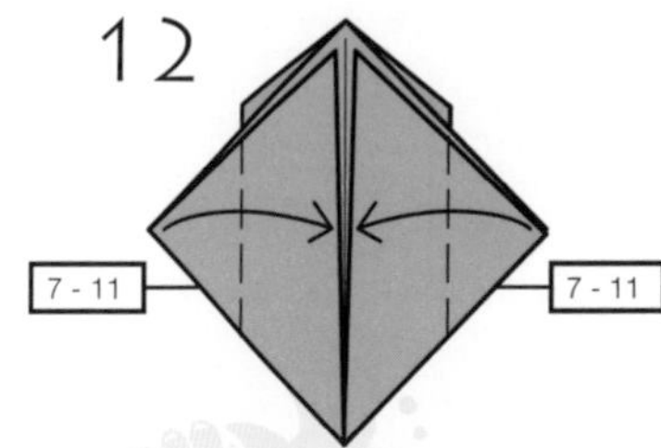

Repeat steps 7-11 on both sides.

13

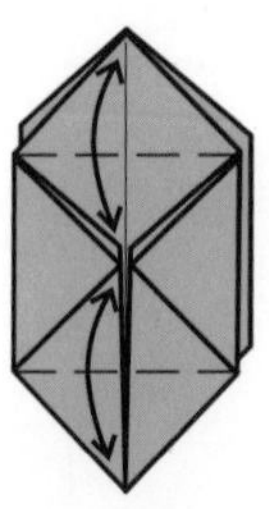

Fold and unfold top and bottom triangles.

14

15

Pull flaps apart. Blow air into the hole in the bottom and shape into 3D cube.

Completed water bomb.

GLIDER

MODEL: TRADITIONAL
DIAGRAM: MATTHEW GARDINER

Paper planes are one of the many wonders of the world. How can a sheet of paper and a few folds become a gravity-defying flying machine? This glider is a simple but stable model that flies well. If you curve the rear corners upwards a little, you accelerate lift, causing it to do loop the loops.

World record holder Ken Blackburn set his record of longest time aloft at the Georgia Dome, USA in 1998. The record is 27.6 seconds of flight from a hand launch.

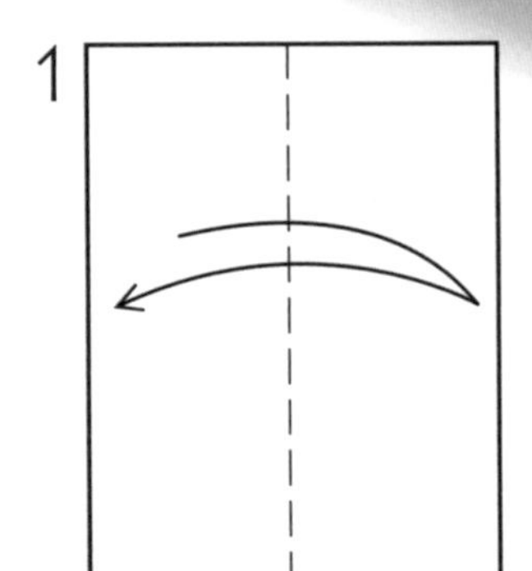

Use an A4 (8.5 x 11in) sheet of paper. Book fold and unfold.

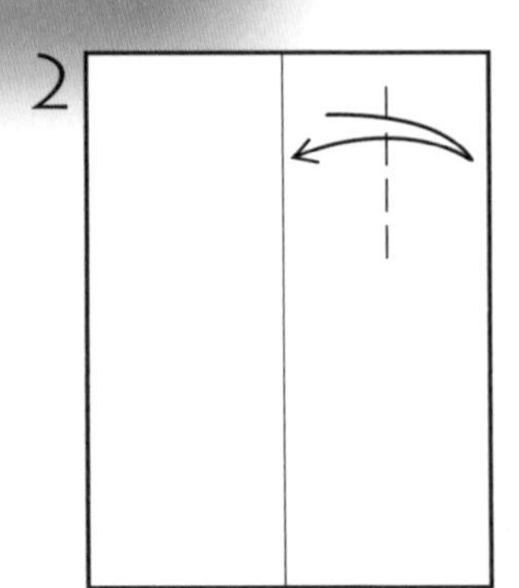

Fold and unfold edge to centre crease. Make only a short crease as shown.

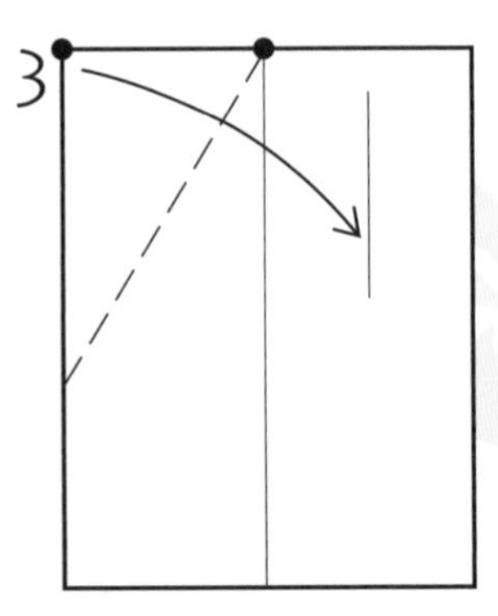

Fold the corner to touch the crease from step 2. Start the fold from the centre crease.

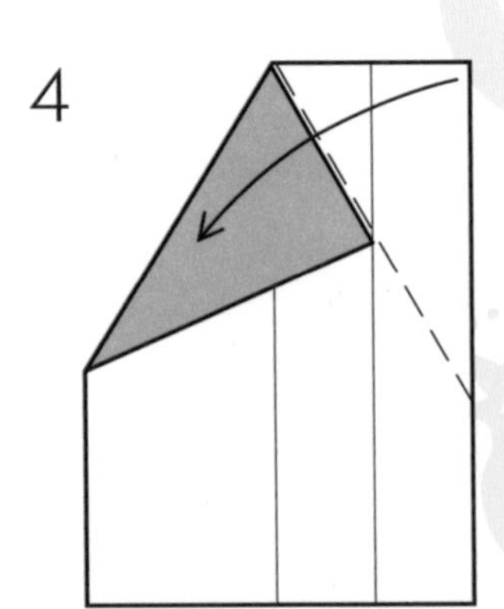

Fold other edge over.

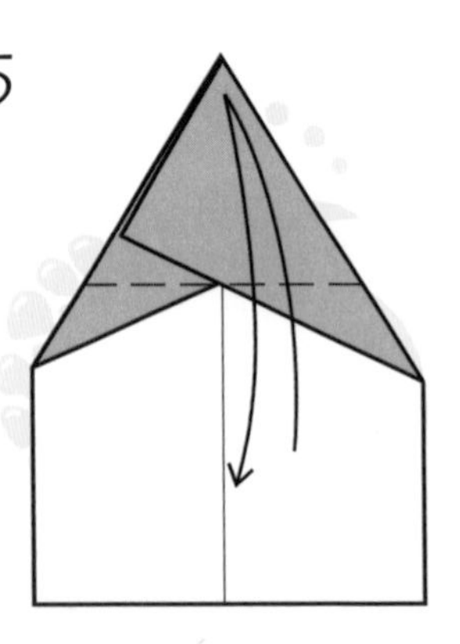

Fold across the intersection of the top layers, and unfold.

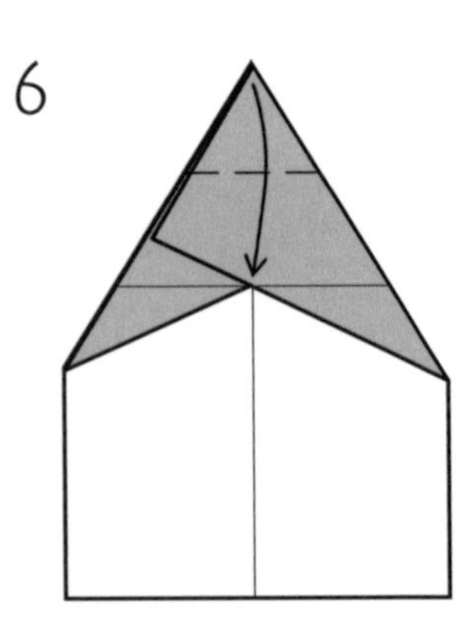

Fold to the previous crease.

7

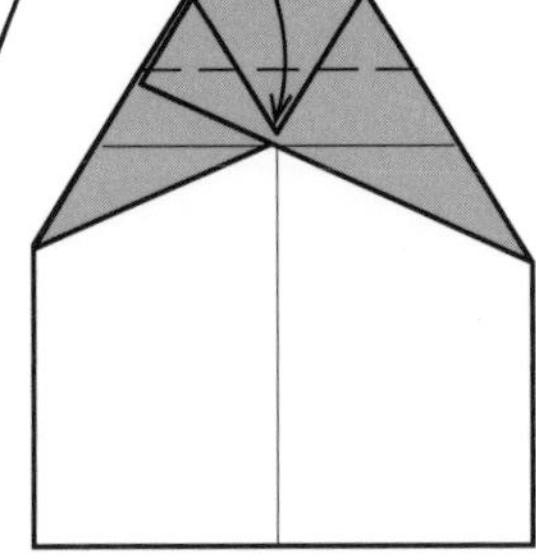

Fold the top edge to meet the intersection.

8

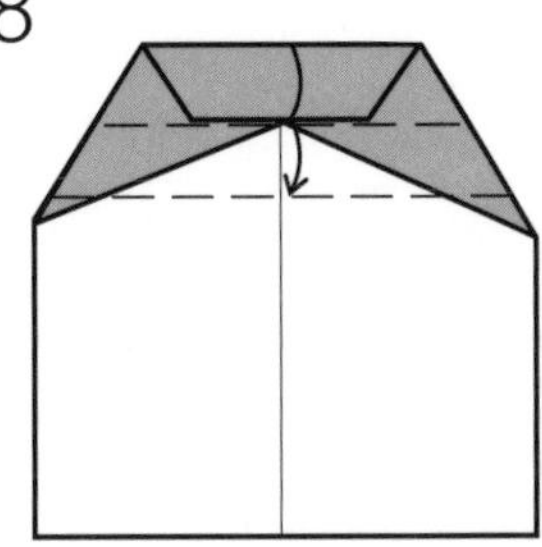

Fold over, and over again.

9

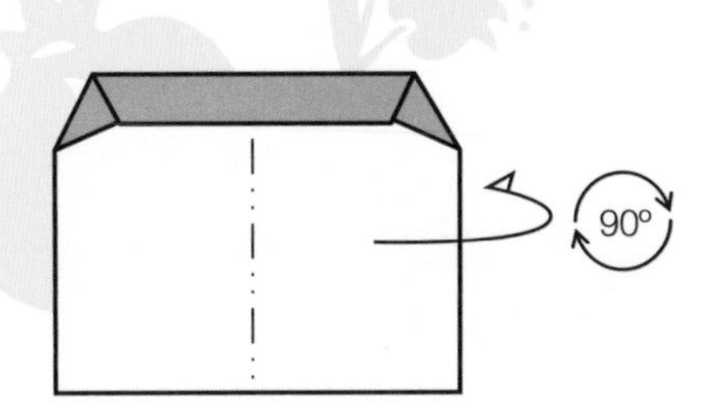

Mountain fold in half.
Rotate 90° degrees.

10

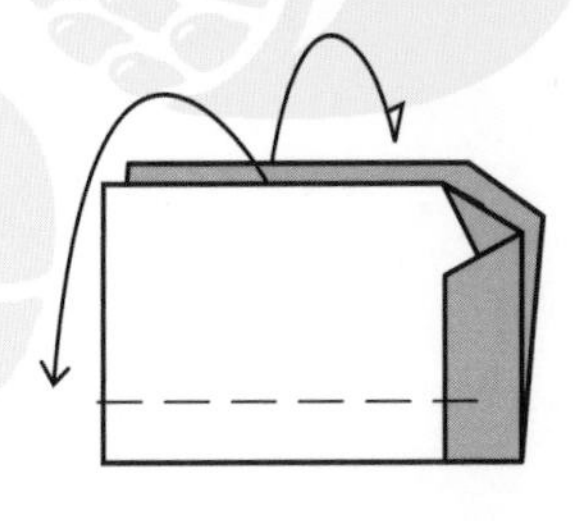

Fold both flaps down about 2 cm from the bottom.

11

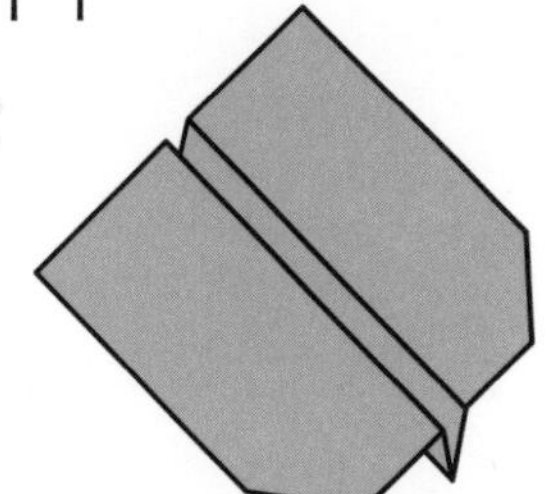

Completed glider.

12

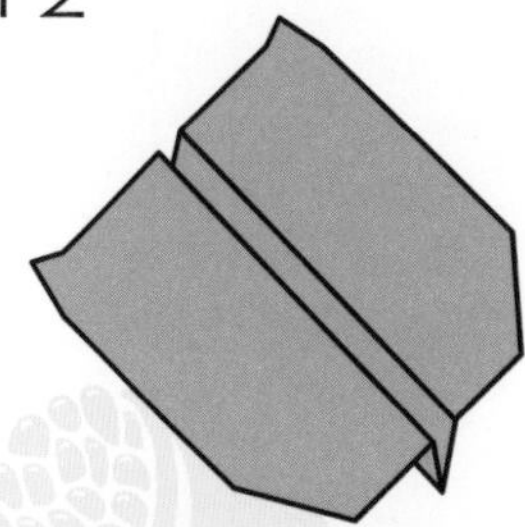

Curve the back corners upwards. This will give the glider more lift, and allow you to do loop the loop tricks.

Jumping Frog

MODEL: Traditional, Japan
DIAGRAM: Matthew Gardiner

The jumping frog is a paper racing game waiting to happen. All you need are a few friends, some jumping frogs and the game is on! High performance frogs can be made from card. Business cards make small dynamic frogs, but index cards are a more foldable size.

At the 2007 Australian Origami Convention, special guest Michael LaFosse used a secret racing frog design to win the Melbourne Paper Cup.

1

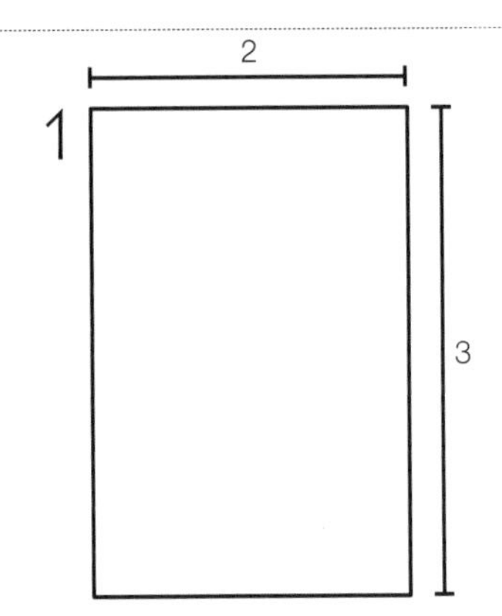

Choose a rectangle piece of paper with a ratio of 2:3. Index cards are a good size.

2

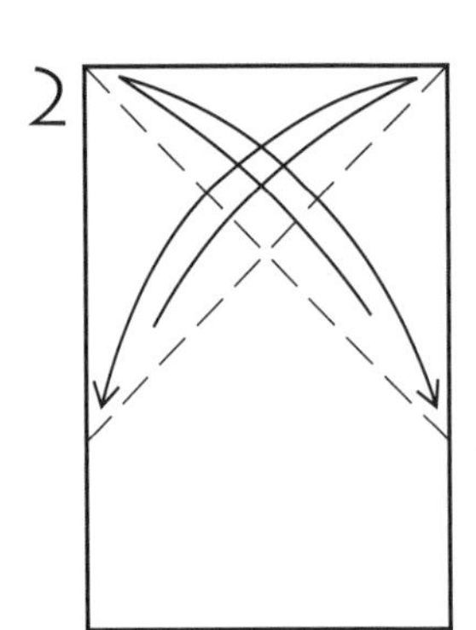

Begin white side up. Fold and unfold diagonally so that the top edge lines up with the side edge. Turn over.

3

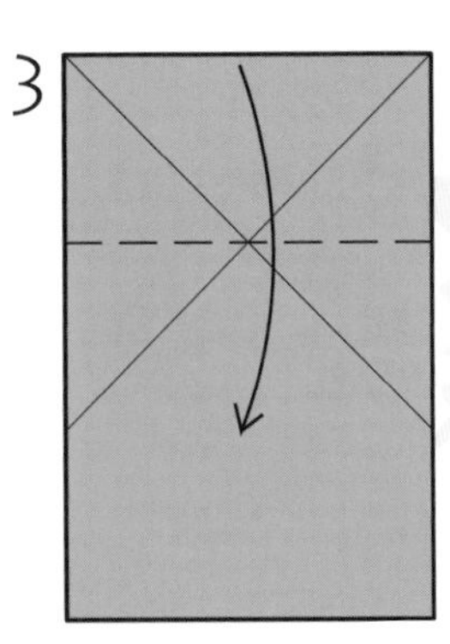

Fold and unfold through the crossing diagonals. Turn over.

4

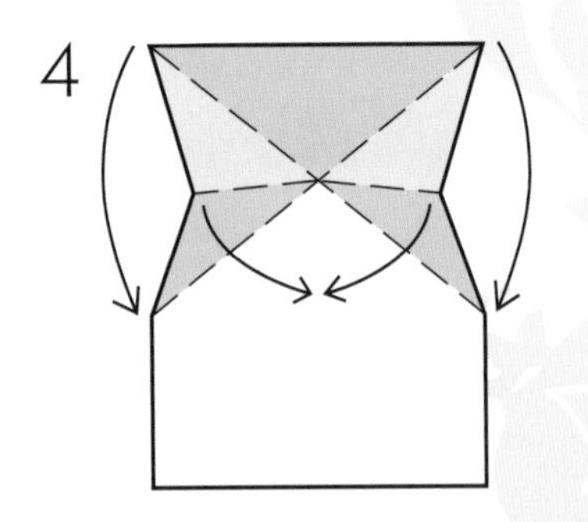

Fold top corners down.
Fold midpoints inwards.

5

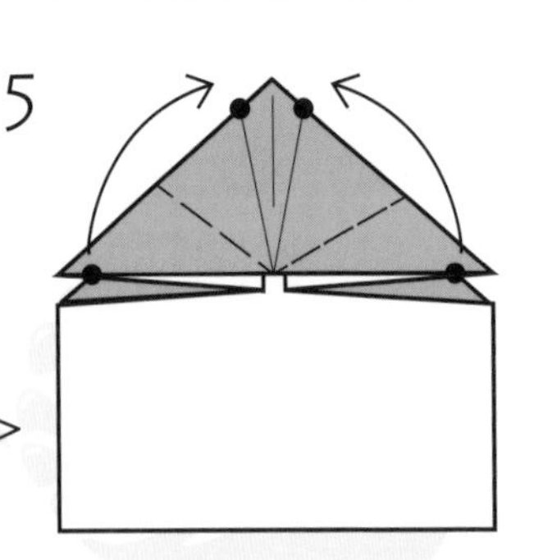

The top triangular shape is called a water bomb base. Fold up the top two corners just short of the centre line, so they point out a little.

6

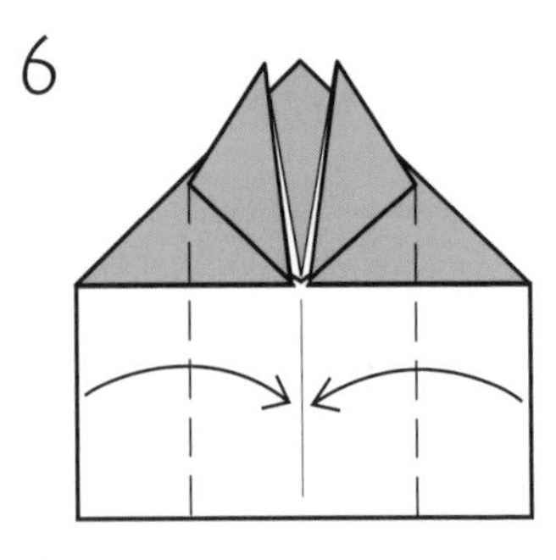

Cupboard fold.

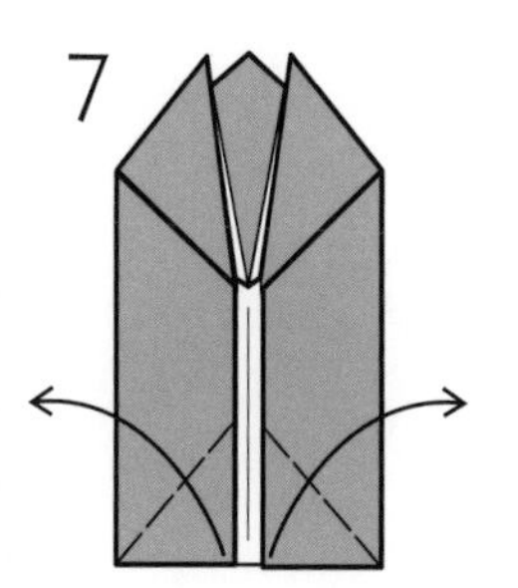

Fold out rear legs.

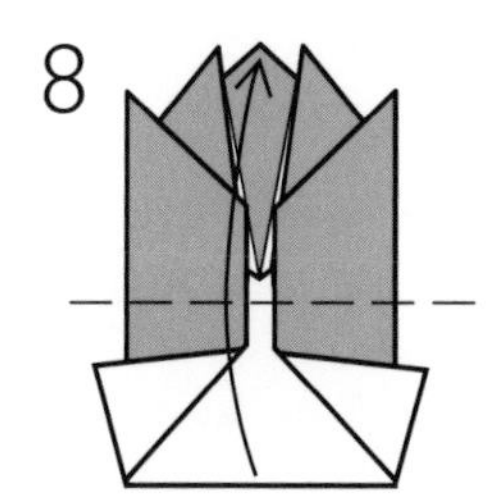

Fold in half, bringing the bottom to the top.

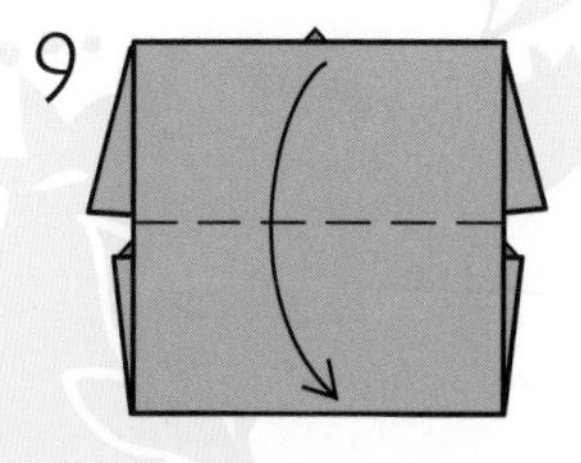

Fold the top layer in half, bringing the top to the bottom.

Turn the model over.
Completed jumping frog.

To make the frog jump gently press and release at the point marked.

Walking Crab

MODEL: Shoko Aoyagi
DIAGRAM: Shoko Aoyagi

The walking crab is a fun design that walks sideways when you tap it. Shoko is well known for her fun origami style – she likes to use stick-on eyes to add character to her origami creations. You cut out circles of white and black paper and glue them together, or use pre-cut circles that are available at office suppliers.

The walking crab is a contemporary Japanese design.

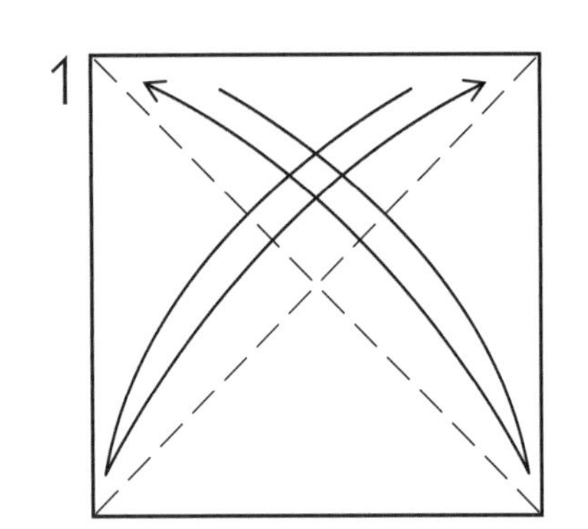

Fold and unfold diagonals. Turn over.

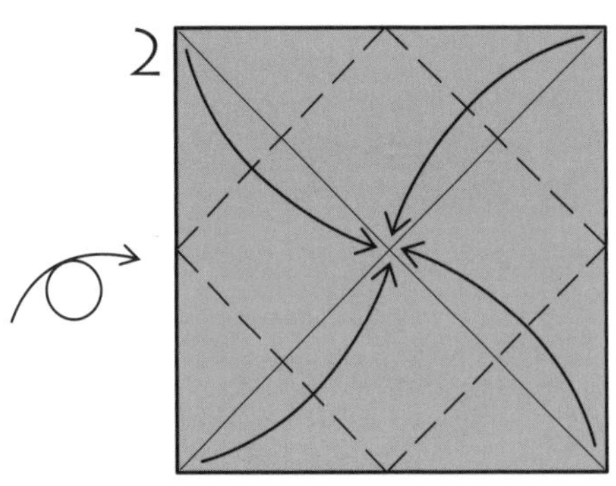

Blintz fold.

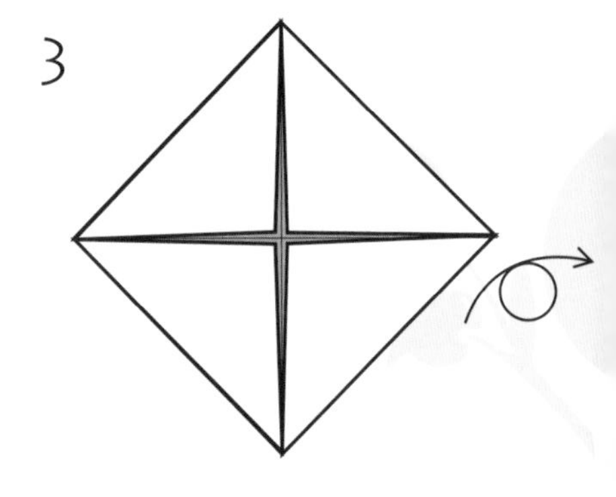

Completed step 2. Turn over.

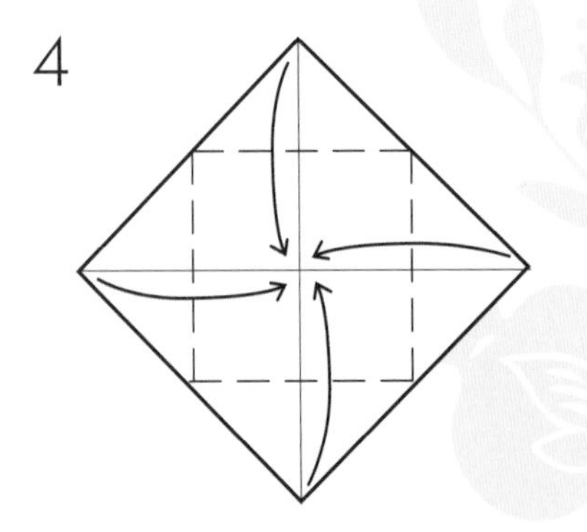

Blintz fold again.

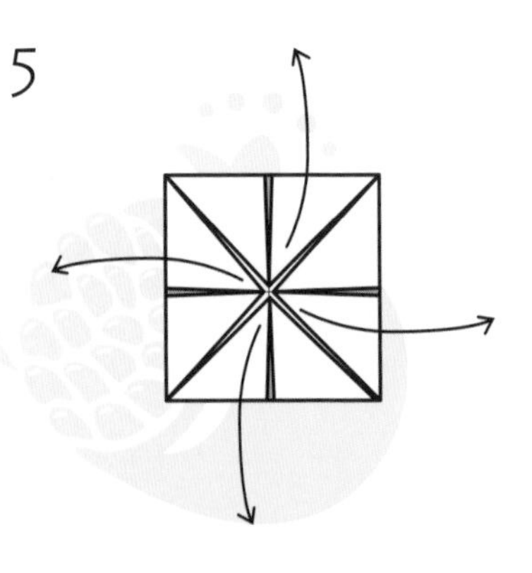

Completely unfold the paper.

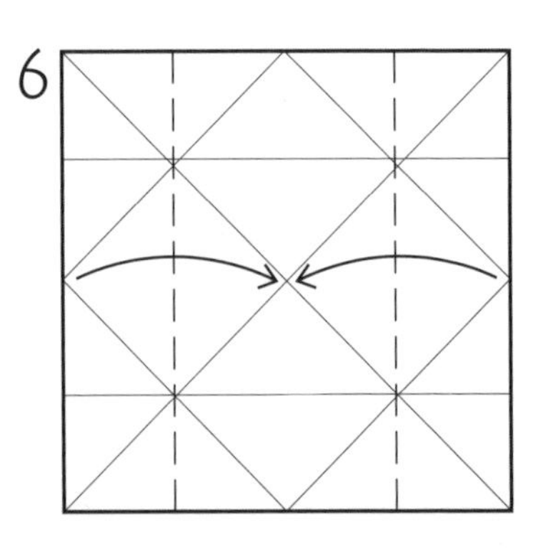

Then fold sides to centre.

7

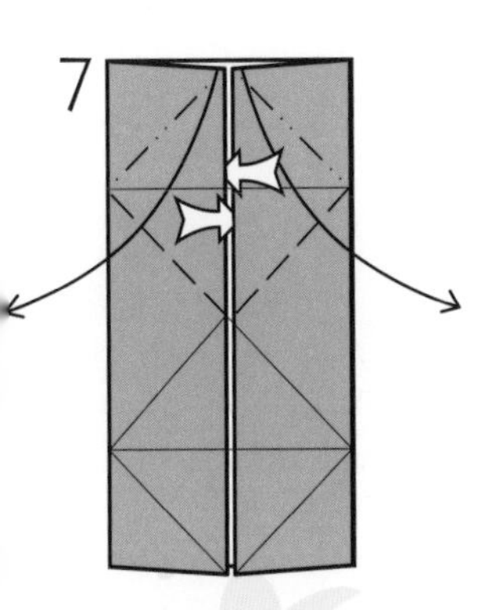

Bring both corners forwards and squash fold.

8

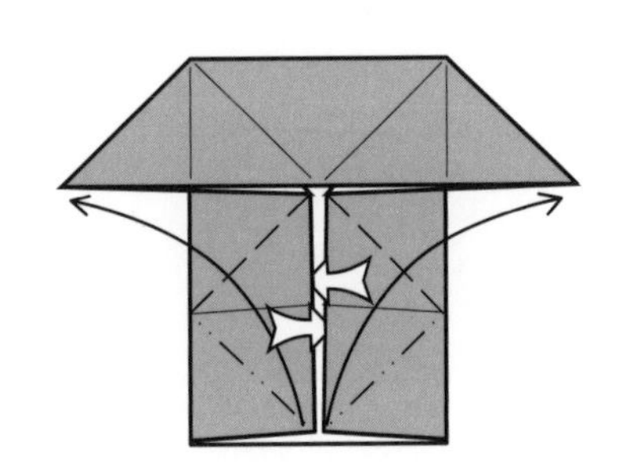

Repeat step 7 on other end.

9

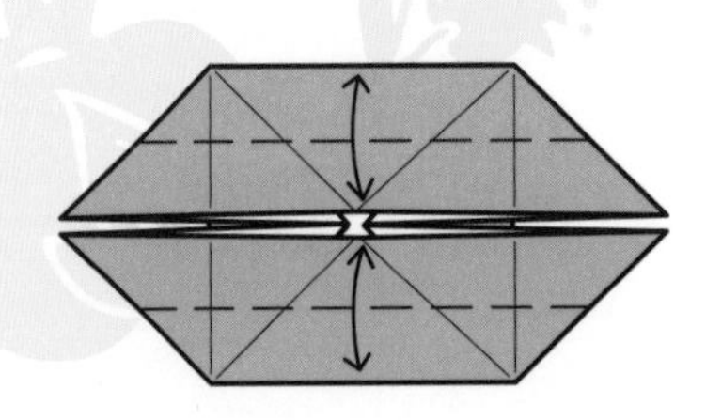

Fold and unfold top and bottom edge to the centre.

10

Open up pockets.

11

This shows the pockets open. Lift up inside corners, and fold the edges outwards.

12

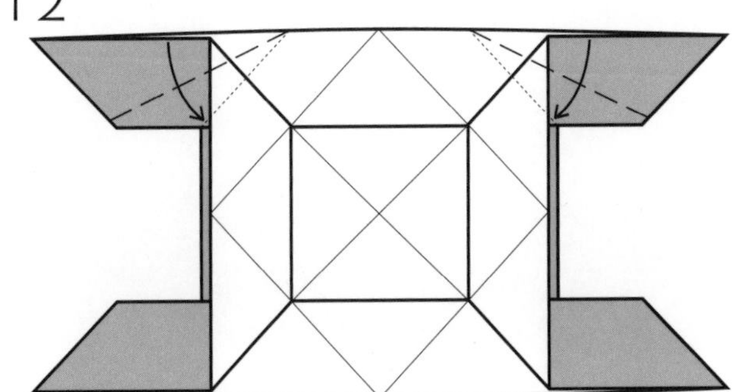

Fold edge to corner.

13

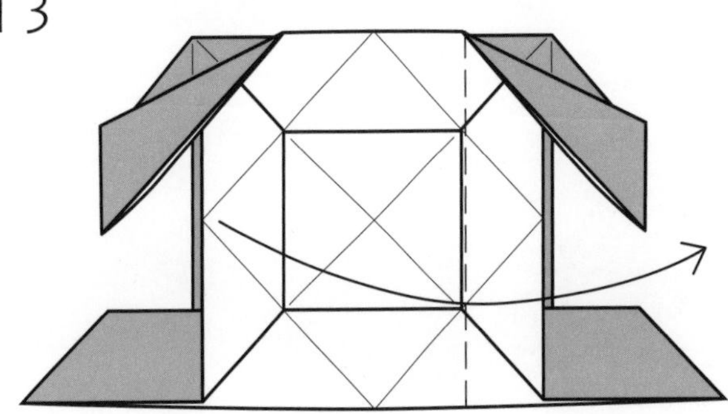

Fold over.

14

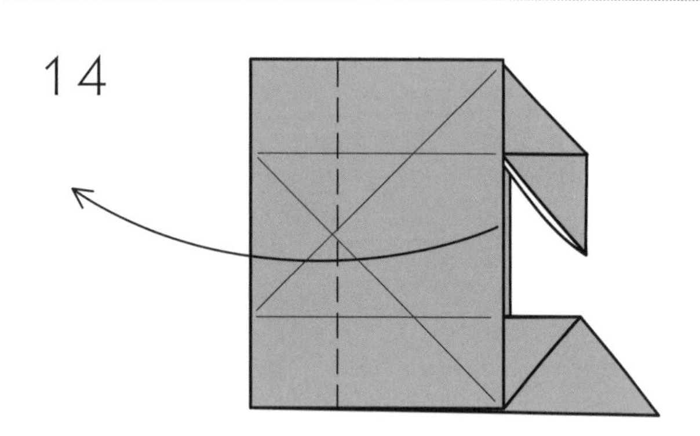

Fold over.

15

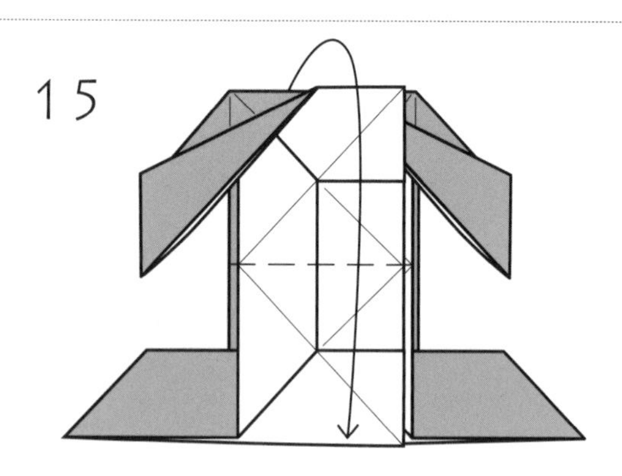

Fold in half through all layers.

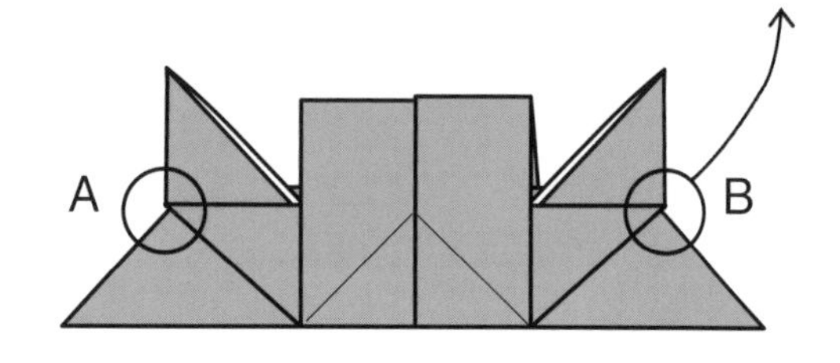

Hold 'A' with one hand. Pull 'B' upwards.

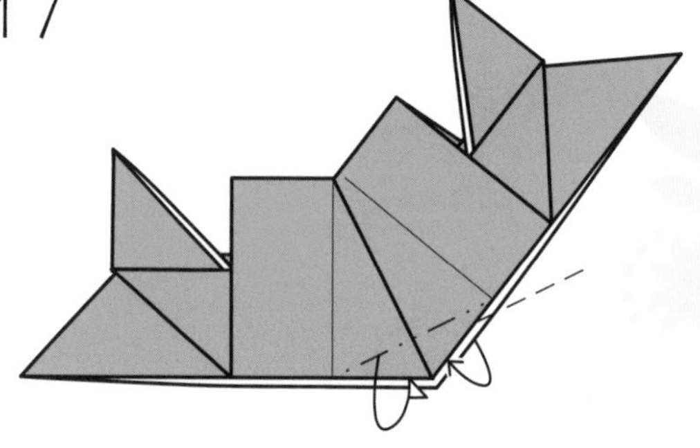

Fold inside the base of the front flap as shown. Repeat on the other side.

18

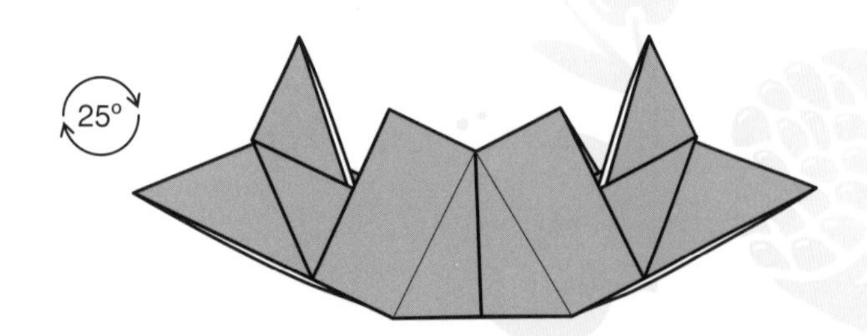

Completed walking crab.

19

When you tap the C, the crab will walk sideways. Attach the round stickers for eyes and draw eyeballs.

BANGER

MODEL: TRADITIONAL, JAPAN
DIAGRAM: MATTHEW GARDINER

This single layer banger could be the alternative to shrill party whistles. It is best made from a sheet of newspaper.

1

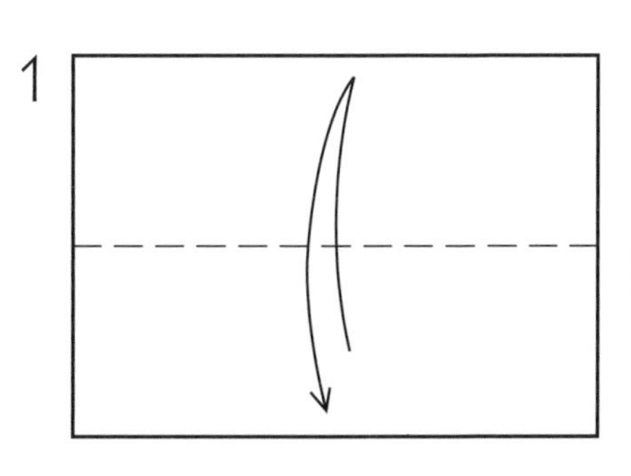

Start with a large thin rectangle. Newspaper works well. Book fold and unfold.

2

Fold corners over.

3

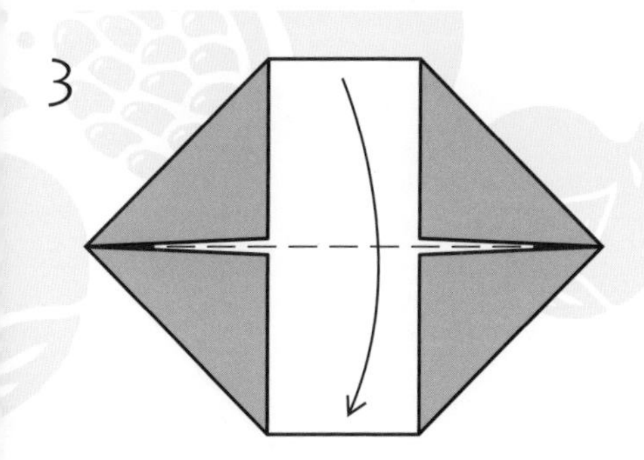

Fold in half.

4

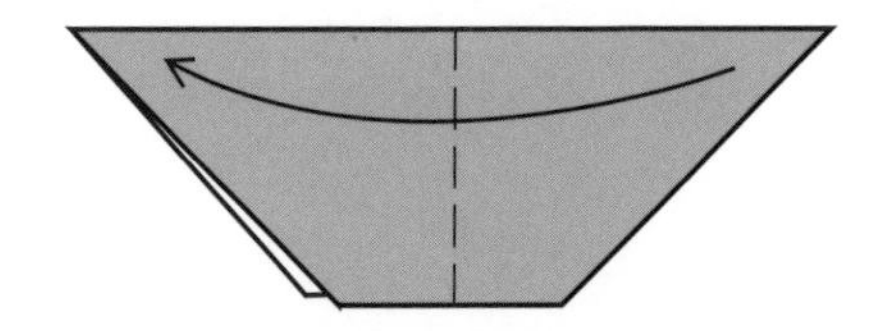

Fold in half again.

5

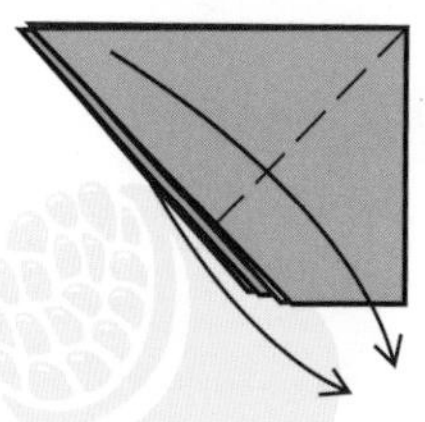

Valley fold front and back points.

6

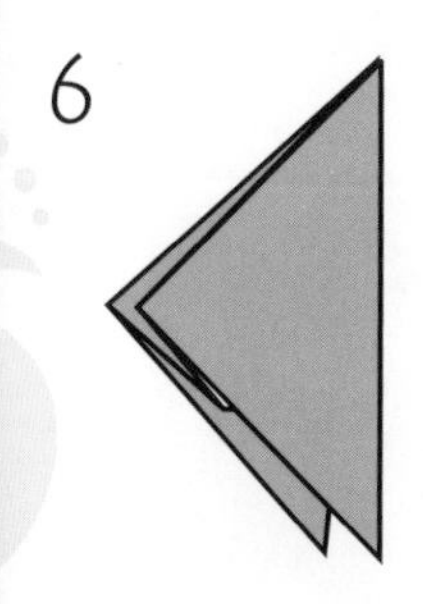

Completed banger.

7

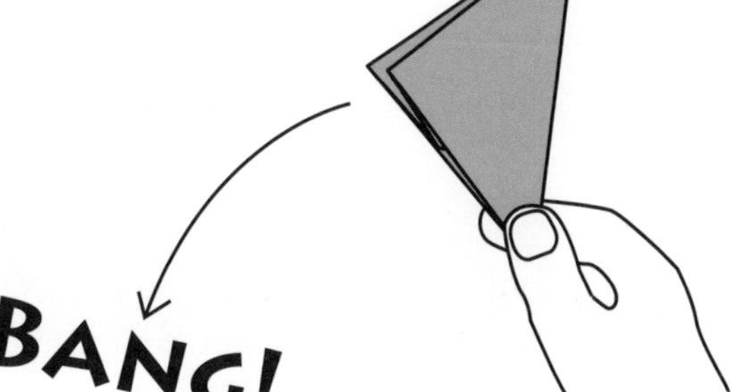

Hold at the points to use.To make a bang, thrust downwards.

FORTUNE TELLER

MODEL: TRADITIONAL, JAPAN
DIAGRAM: MATTHEW GARDINER

The fortune teller, also known as the "cootie catcher" or "salt cellar", is perhaps the best known origami game in the west. The game, played by children, uses colours and numbers to magically reveal the player's fortune.

The fortune teller is best made from a 30cm (12in) square of white paper.

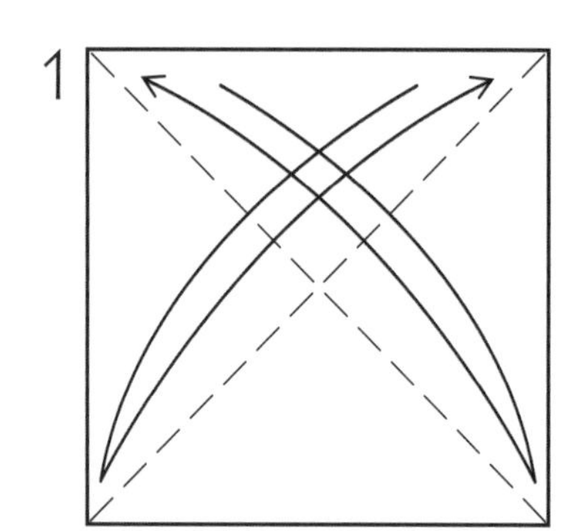

Fold and unfold diagonally.

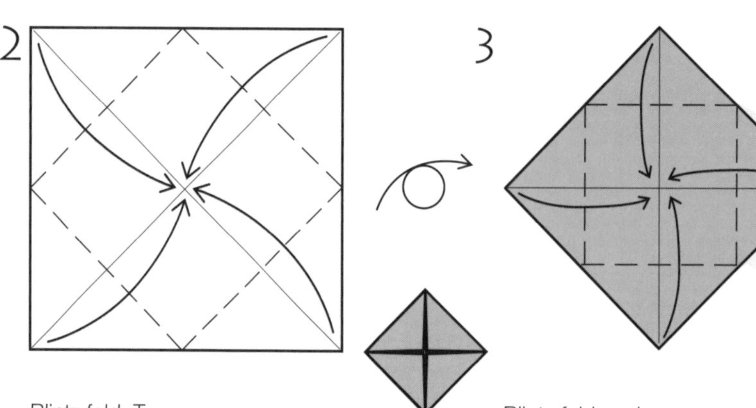

Blintz fold. Turn over.

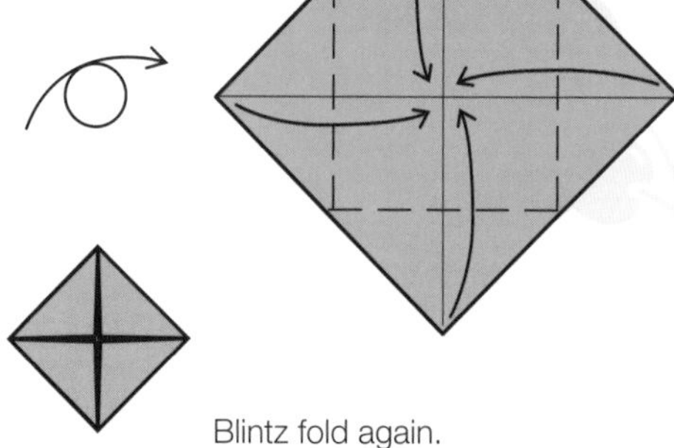

Blintz fold again.

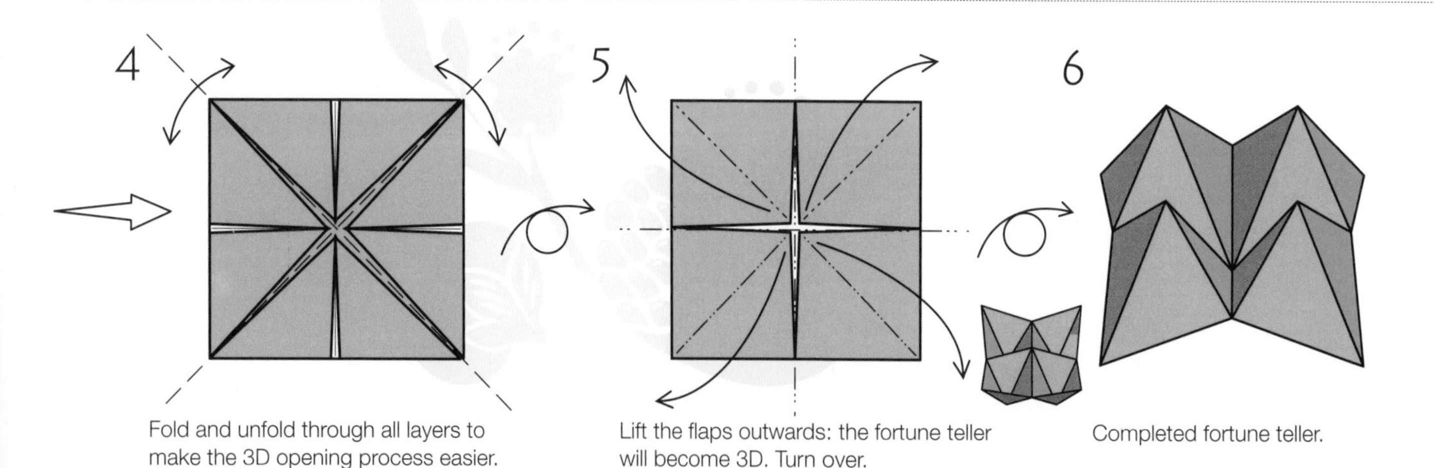

Fold and unfold through all layers to make the 3D opening process easier. Turn over.

Lift the flaps outwards: the fortune teller will become 3D. Turn over.

Completed fortune teller.

HOW TO PLAY:

DRAW

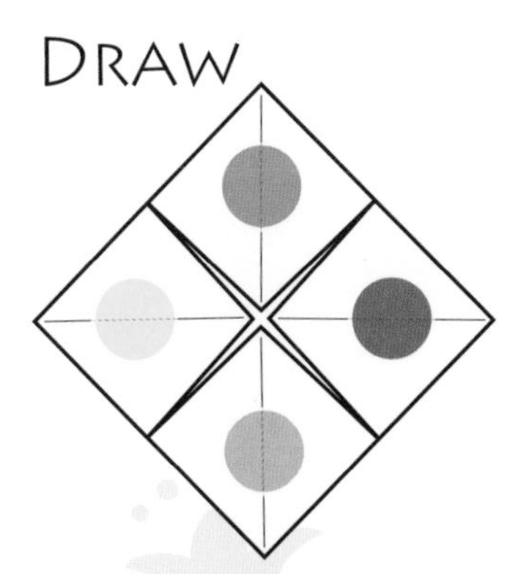

Flatten the model to step 5. Decorate your fortune teller with four colours.

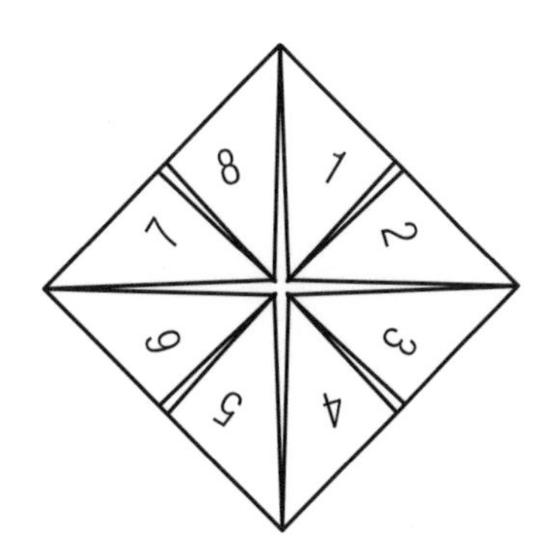

Turn over, and write the numbers from 1 to 8 on each of the triangles.

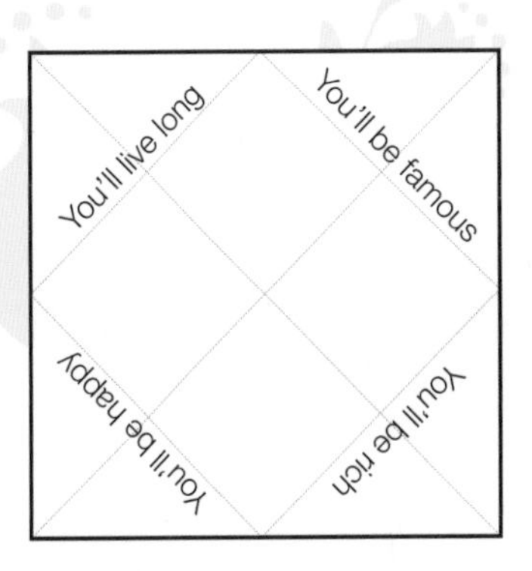

Open up all the points and write in your fortunes. Write one for each number.

MOVE

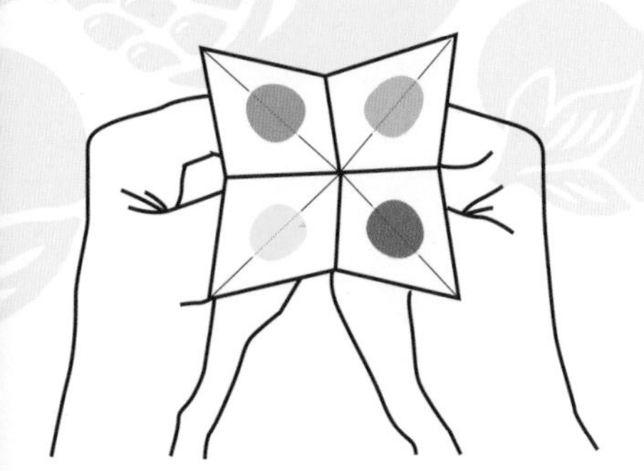

The "start" position. Thumbs and forefingers of both hands are together.

A

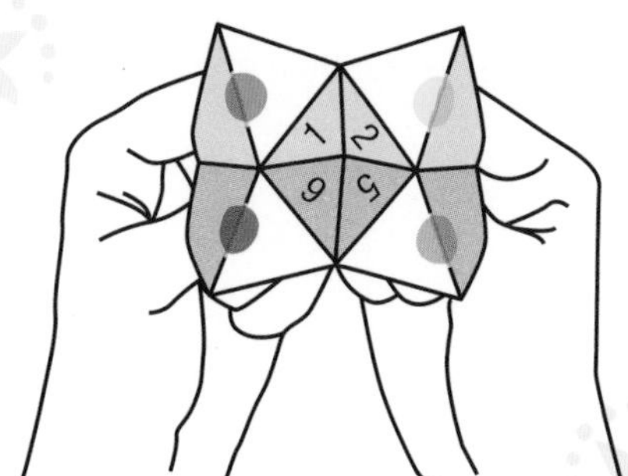

One count/letter. Thumbs and forefingers of each hand are together.

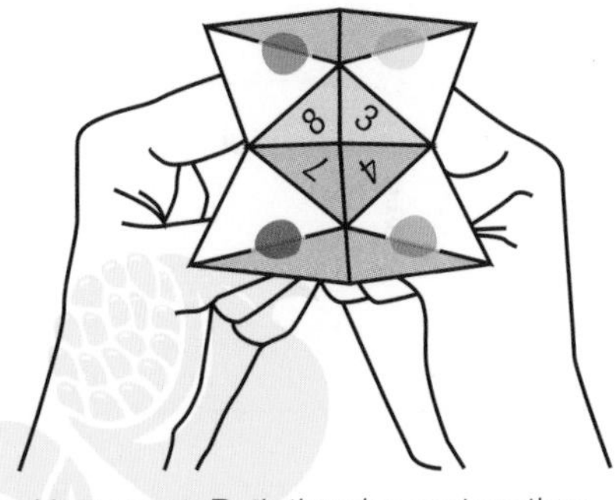

Next count. Both thumbs are together, and both forefingers are together.

PLAY

Begin in the "start" position.

Ask your friend to pick a colour.

Spell out the colour, letter by letter, and as you say each letter, alternate between the positions shown in B and C with the fortune teller, as shown above.

Ask your friend how many boyfriends/girlfriends they have, and count the number they say.

Ask your friend to pick a number. Unfold the flap that has the number, and read their fortune.

You can make up lots of fun fortunes.

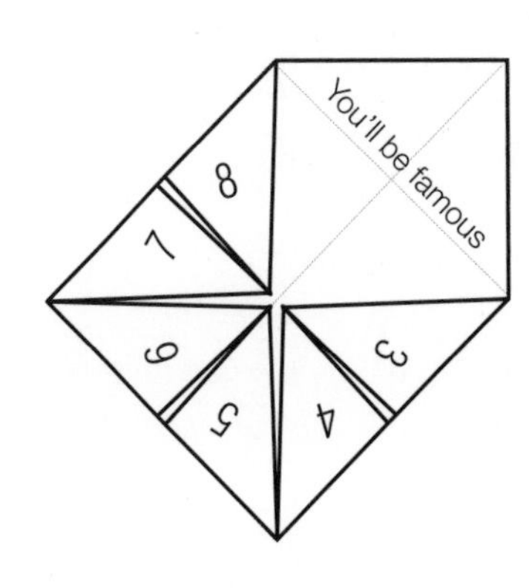

Fox

MODEL: TRADITIONAL, JAPAN
DIAGRAM: MATTHEW GARDINER

The fox is a cunning creature. In Japanese mythology, foxes possess magical abilities and wisdom, and some have the ability to change into human form. This fox is a fun little hand puppet that gives the wearer special fox abilities. Use this puppet with care, and respect the animals of the world.

The Japanese say that a sunshower (rain falling from a clear sky) is the sign of a fox wedding.

1

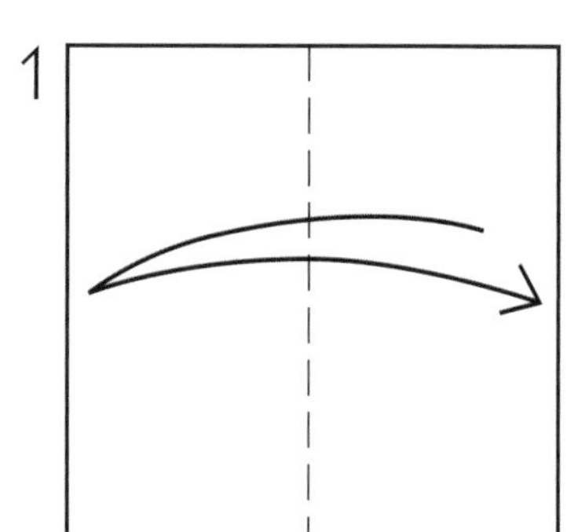

Book fold and unfold.

2

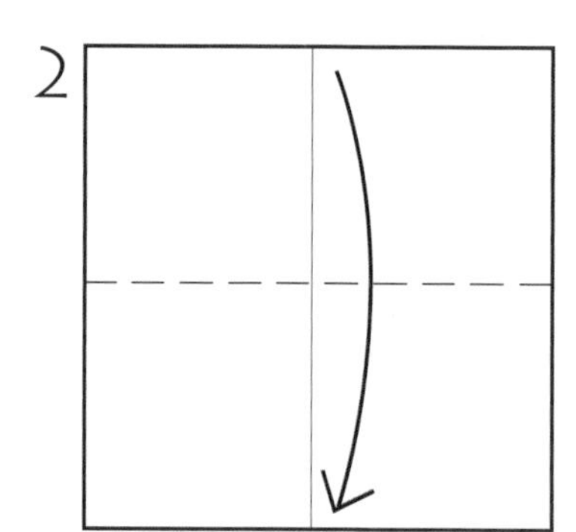

Book fold.

3

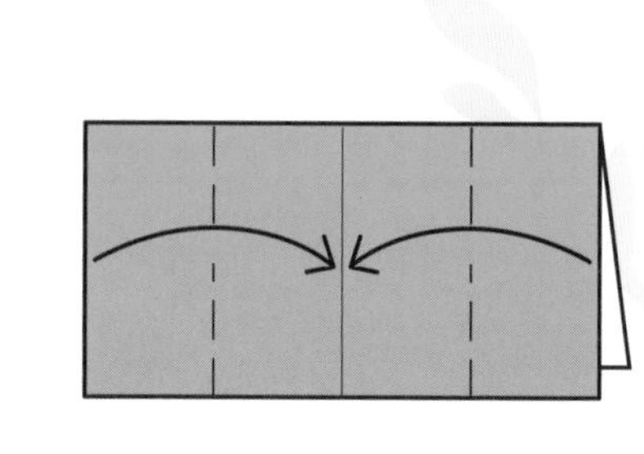

Cupboard fold.

4

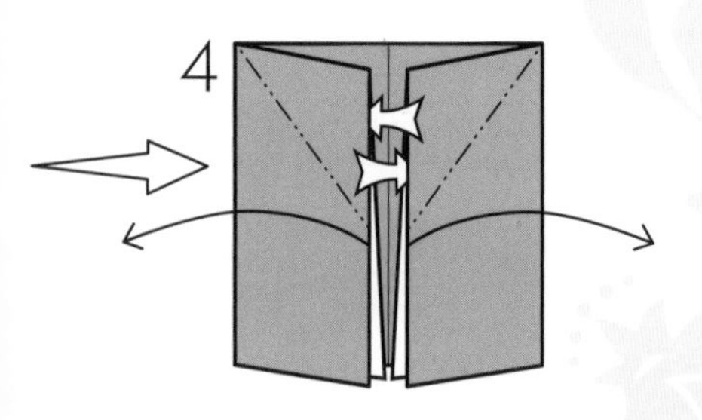

Open up the pocket and squash fold.

5

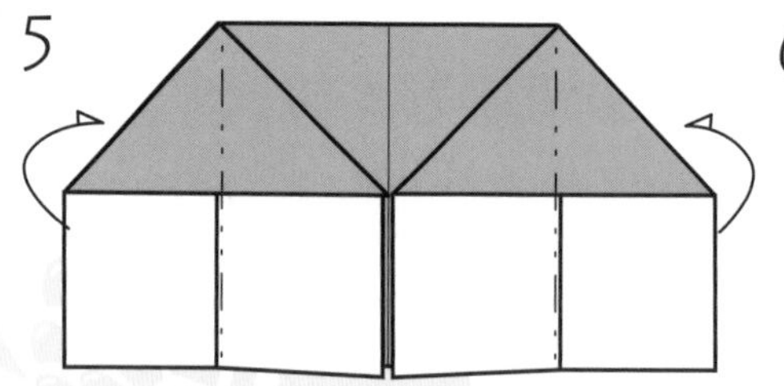

Mountain fold sides.

6

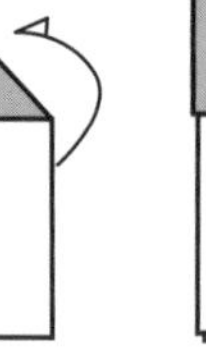

Fold up corner of top layer.

7

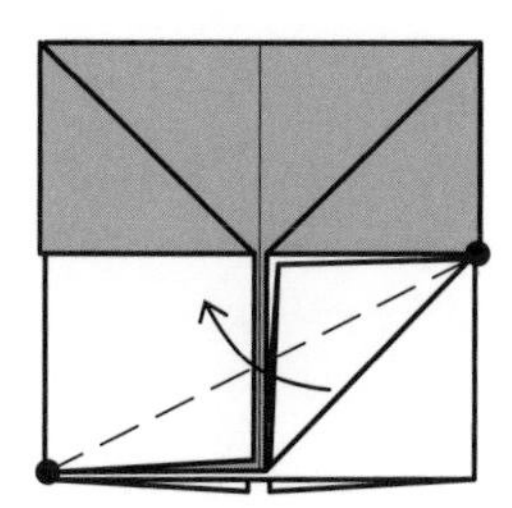

Fold up.

8

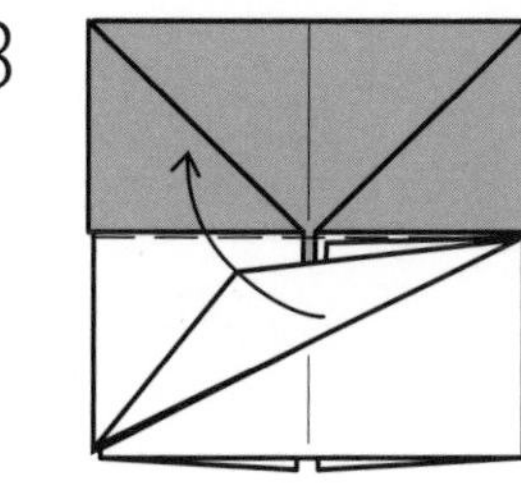

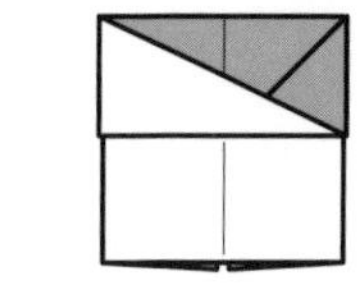

Fold up again.
Turn over.

9

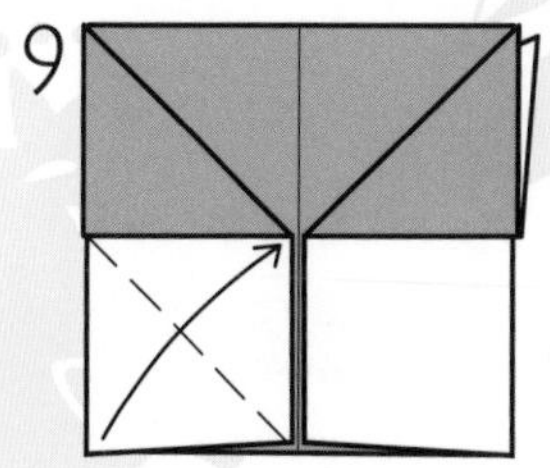

Fold up corner.

10

Fold up.

11

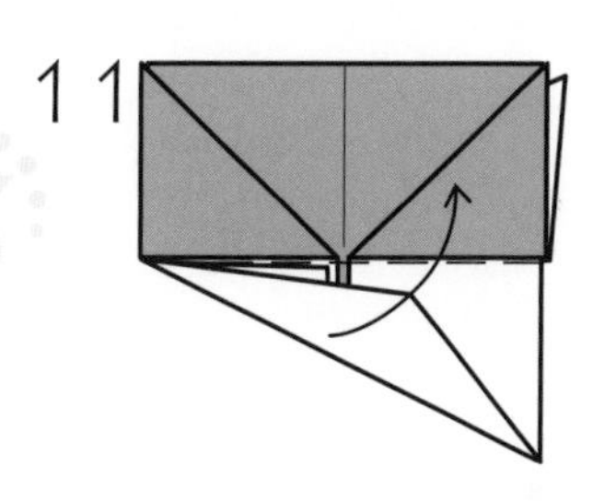

Fold up again.

12

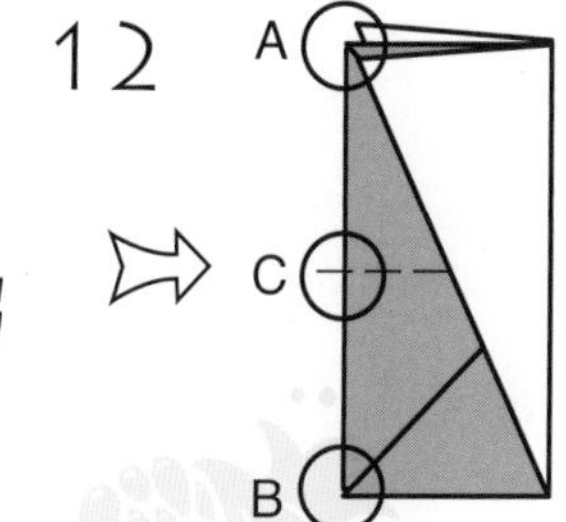

Push point C further in so point A and B touch.

13

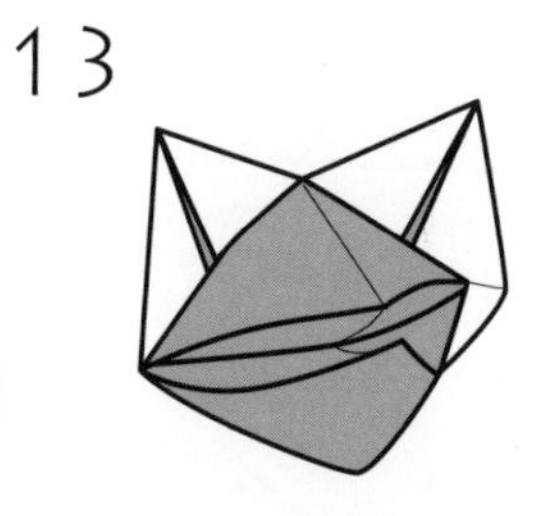

Completed fox.

14

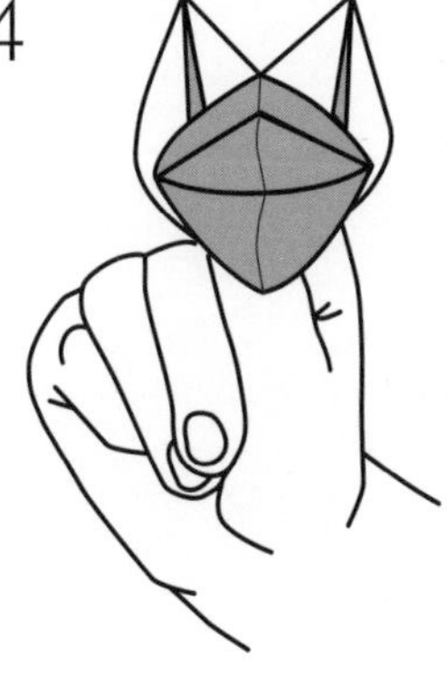

Insert your hand in the back and use as a puppet.

PUPPETS

MODEL: TRADITIONAL, JAPAN
DIAGRAM: MATTHEW GARDINER

This model can make two types of animal finger puppets – a cat and a pig. Fold them from a 15cm (6in) square of paper, and carefully draw the faces on your puppets. Make a group of puppets and invent your own characters for these lovable creatures.

The art of puppetry is a rich tradition of story-telling, popular with both young and old.

1

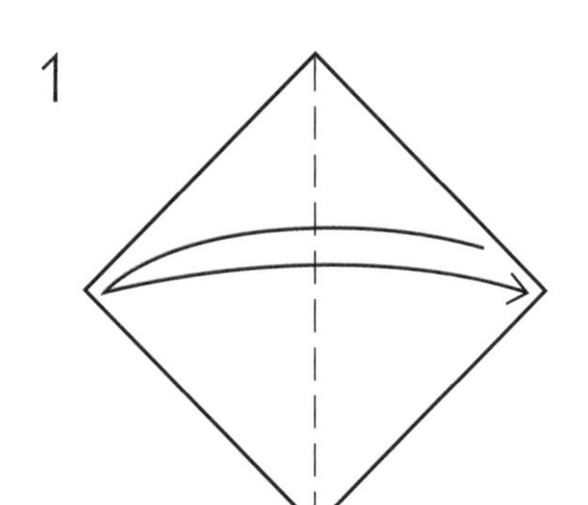

Fold and unfold diagonal.

2

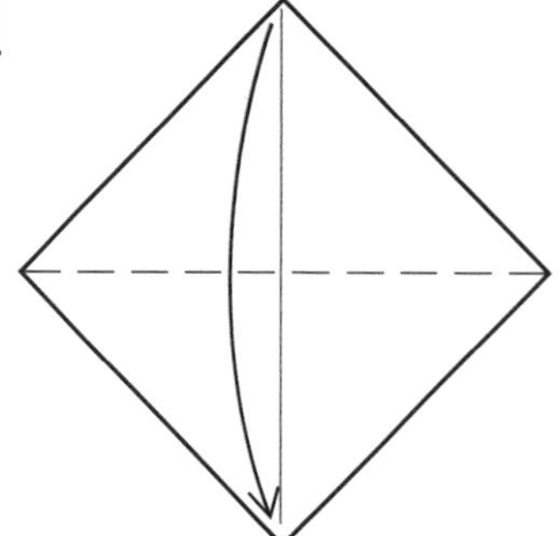

Fold in half diagonally.

3

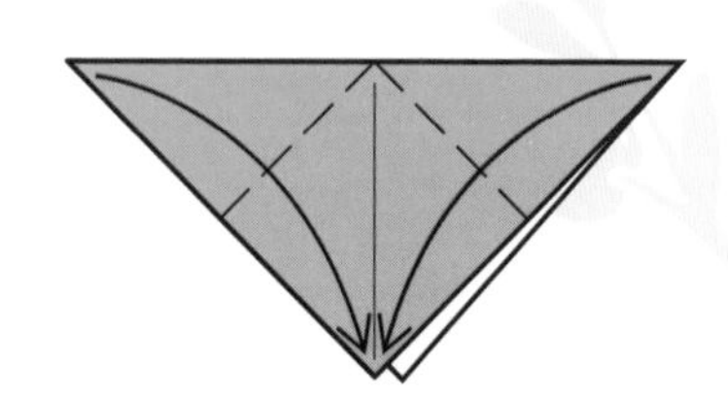

Fold side corners down to meet bottom corner.

4

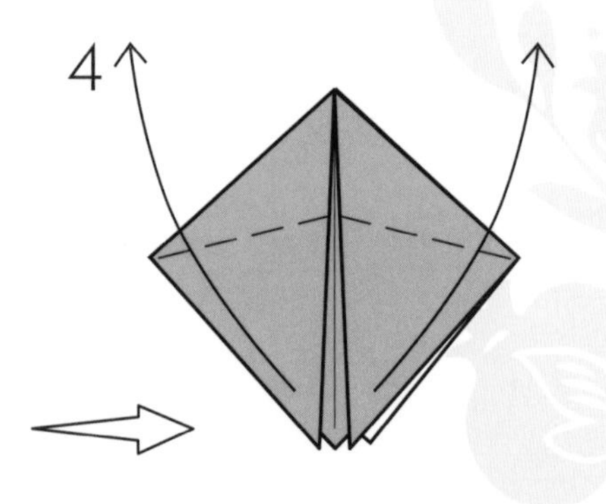

Fold two flaps up.

5

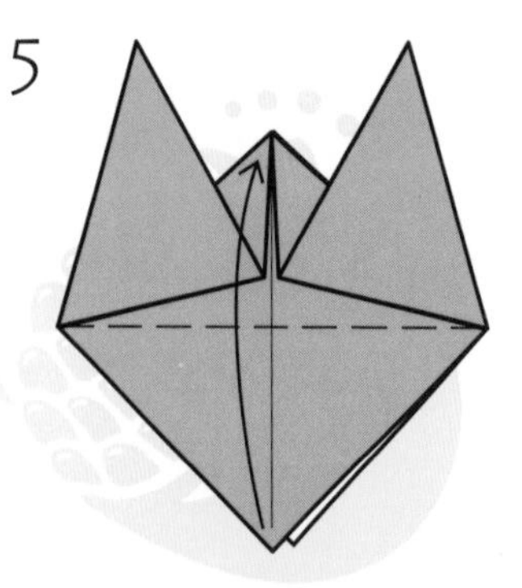

Fold top flap up.

6

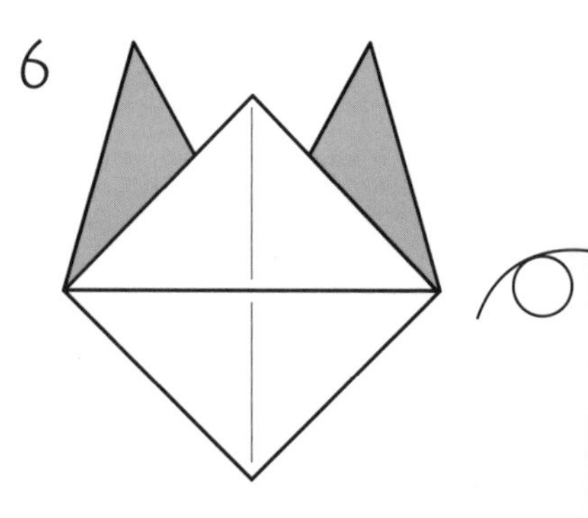

Fold top flap up. Turn over.

7

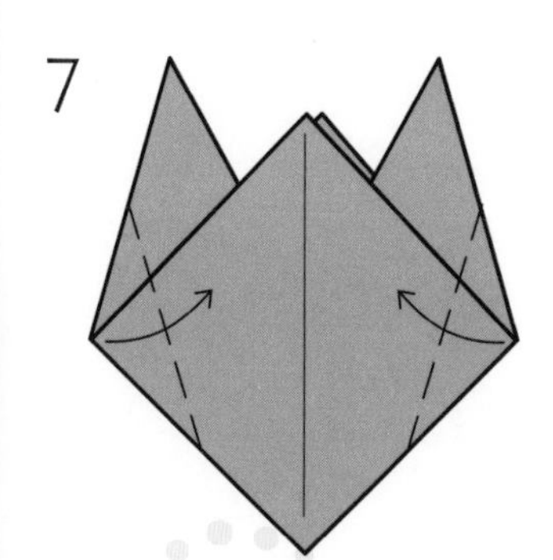

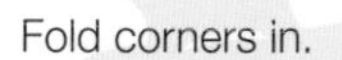

Fold corners in.

8

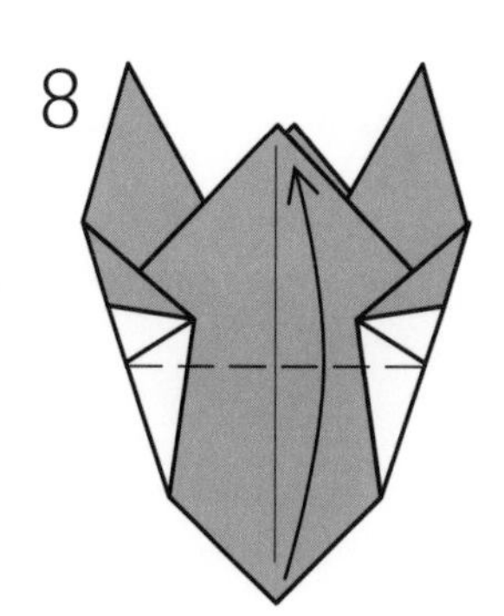

Fold up.

9

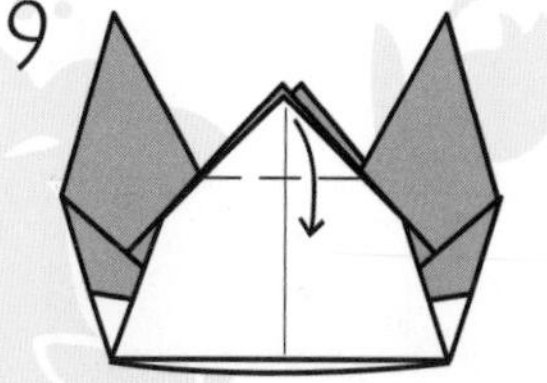

Fold all top layers down.
Turn over.

10

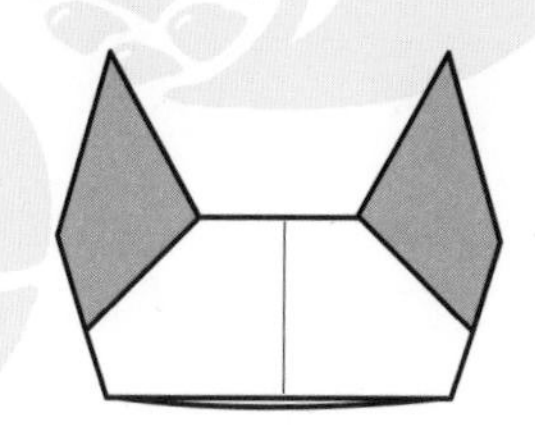

Completed cat face.

11

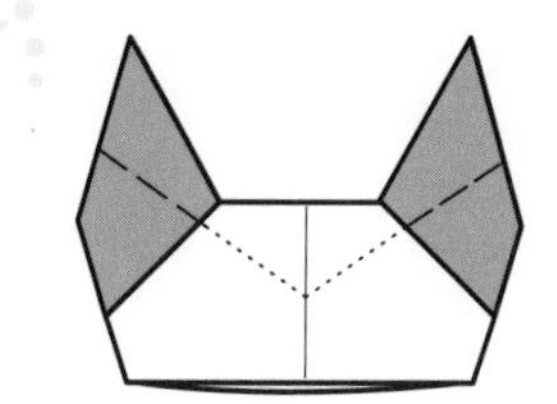

To make a pig face, fold ears over.

12

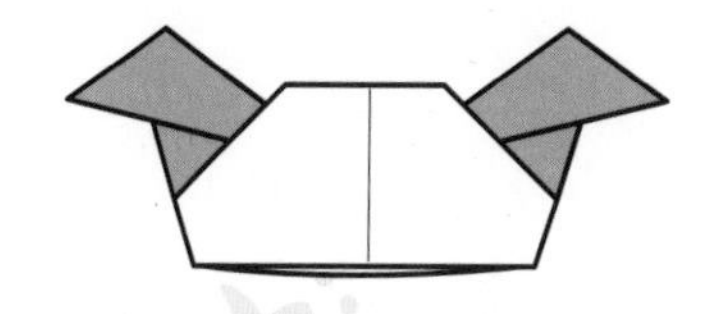

Completed pig face.

13

Draw a cat face and use as a finger puppet.

14

Draw a pig face and use as a finger puppet.

TALKER

MODEL: TRADITIONAL, JAPAN
DIAGRAM: MATTHEW GARDINER

The origami talker looks like a little mouth. There is a whole range of talking origami models, and this is perhaps one of the simplest and easist to make.

The talker looks best when folded from a duo-toned paper.

1

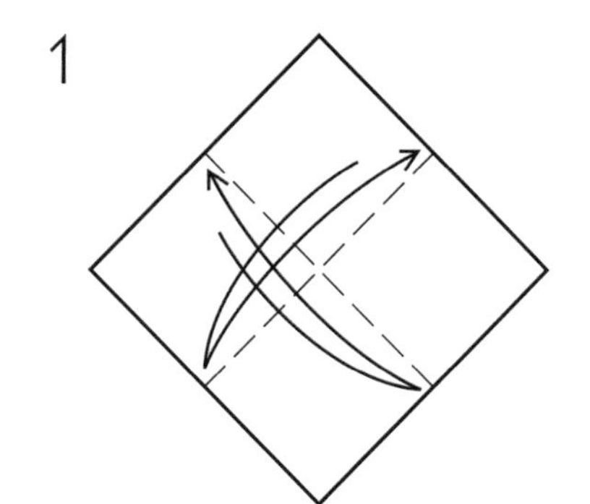

Book fold and unfold.

2

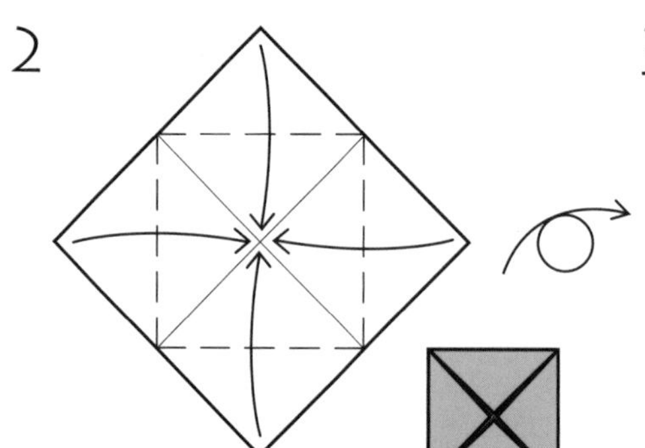

Blintz fold. Turn over.

3

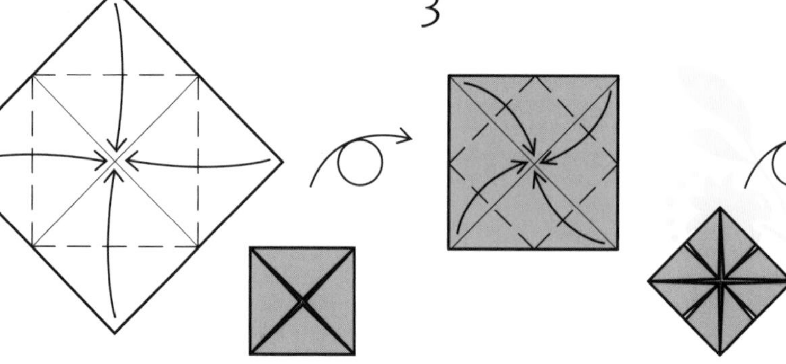

Blintz fold again. Turn over.

4

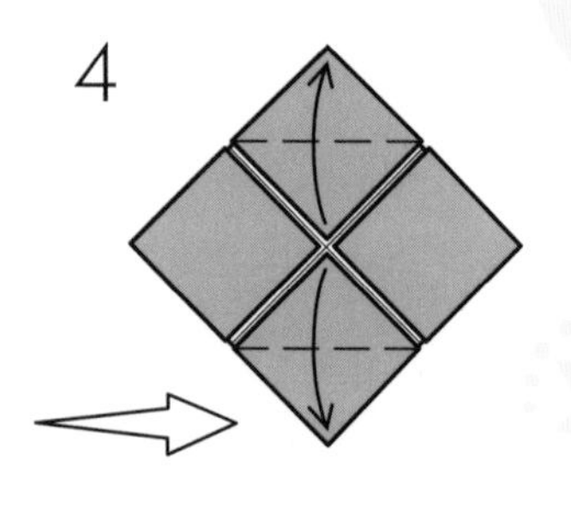

Fold top layer only.

5

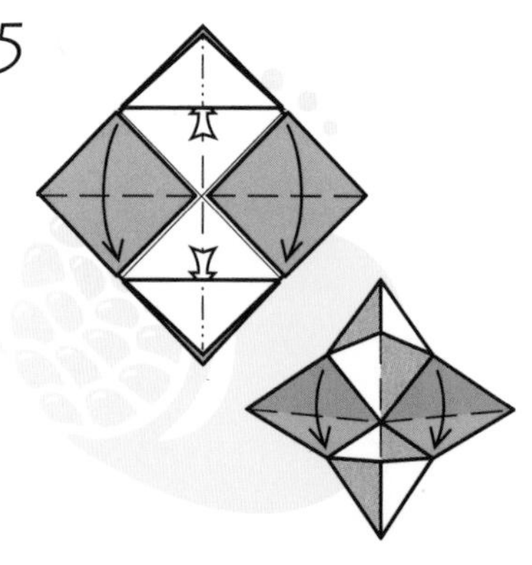

Poke your finger into the white pockets and lift up, then fold the model in half.

6

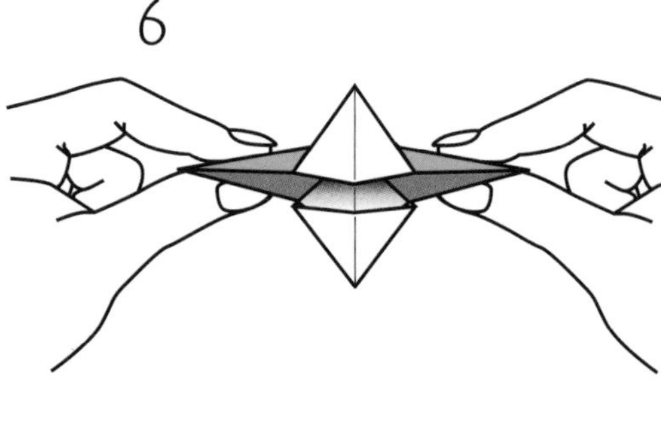

Completed talker. Hold as shown and push and pull the mouth together to make the talker talk.

Masu Box

model: Traditional, Japan
diagram: Matthew Gardiner

The masu box is a very practical origami model. Traditionally it was used as a measure for rice, as certain sheet sizes produced a set volume of rice. The masu, as you will see later in this section, has many new variations, and perhaps the best variation is that by making a slightly bigger or smaller box, you can make a lid or a base.

The masu box is handy for holding almost anything.

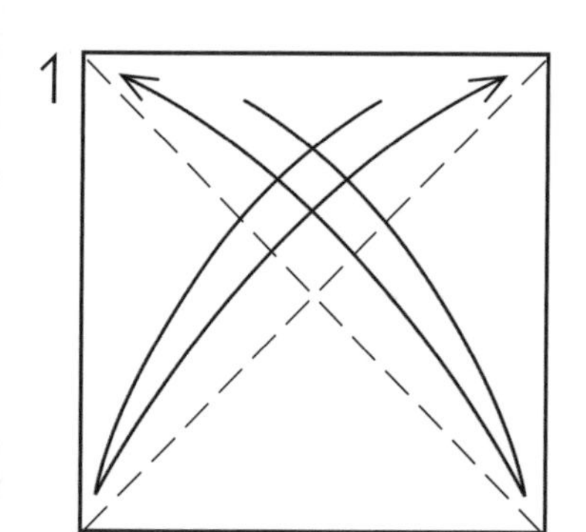

Begin white side up. Fold and unfold diagonals.

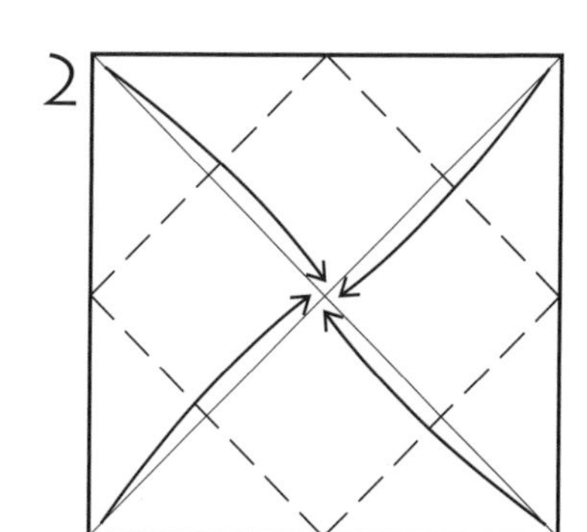

Blintz fold.

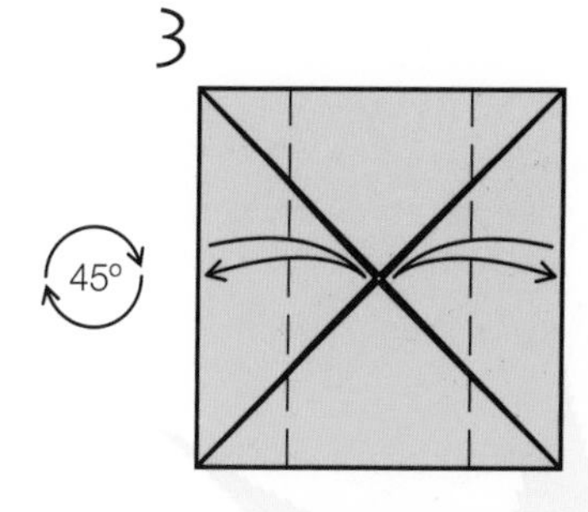

Cupboard fold and unfold.

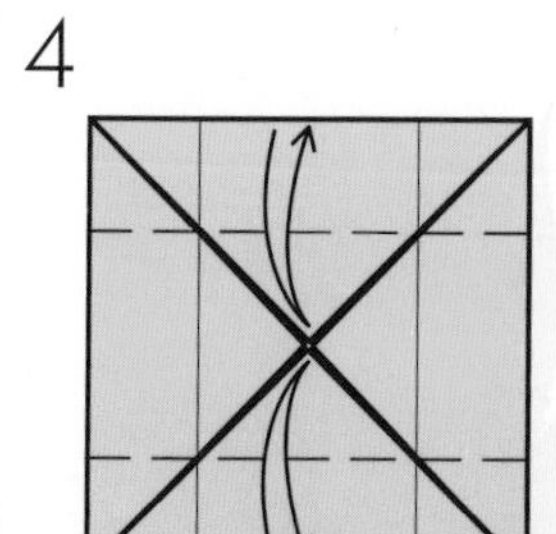

Cupboard fold and unfold the other edges.

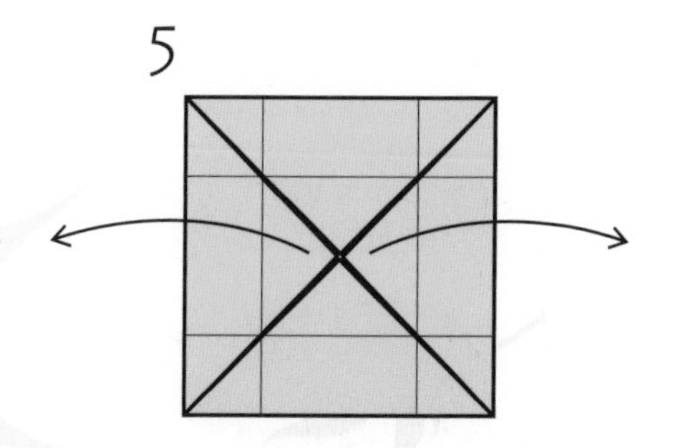

Unfold two side points.

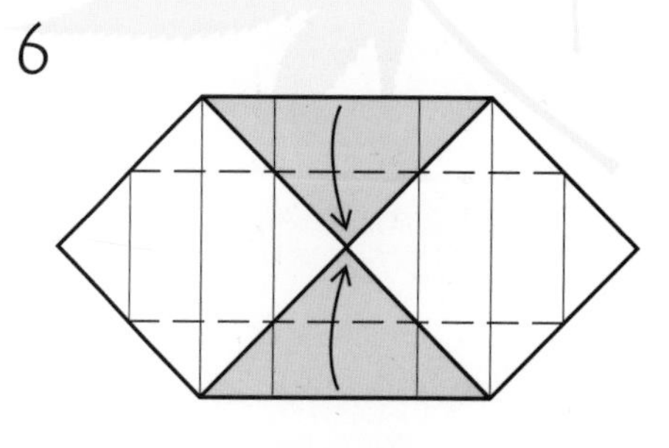

Fold on existing creases.

The Masu Box

MODEL: TRADITIONAL, JAPAN
DIAGRAM: MATTHEW GARDINER

7

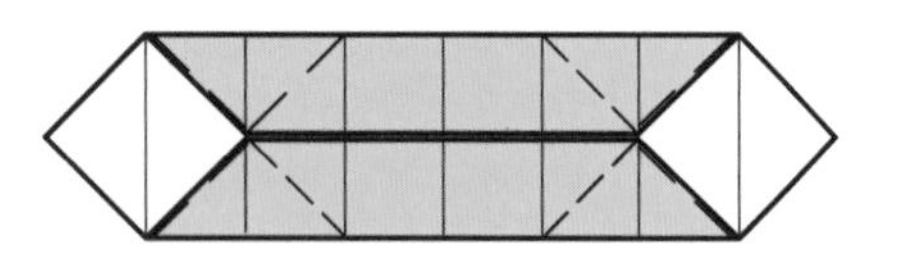

Fold and unfold on diagonals.

8

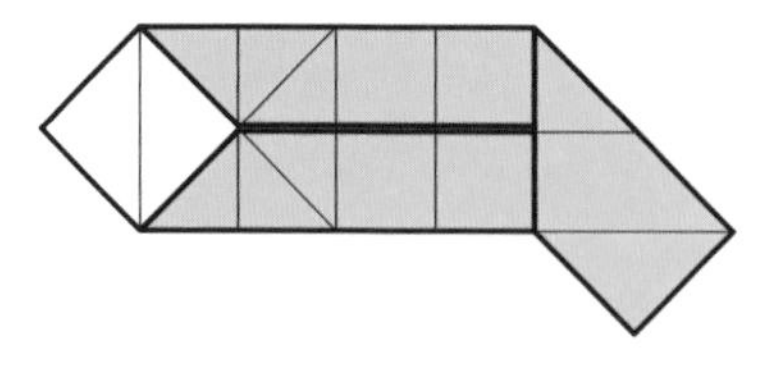

Step 7 in progress.

9

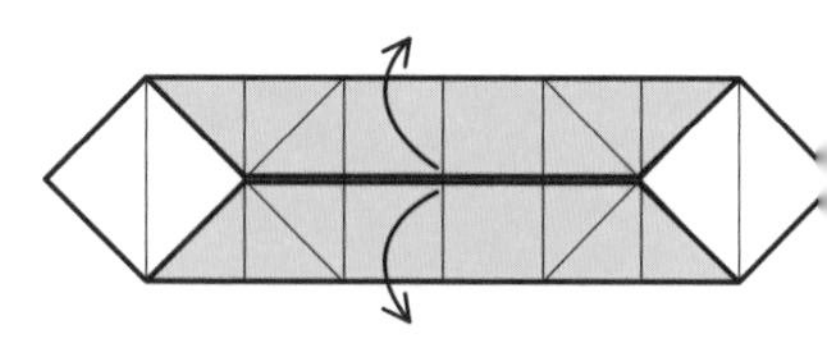

Lift sides to 90º.

10

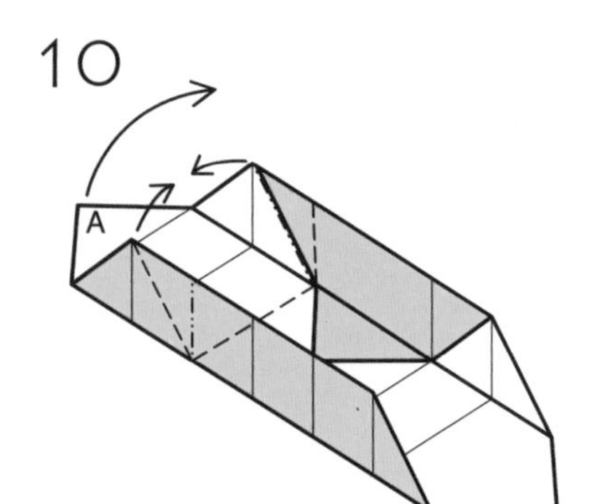

To make the side of the box, lift point A upwards – the existing sides will naturally collapse to points.

11

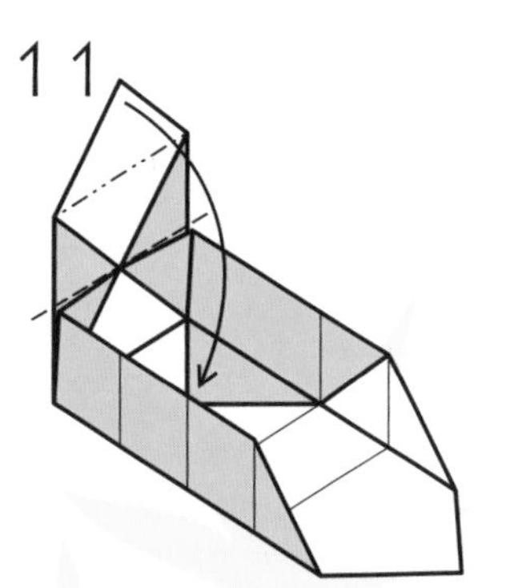

Fold the point down into the box, and press the point to the centre.

12

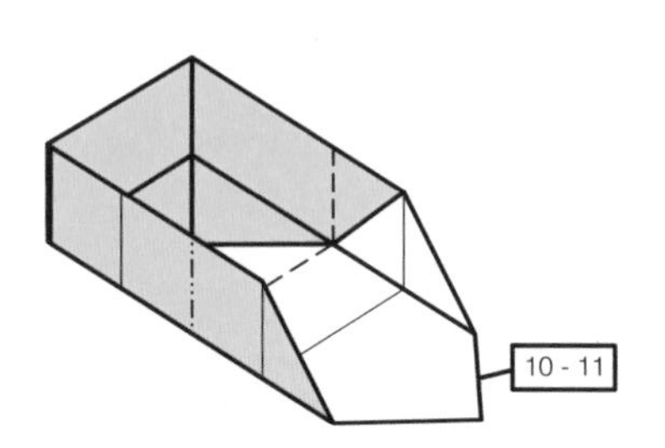

Repeat steps 10-11 on this side.

13

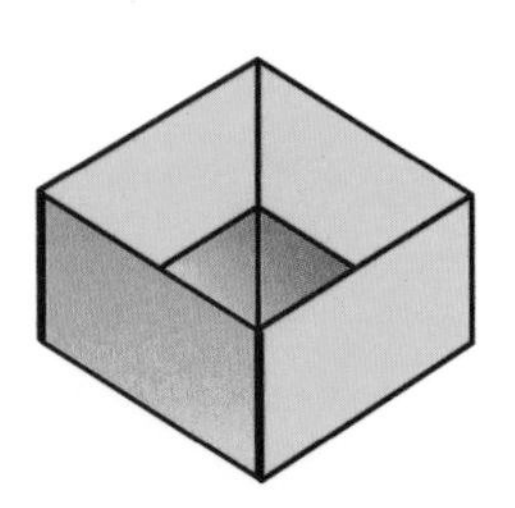

Completed masu box.

Star Box Masu

MODEL: DARREN SCOTT
DIAGRAM: DARREN SCOTT

This box lid fits the traditional masu box. There are lots of possible variations – see what you can create yourself. To get a perfect fit, make this lid first, and then trim the same size sheet by one eighth and make the masu box.

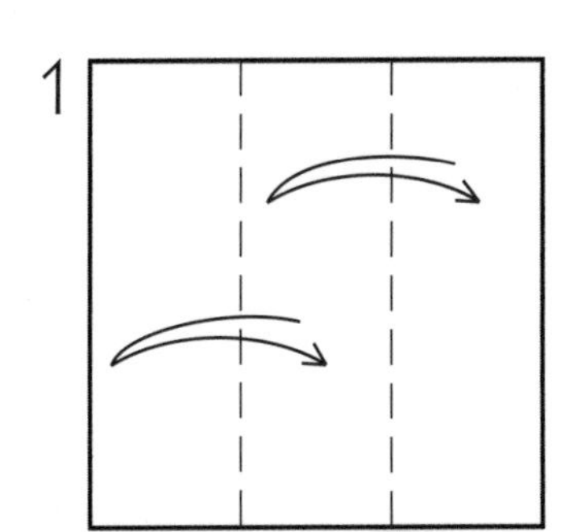

Start with the square white side up and divide into thirds and unfold.

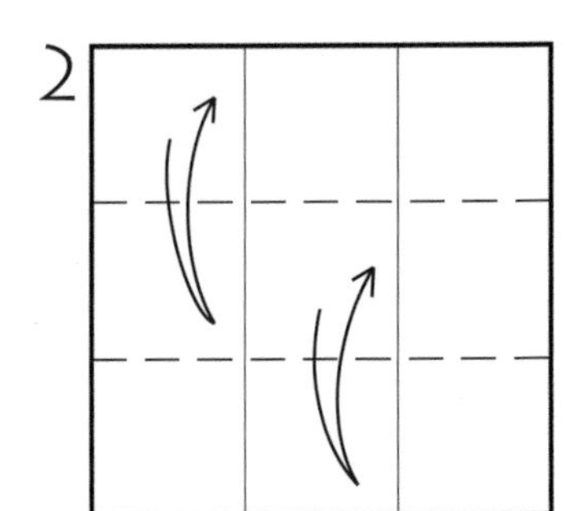

Divide into thirds in the horizontal direction and unfold.

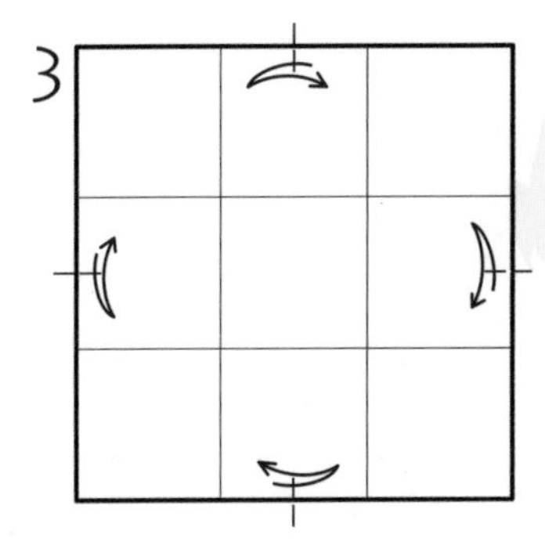

Make small pinches at the midpoint on all four sides.

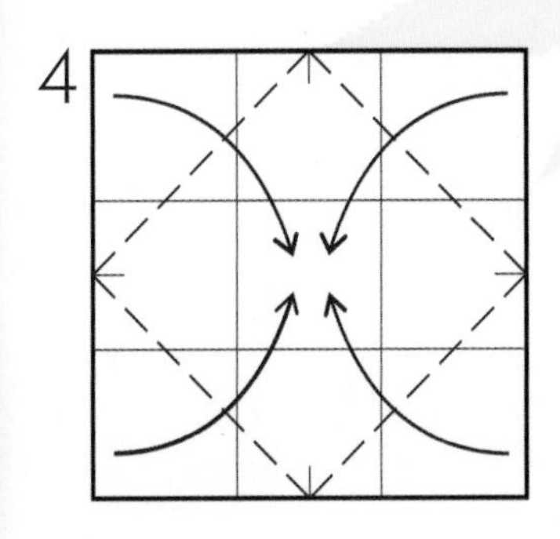

Using the creases in step 3 blintz fold.

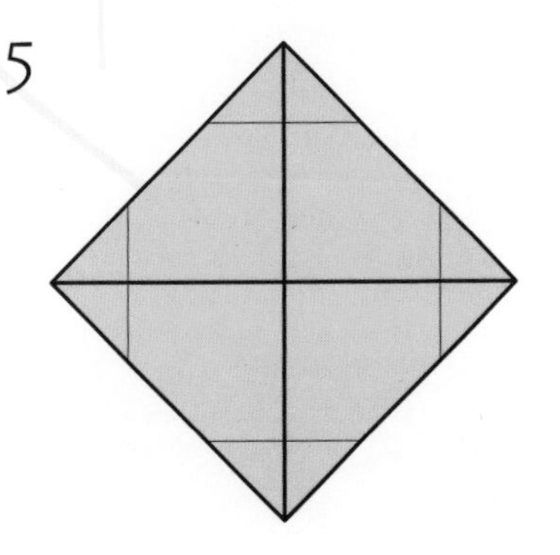

This should be the result. Now turn over.

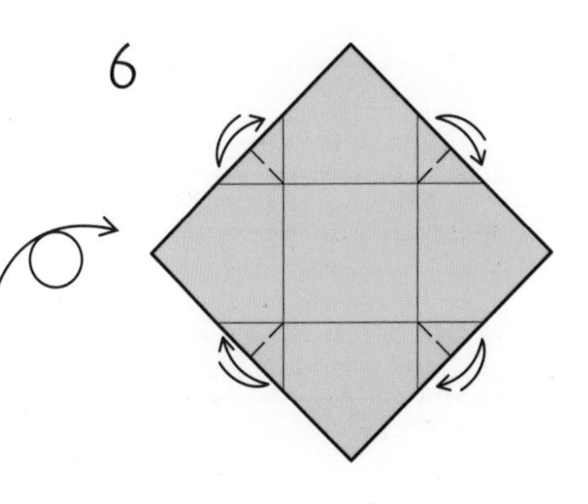

Make four more small creases.

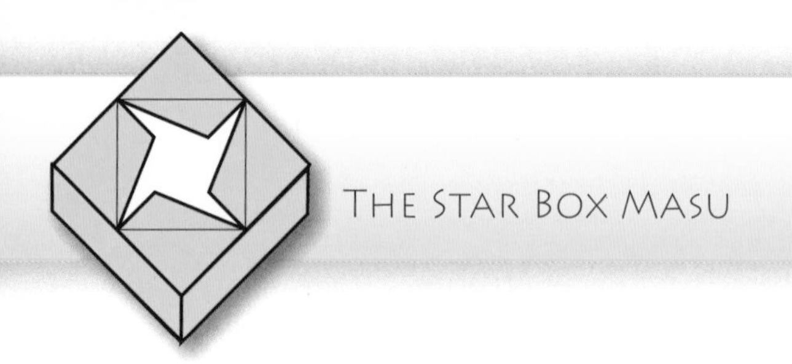

The Star Box Masu

MODEL: DARREN SCOTT
DIAGRAM: DARREN SCOTT

7

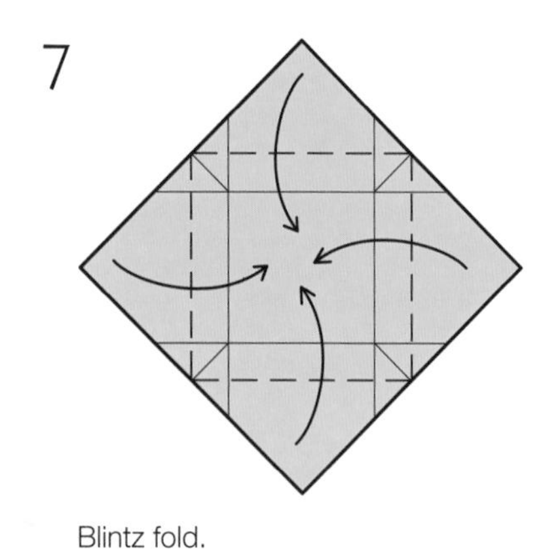

Blintz fold.

8

Fold and unfold over existing creases. These will form the edges of the box. Turn over.

9

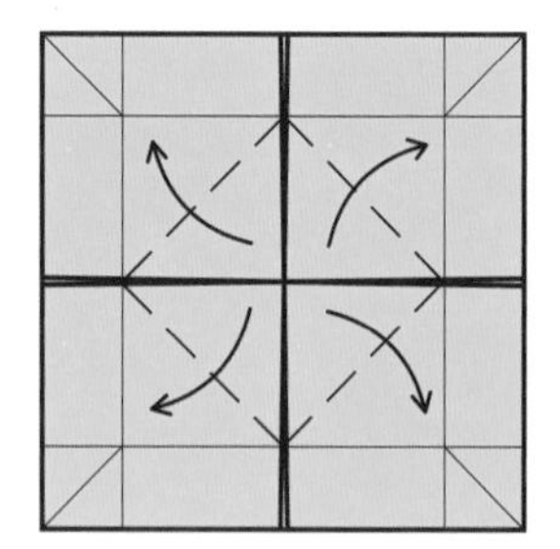

Fold the corners from the middle to the corners made by the creases.

10

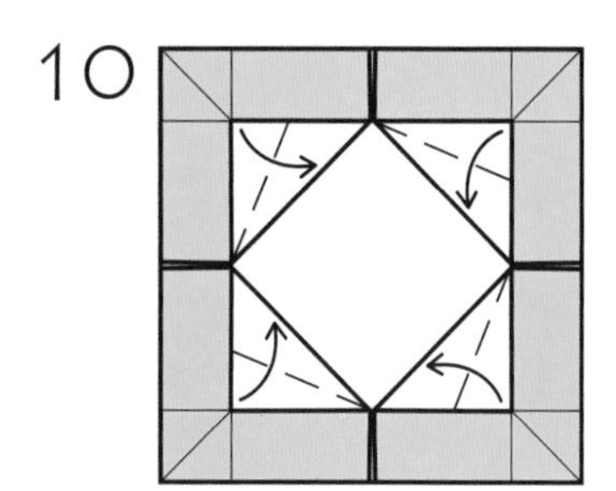

Fold the corner of each flap to meet the edge of the crease.

11

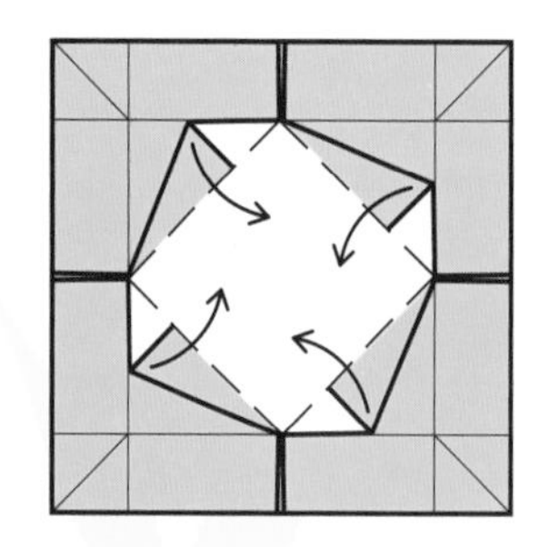

Fold each flap along the existing crease.

12

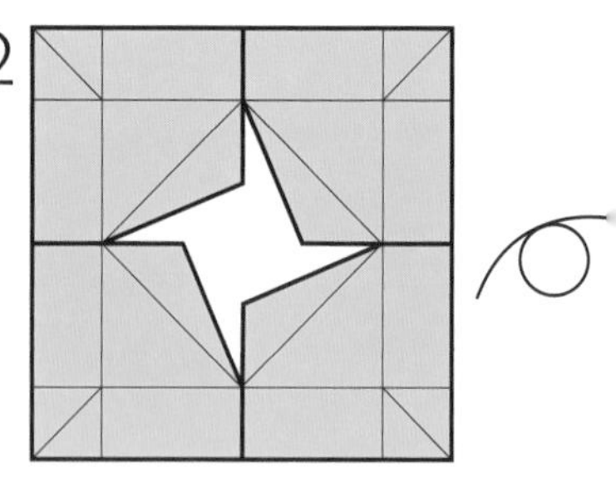

This should be the result. Turn over.

13

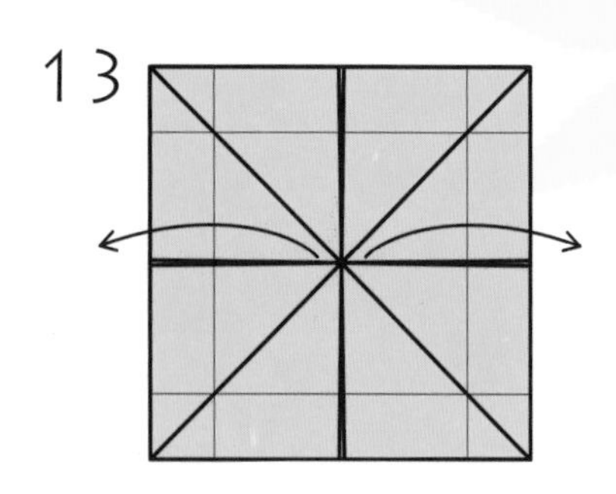

Open out the two side points.

14

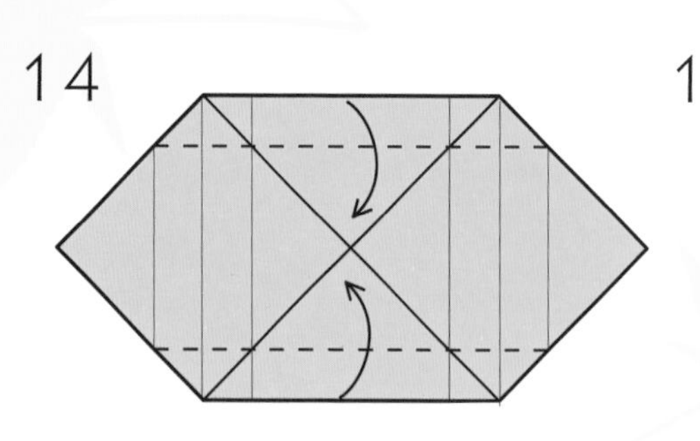

Fold the edges upwards to 90°.

15

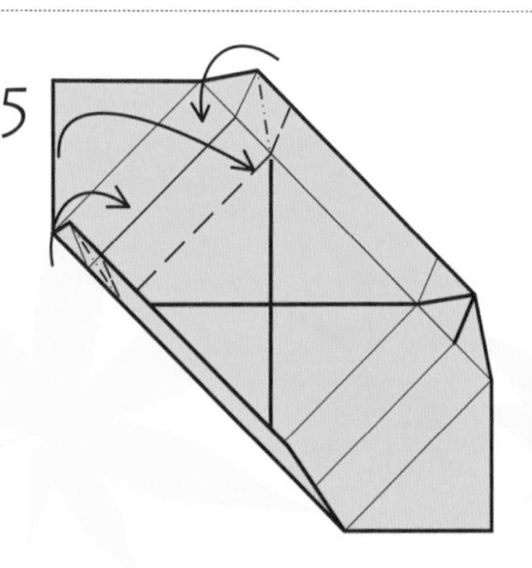

Using the existing creases lift the flap upwards and then bring the edges towards the centre.

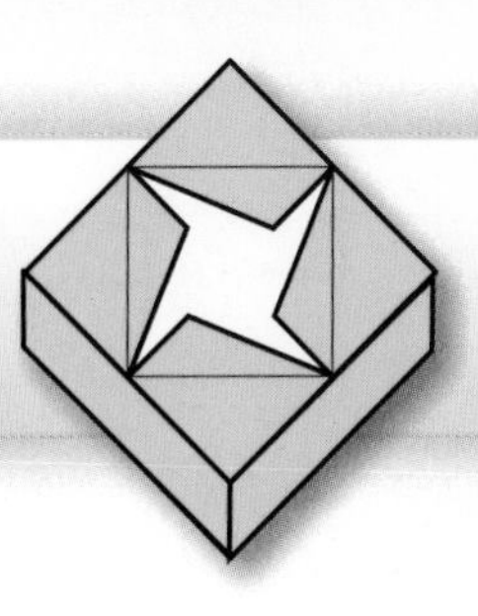

16

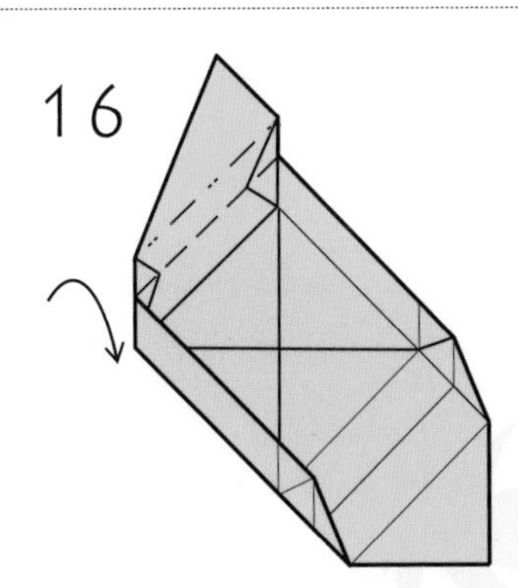

Now that you have formed the edge you need to lock the corners in place. This is done by making two folds along existing creases.

17

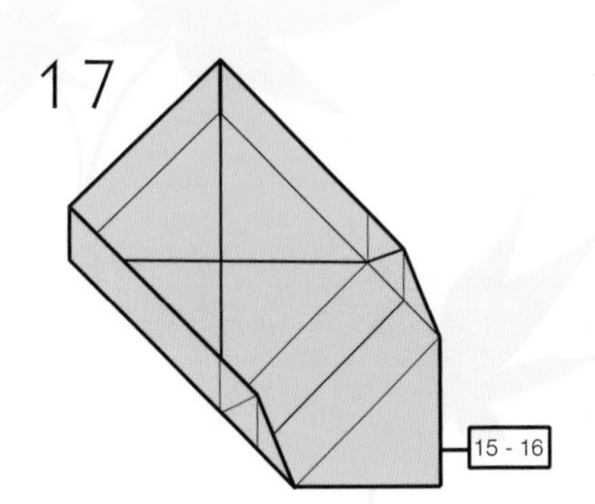

Repeat steps 15-16 on the other end.

18

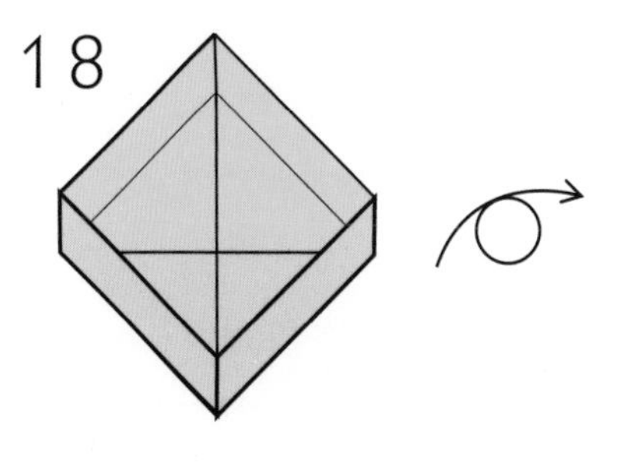

Turn over.

19

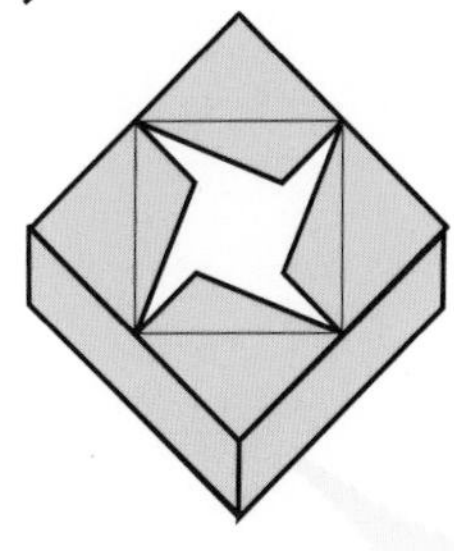

Complete star masu box.

20

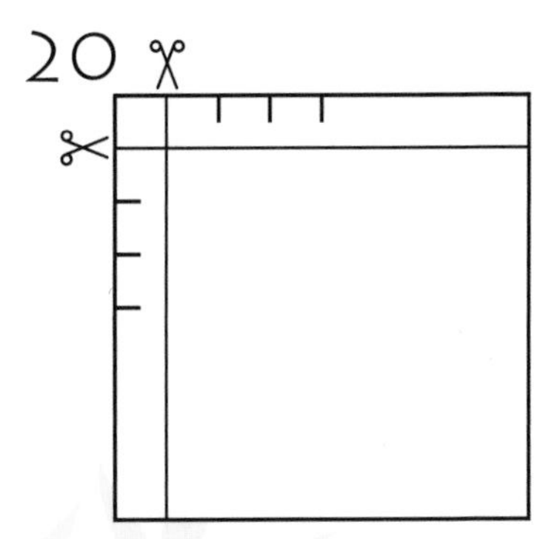

Trim 1/8 (one eighth) off the same size sheet to make the base.

21

Use the trimmed sheet to fold the masu. The base will fit in the star box masu.

Heart Box

MODEL: Darren Scott
DIAGRAM: Darren Scott

The Valentine masu is a nice gift for someone special and even better when it's filled with delicious chocolates.

1

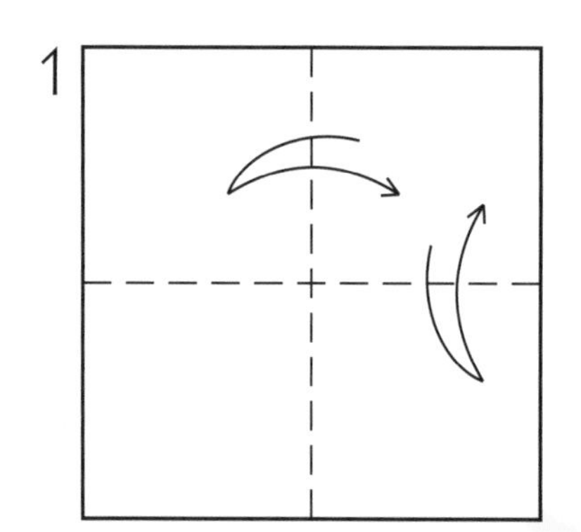

Start with paper white side up and book fold and unfold.

2

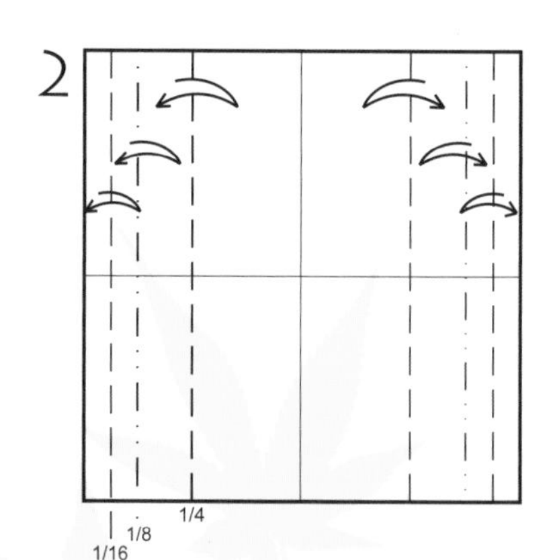

Make the following creases and unfold.

3

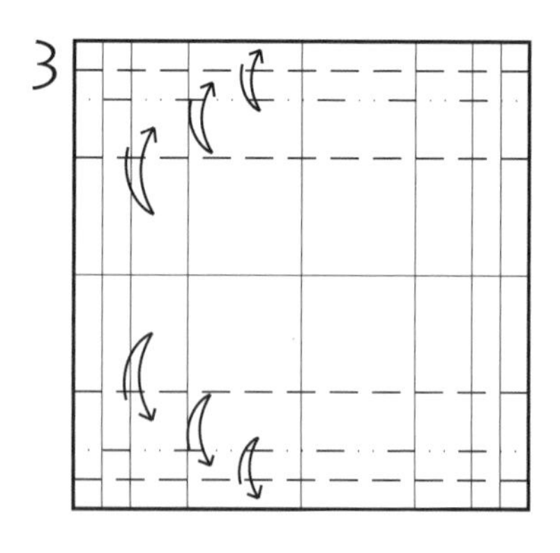

Repeat step 2 in the horizontal direction

4

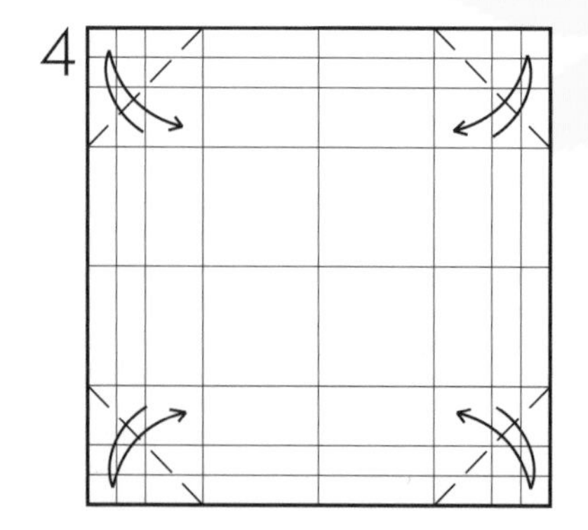

Make the small diagonal creases and unfold.

5

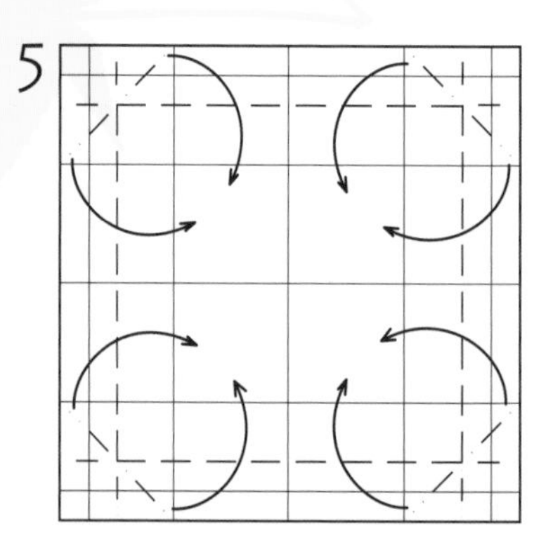

Fold on the existing creases to make preliminary bases on each corner.

6

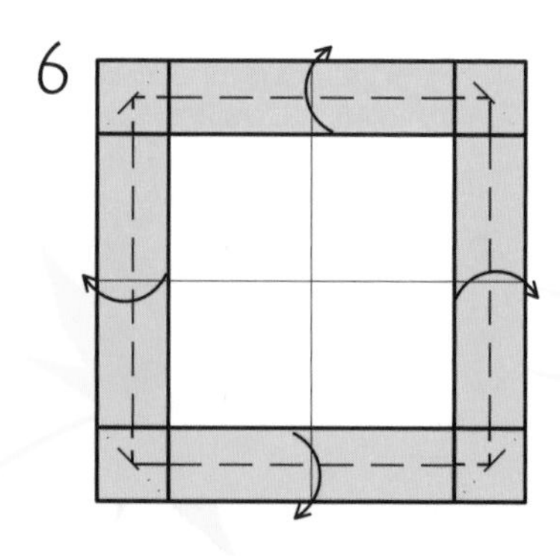

Valley fold along the existing 1/16th creases to hide the colored paper. This extends under the preliminary base.

7

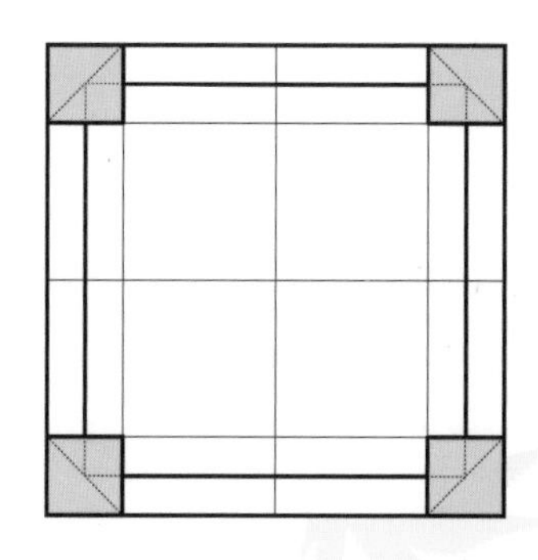

This should be the result. Note that the dotted lines show the layers of paper underneath. Turn over.

8

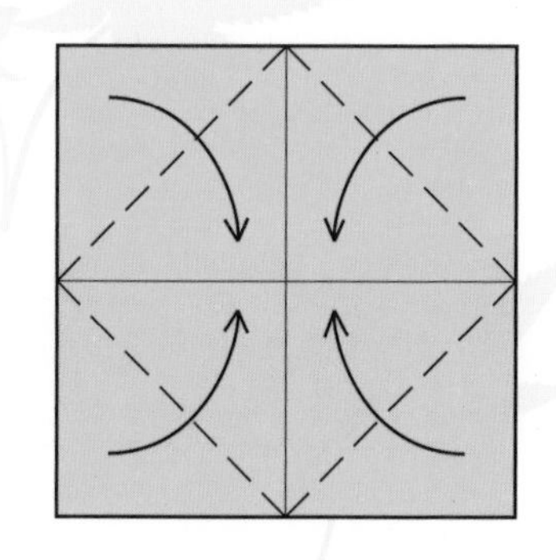

Blintz fold.

9

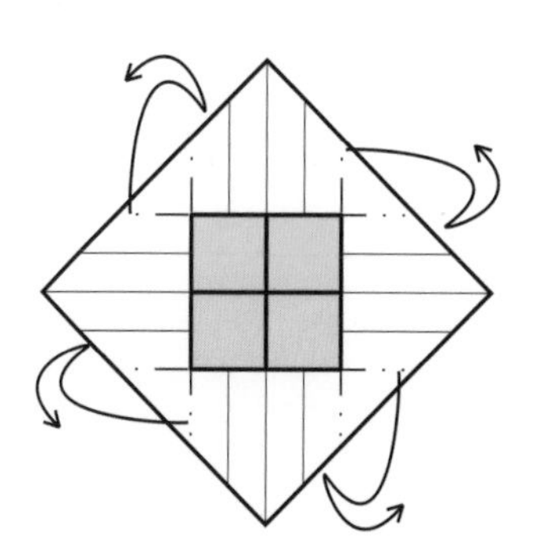

Fold along the existing 1/8th creases and unfold.

10

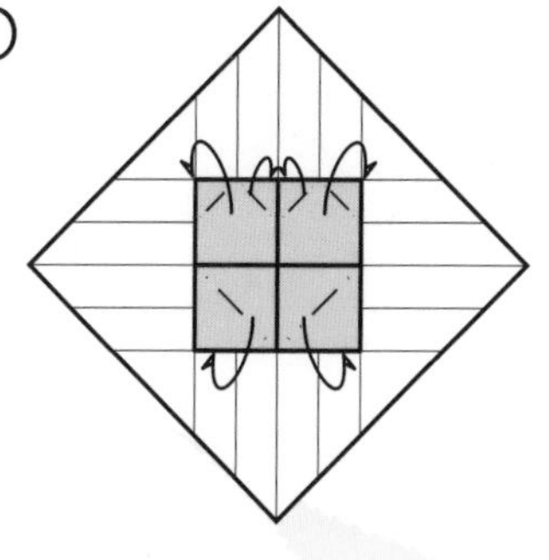

Fold the corners under to begin forming the heart.

11

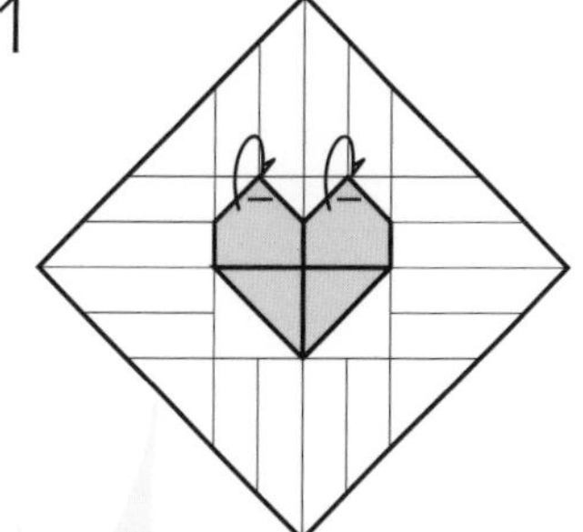

Fold the tips of the heart over to finish forming the heart. Turn over.

12

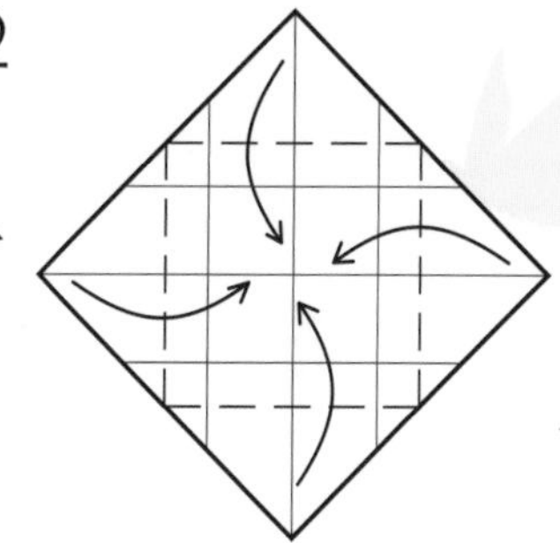

Blintz fold again.

13

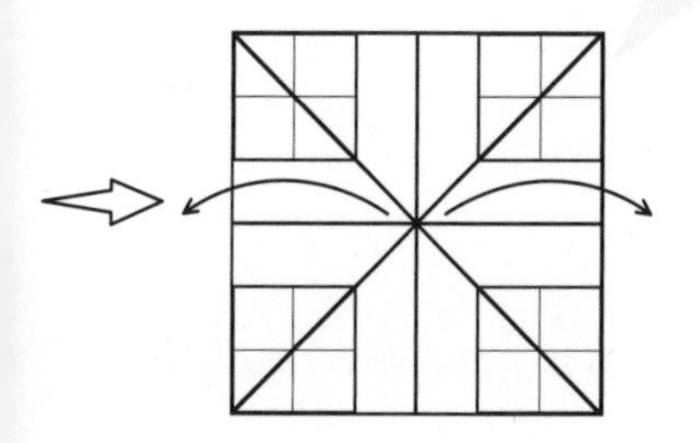

Unfold the left and right flaps.

14

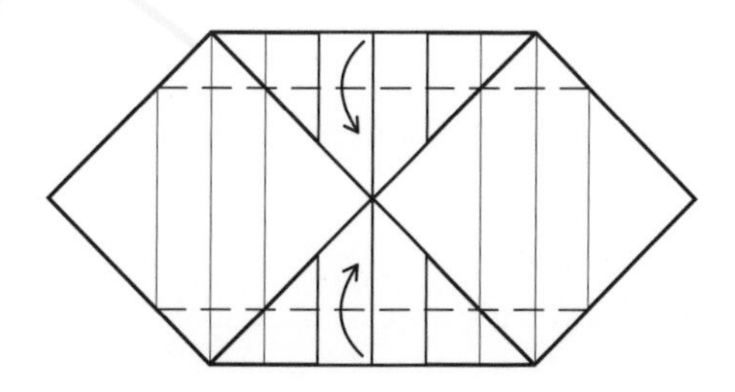

Fold the top and bottom edges up to 90°.

15

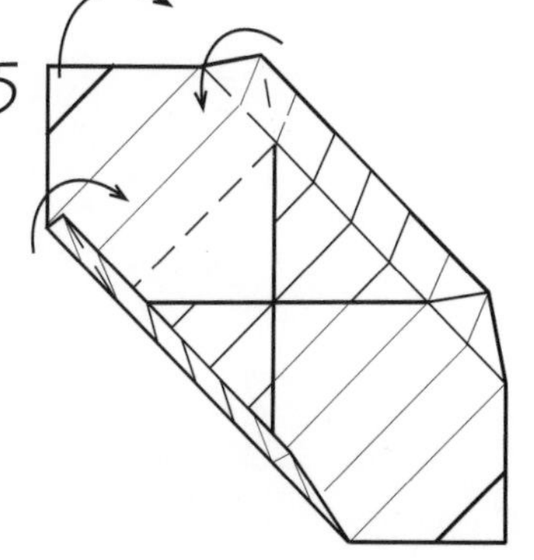

Using the existing creases lift the point up and fold the edges to the centre.

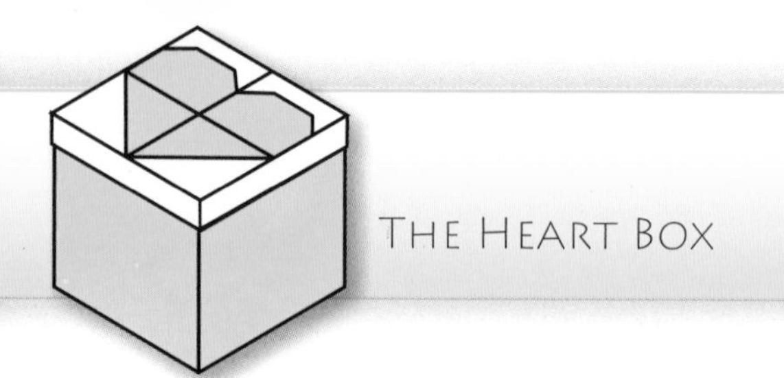

The Heart Box

Model: Darren Scott
Diagram: Darren Scott

16

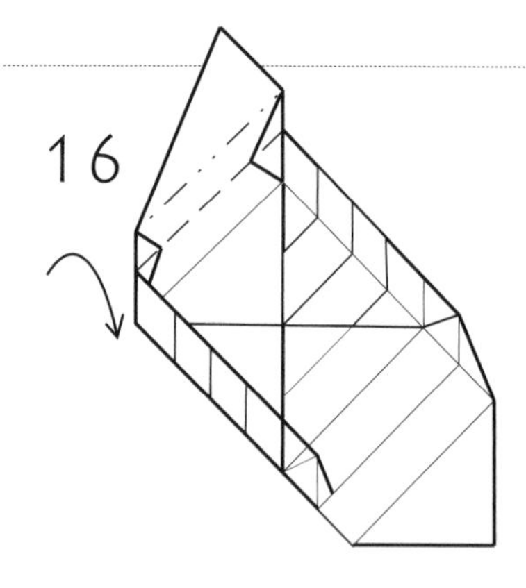

Now that you have formed the edge you need to lock the corners in place. This is done by making two folds along existing creases.

17

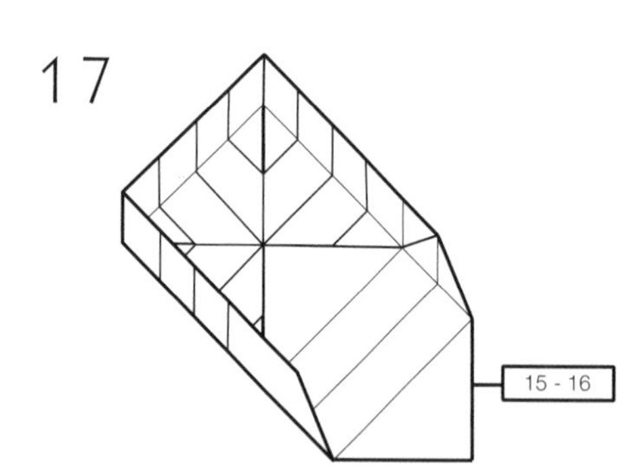

Repeat steps 15-16 on the other end.

18

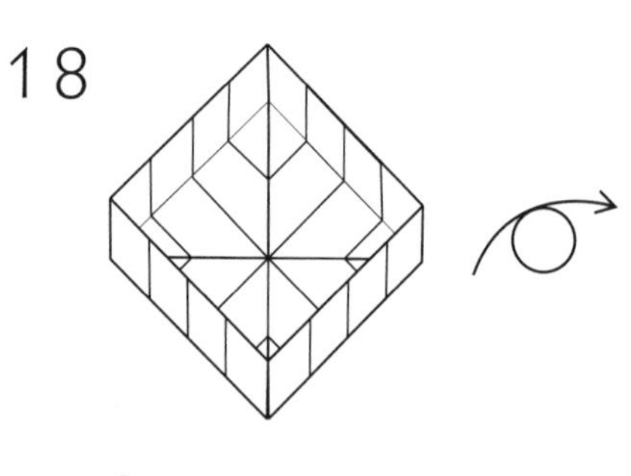

Completed step 17. Turn over.

19

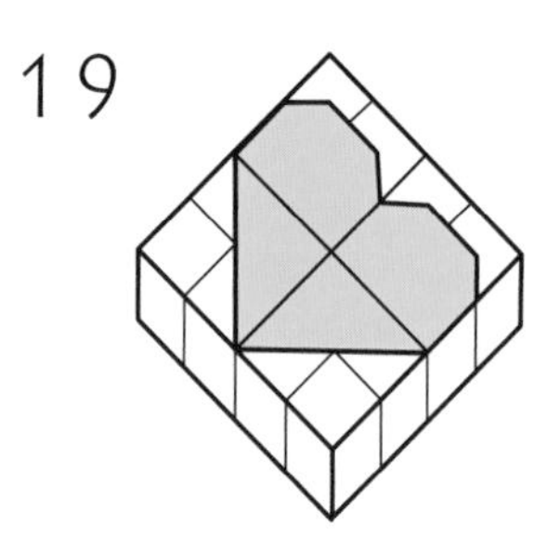

The lid is complete. Let's make the base.

20

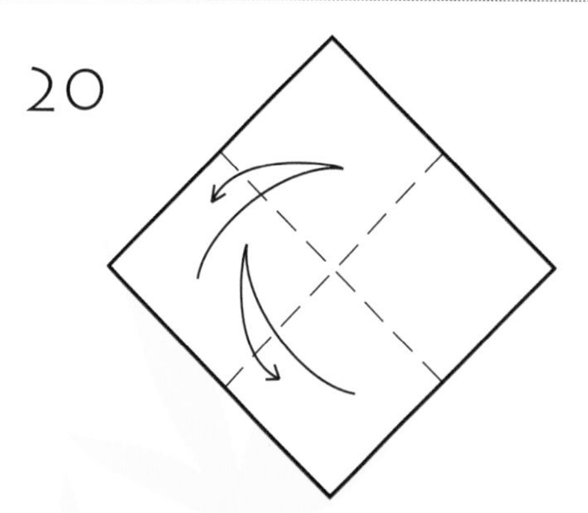

Start with a square white side up. Book fold and unfold.

21

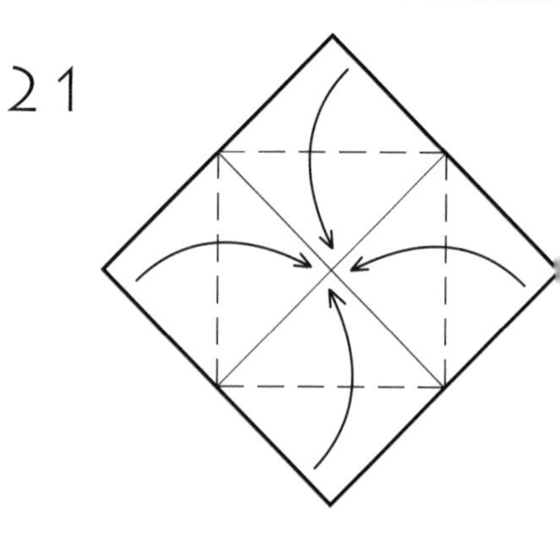

Blintz fold.

22

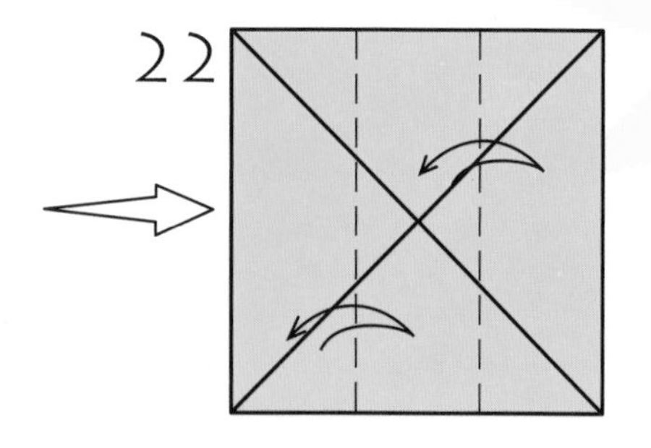

Divide the square into thirds horizontally and unfold.

23

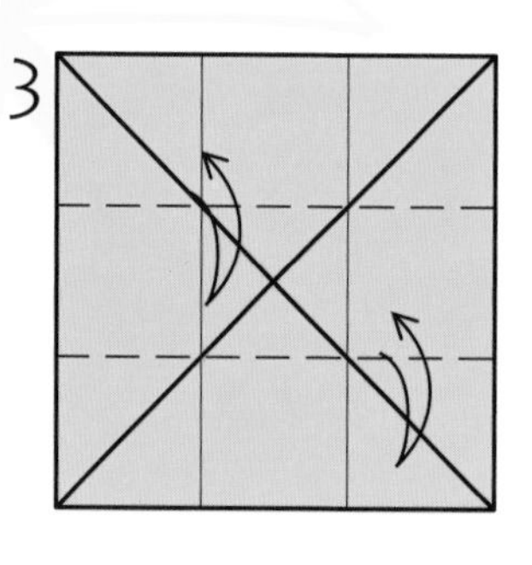

Now divide the paper into thirds vertically and unfold.

24

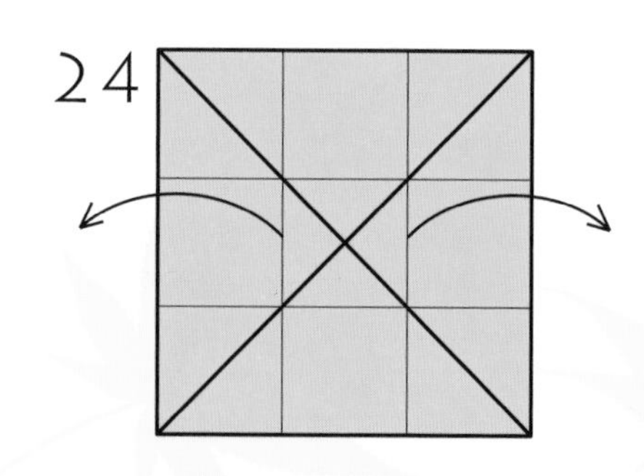

Unfold the left and right flaps.

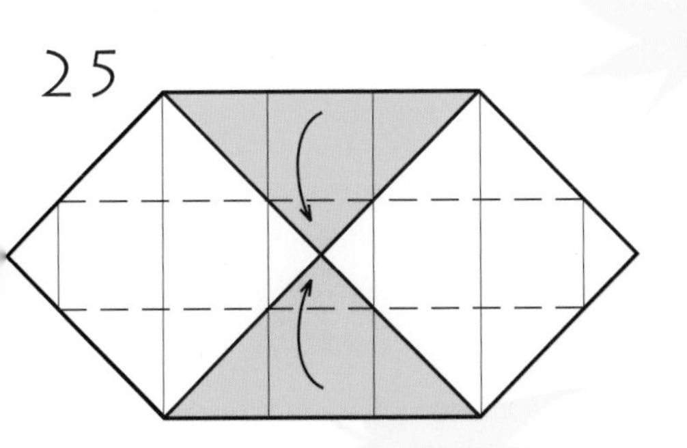

This process is very similar to forming the lid. Fold the sides up to 90°.

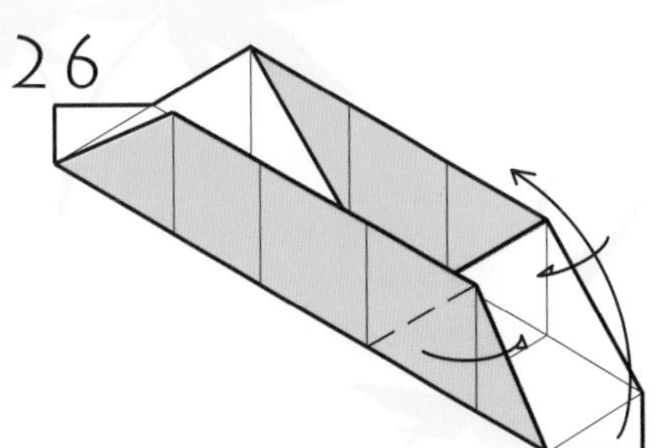

Using the existing creases form the side of the box.

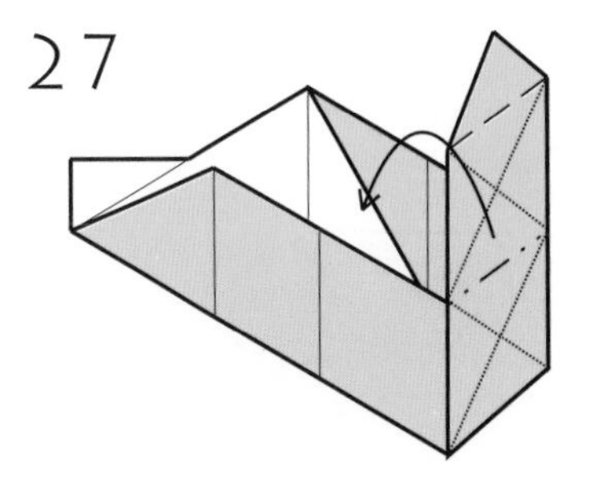

Tuck the flap inside to lock the side in place.

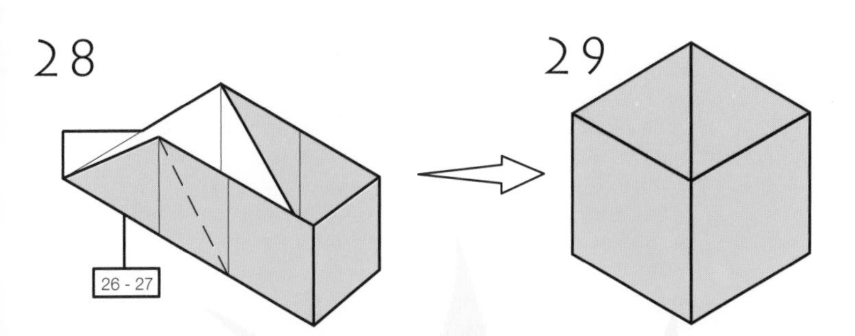

Repeat steps 26-27 on the other end.

The box is complete and we can add the lid.

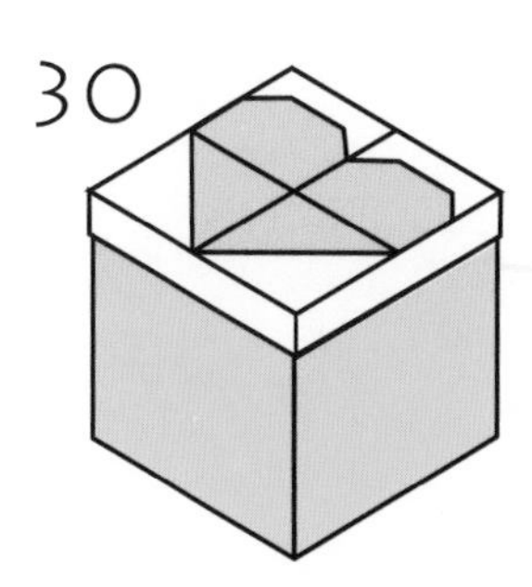

Completed heart box.

TWIST BOX

MODEL: DARREN SCOT
DIAGRAM: DARREN SCOT

The twist box uses a special origami technique called a twist fold, made famous by Mr Kawasaki's origami rose.

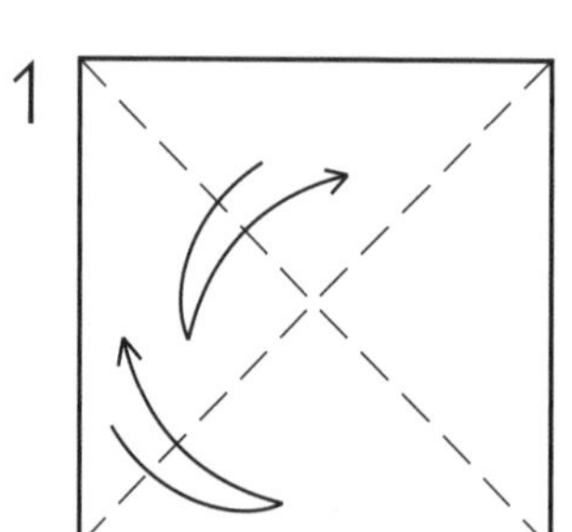

Start white side up. Fold and unfold diagonals.

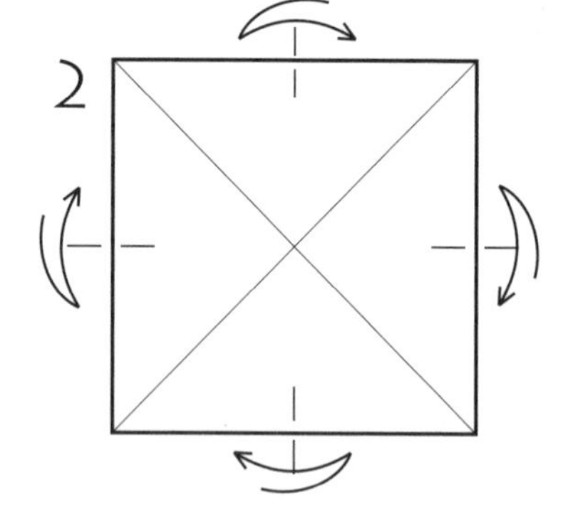

Pinch the midpoints on all four sides.

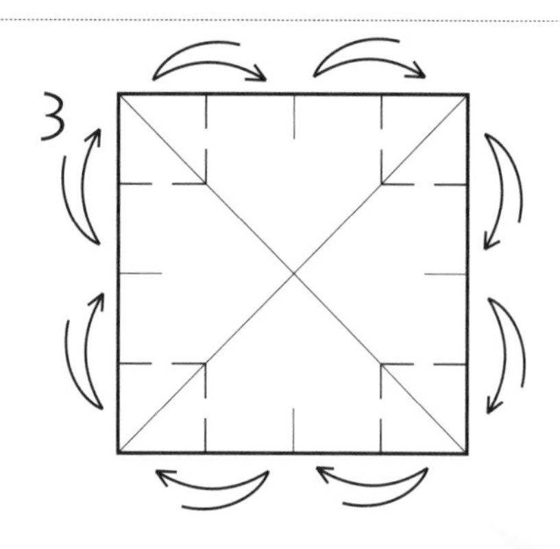

Using creases from step 2, crease from the outer edge to the diagonal.

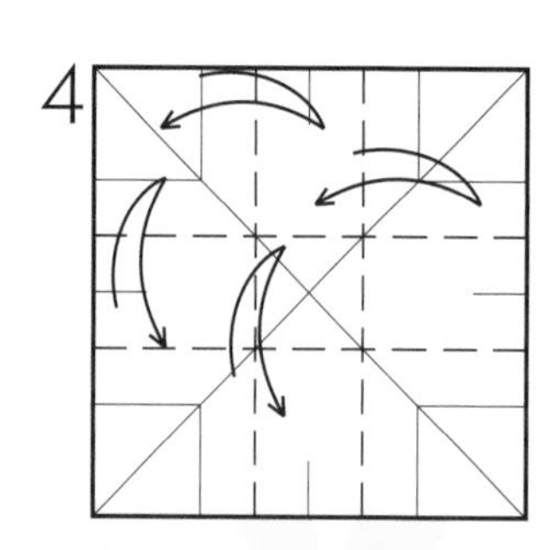

Using creases from step 2, crease from the outer edge to the diagonal.

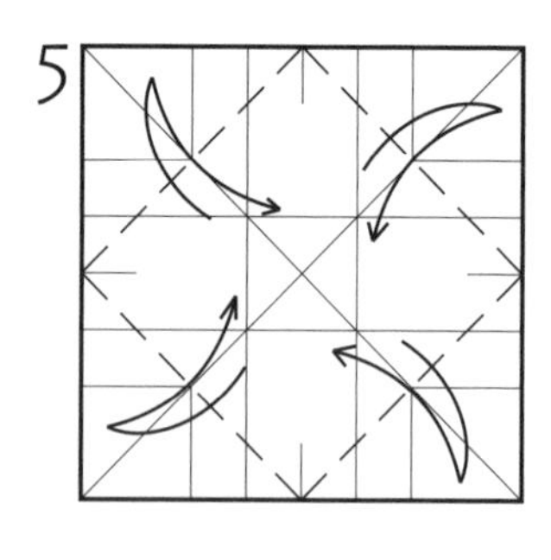

Blintz fold and unfold.

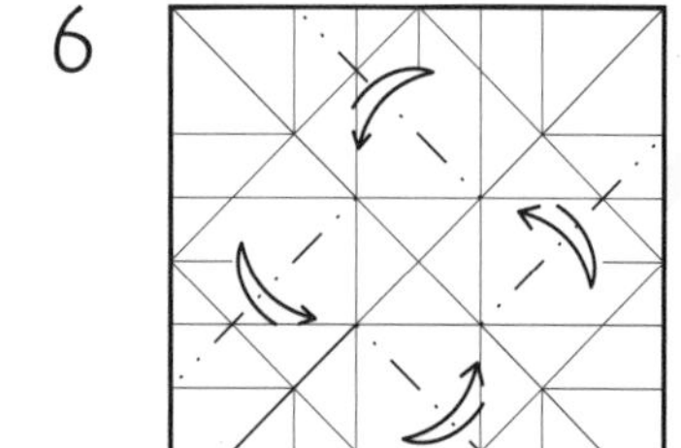

Make more diagonal folds and unfold.

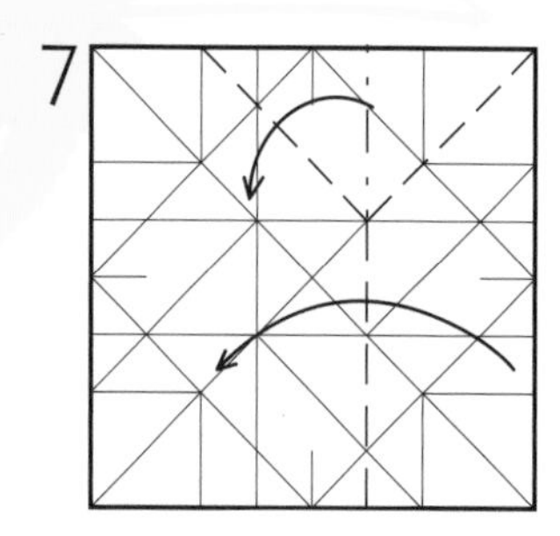

Using existing creases, fold the right edge. See the result in the next diagram.

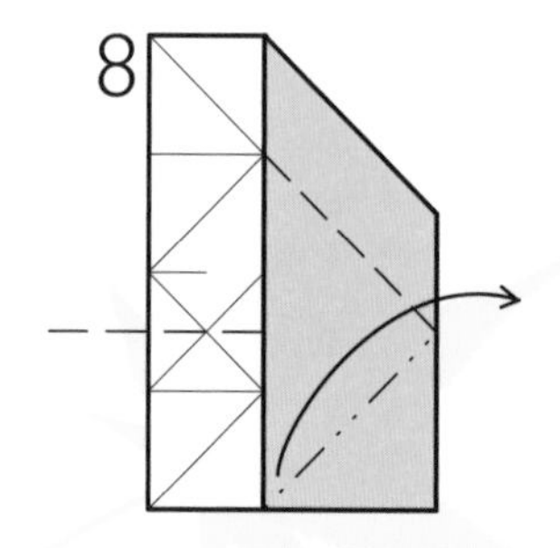

Using existing creases, lift layer up and squash fold to the right.

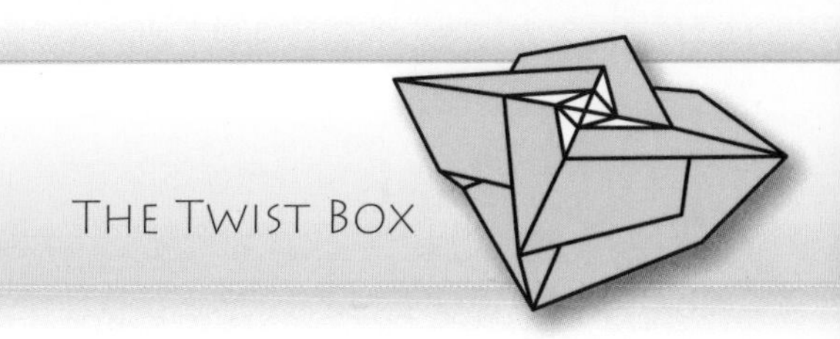

9

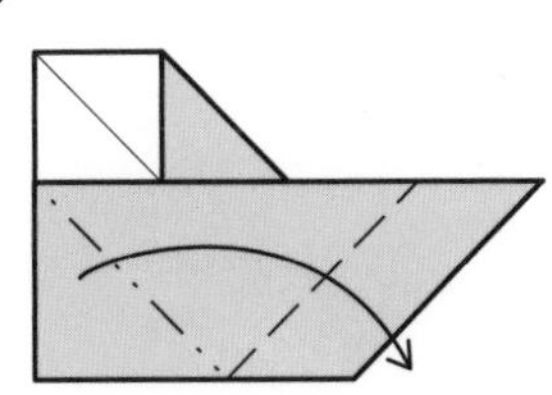

Repeat step 8 on the next point.
Look carefully at the next step as the model will not sit flat.

10

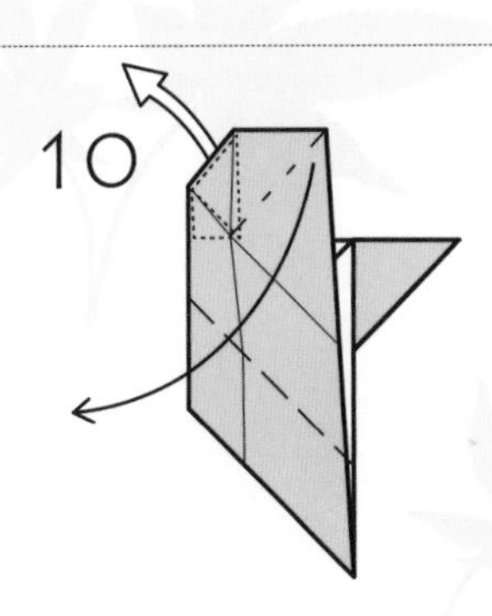

Repeat step 8 on the top point.
Pull out the trapped point from behind.

11

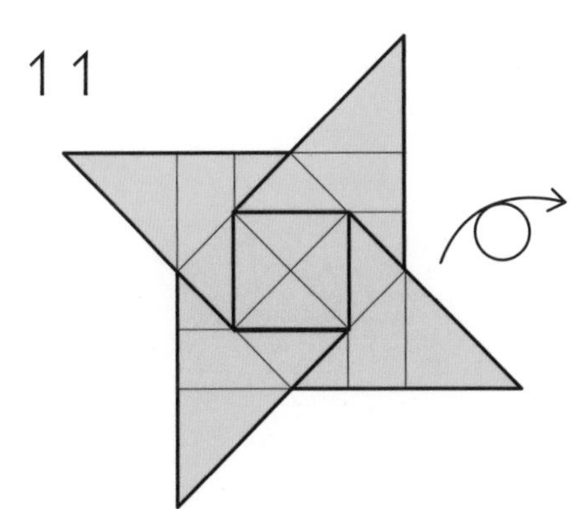

For reference, this is the result when viewed from the bottom. Turn over.

12

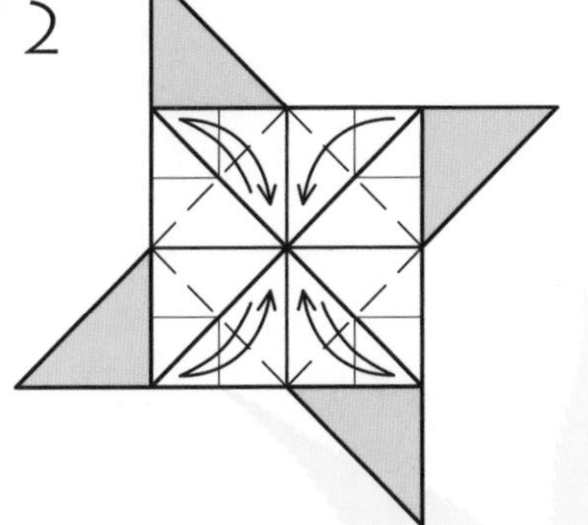

Fold all the corners inwards.
Unfold all except one.

13

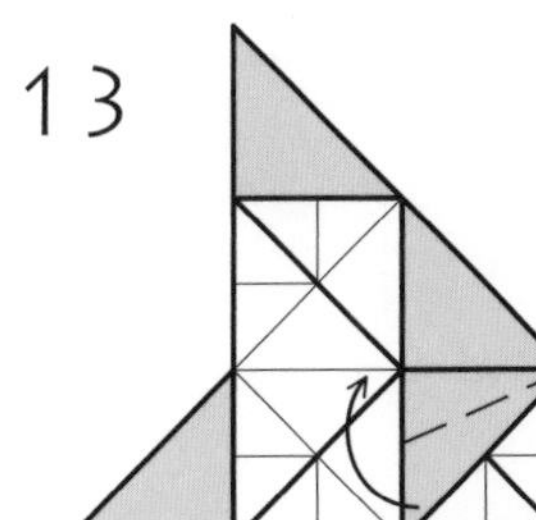

Fold the flap upwards to the centre edge.

14

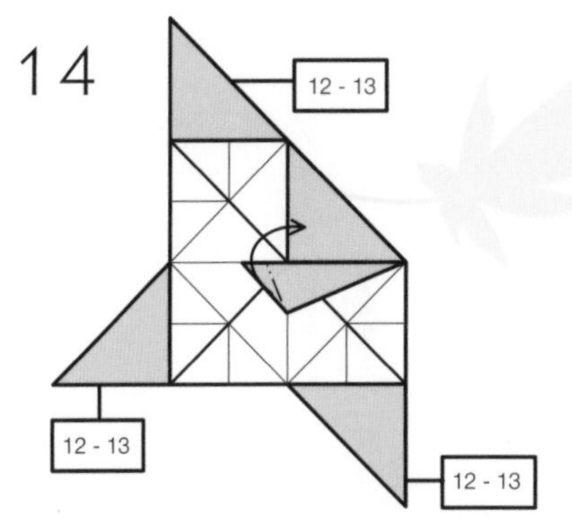

Make the small outside reverse fold.
Repeat steps 12-13 on the remaining three sides.

15

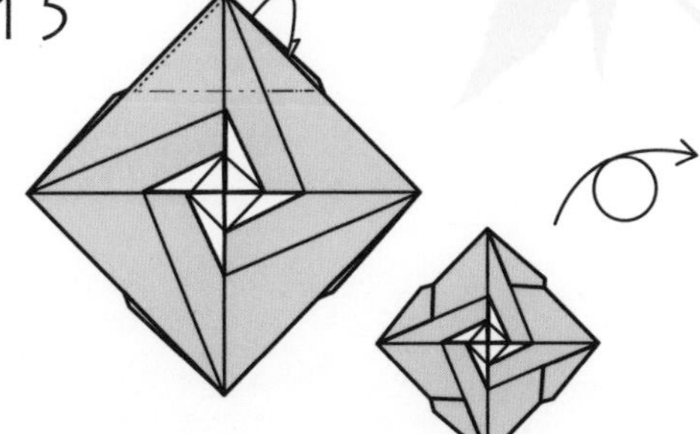

Lock the top in place by weaving the four white triangles. Then fold the mostly hidden corner flap behind. Repeat with the remaining three hidden corner flaps. Turn over.

16

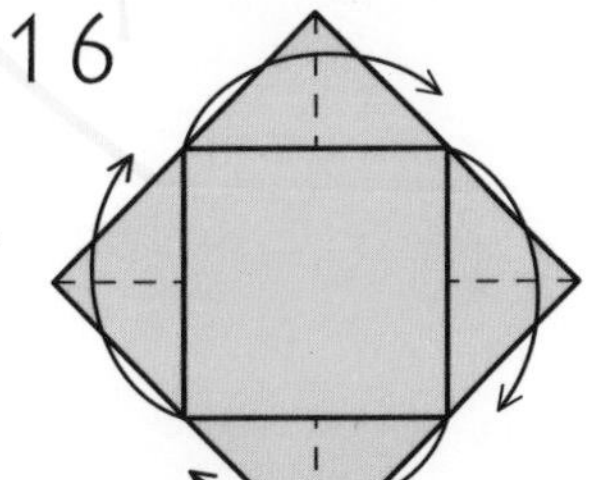

Make the box 3D by twisting the top square and pulling it upwards. Turn over.

17

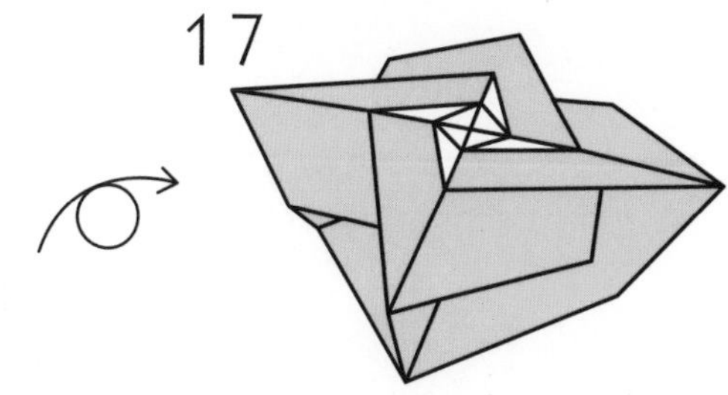

Completed twist box.

Lunch Bag

MODEL: DARREN SCOTT
DIAGRAM: DARREN SCOTT

The no-glue lunch bag will come in handy for storing all sorts of things, not just your lunch. Try varying the width and height of the paper you start with to suit the object you want to store.

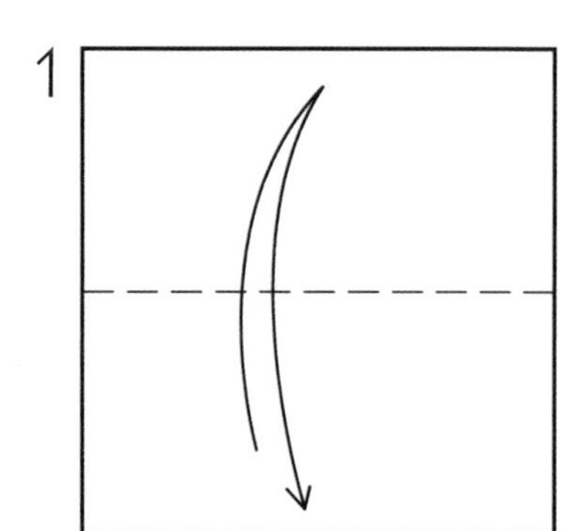

1 Start with a square white side up. Book fold and unfold.

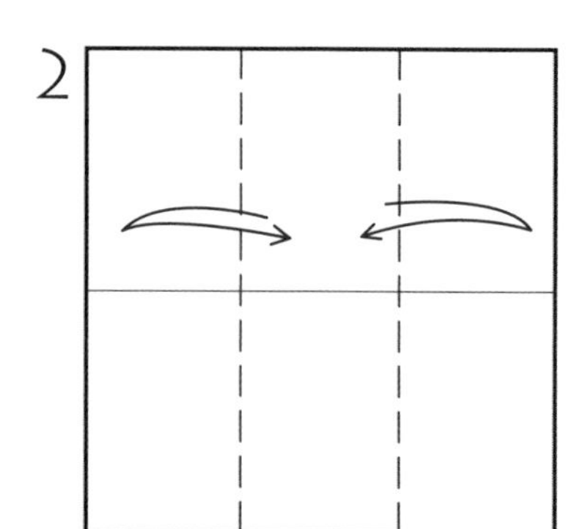

2 Divide the square into thirds vertically, and unfold.

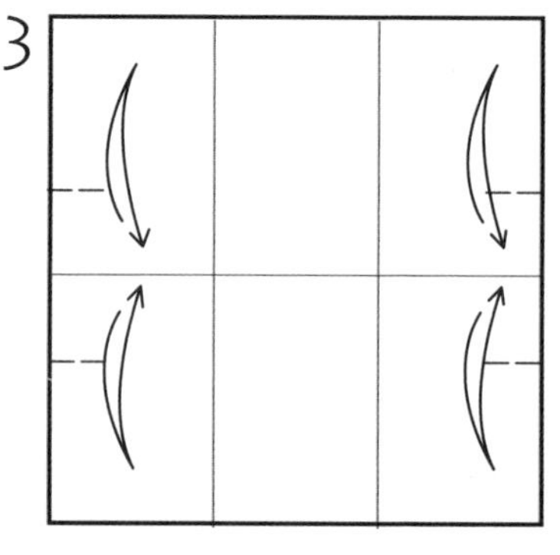

3 Divide the square into thirds horizontally. This time just make small pinch marks at the edges.

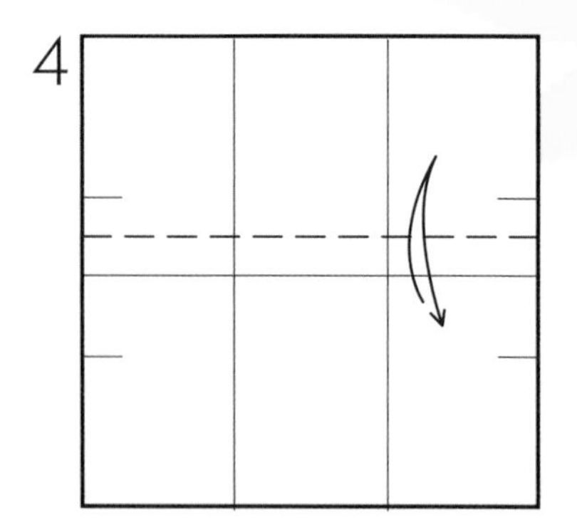

4 Make a fold between the top pinch mark and the centre crease. Unfold.

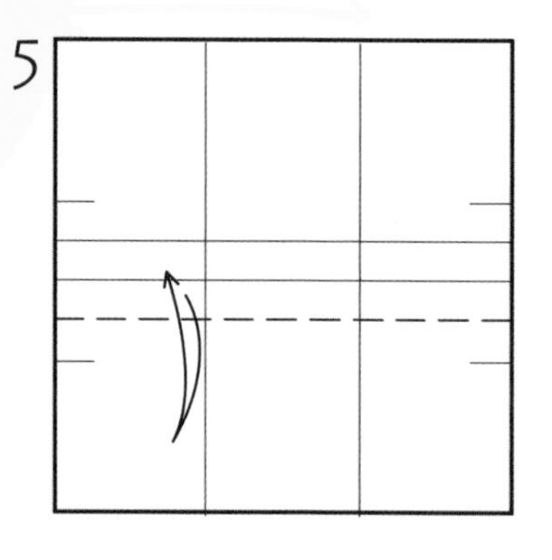

5 Repeat step 4 using the bottom pinch marks.

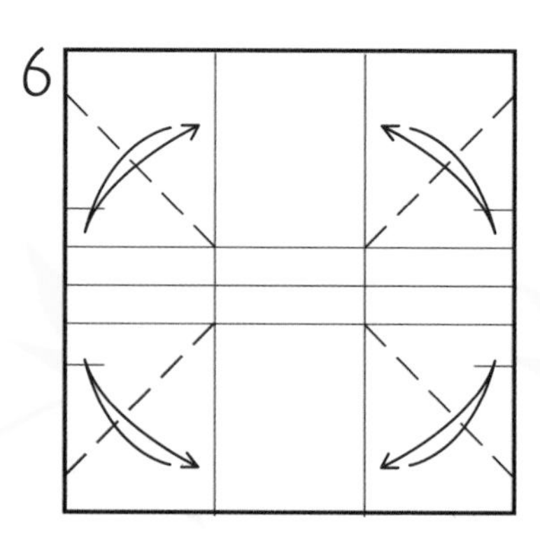

6 Create the diagonal creases and unfold.

7

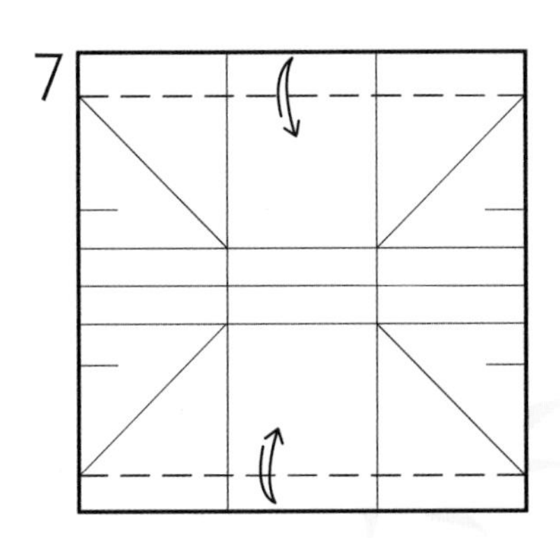

Using the diagonal creases as landmarks, fold the top and bottom edges. Unfold.

8

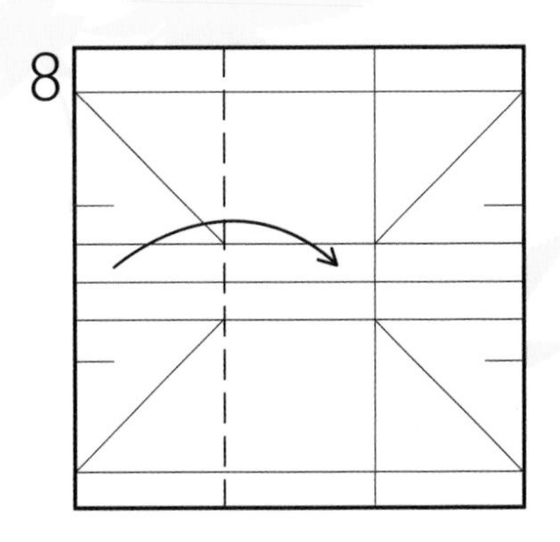

Fold a third to the right using the crease made in step 3.

9

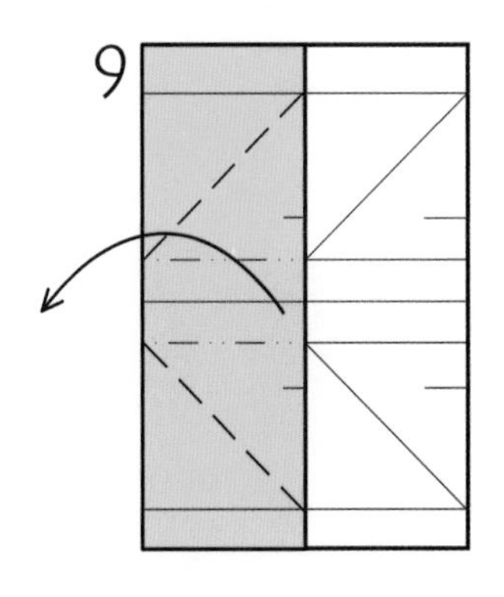

Using the existing creases start forming the side of the bag.

10

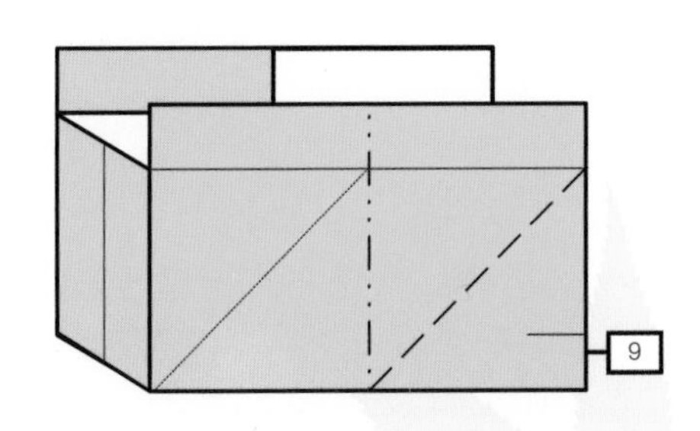

This should be the result. Repeat step 9 on the right-hand side.

11

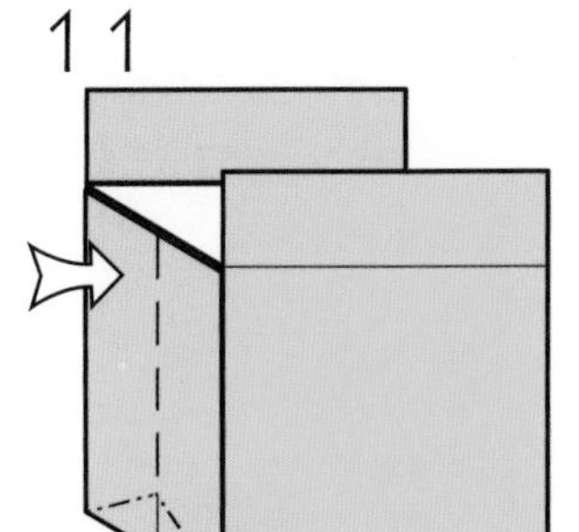

Push the side edge inwards and bring the top edges together.

12

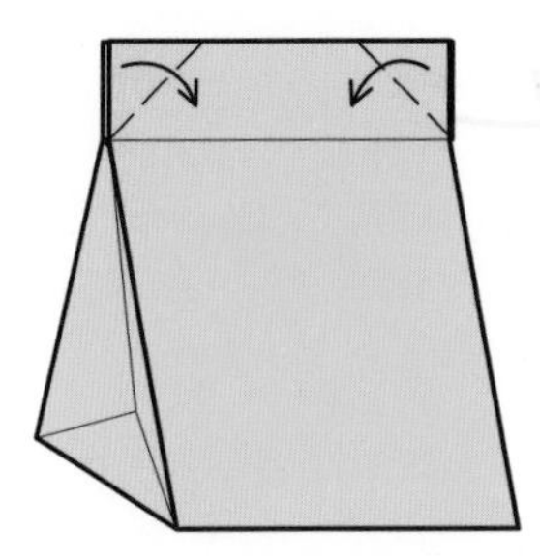

Fold the corners down to meet the creases made in step 7.

13

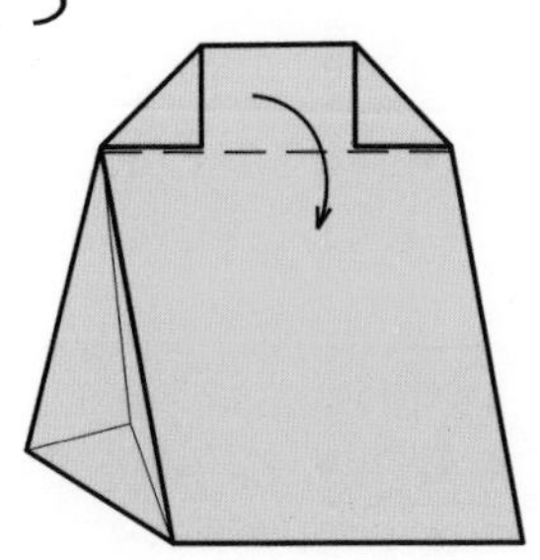

Refold the creases made in step 7.

14

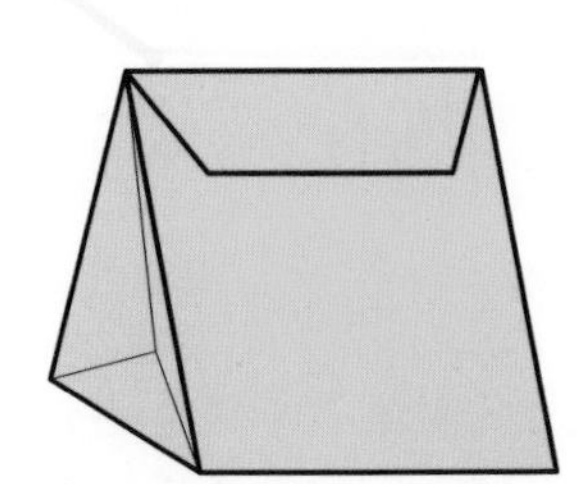

Completed lunch bag.

BOOKMARK

MODEL: GARETH LOUIS
DIAGRAM: GARETH LOUIS

The chequered bookmark is a useful and decorative bookmark that slips over and locks onto a page. This unique and practical kind of bookmark is a favourite subject for origami designer Gareth Louis.

The chequered bookmark will keep your page marked for you in paper folding style.

1

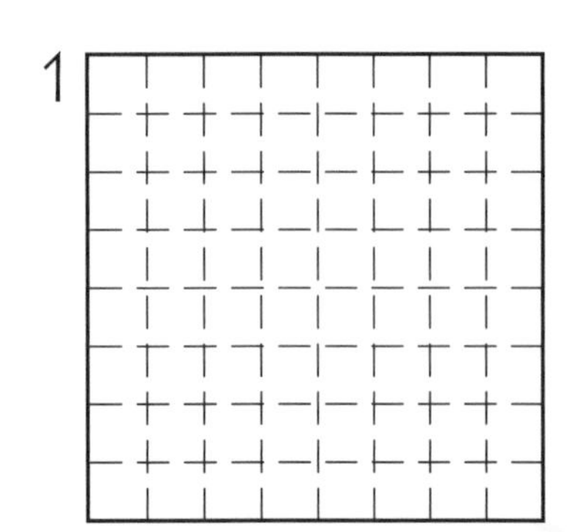

White side up. Pre-crease into a grid of eighths.

2

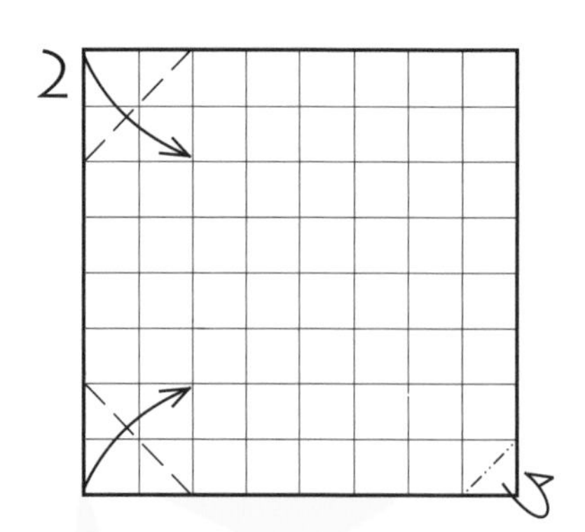

Valley fold the two left corners, and mountain fold the bottom right corner.

3

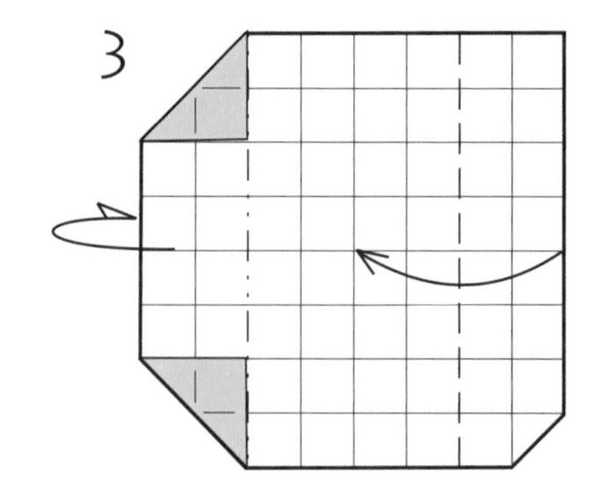

Mountain fold on the left side, and valley fold on the right.

4

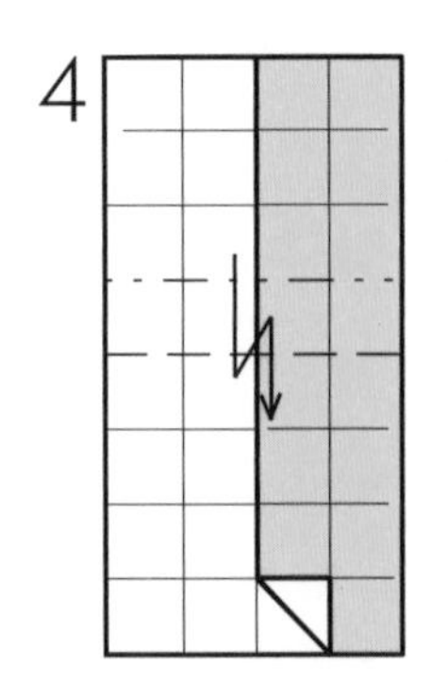

Pleat downwards.

5

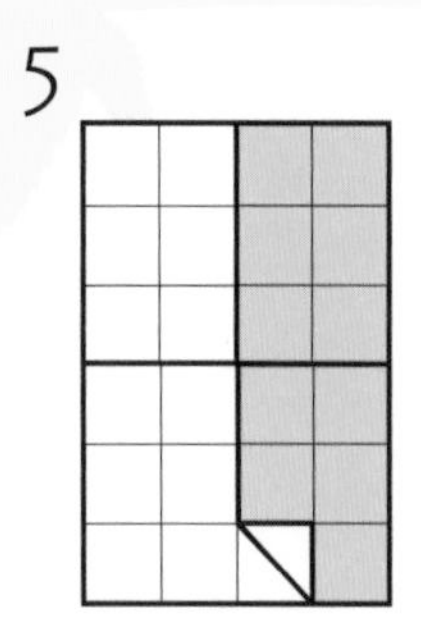

Completed step 4. Turn over.

6

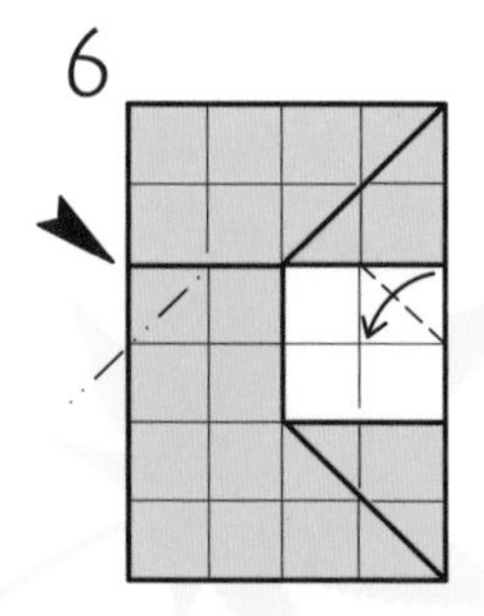

Reverse fold on the left point and valley fold on the right-hand side.

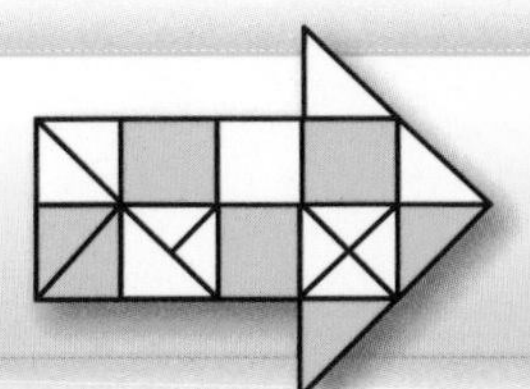

7

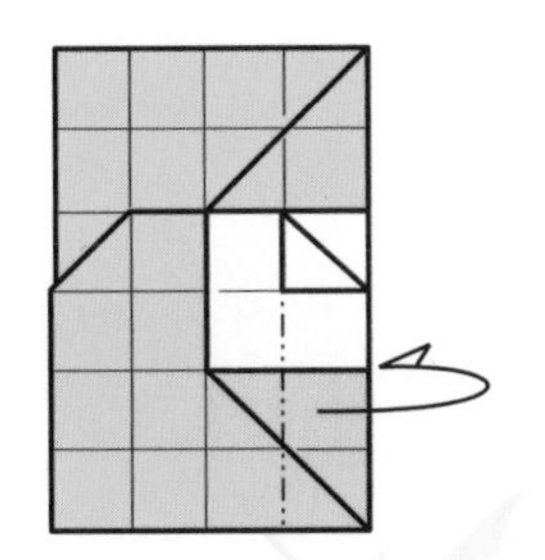

Mountain fold behind.

8

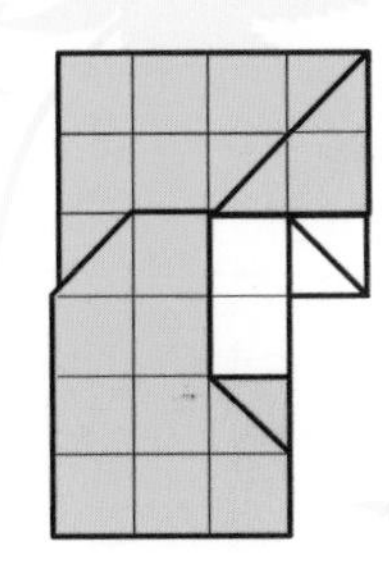

Completed step 7. Turn over.

9

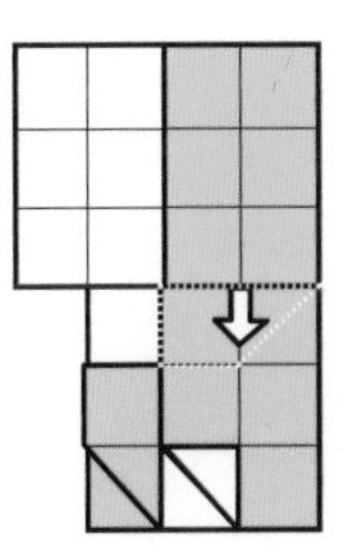

Pull out hidden layers from beneath.

10

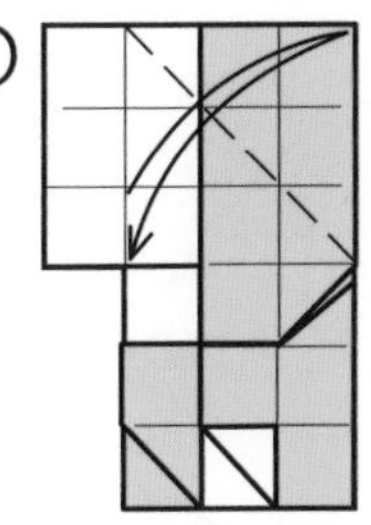

Pre-crease top right corner.

11

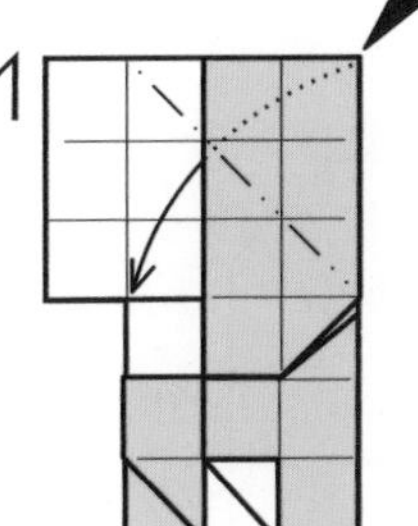

Reverse fold on creases from step 10.

12

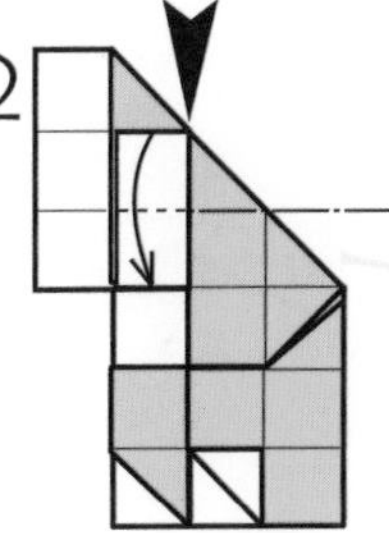

Reverse fold inside.

13

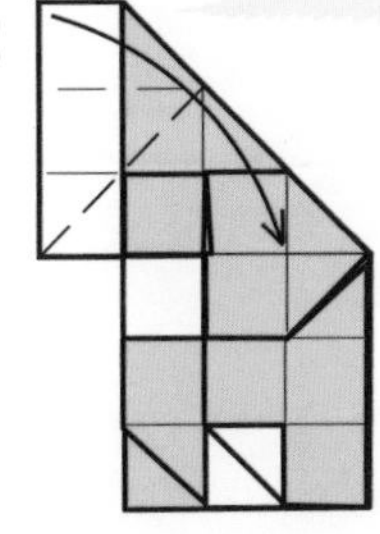

Valley fold top right flap.

14

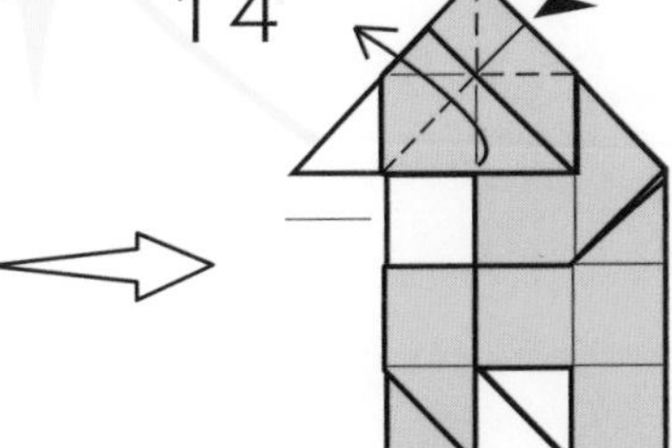

Collapse upwards by valley folding and making a reverse fold at the end.

15

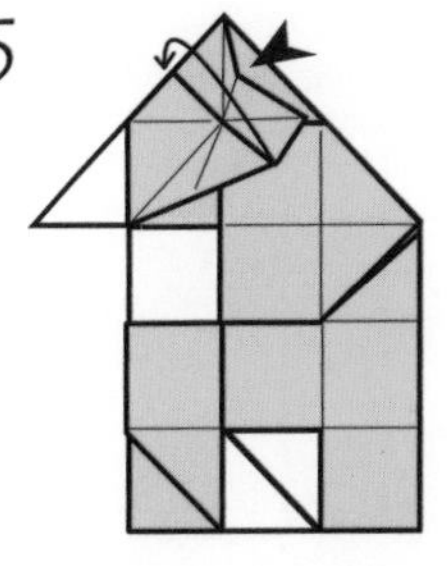

Step 14 in progress. The black arrow shows where to make the reverse fold.

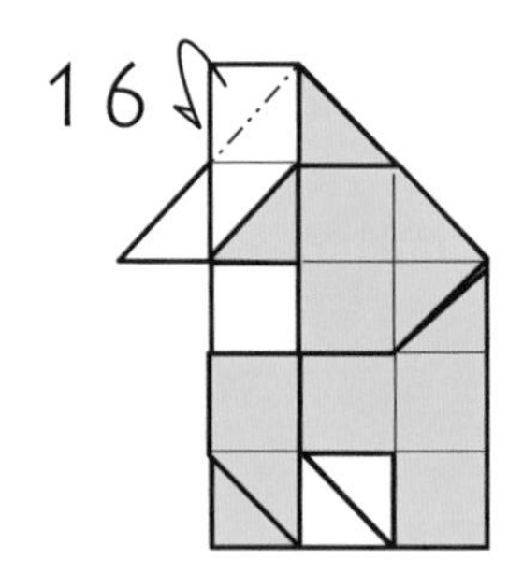

Mountain fold corner into the pocket behind.

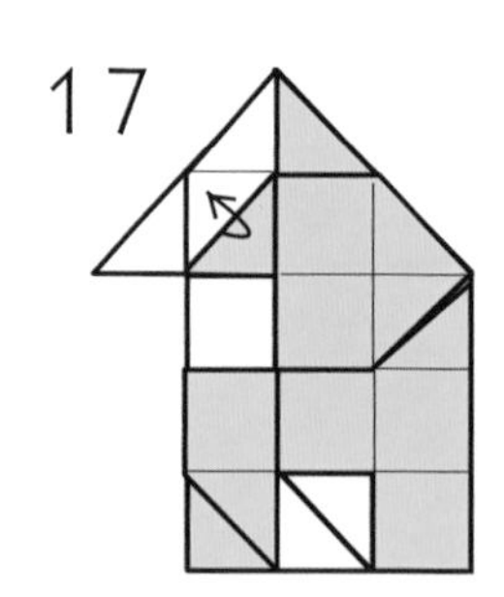

Pull out the coloured layer from behind.

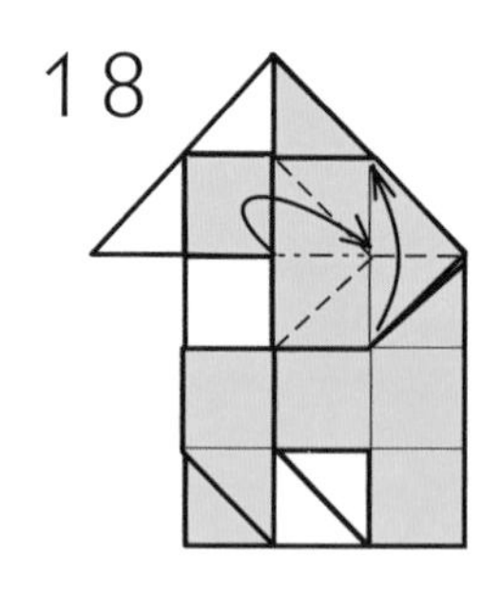

Valley fold up while incorporating a reverse fold.

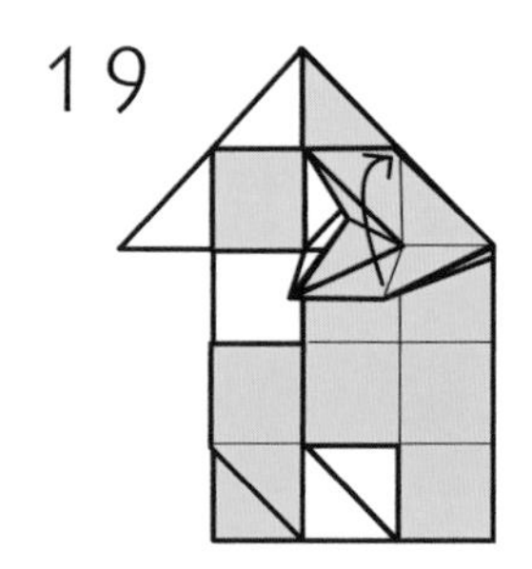

Collapsing in progress.

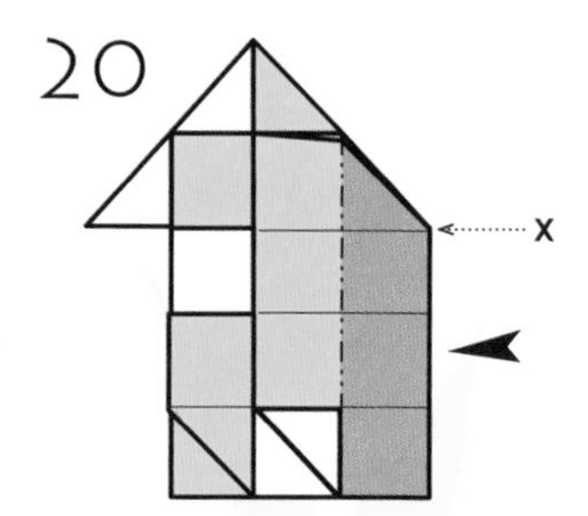

Open sink the darkened portion, but leave point X as it is, sticking out.

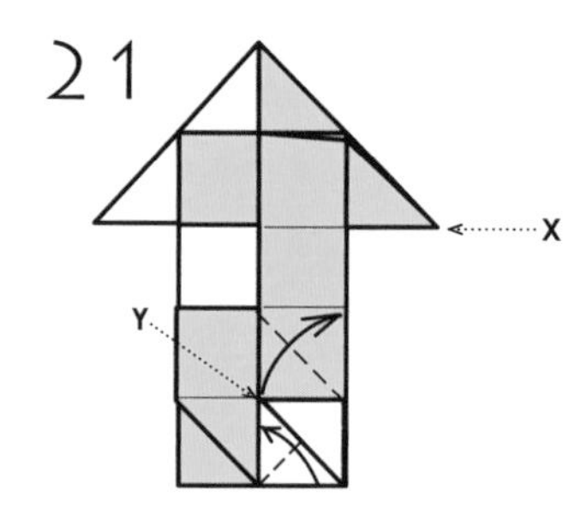

After the sink, you can still see point X. Valley fold point Y, at the same time swivelling the bottom white triangle.

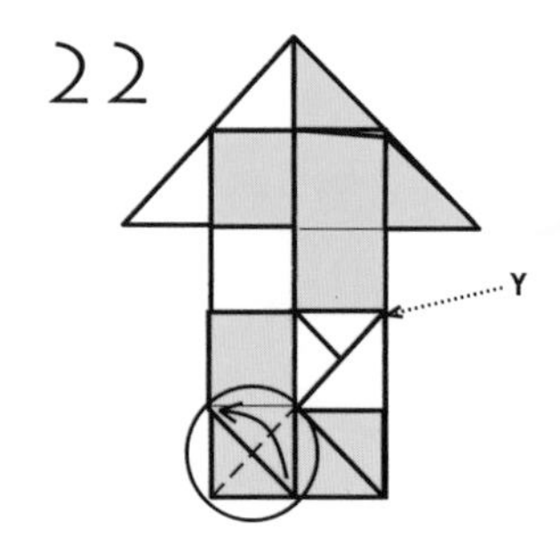

Note the new location of corner Y. Valley fold the lower corner to effect a colour change.

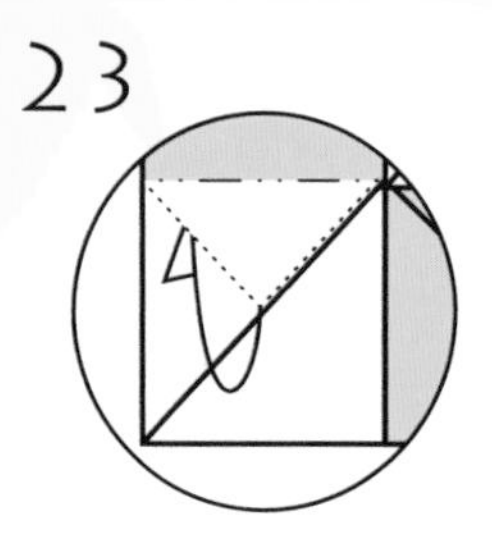

Close-up X-ray view: Mountain fold a tiny tip beneath the white layer. (It will help if you loosen the side flaps.)

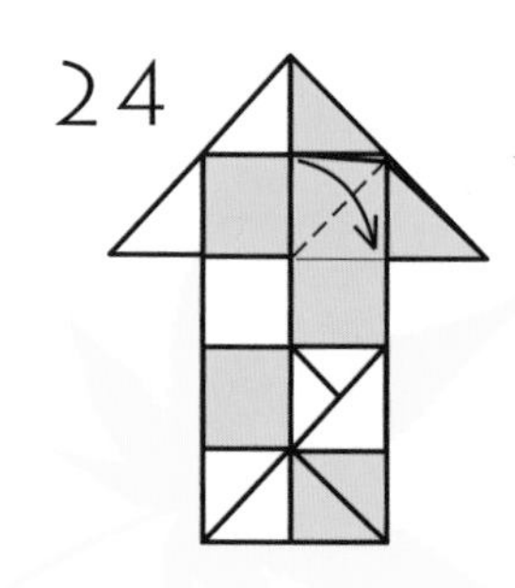

Valley fold for one last colour change.

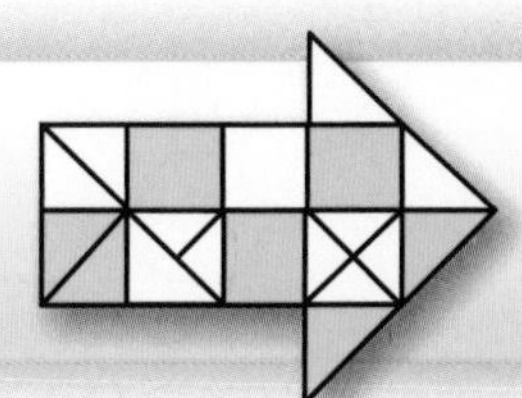

25

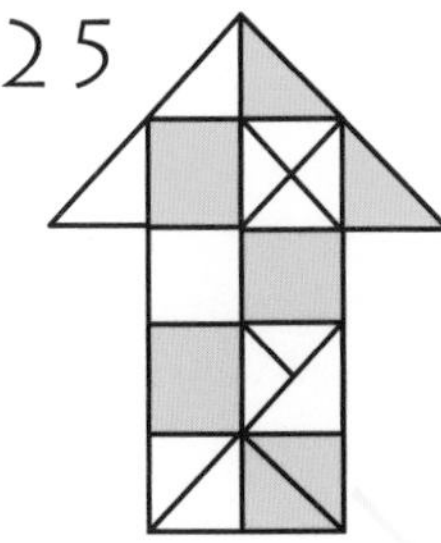

Completed chequered arrow.

26

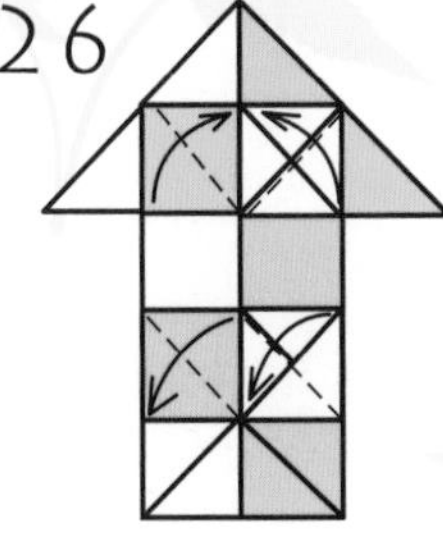

To transform the pattern into a plain simple two coloured arrow, just flip the flaps as shown.

27

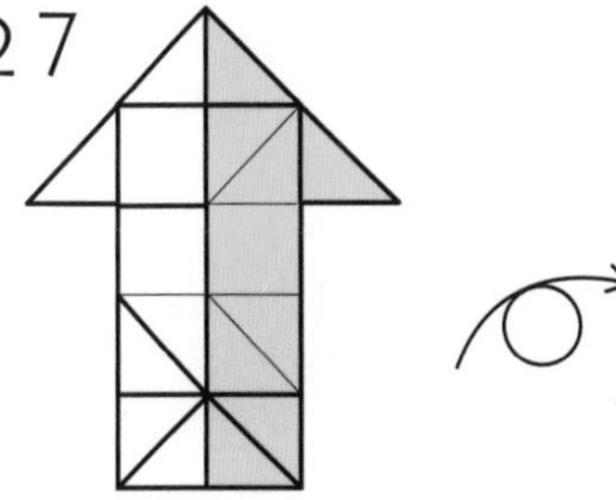

And no fancy patterns, just a normal two coloured arrow. Either way, turn over...

28

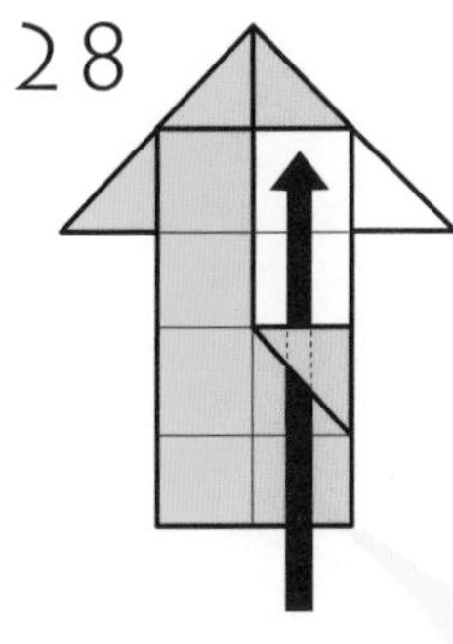

...and you will note the pocket to slip into a page.

29

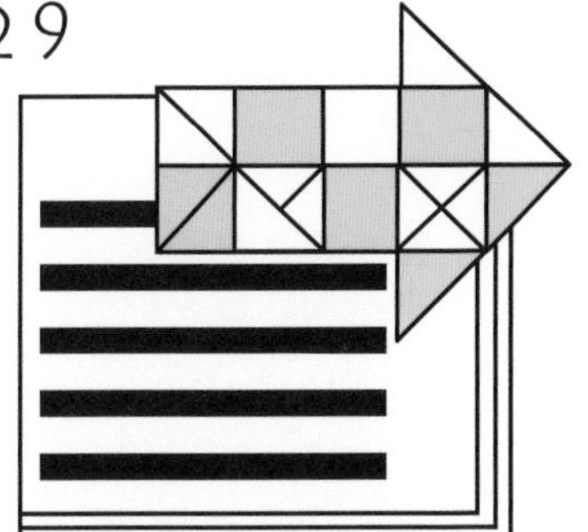

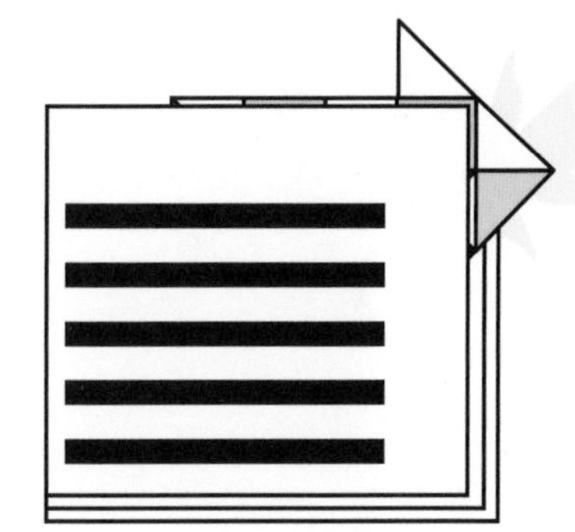

Slotted into a book, this model makes a very nice bookmark.

Pouch

MODEL: Darren Scott
DIAGRAM: Darren Scott

This pouch is an ideal way to store your origami paper. To store 7.5cm squares, start with a sheet of A4 paper. If you don't have any A4 paper handy, a rectangle that's 20 x 30cm (8.3 x 11.2in) will do just fine. This model can even be made large enough to store regular documents.

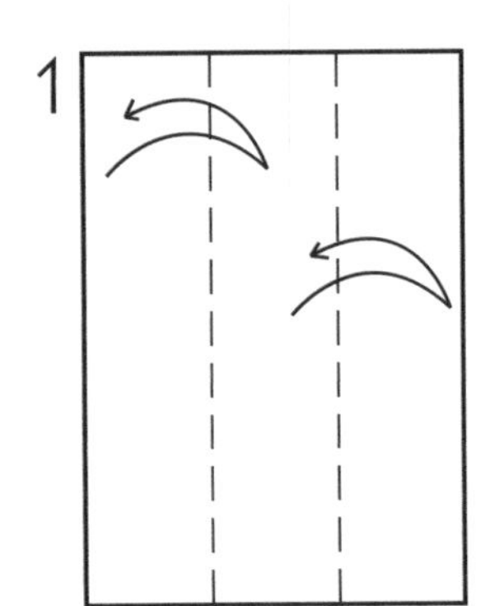

Start with a rectangle A4 or 1:1.5 white side up. Divide into thirds vertically and unfold.

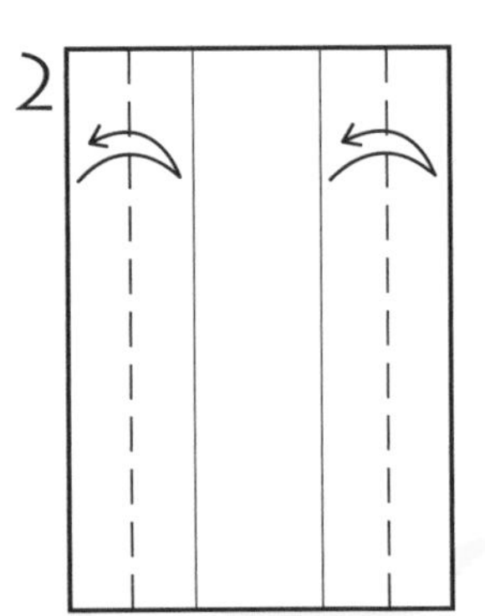

Divide the outer thirds in half and unfold.

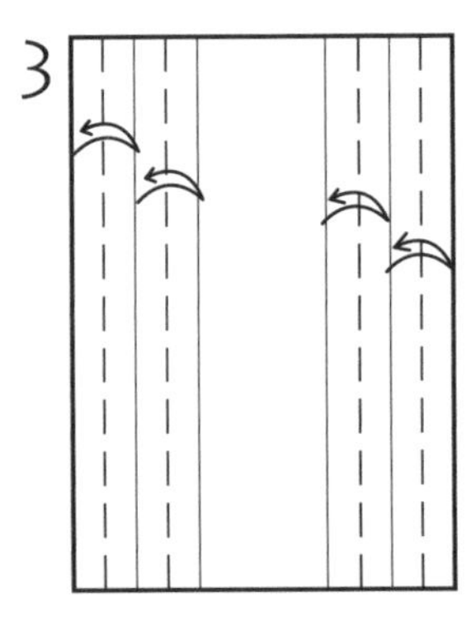

Divide the outer thirds in half again and unfold.

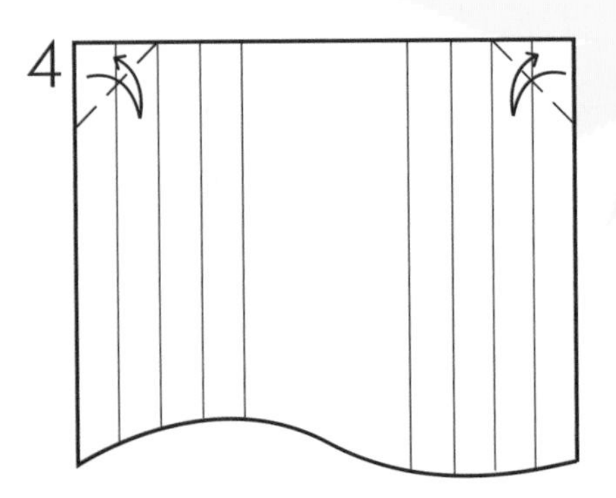

For the next steps we will be looking at the top only. Fold the corners and unfold.

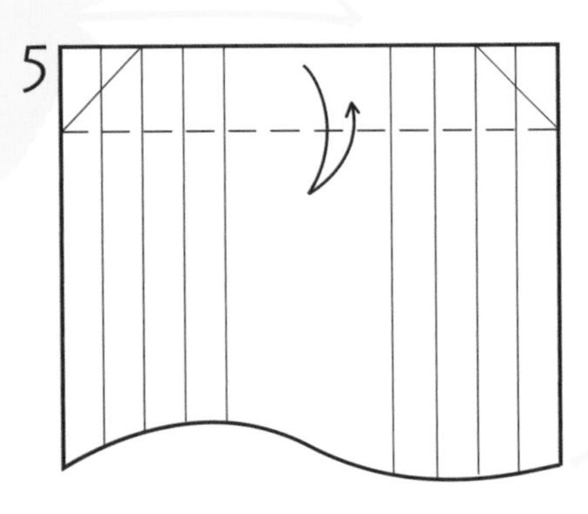

Use the crease marks from step 4 and fold all the way across and unfold.

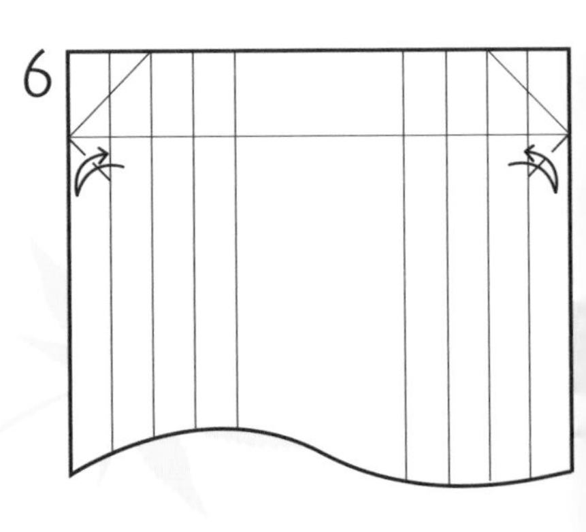

Make two small diagonal creases.

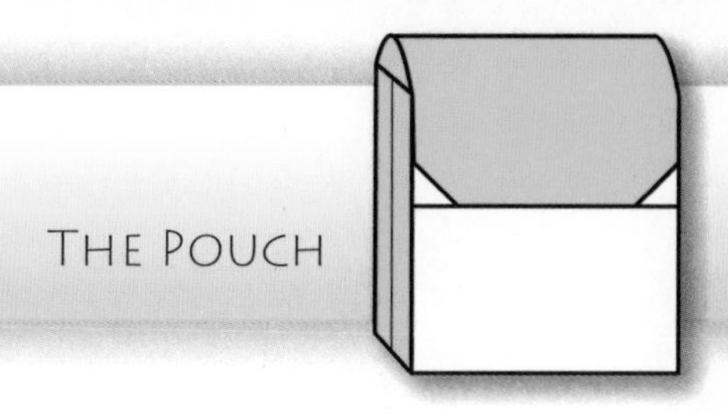

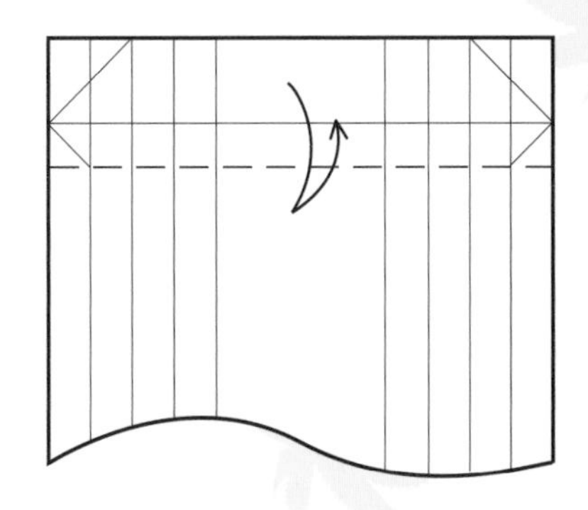

Using creases from step 6 make the horizontal crease and unfold.

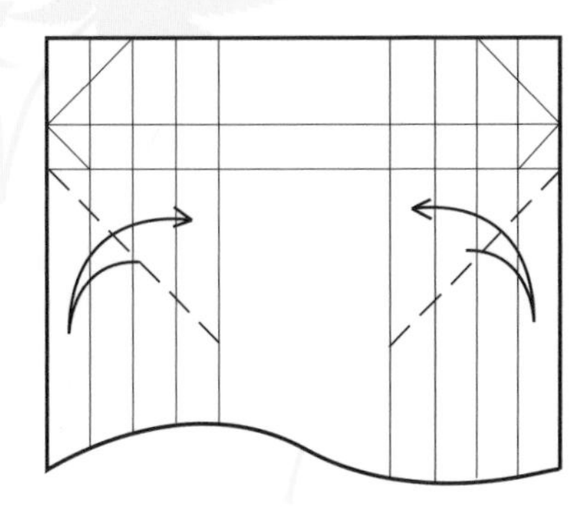

Create the diagonal creases and unfold.

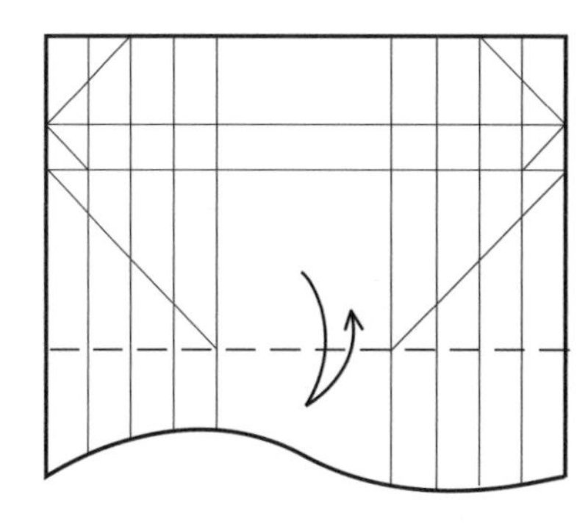

Using creases from step 8 make the horizontal crease and unfold.

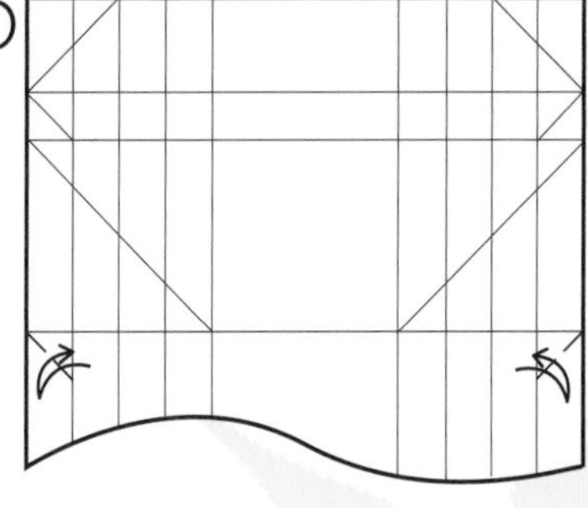

Fold and unfold.

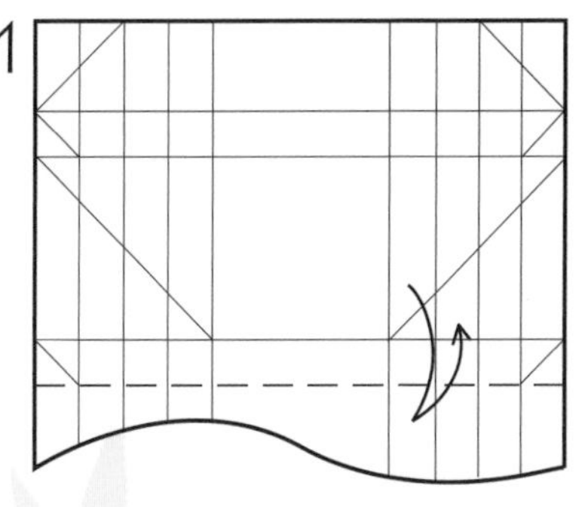

Fold and unfold.

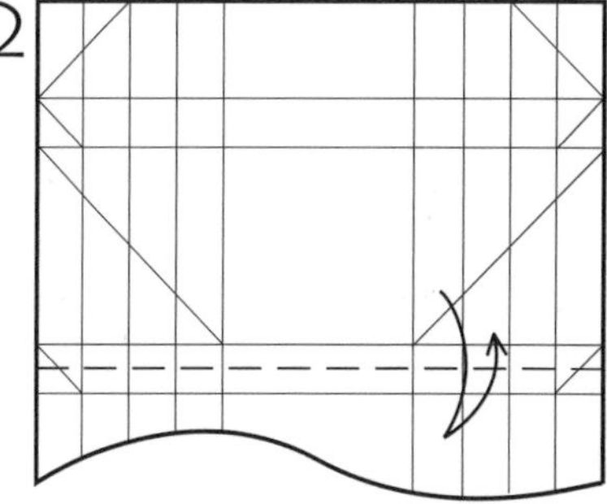

Bring the crease from step 9 and step 11 together to create the new crease.

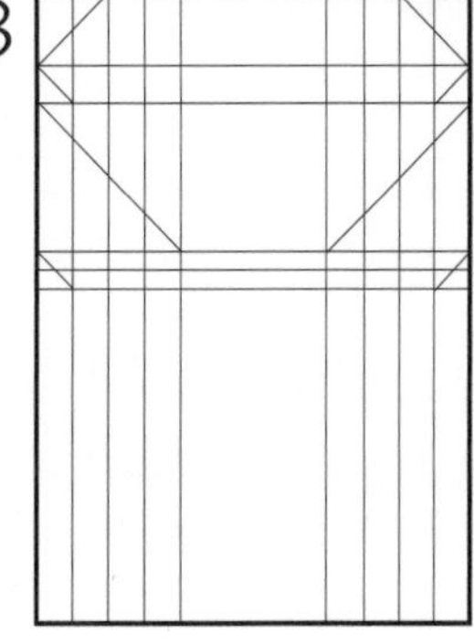

This is the result. Now we will work on the bottom of the sheet.

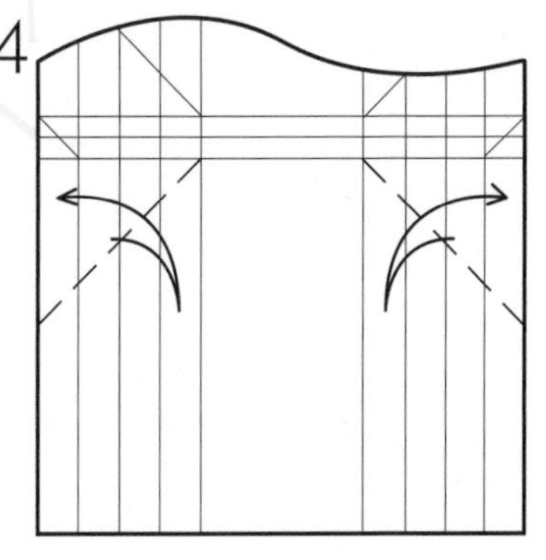

Create more diagonal creases.

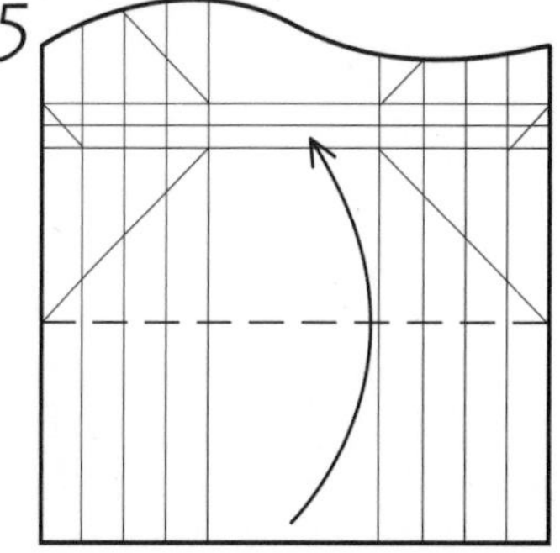

Using the diagonals fold the bottom edge upwards.

The Pouch

MODEL: DARREN SCOT

DIAGRAM: DARREN SCOT

16

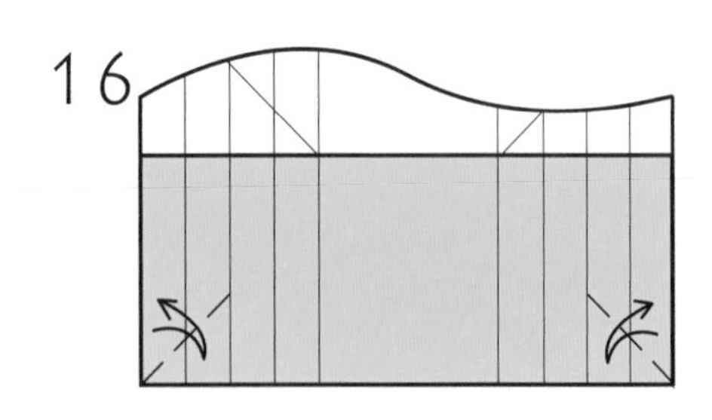

Create more diagonal creases and unfold.

17

Fold the bottom edge back down using step 16 as a guide.

18

Fold the bottom edge up to meet the crease made in step 11.

19

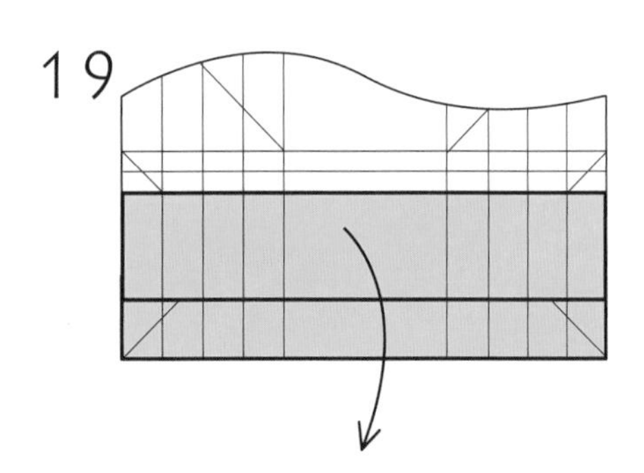

The pre-creasing is now complete. Unfold completely.

20

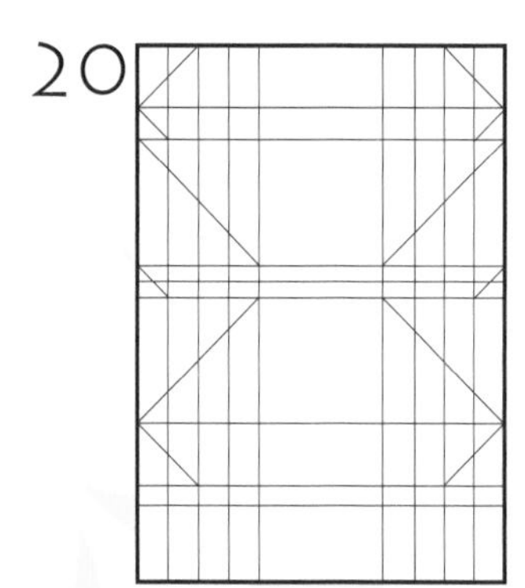

The pre-creased sheet will look like this.

21

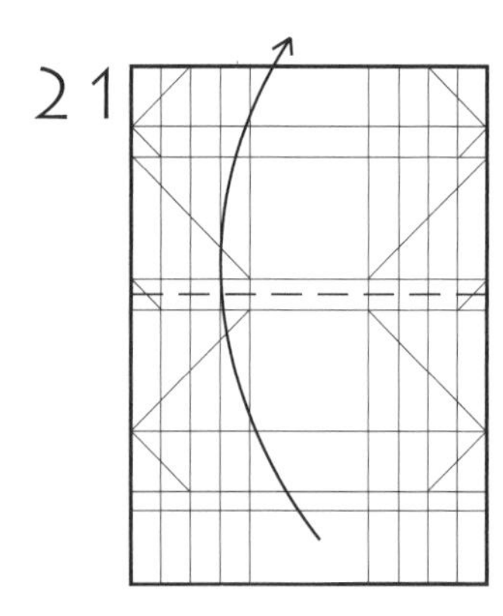

Fold the bottom upwards along the crease made in step 12.

22

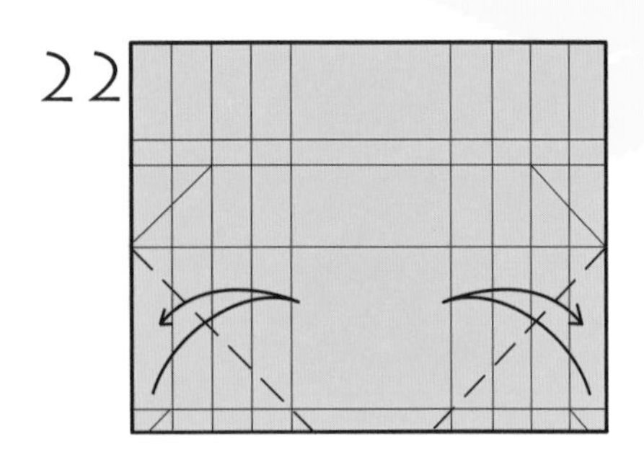

Fold along the diagonals and unfold. These are existing creases.

23

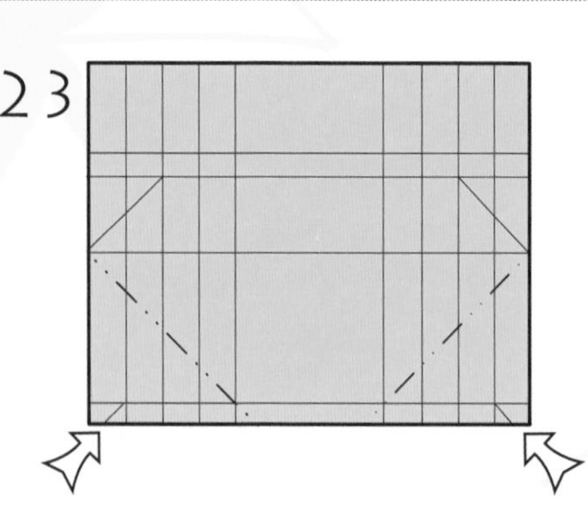

Sink the corners.

24

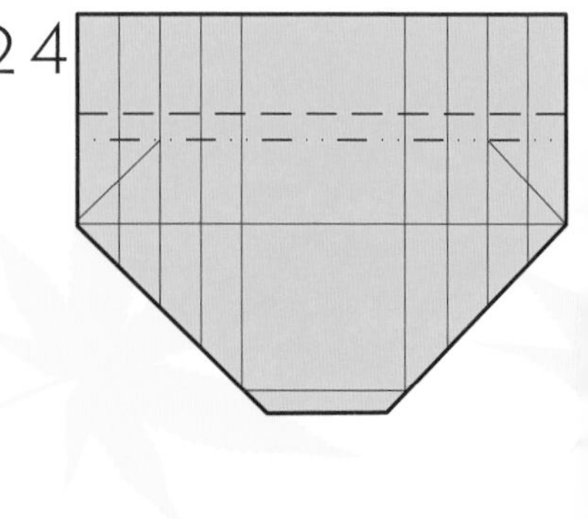

Make a small crimp using creases made in steps 17-18.

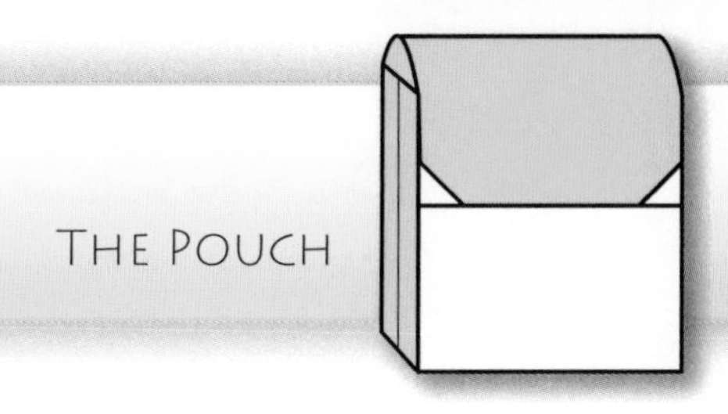

25

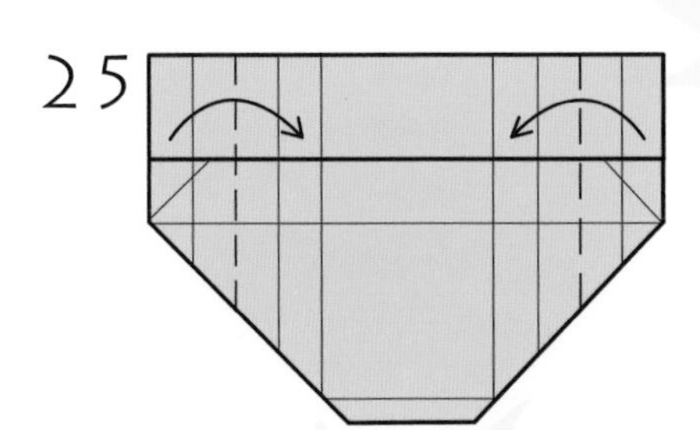

Fold the outside edges on the top layer in using existing creases.

26

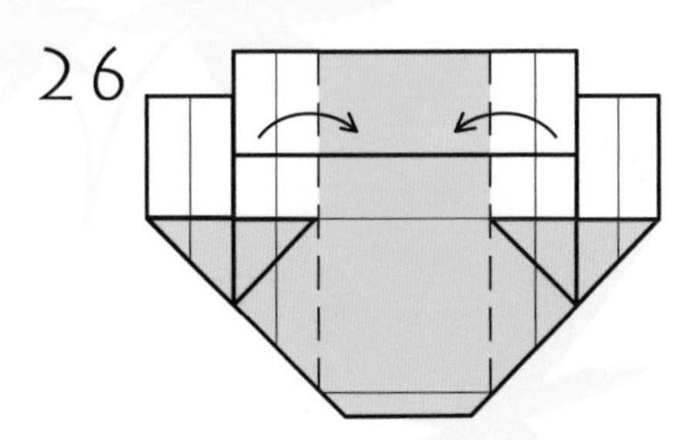

Fold the top layer in again using existing creases.

27

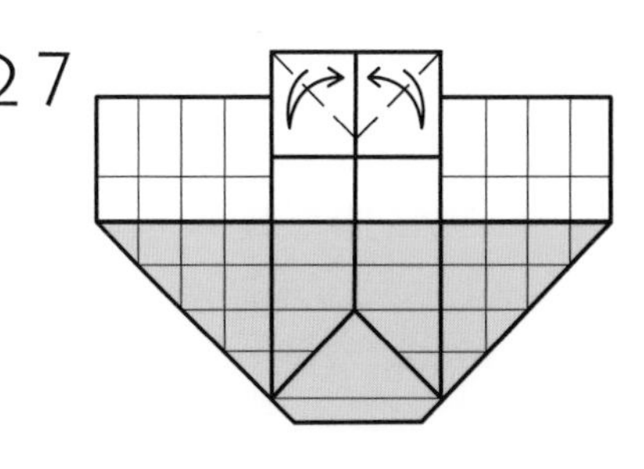

Make the diagonal creases. These will be used in the next step to lock the flap in place.

28

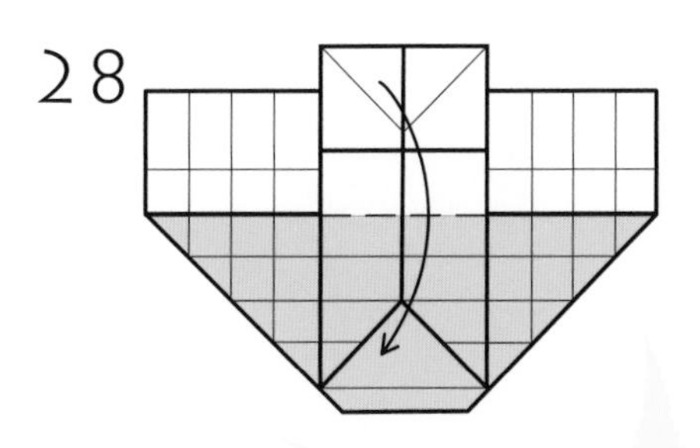

Fold the front flap downwards. Use the triangles from step 27 to lock the flap in place.

29

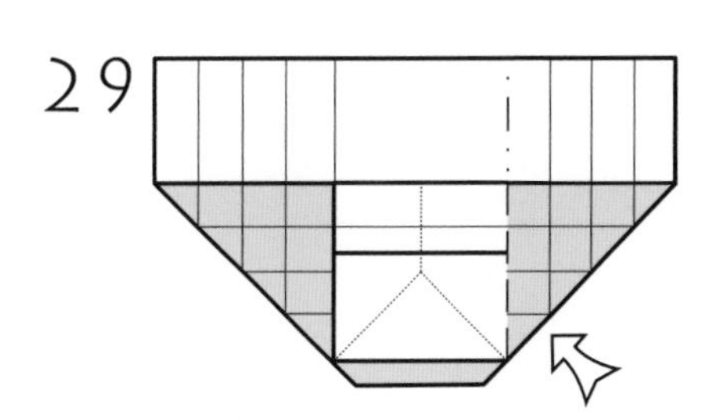

Fold the right-hand flap inwards using the existing creases. This is an inside reverse fold.

30

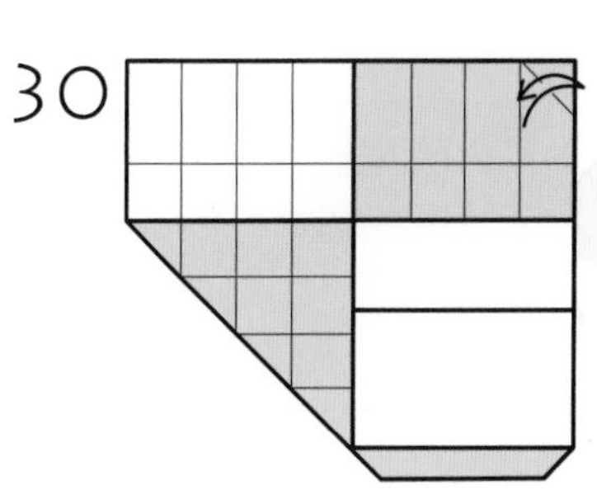

Make the small diagonal crease and unfold.

31

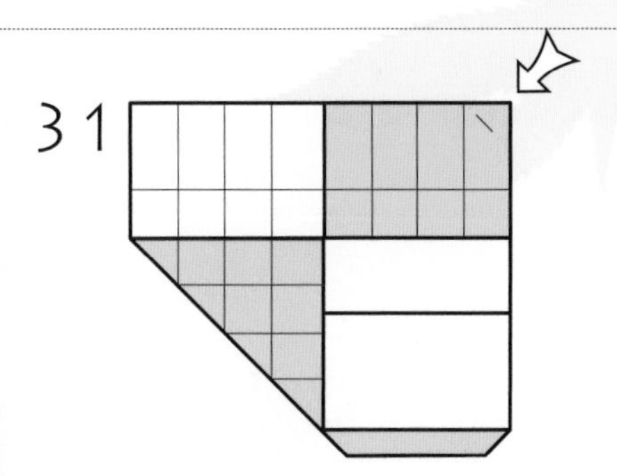

Inside reverse fold the top corner.

32

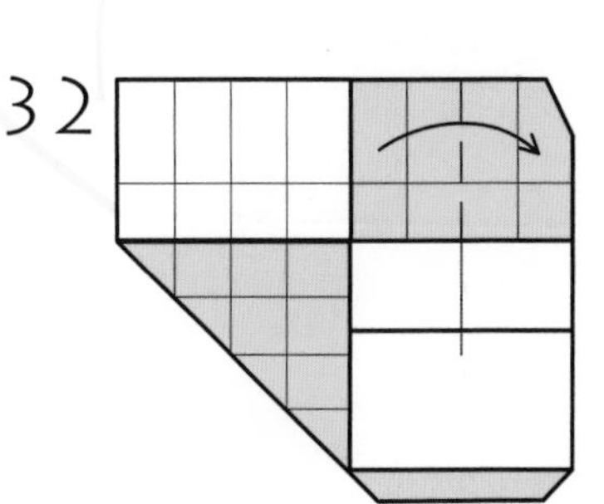

Fold the whole inner layer to the right.

33

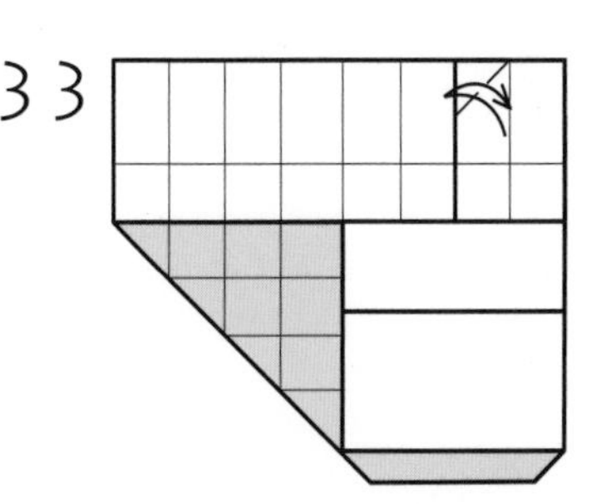

Make another small diagonal crease and unfold.

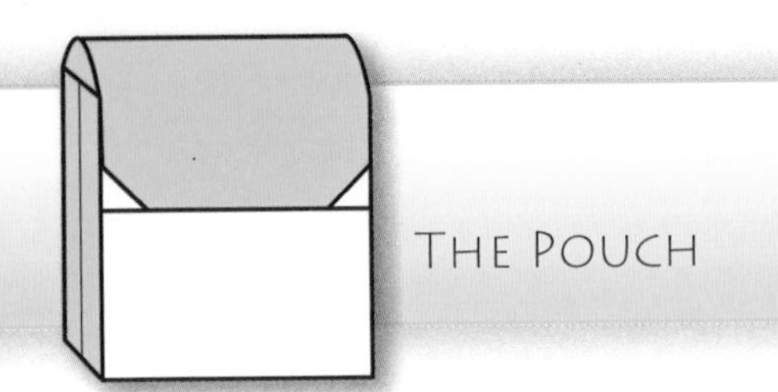

The Pouch

MODEL: Darren Scott
DIAGRAM: Darren Scott

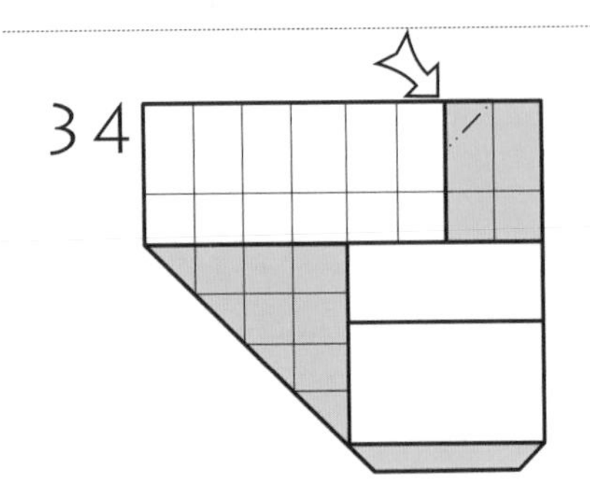

Inside reverse fold the corner.

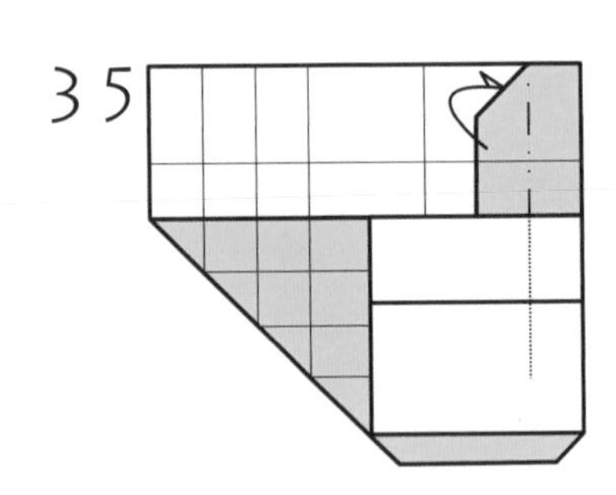

Fold the middle layer back to lock it into place.

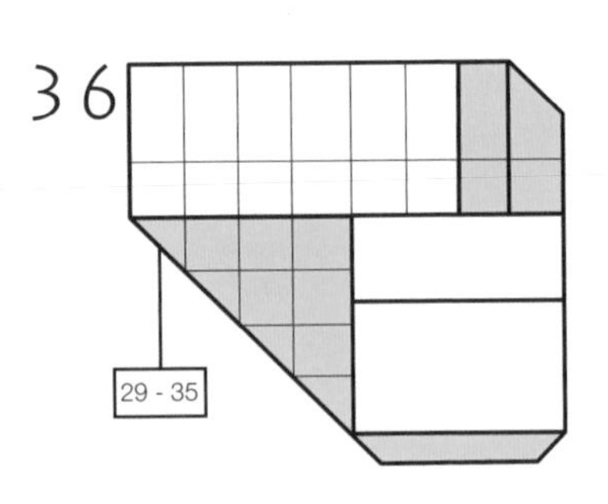

This will be the result. Now repeat steps 29-35 on the left.

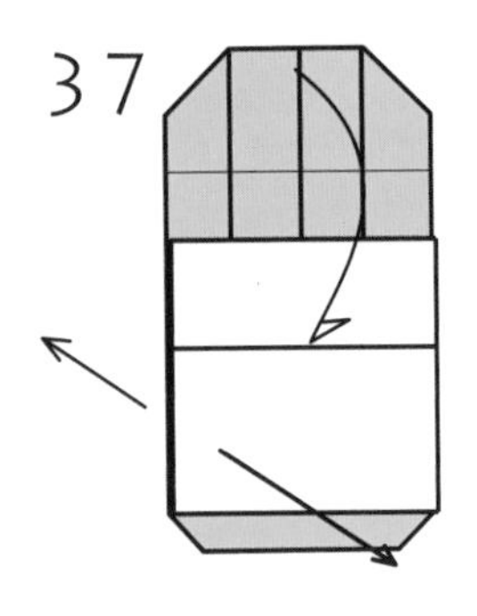

Tuck the flap into the front pocket and expand the pouch.

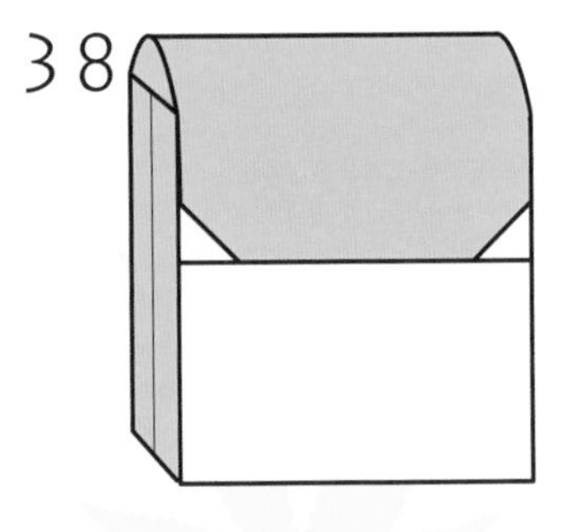

Completed pouch.

MANDARIN DUCK

MODEL: STEVEN CASEY
DIAGRAM: STEVEN CASEY

The mandarin duck is inspired by a traditional model. The mandarin duck is a migratory bird, and flies to southern China and Japan during the winter months. The male mandarin duck has very distinctive patterning on its head, so use a decorative sheet of paper.

A Chinese proverb relates loving couples to 'two mandarin ducks playing in water'.

1

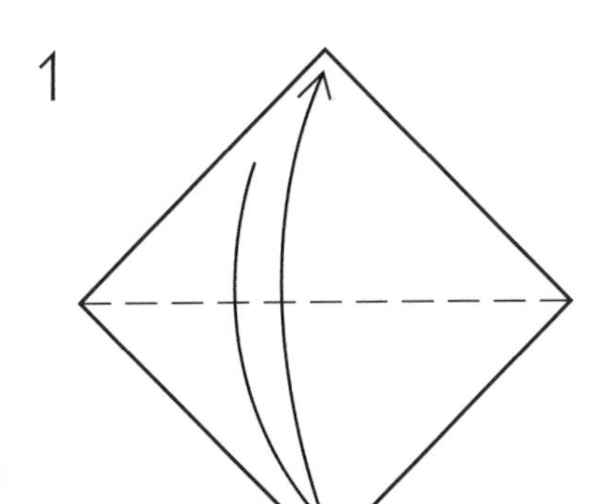

Start with white side up. Fold and unfold diagonal.

2

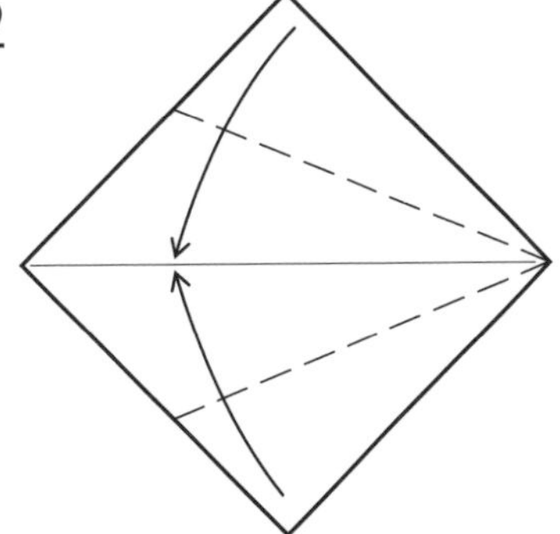

Fold both sides to the middle.

3

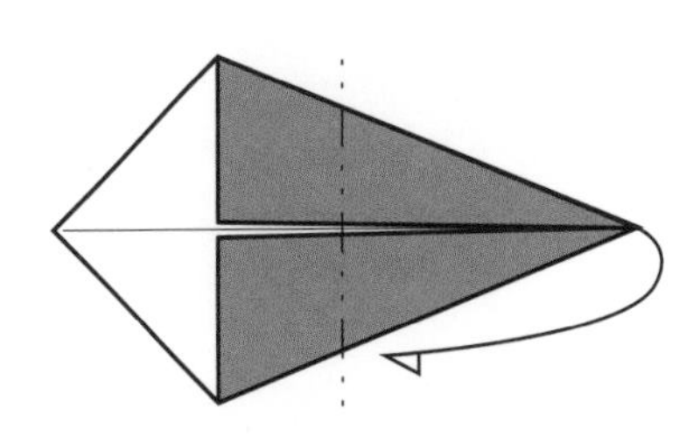

Mountain fold in half behind.

4

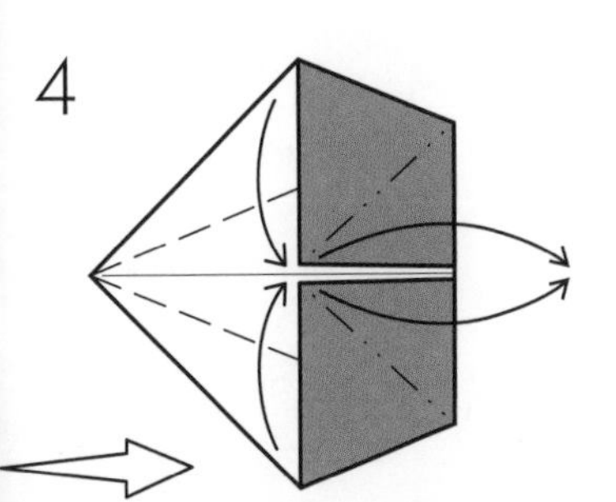

Squash fold both sides.

5

Mountain fold the back layer behind.

6

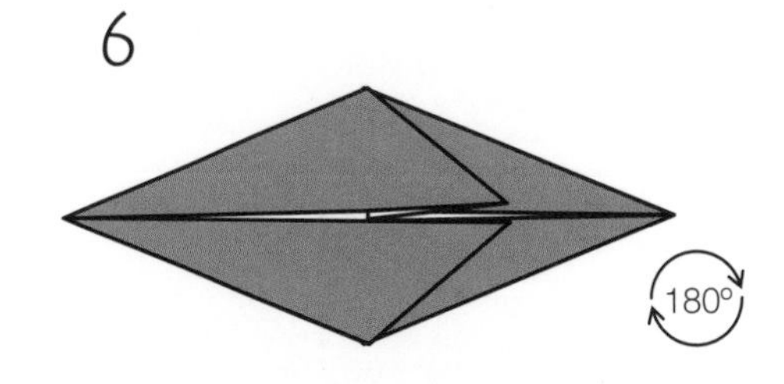

This is known as the fish base. Rotate 180°.

7

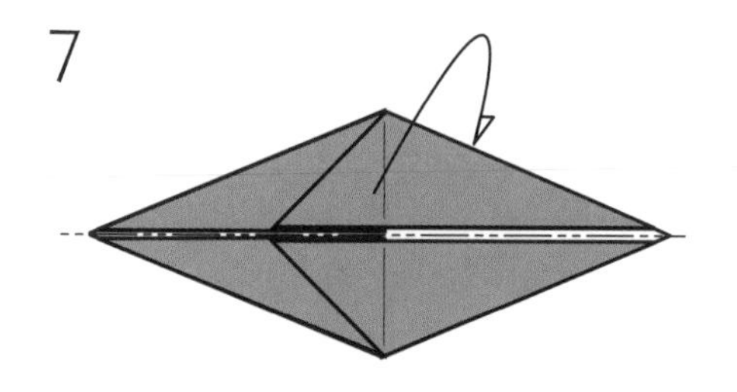

Fold top half behind.

8

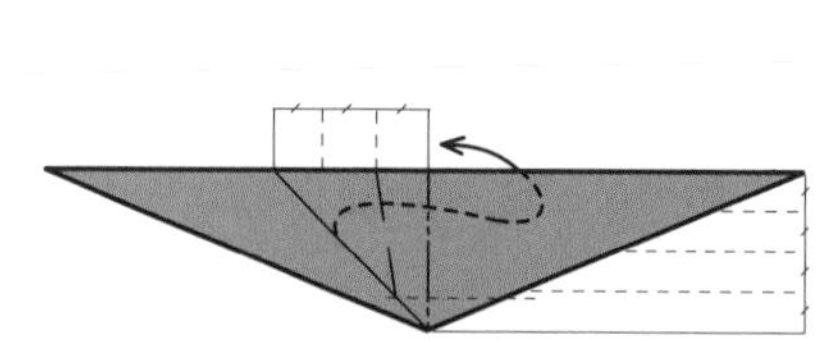

Double reverse fold small flaps. Repeat behind.

9

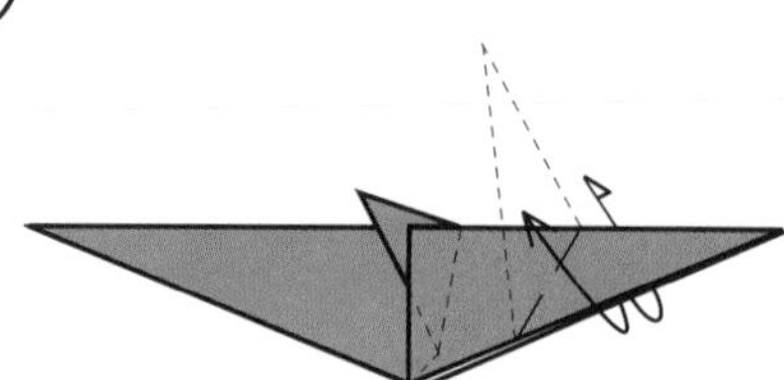

Outside reverse right point.

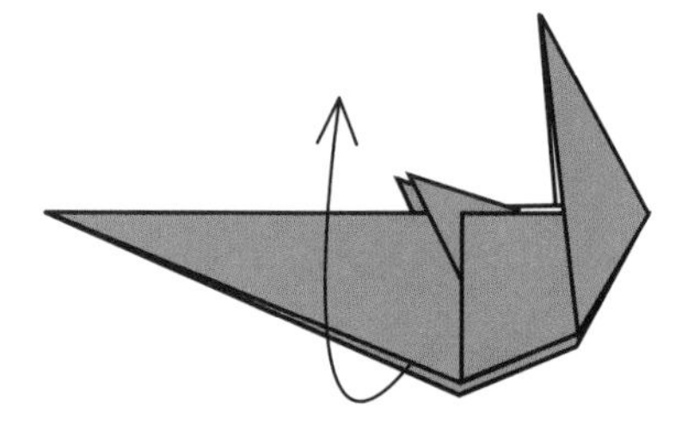

Lift layer upward.

11

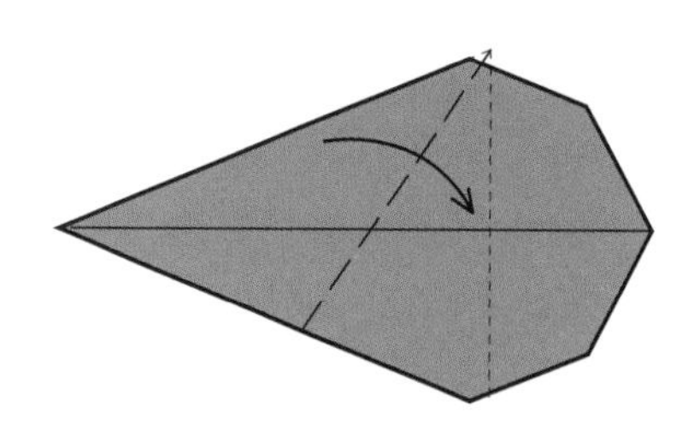

Fold top edge in line with dotted vertical line.

12

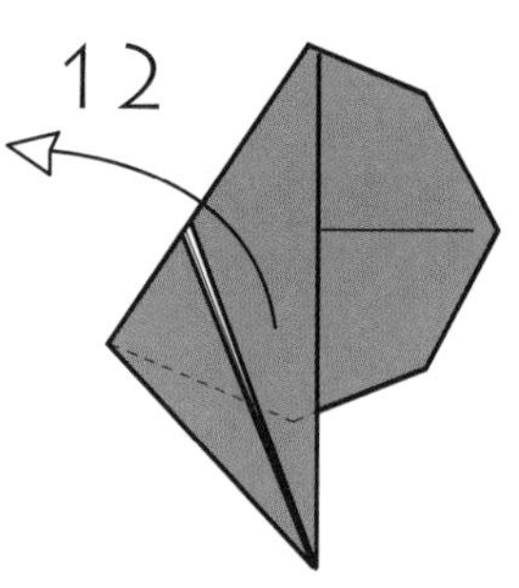

Unfold.

13

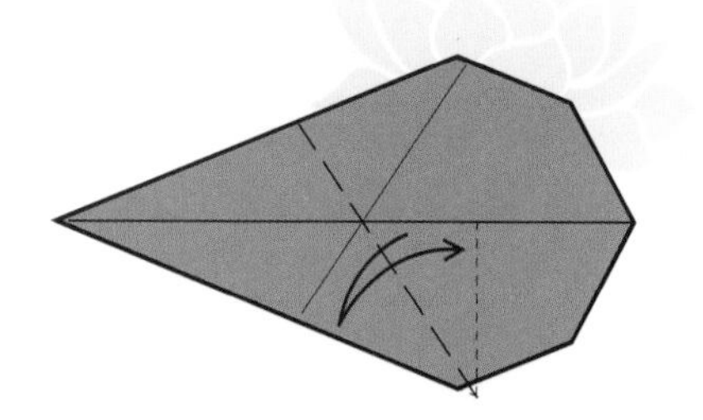

Repeat in other direction.

14

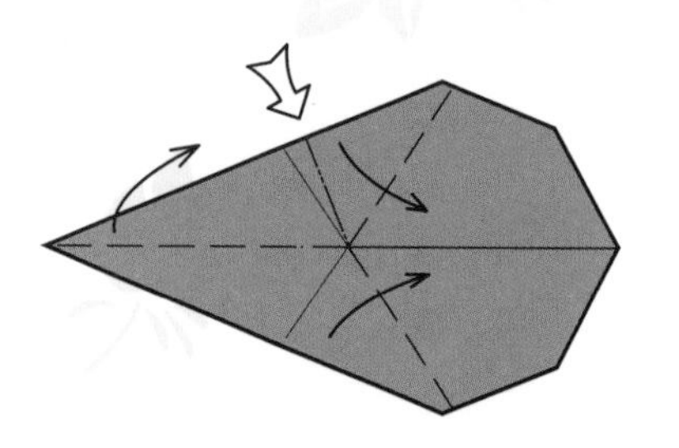

Rabbit ear on existing creases.

15

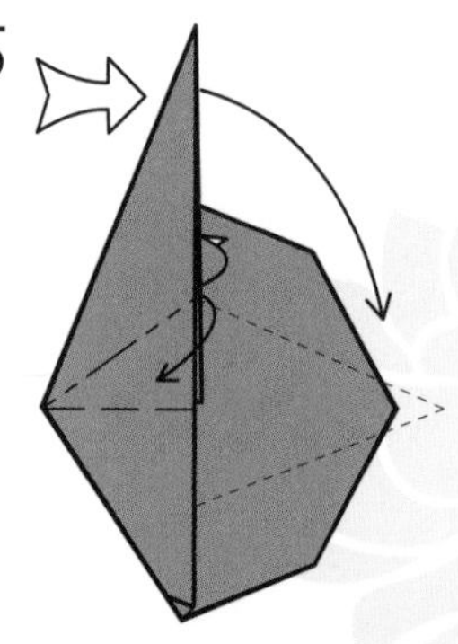

Lift the point upwards and squash fold.

16

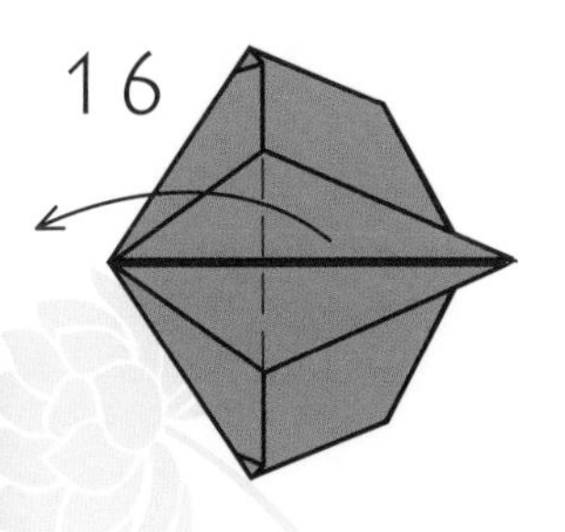

Valley fold the top point to the left.

17

Fold top half down in front.

18

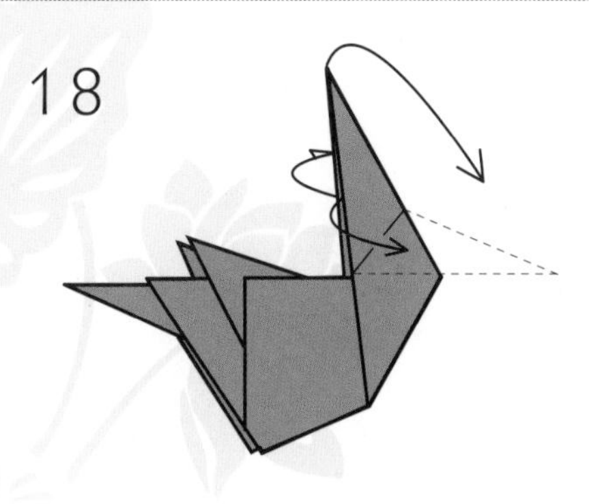

Outside reverse.

19

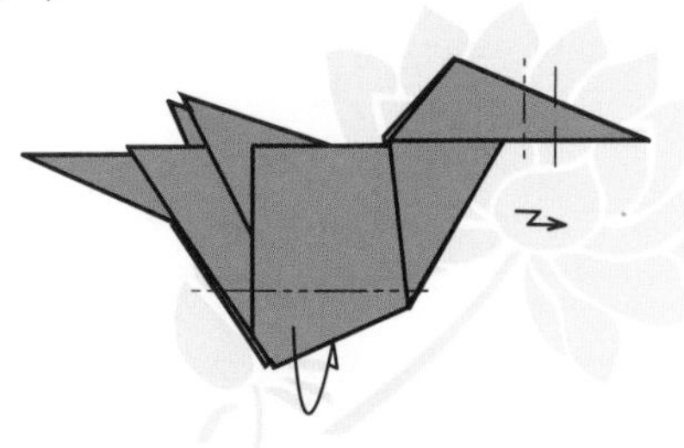

Fold bottom edge under and into body.
Double reverse point to form bill.

20

Completed mandarin duck.

Labrador

MODEL: Steven Casey
DIAGRAM: Steven Casey

The labrador is a smart dog: obedient, energetic, affectionate and faithful. Use a large sheet 30cm (12in) or larger of black, brown or golden paper to make your favourite coloured labrador.

The labrador breed is so intelligent and reliable that they make up about 60% of all guide dogs.

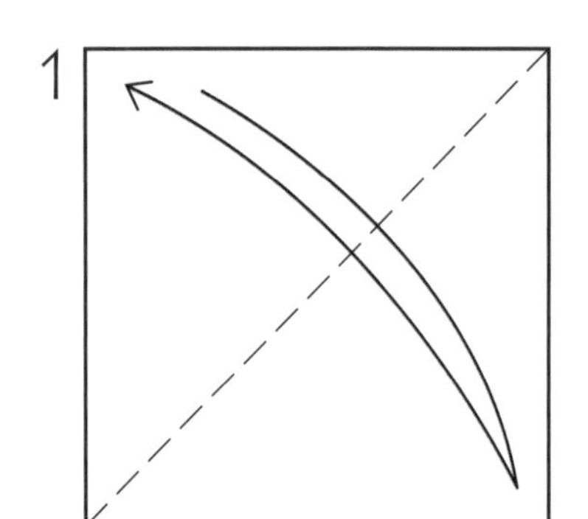

Begin white side up.
Fold and unfold diagonal.

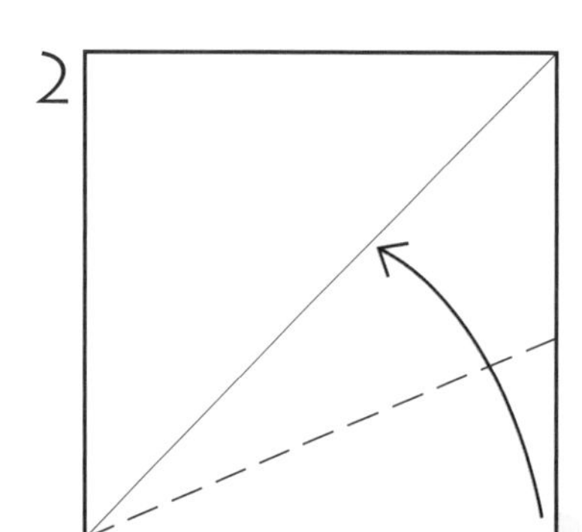

Fold bottom edge to diagonal crease.

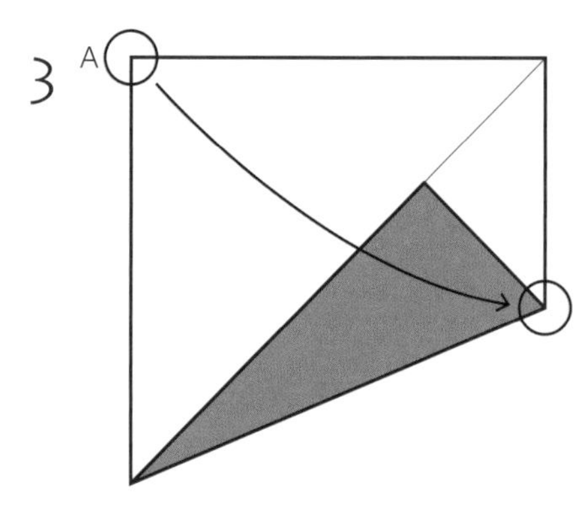

Fold point A to point B, make a small crease at top.

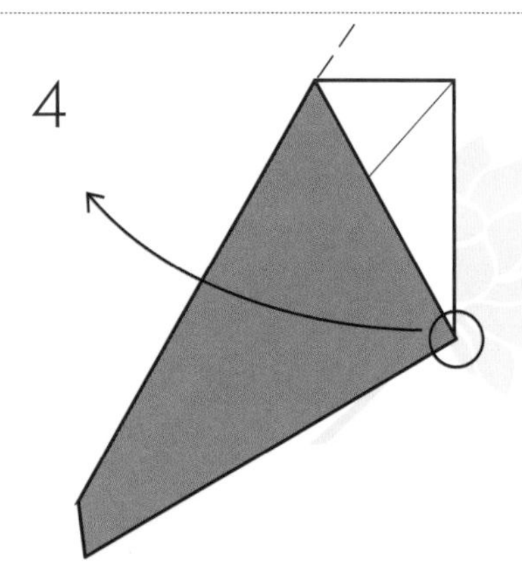

The top left corner marks one third.

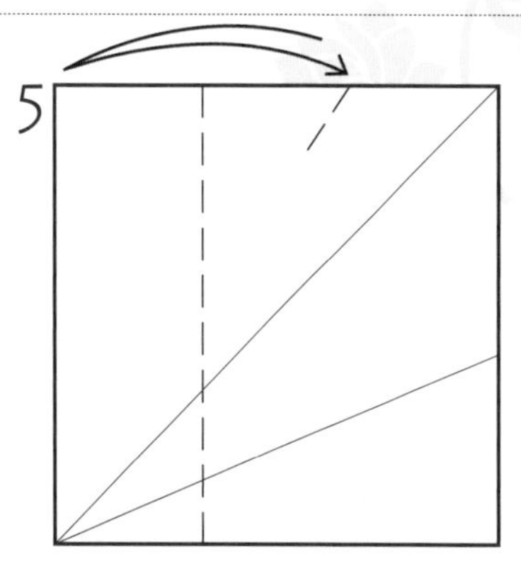

Fold the edge to meet the third.

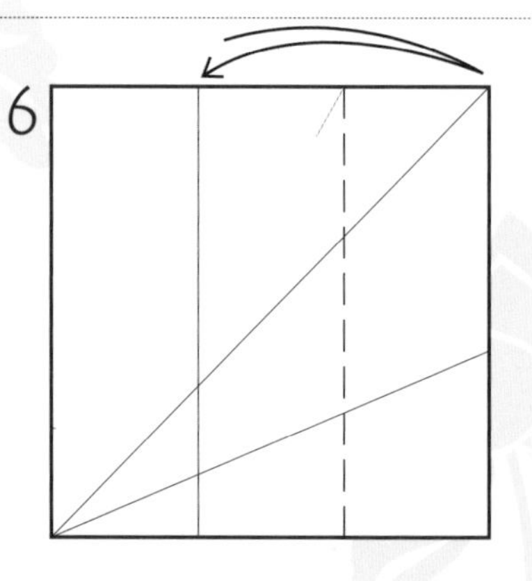

Fold the other edge to meet fold from step 5.

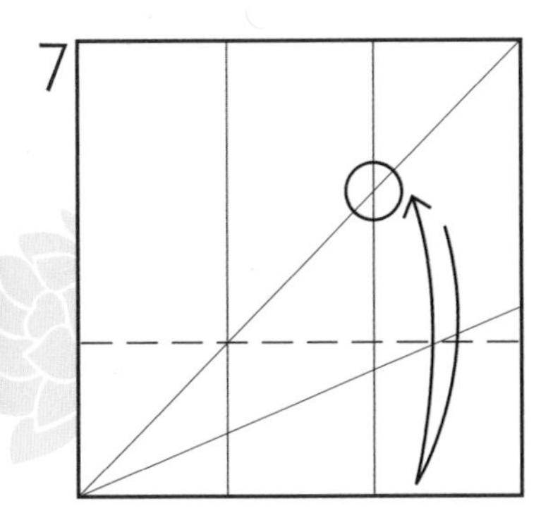

Fold the bottom edge to meet the marked intersection, then unfold.

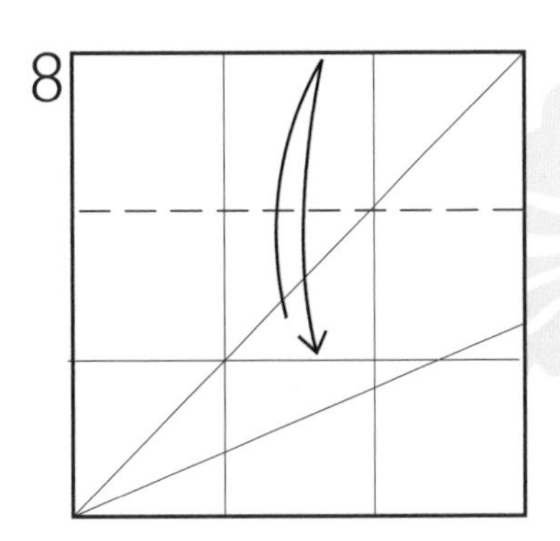

Fold top edge to meet fold from step 7.

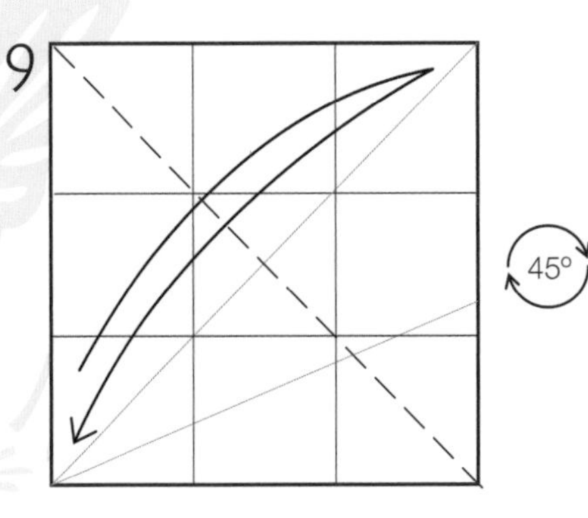

Fold and unfold diagonal. Rotate 45°.

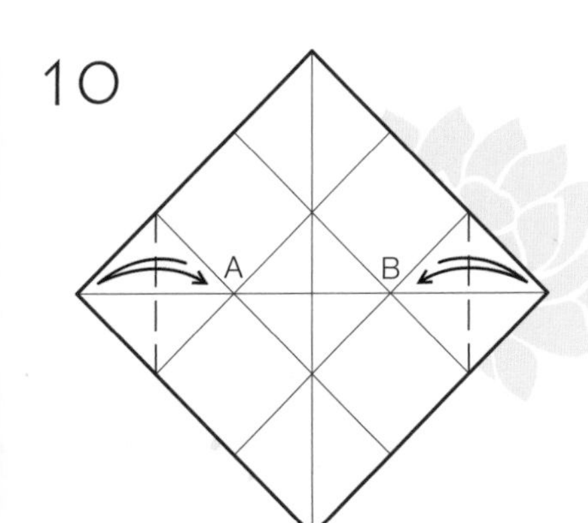

Fold side corners to points A and B then unfold.

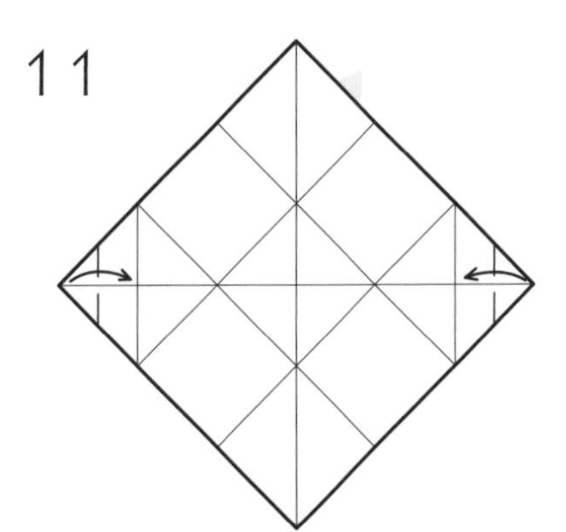

Fold side corners to crease made in step 10.

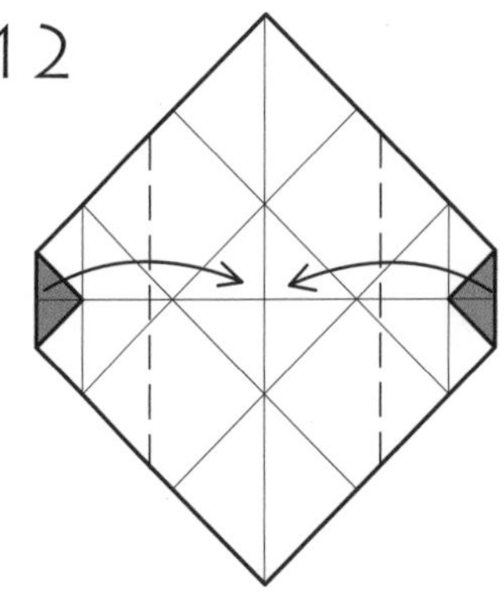

Fold sides into the centre.

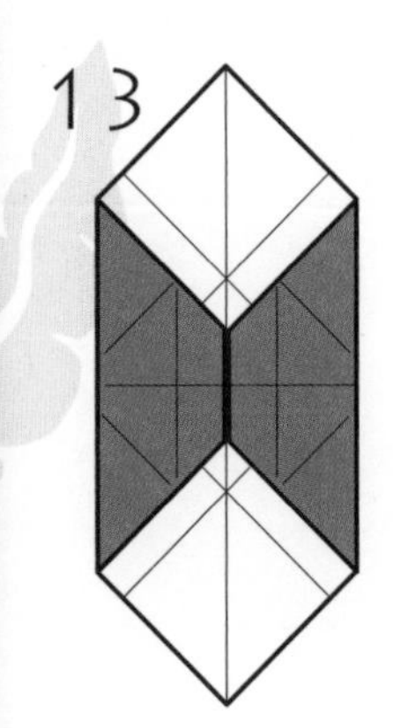

Rotate model 90°.

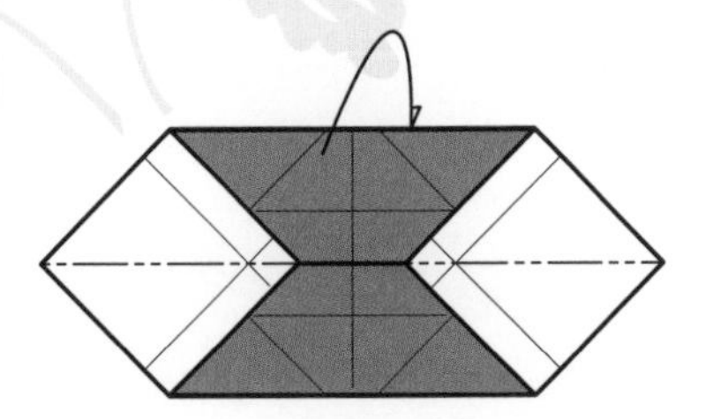

Mountain fold top half behind.

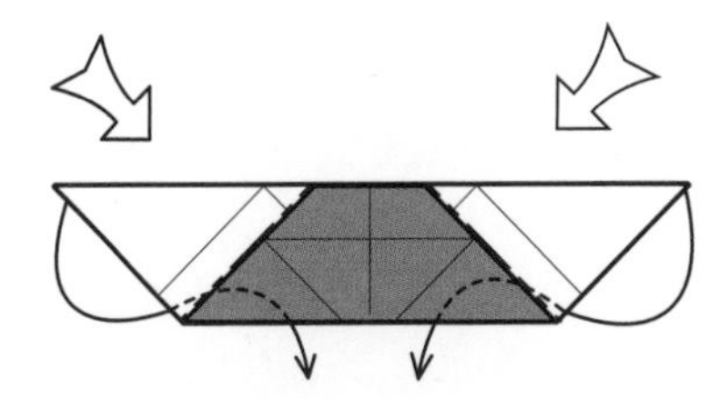

Reverse fold side flaps. Next step changes scale.

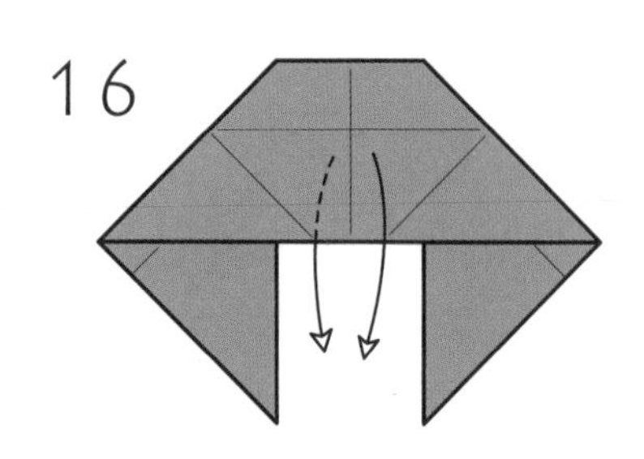

Fold single flaps down in front and behind.

17

Sink top section. Unfold the corner from behind.

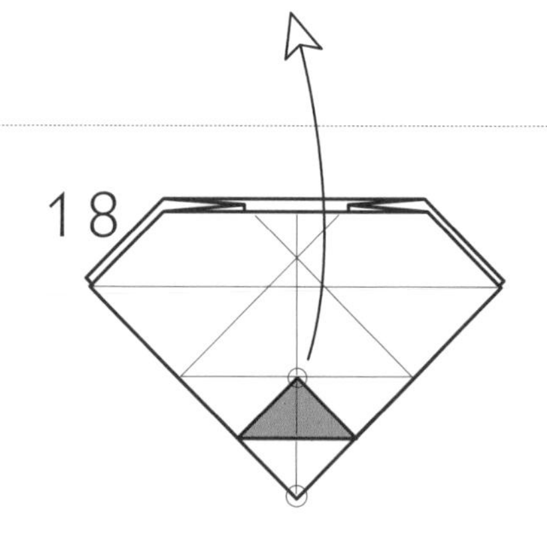

Hold lower corner and pull upper corner to open out model completely. Scale is reduced next step.

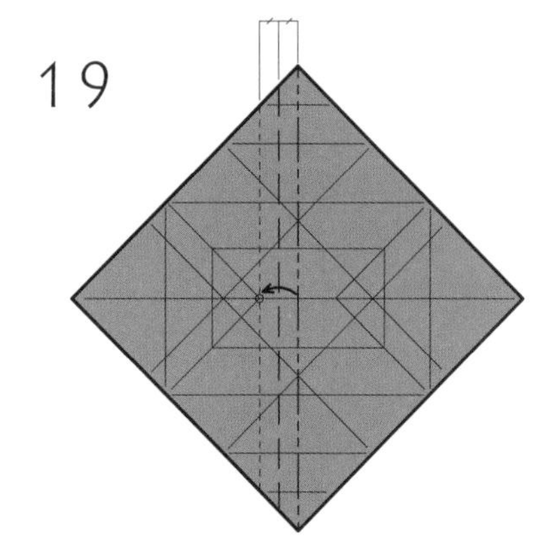

Add a diagonal pleat.

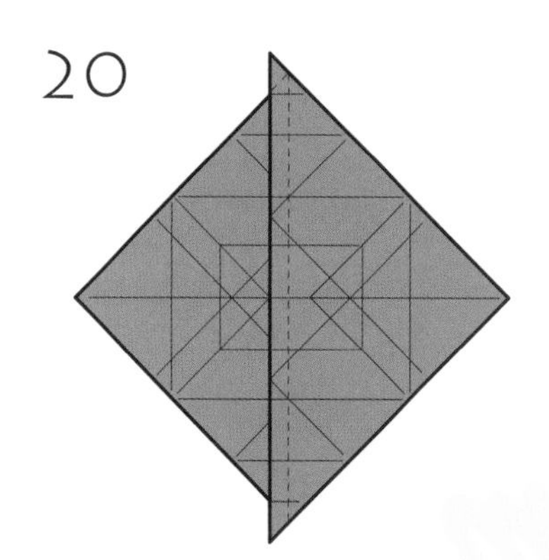

Turn over top to bottom.

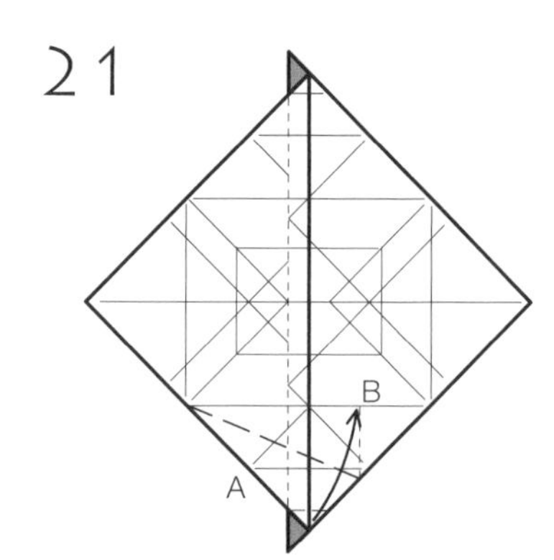

Fold edge A to crease B.

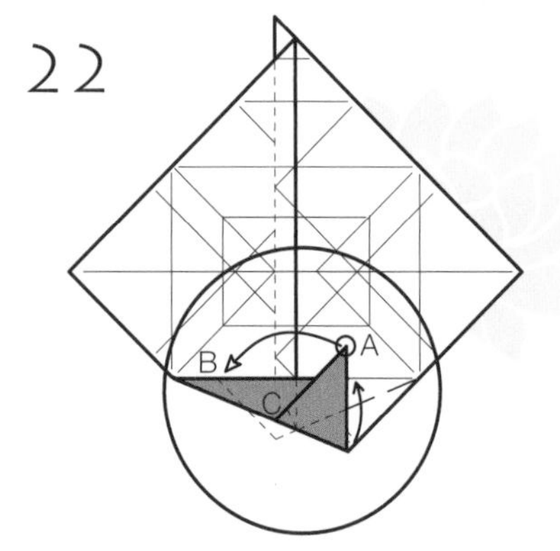

Grab point A and rotate until it touches raw edge B. Corner C drops down.

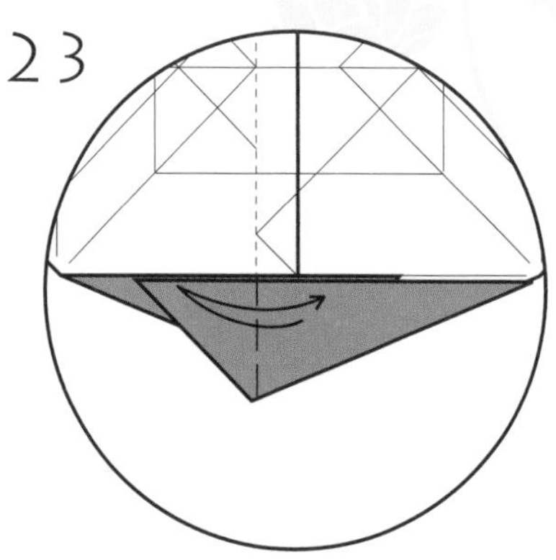

Pre-crease.

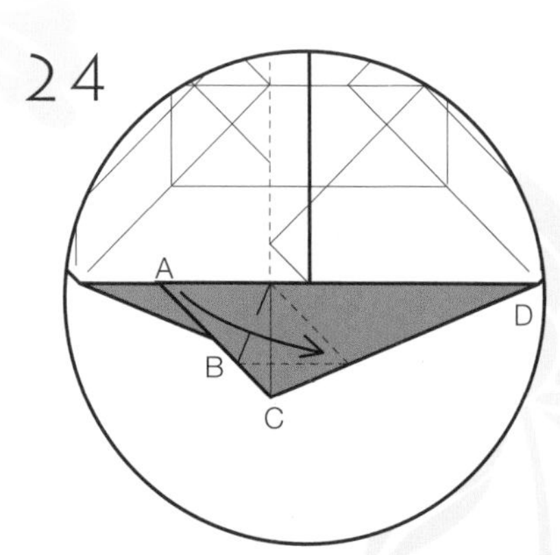

Fold point A to touch the diagonal line C-D. The line A-B should be horizontal.

25

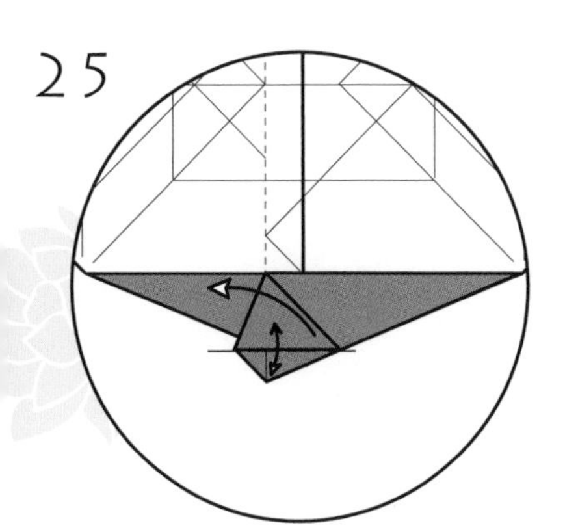

Pre-crease lower edge. Unfold the upper flap.

26

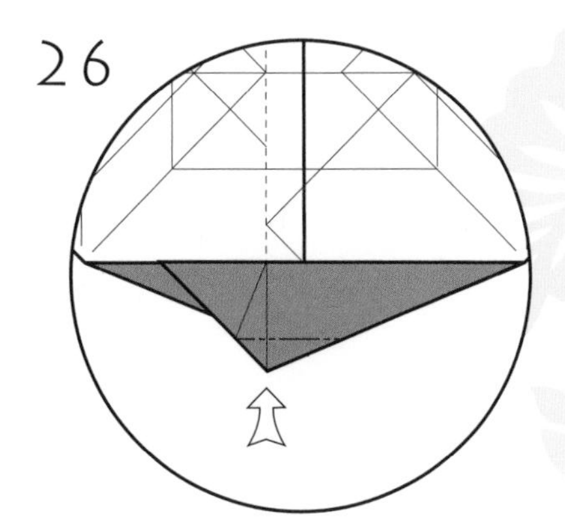

Sink lower edge.

27

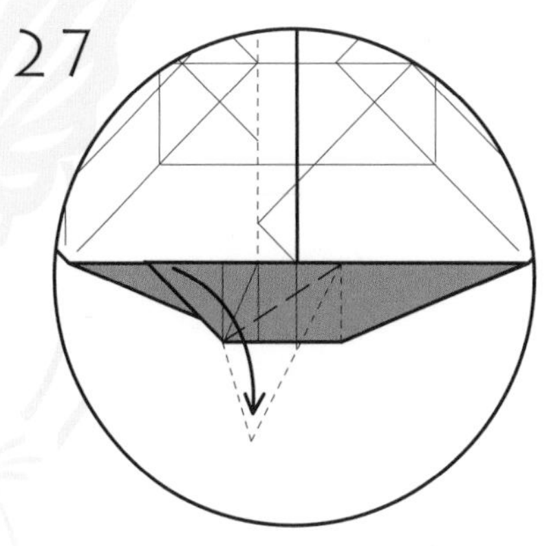

Fold flap down. The layers behind separate and flatten.

28

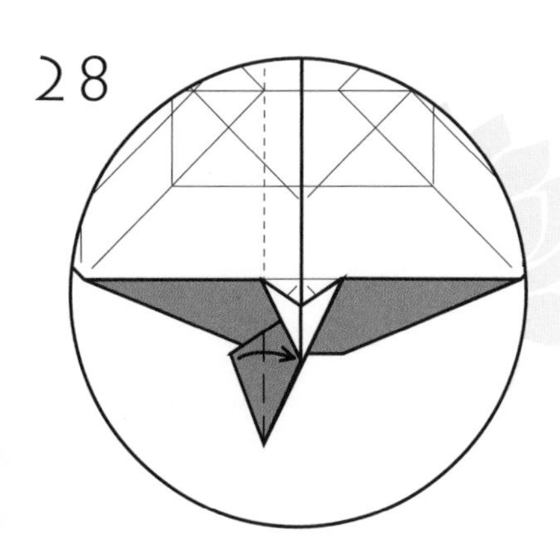

Valley fold to narrow flap. Next step shows full view.

29

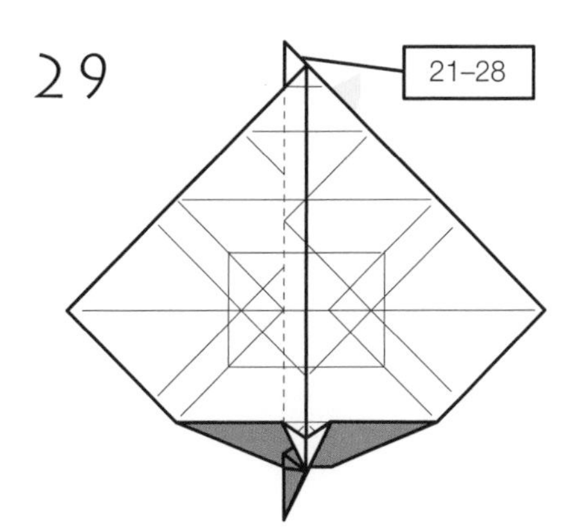

Repeat steps 21–28 on the top half of the model.

30

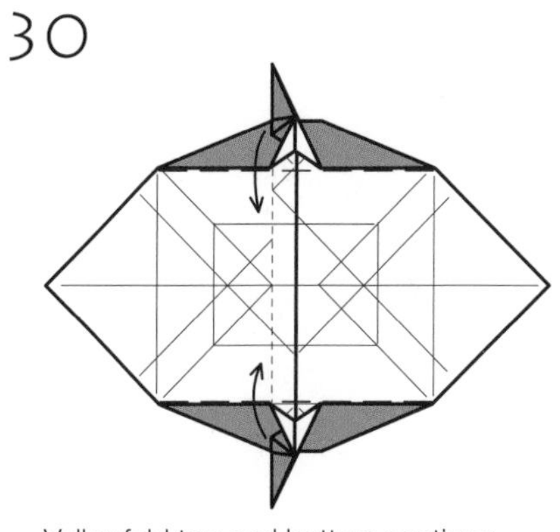

Valley fold top and bottom sections inward.

31

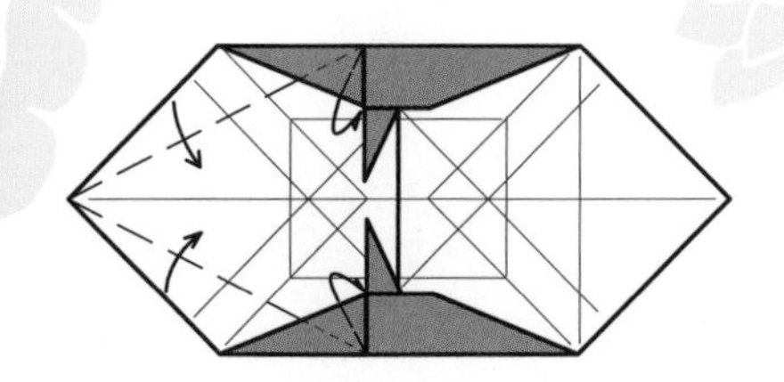

Swivel fold.

32

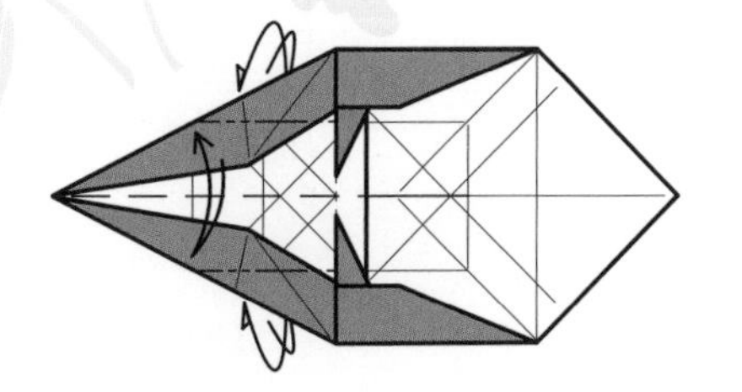

Add some additional creases.

33

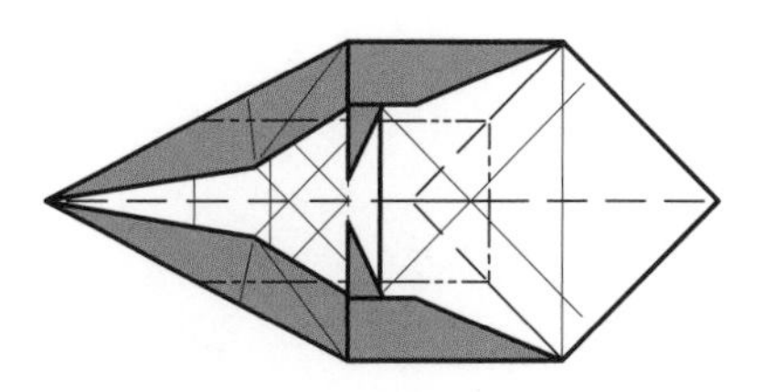

Collapse using existing creases.

34

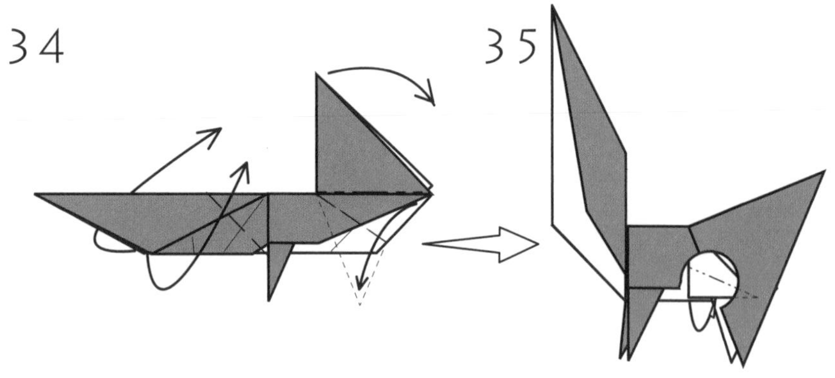

Outside reverse fold. Crimp right flaps down.

35

Cut-away view: Bisect inside triangle and then reverse fold.

36

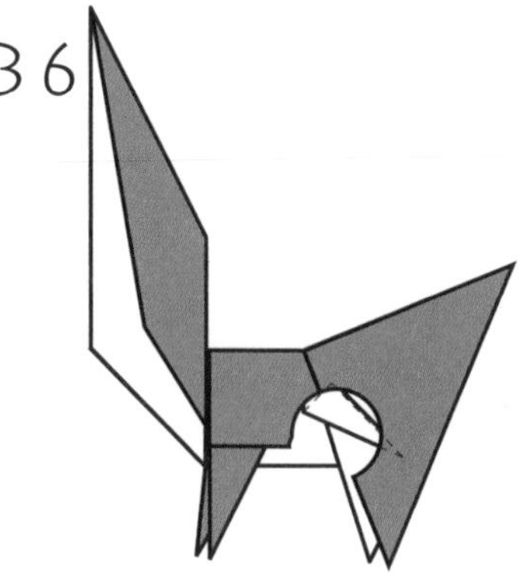

This is the result.

37

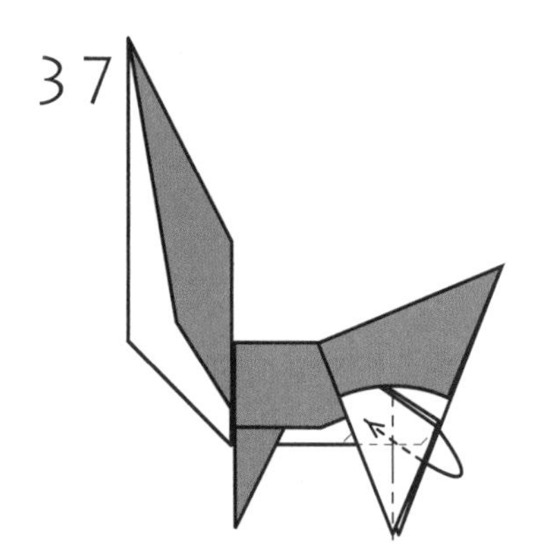

Cut-away view: Reverse fold inside corner. Repeat on other side.

38

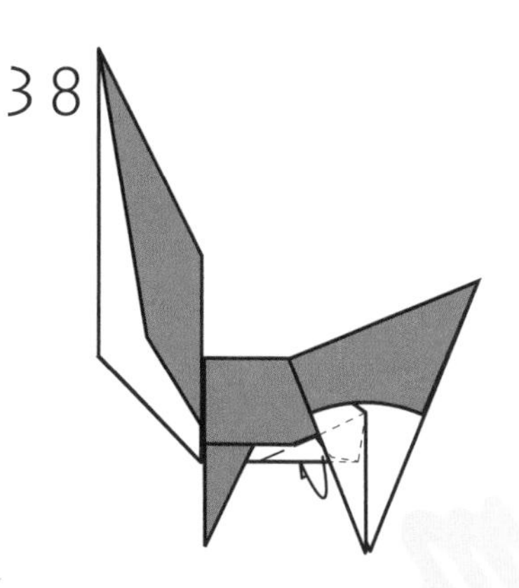

Fold lower flap up into the body. Repeat on other side.

39

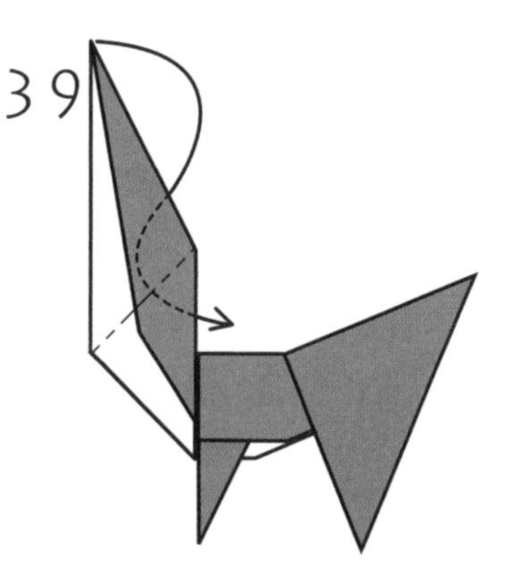

Reverse fold head section.

40

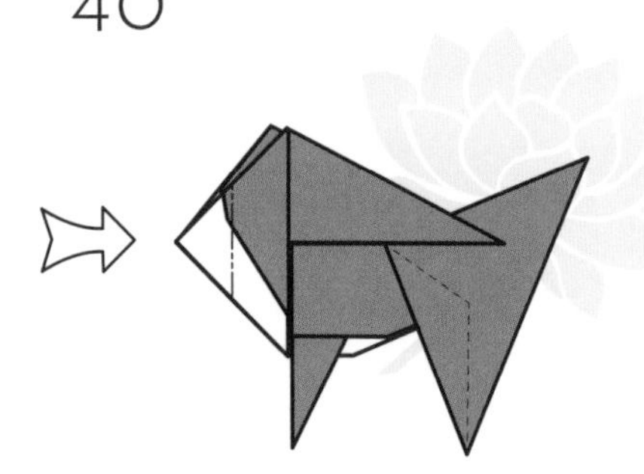

Open sink.

41

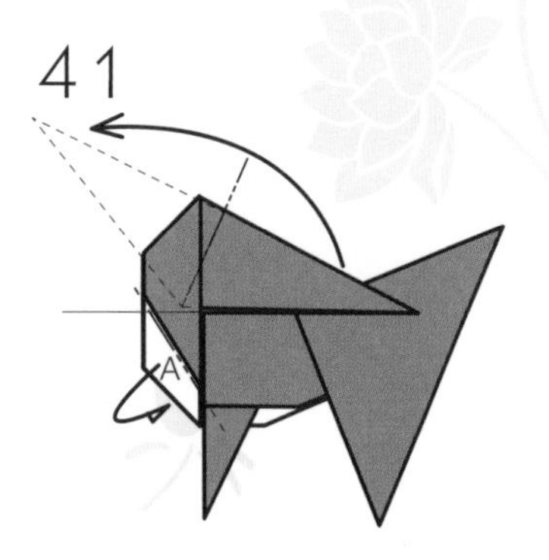

Reverse fold head point. Tuck flap A into body. Repeat on other side.

42

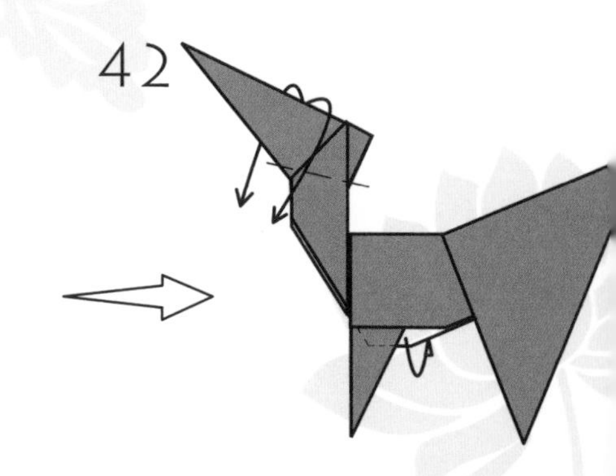

Tuck flap up into body. Outside reverse fold head.

43

Double reverse fold to form muzzle.
Reverse fold tail.

44

Add crimp to form ears. Narrow tail and legs with a swivel fold. Inside reverse fold to shorten the nose.

45

Reverse fold tail, and use inside reverse folds to shape ears.

46

Tuck in flap at base of tail.
Crimp hind legs.

47

Crimp all feet. Narrow tail.

48

Completed labrador.

MOUSE

MODEL: STEVEN CASEY
DIAGRAM: STEVEN CASEY

The mouse is a member of the rodent family. This mouse resembles the well-known common house mouse, with alert ears and a long tail. Attempt this model first with a 30cm (12in) sheet before progressing onto a smaller sheet size for a life-size mouse.

The mouse is regarded as the third most successful mammal on the planet, due to its ability to adapt to almost any environment.

1

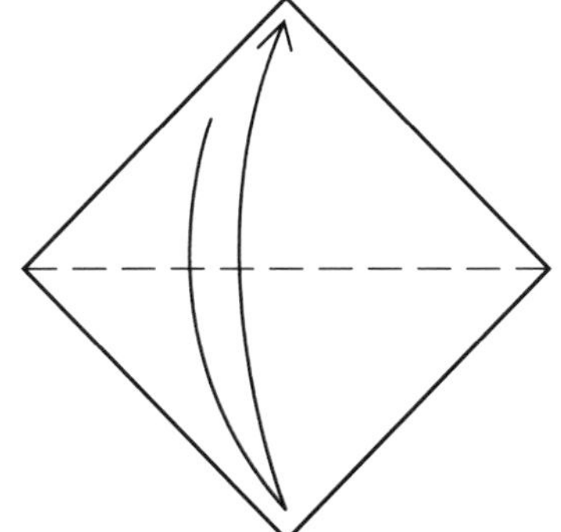

Begin white side up.
Fold and unfold diagonal.

2

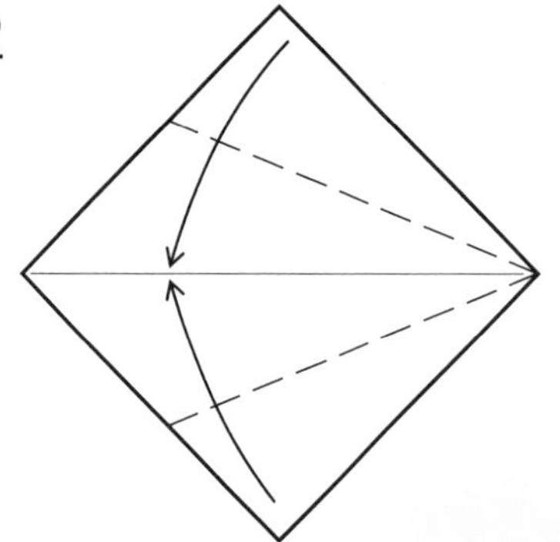

Fold both sides to the middle.

3

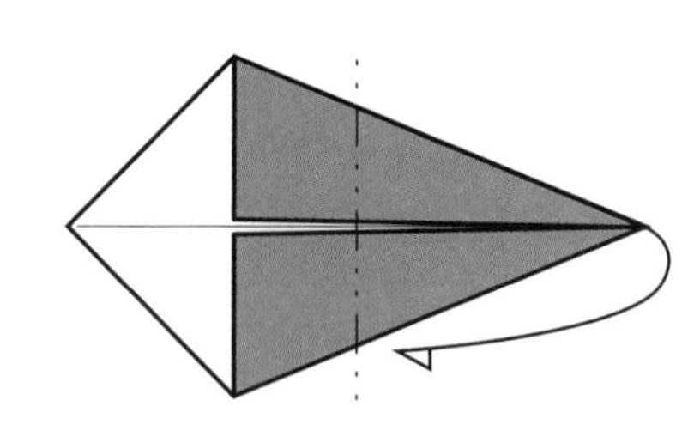

This is known as the kite base.
Mountain fold in half.

4

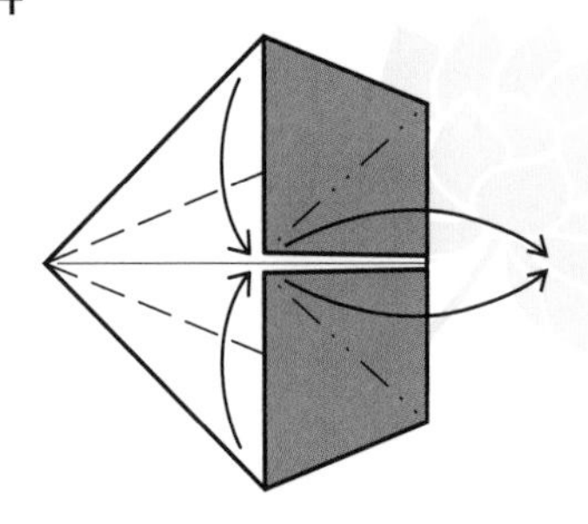

Squash fold both sides.

5

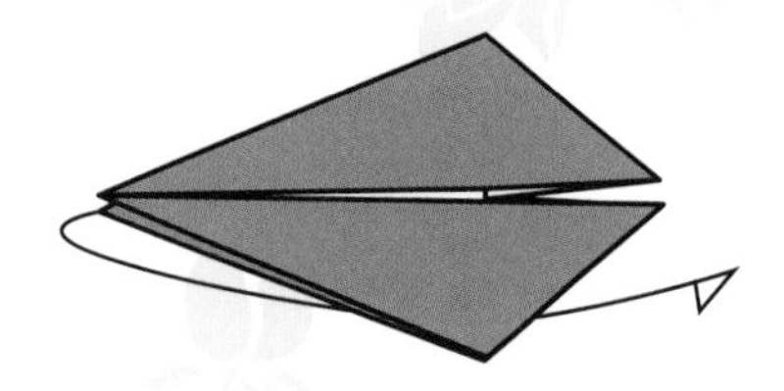

Mountain fold the point behind.

6

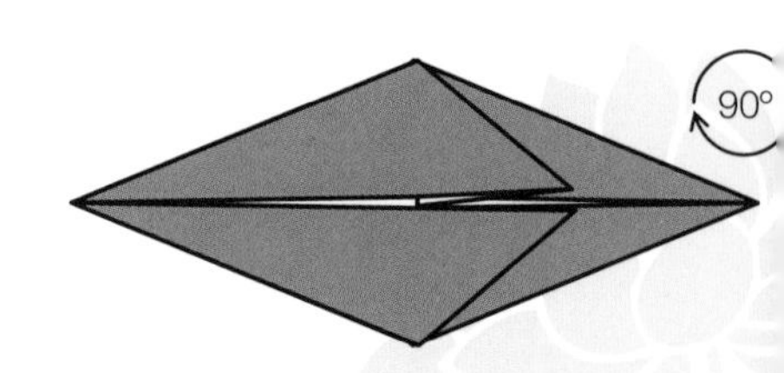

This is known as the fish base.
Rotate 90°.

7

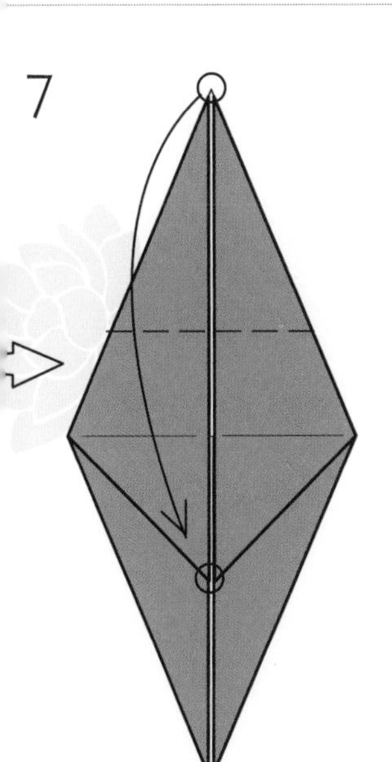

Fold the top down to the tip of the small triangles.

8

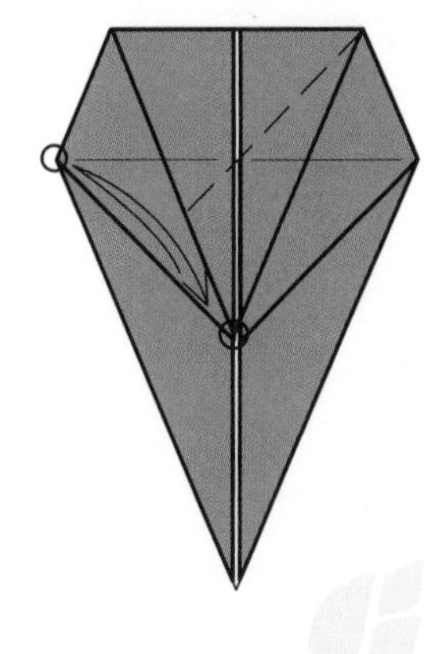

Bring the middle point to the outside corner then unfold.

9

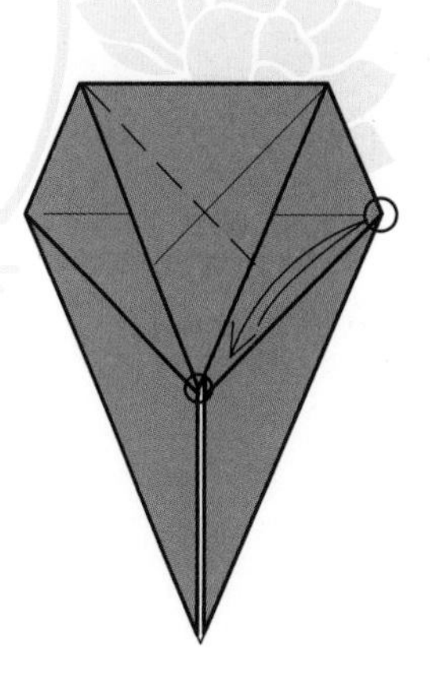

Repeat step 8 in the other direction.

10

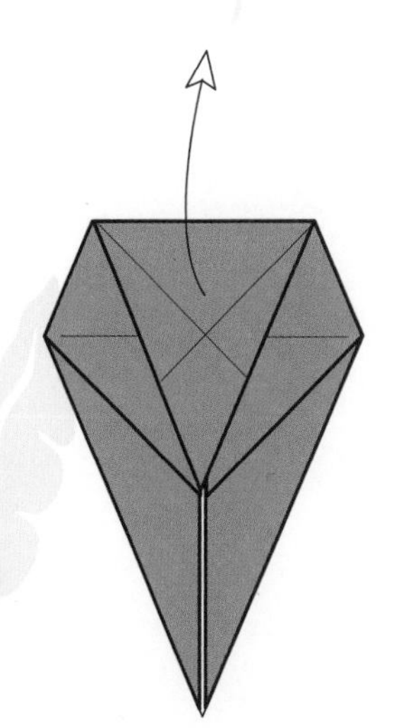

Unfold point to original position.

11

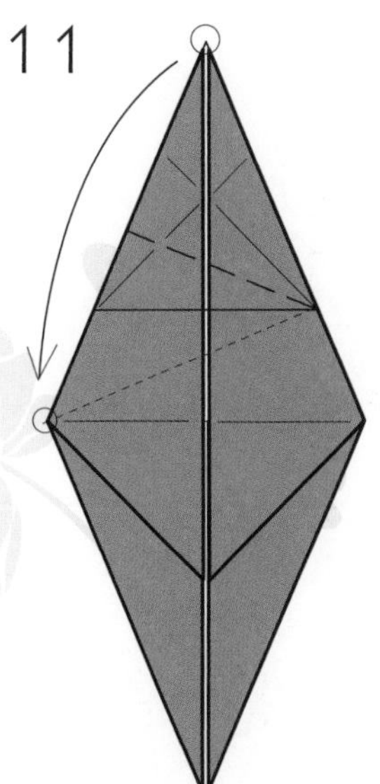

Fold tip down to corner.

12

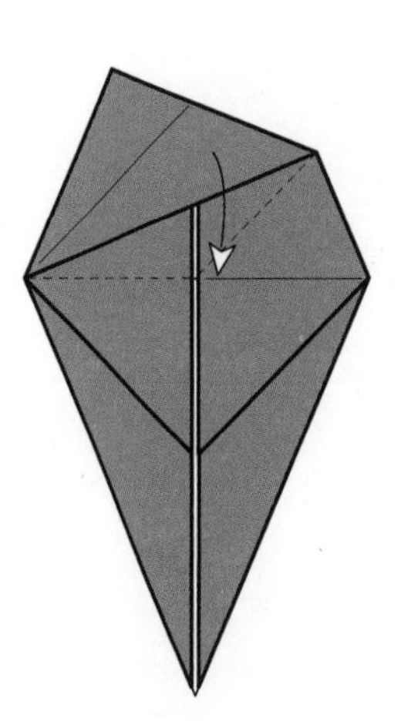

Ease out extra paper.

13

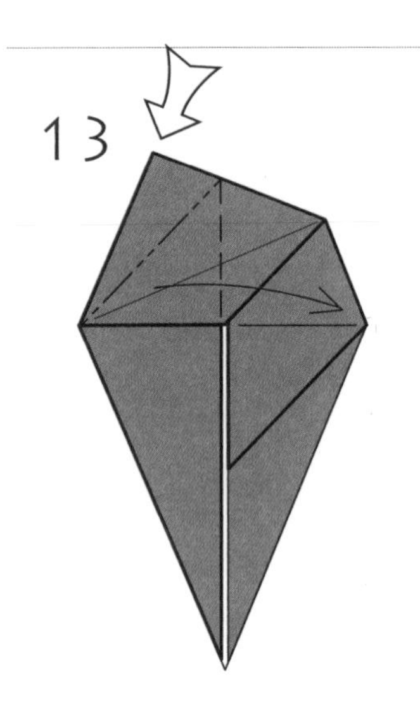

Fold the top layer across, to make a squash fold on the top point.

14

Pull out extra paper.

15

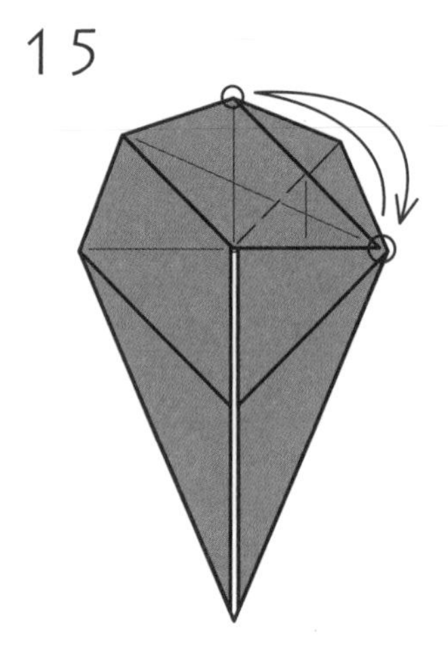

Pre-crease.

16

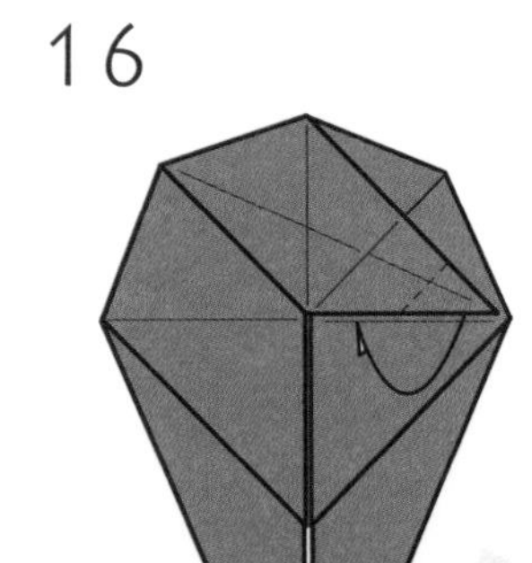

Inside reverse.

17

Do another inside reverse fold.

18

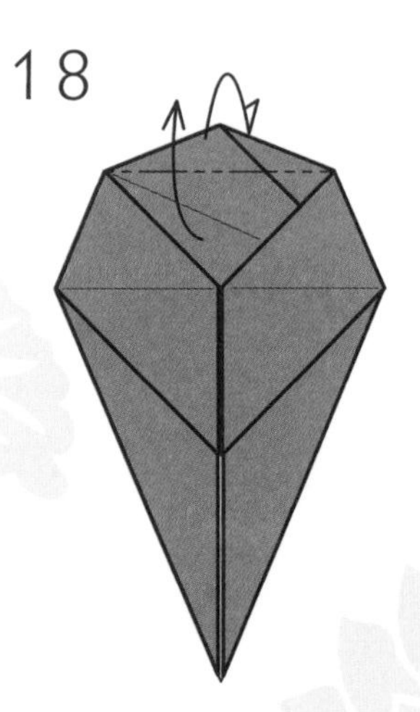

Flip back.

19

Valley fold small flaps up.

20

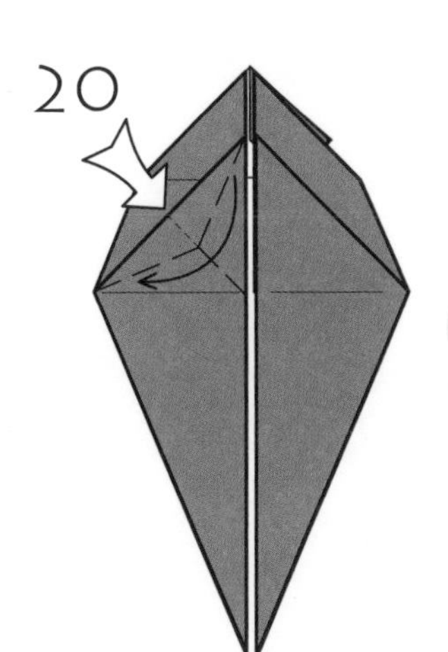

Rabbit ear the top layer.

21

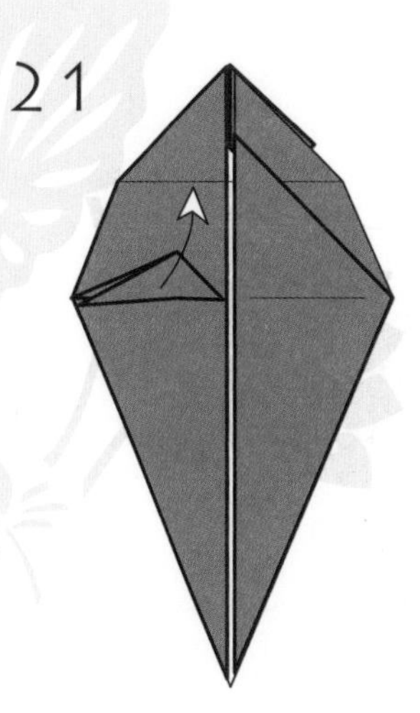

Unfold the rabbit ear.

22

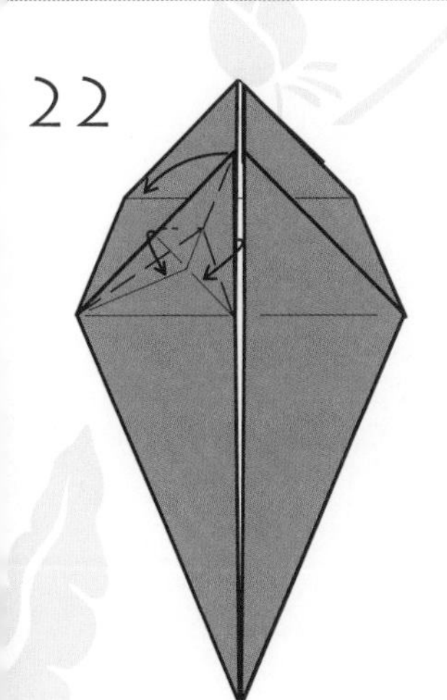

Add a new rabbit ear around the creases of the original. Place the tip near the side corner.

23

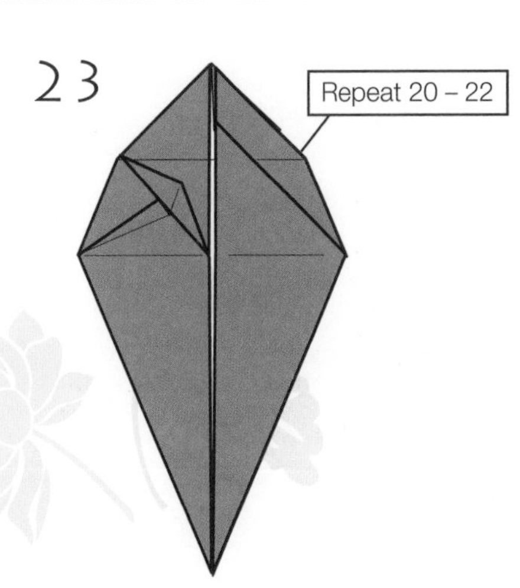

Repeat the folds on the right-hand flap.

24

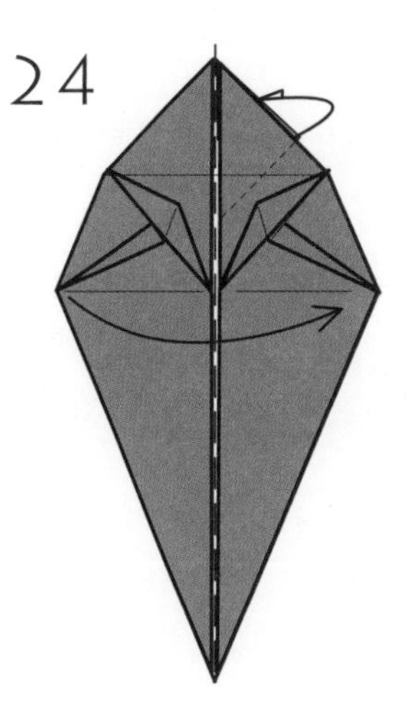

Fold in half. Allow hidden flap on the right to flip behind to the left.

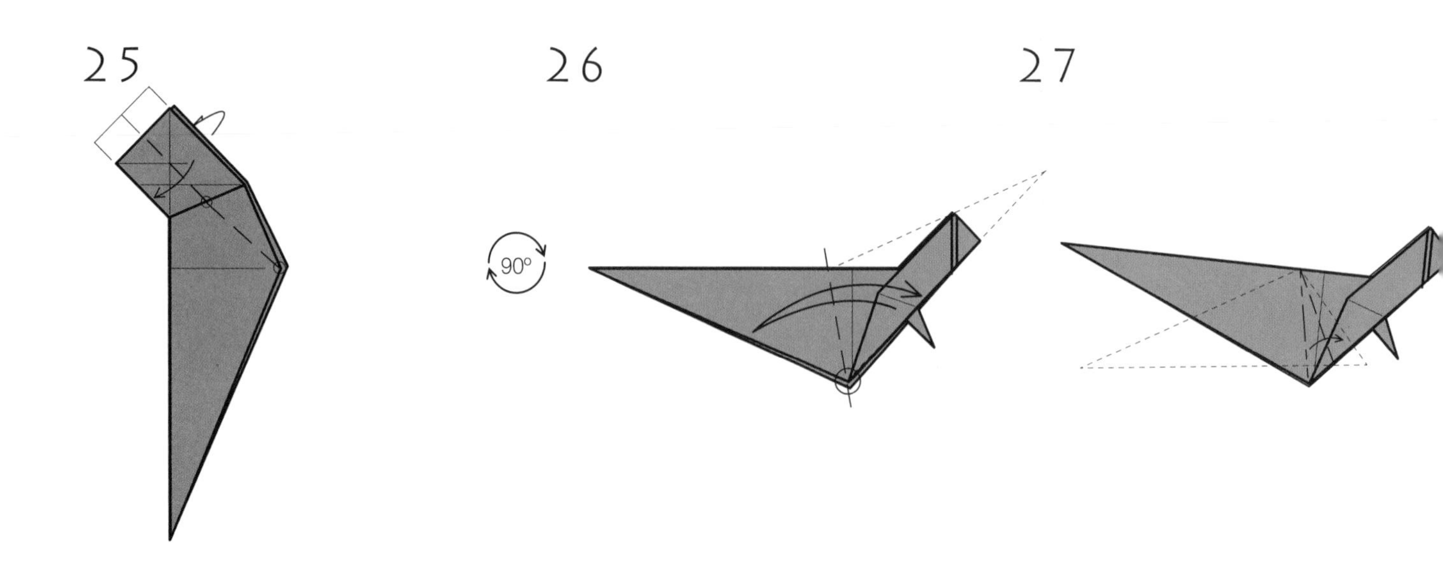

Valley fold in front, mountain fold behind. Rotate to position in next step.

Fold the lower left edge in line with the right. The crease runs through the lower corner.

Crimp back legs and tail section.

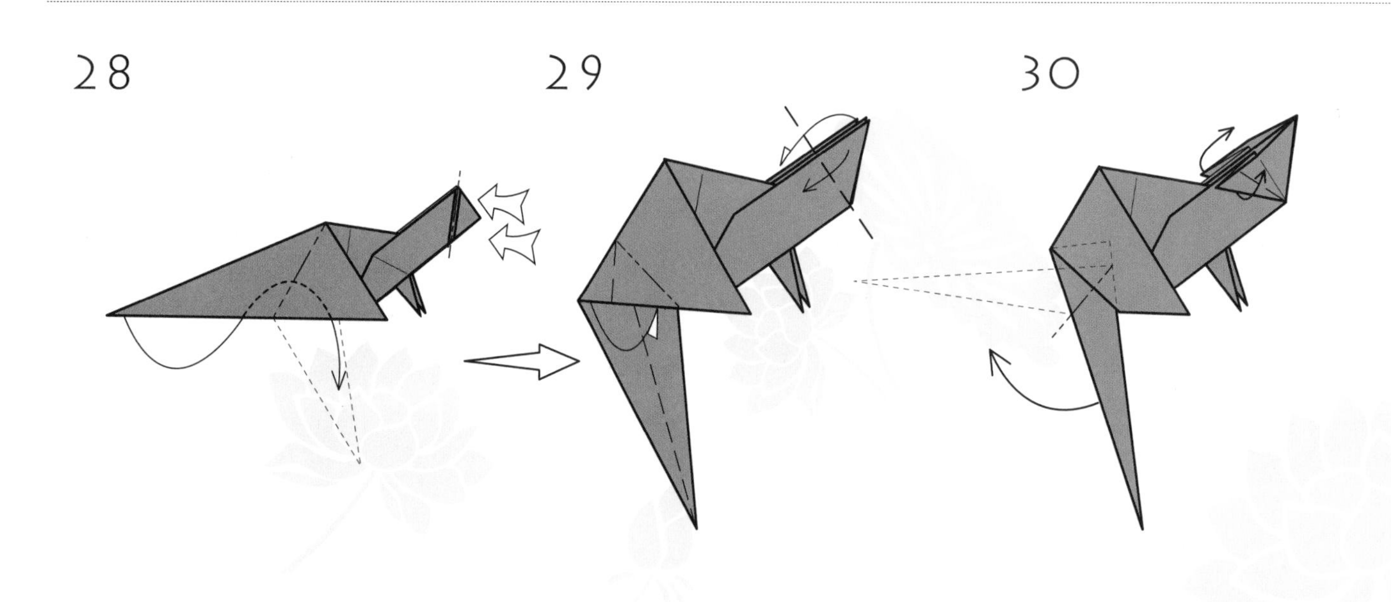

Reverse fold tail. Push in two corners.

Swivel fold tail on both sides. Fold ears back.

Reverse fold tail. Fold ear flaps forward.

31

Crimp head down. Swivel fold tail. Repeat behind.

32

Tuck the back points into the body and close sink the top point. Curl the tail.

33

Completed mouse.

RABBIT

MODEL: STEVEN CASEY
DIAGRAM: STEVEN CASEY

The rabbit is a small mammal found in many parts of the world. Rabbits have long ears which they use to listen for predators. This rabbit by Steven Casey has all four legs, a white tail and long ears. It is best folded from a 30cm (12in) sheet or larger, as there are many detailed folds. Use a sheet with the same colour on both sides to get a completely single coloured model.

The rabbit is a quick runner, and an even quicker breeder. Baby rabbits take only a month to gestate. A single rabbit can give birth to a normal size litter of seven babies about five times per year.

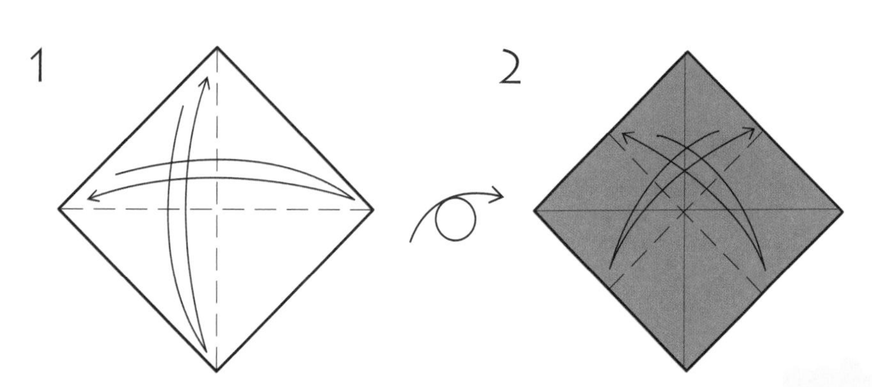

Begin white side up.
Fold and unfold diagonals. Turn over.

Book fold and unfold.

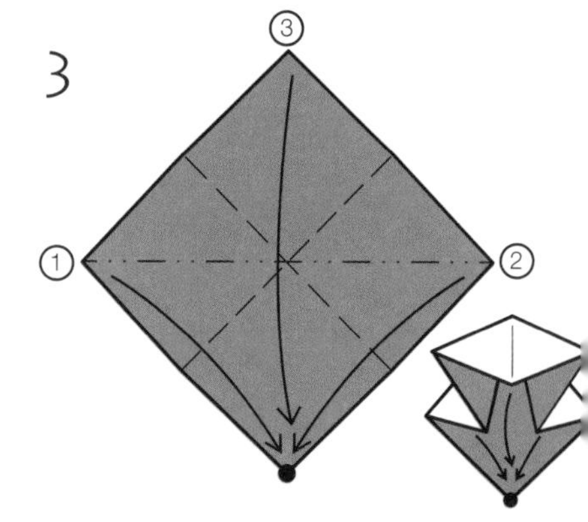

Bring three corners down to meet bottom corner. Start with corners 1 and 2 together followed by corner 3.

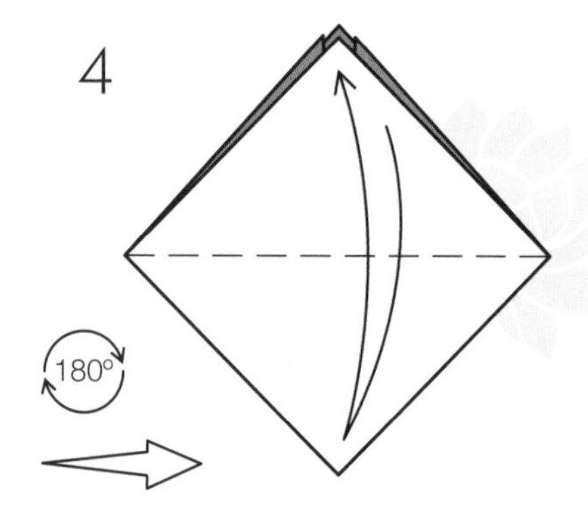

Rotate 180° so the open points are at the top. Fold single layer down then unfold.

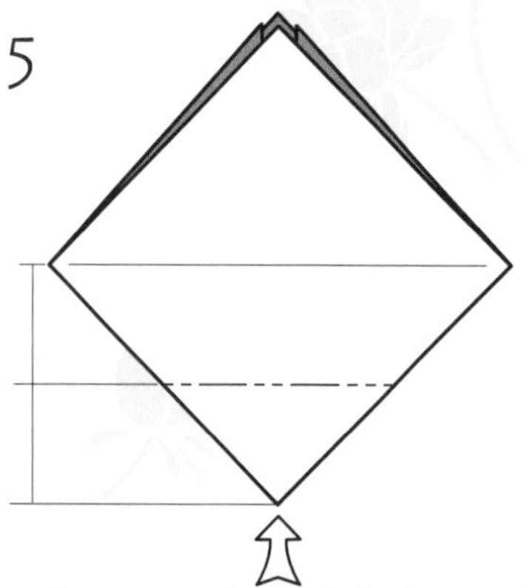

Pre-crease, then sink the bottom tip.

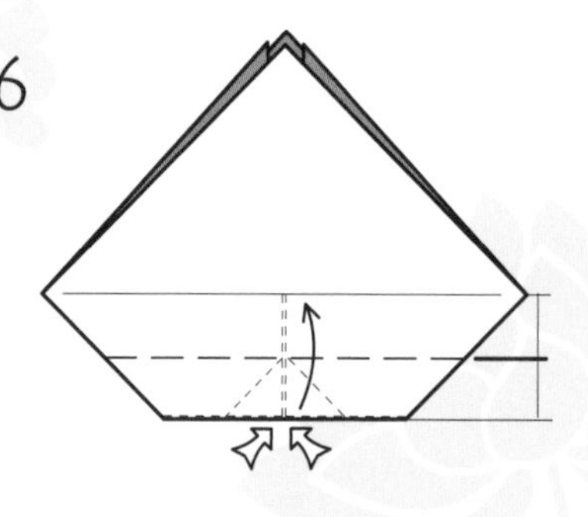

Valley fold upper layer and spread squash fold hidden corners.

7

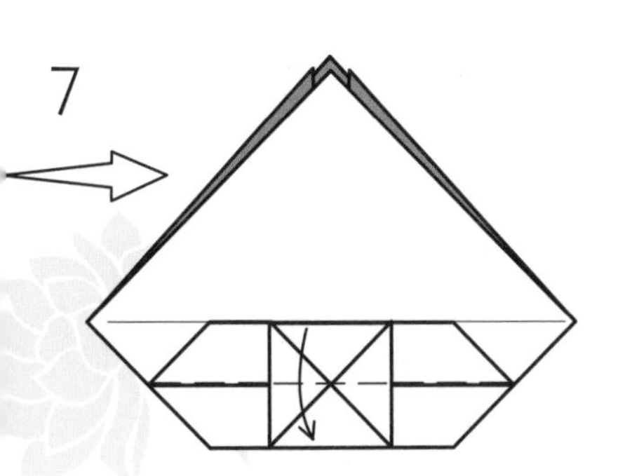

Fold upper layer down.

8

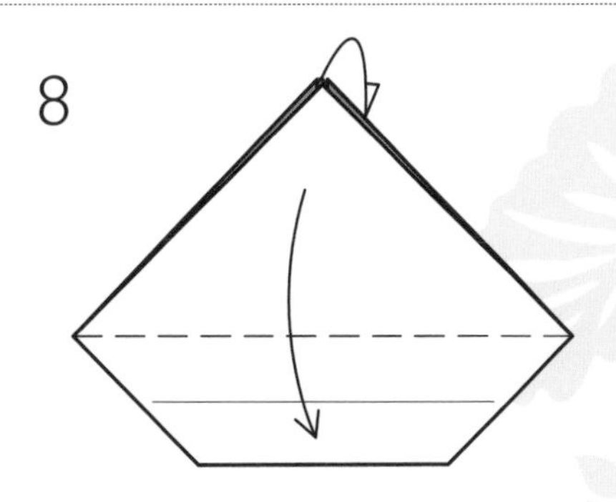

Fold single flap down in front and behind.

9

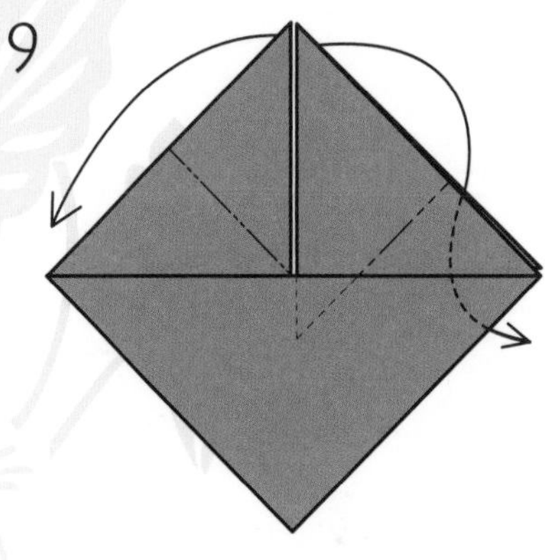

Reverse fold both points as shown.

10

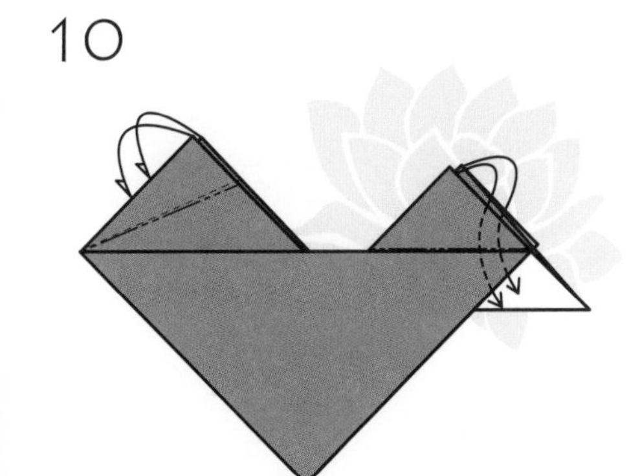

Reverse fold two left flaps and two right flaps.

11

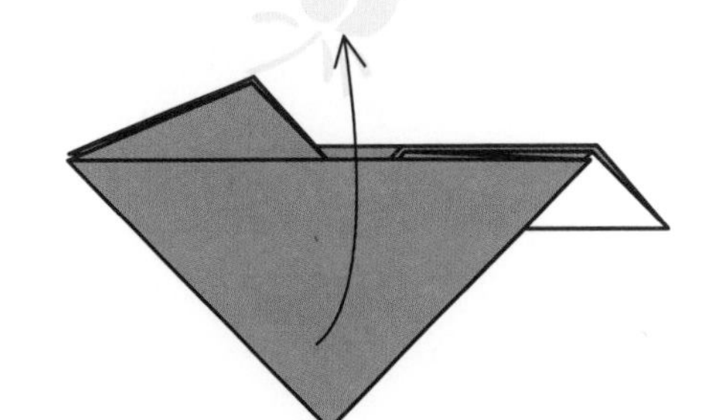

Fold single layer up.

12

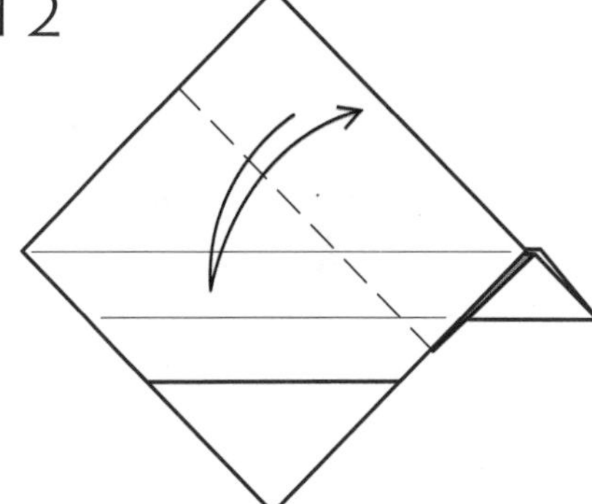

Pre-crease.

13

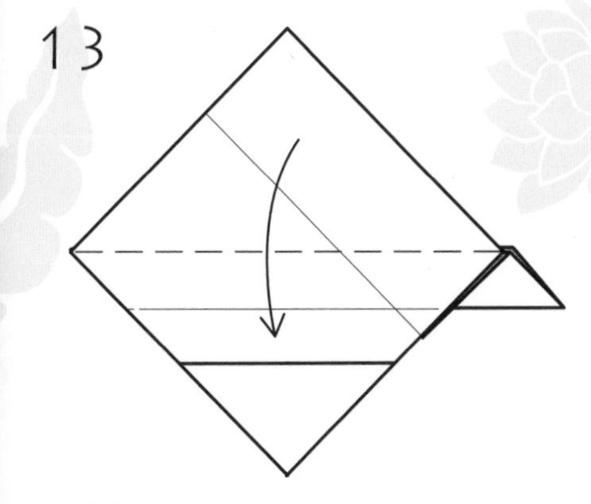

Valley fold top point down.

14

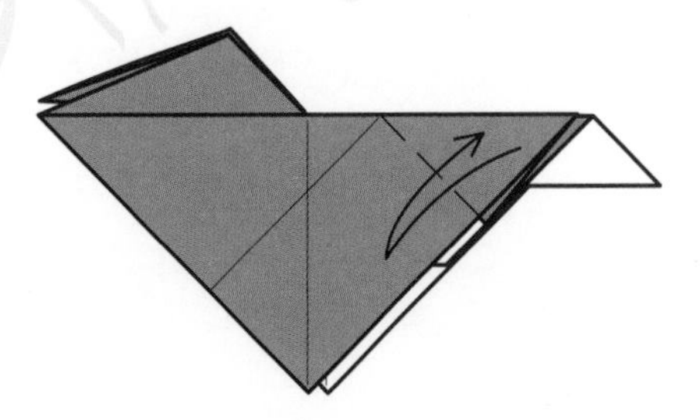

Fold triangle flap down, then unfold.

15

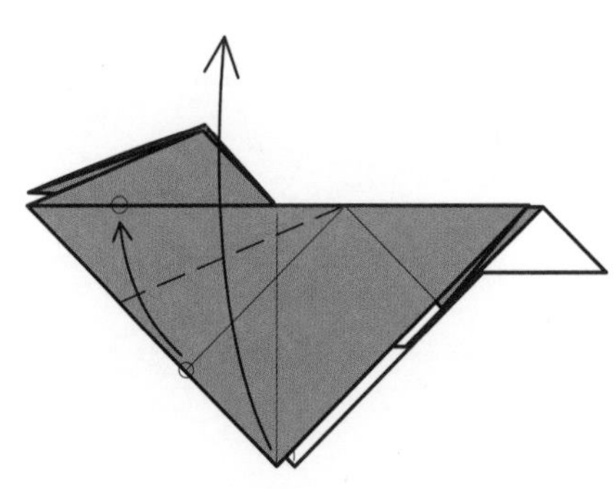

Bring points together with a valley fold. The layer will become 3D.

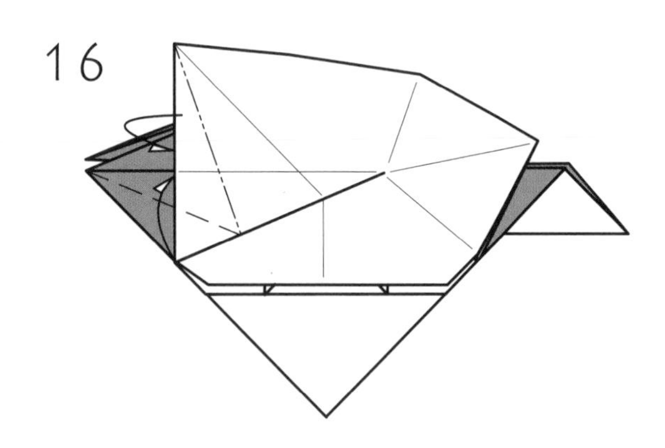

Swivel fold.

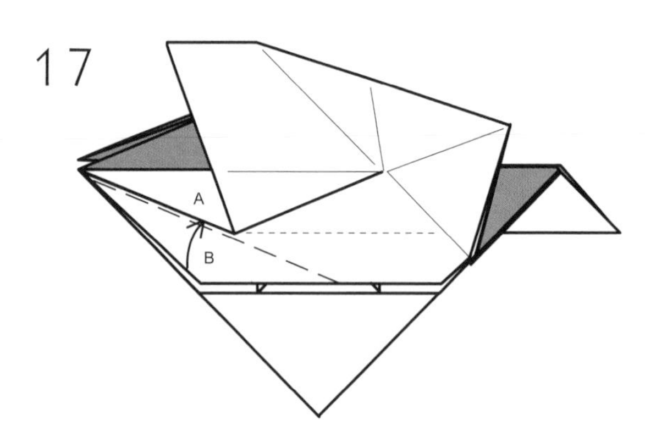

Tuck B under A.

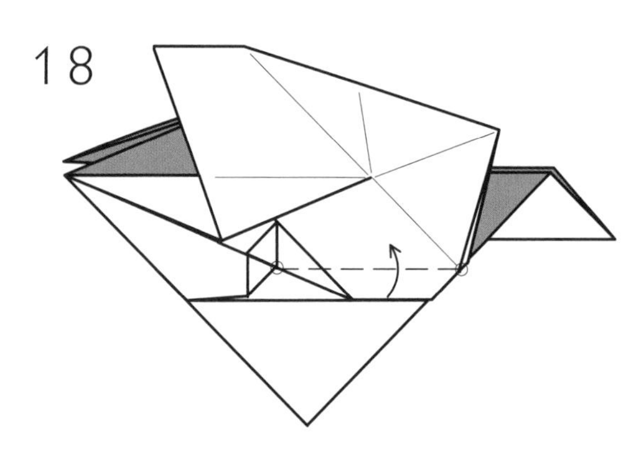

Valley fold edge inwards.

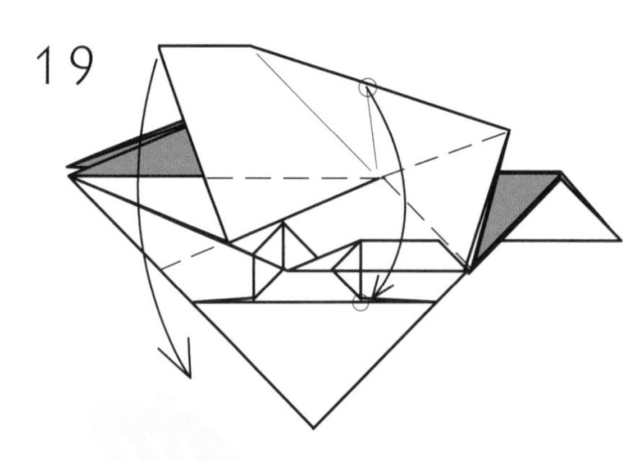

Bring the top flap down. Align the circled points.
At this stage the flap will not lie flat.

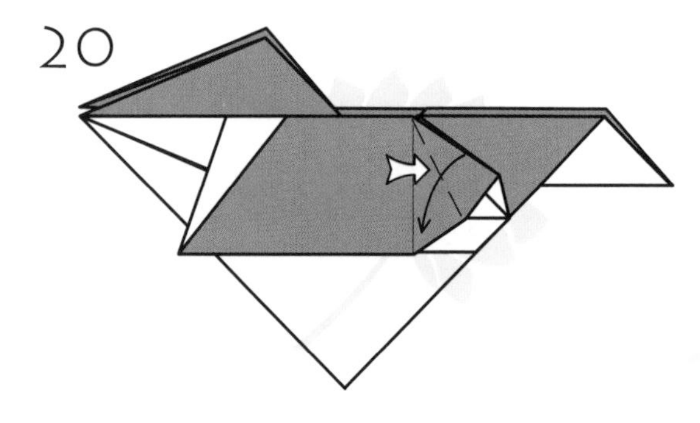

Push in where shown and fold the edge down
to meet the crease.

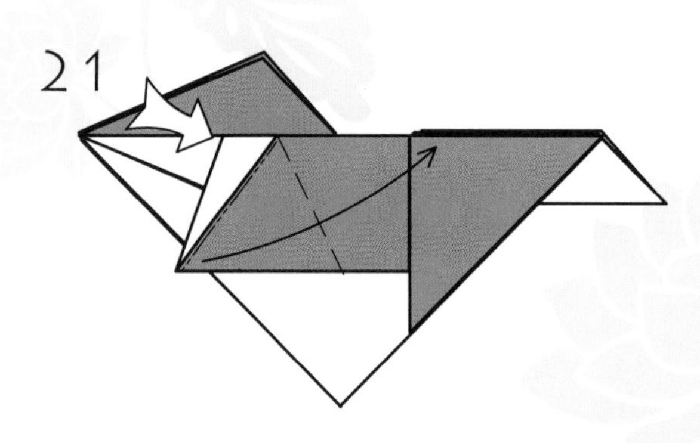

Squash fold.

22

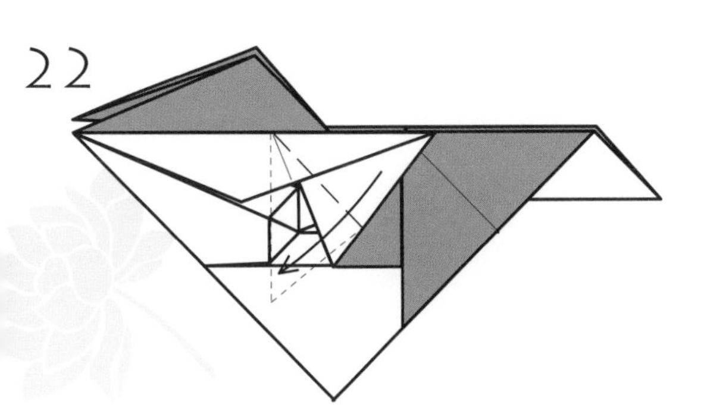

Fold flap down.

23

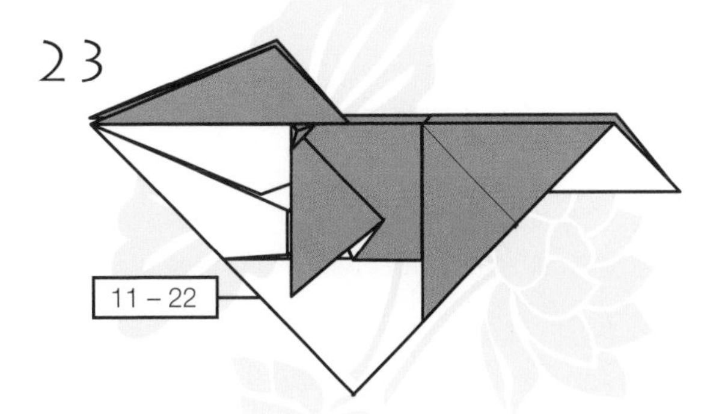

Repeat steps 11–22 behind.

24

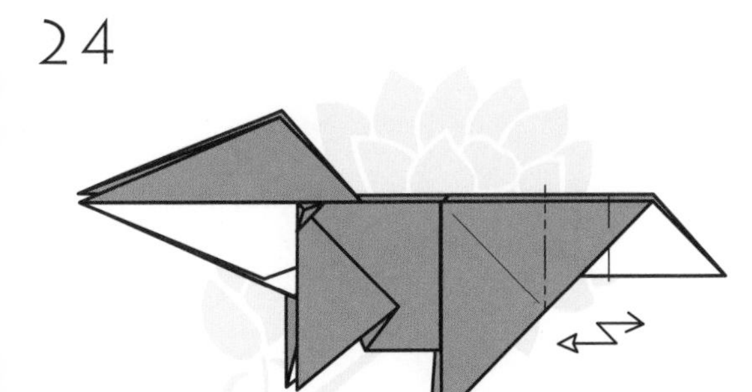

Pleat tail section then unfold.

25

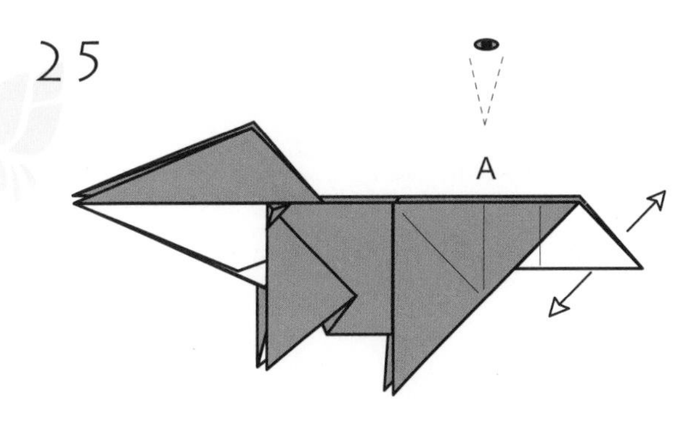

Open out tail section.

26

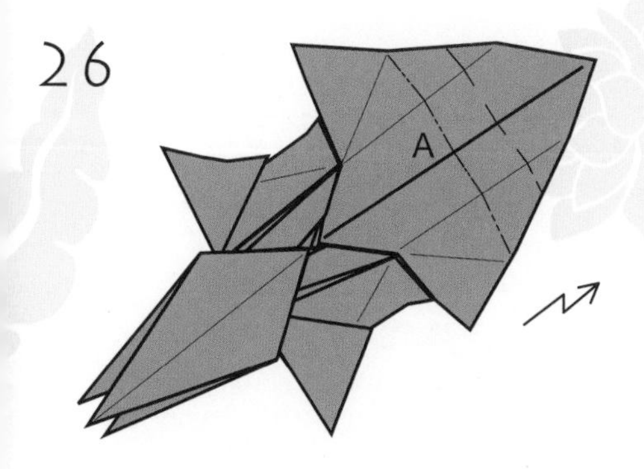

View from arrow A. Pleat tail section.

27

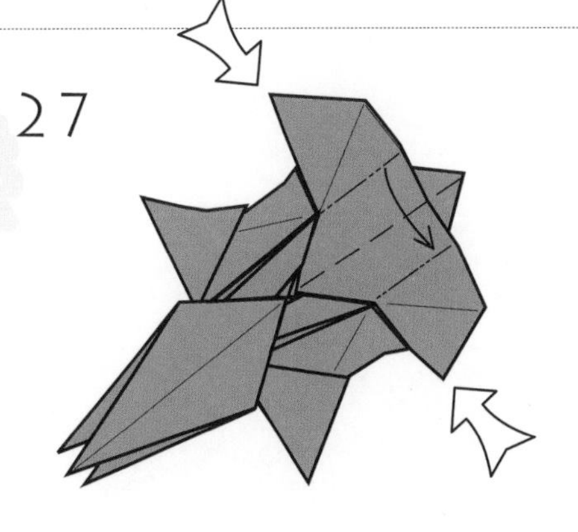

Push sides together.

28

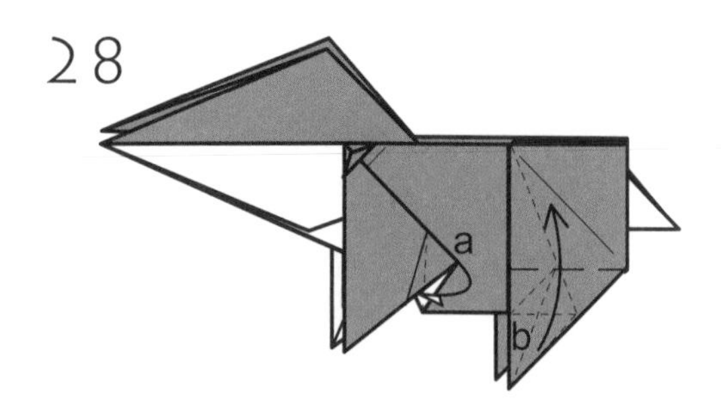

Push in corner A and lift flap B, squashing layers underneath.

29

Fold upper flap back down.

30

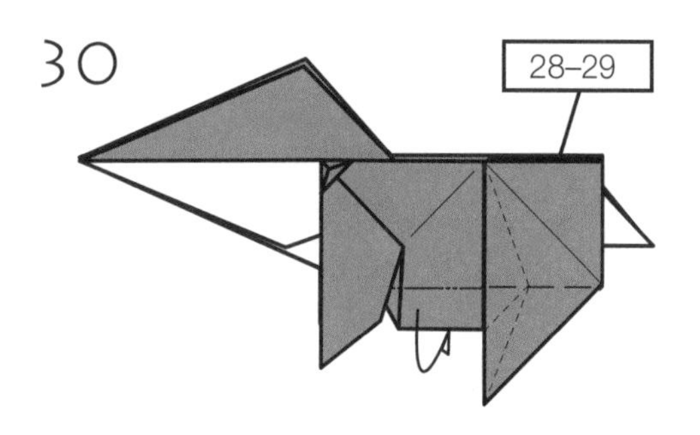

Repeat steps 28–29 behind. Fold flap under in line with inner edge. Repeat behind.

31

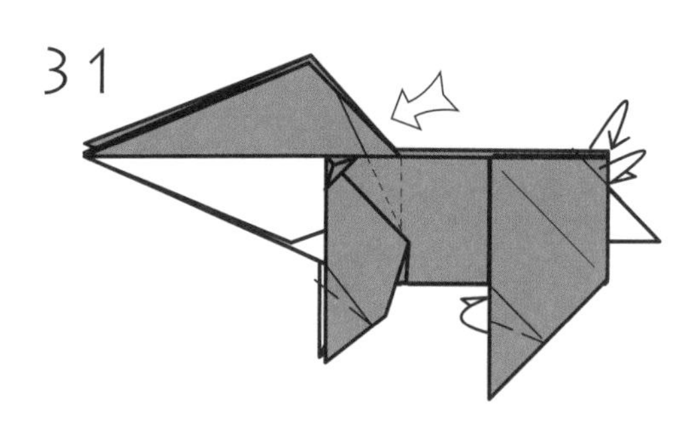

Sink the back of the head. Crimp front and back feet, and tuck in corners near tail.

32

Valley fold ear flaps. Shorten the tail with a reverse fold.

33

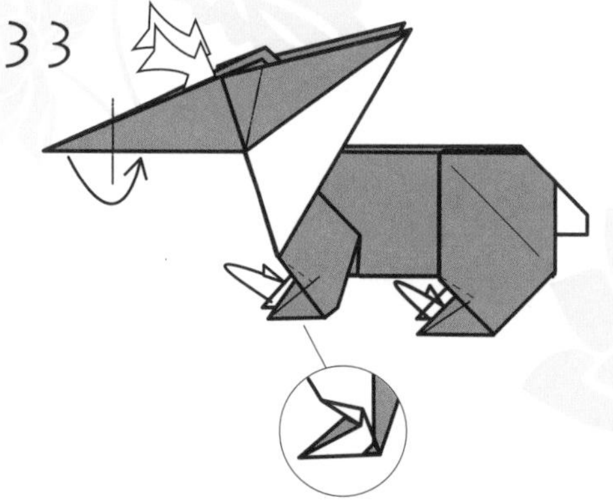

Shorten the head with an outside reverse. Sink the inner corners between the ears. Narrow the feet. Note the swivel that forms underneath.

Fold the nose point under again.

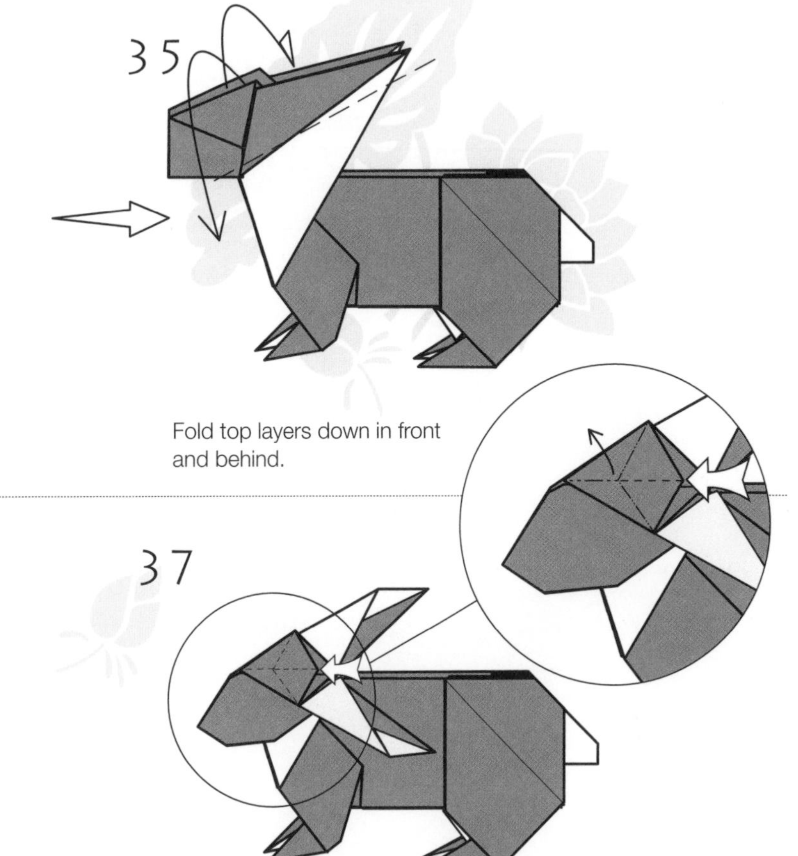

Fold top layers down in front and behind.

Tuck in the lower corners of the head. Lightly bend the front ear down.

Push in where indicated to pop out extra paper. Bring the ears together.

Tuck the lower edges of the ears inside, repeat behind. Shape the body by pressing along the top and underside of the rabbit.

Completed rabbit.

TURTLE

MODEL: STEVEN CASEY
DIAGRAM: STEVEN CASEY

The turtle is a member of the reptile family. Its bony shell gives it shelter from predators, and its webbed feet allow it to swim quickly in water, but still walk on land for nesting. Use a 30cm (12in) or larger sheet for this model, as there are a few layers in the head and tail, and the details require more paper.

The turtle cannot breathe in water, but it can hold its breath for a long time.

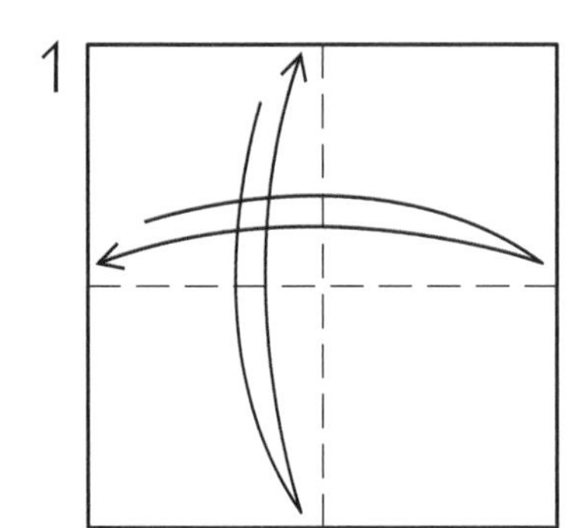

Begin white side up.
Book fold and unfold.

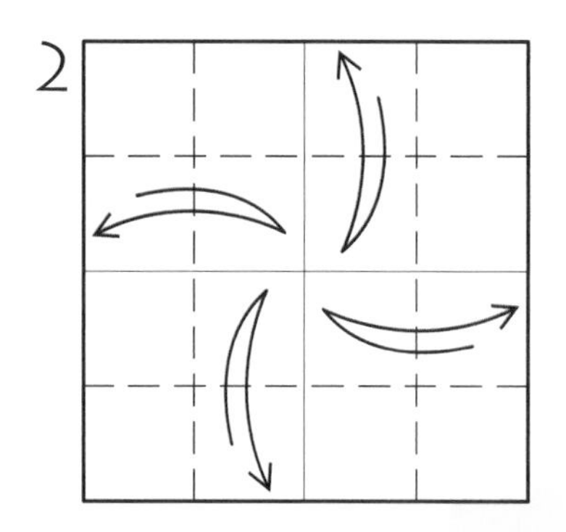

Fold each edge into the centre then unfold.

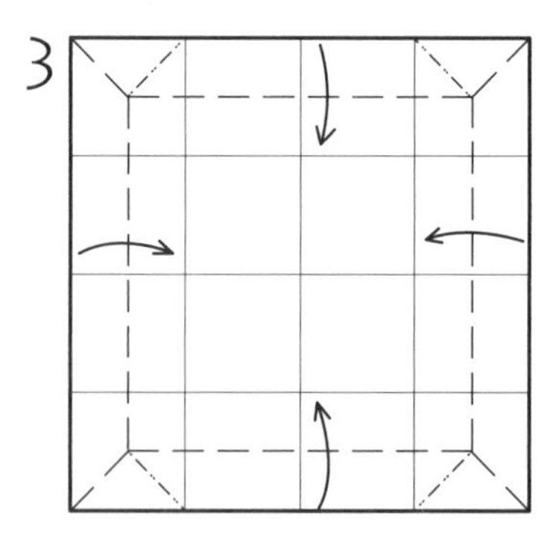

Fold edges in, and rabbit ear corners.

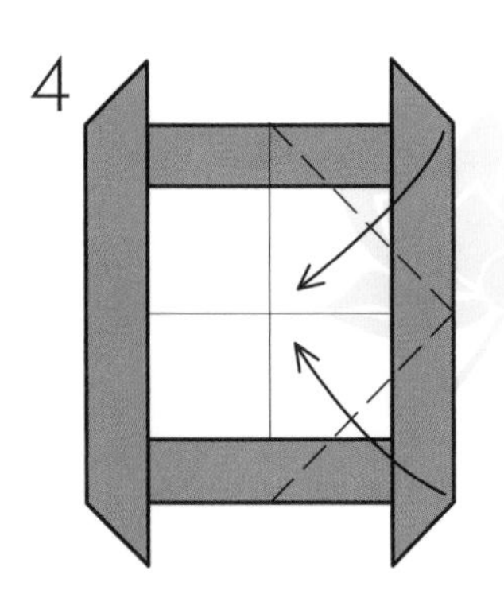

Fold right corners into centre.

Completed step 4. Turn over.

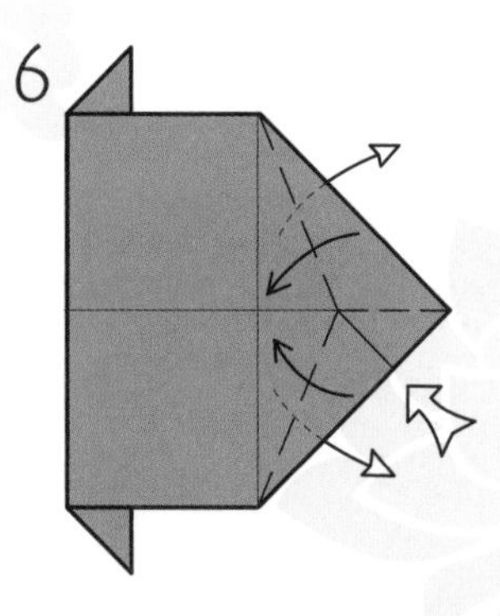

Rabbit ear on right side. Allow layers from behind to flip out.

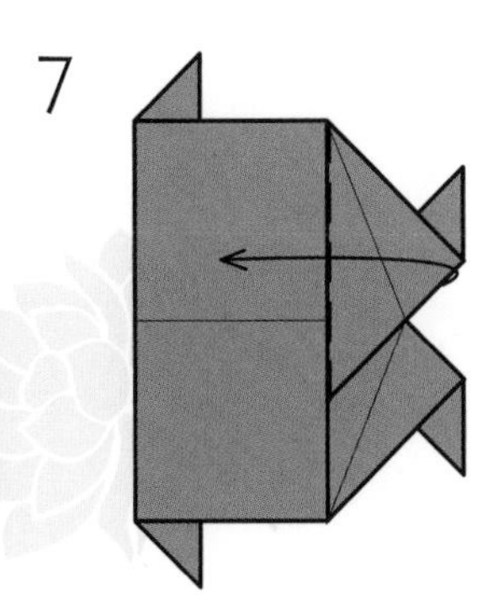

Fold single flap over to the left.

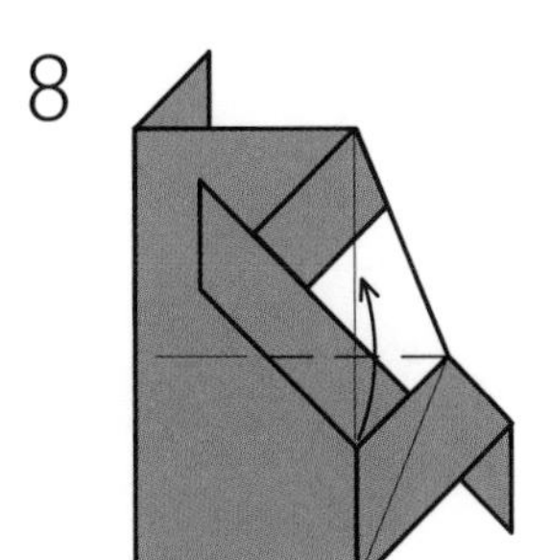

Fold small flap upwards.

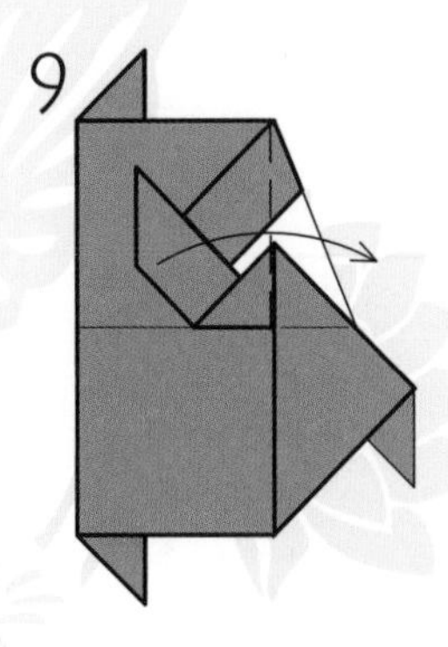

Fold flap over to the right.

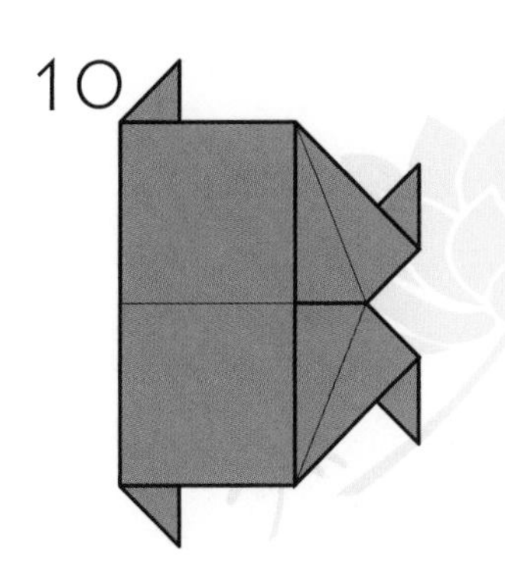

Turn over top to bottom.

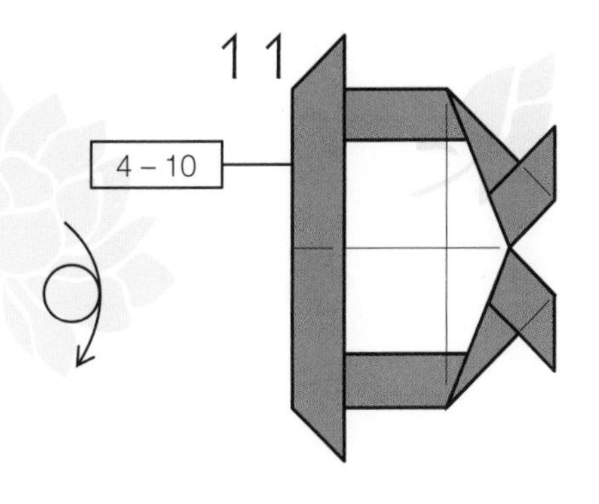

Repeat steps 4–10 on the left half of the model.

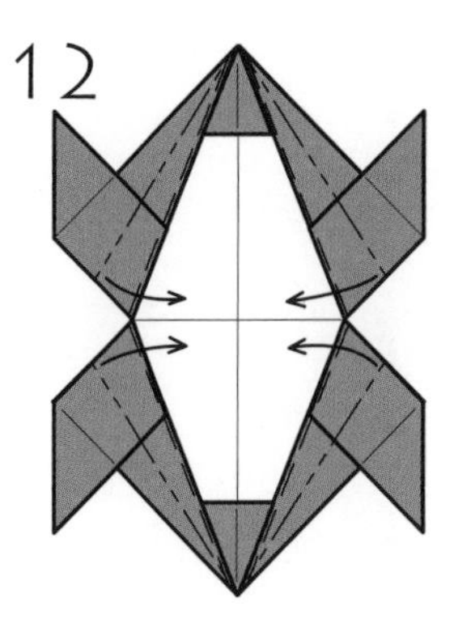

Crimp all four flaps.

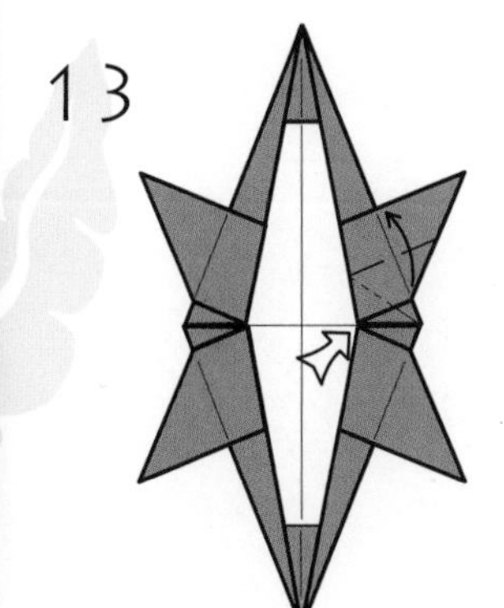

Squash fold.

Repeat step 13 on remaining flaps.

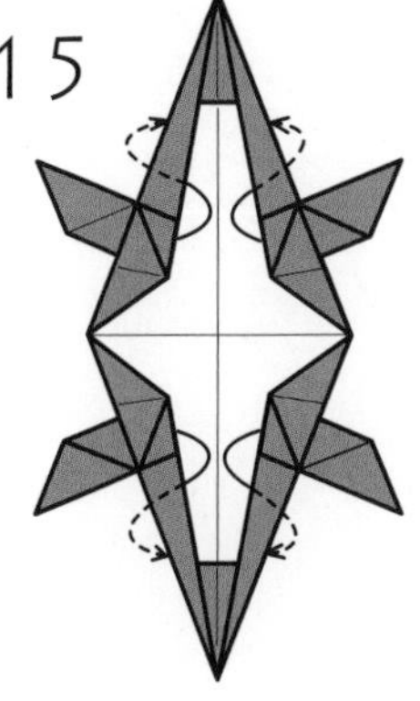

Tuck flaps under the white layer. The top flaps go between the small hidden flap and the white layer.

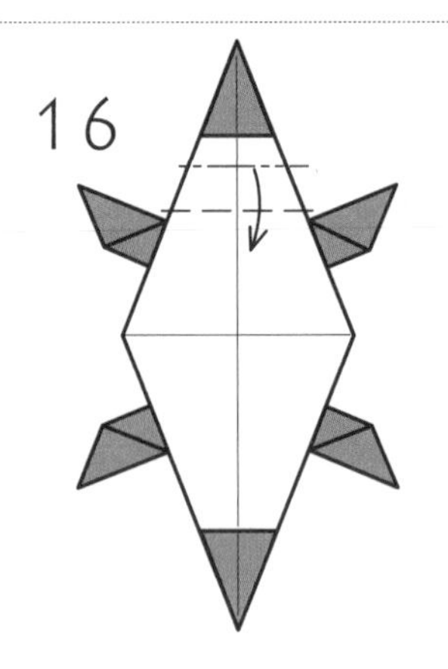

16

Pleat top point.

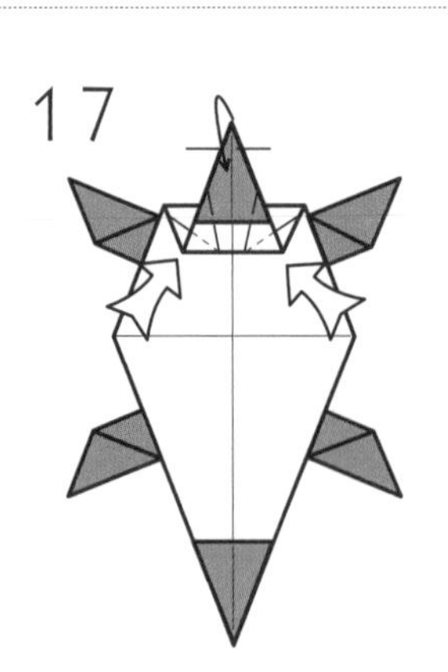

17

Squash fold corners. Valley fold the top point down.

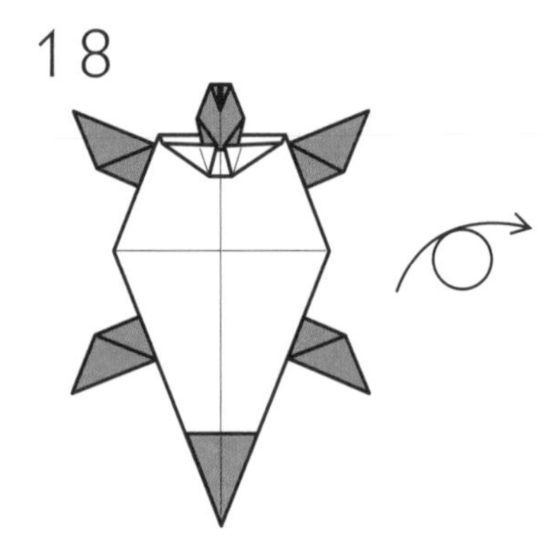

18

Turn over.

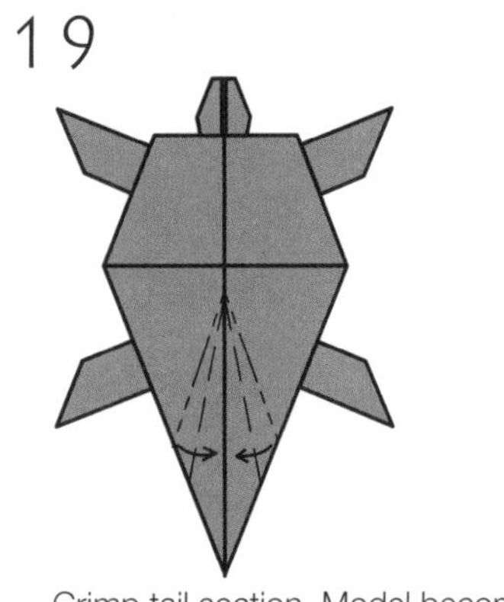

19

Crimp tail section. Model become 3D.

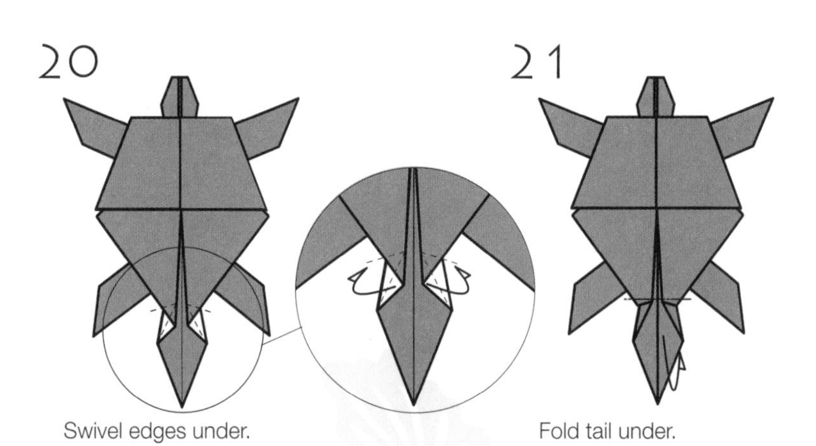

20

Swivel edges under.

21

Fold tail under.

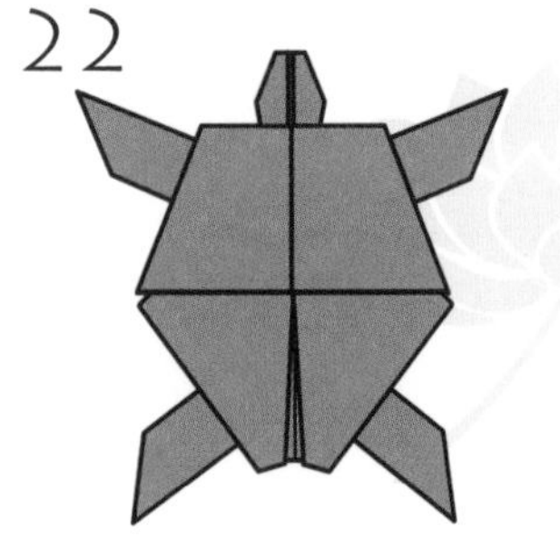

22

Completed step 21. Turn over.

23

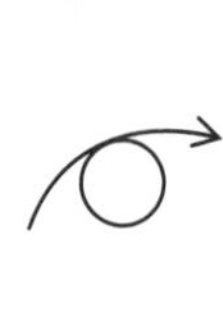

Valley fold tail. Turn over.

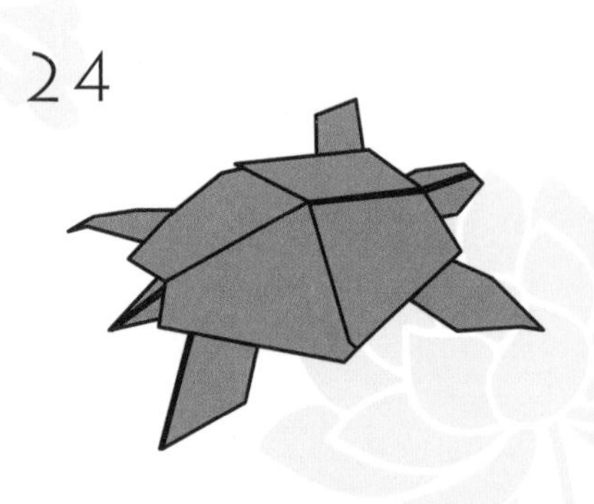

24

Completed turtle.

KUSUDAMA

MODEL: TRADITIONAL, JAPAN
DIAGRAM: MATTHEW GARDINER

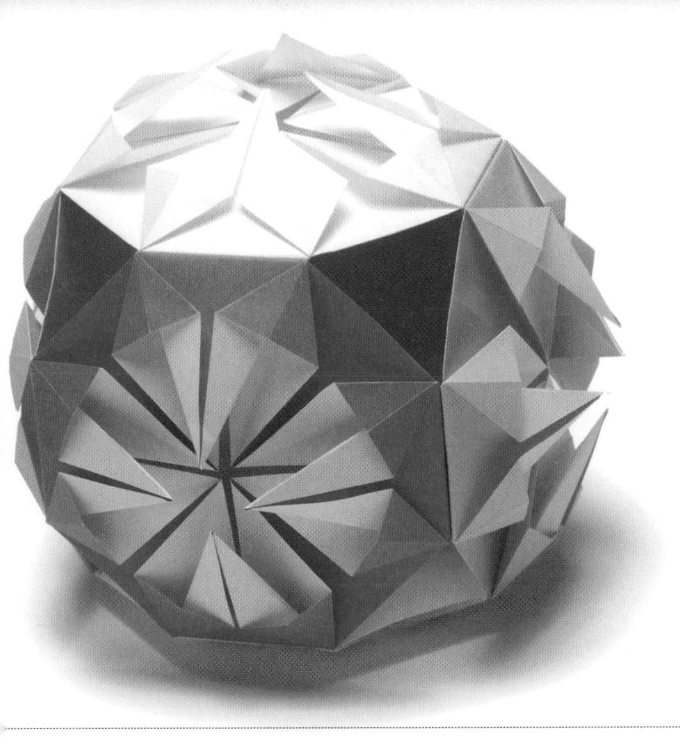

The kusudama is a traditional origami decoration with a very geometric feel. The kusudama is often thought to be the precursor to unit origami. This model requires glue to complete the assembly.

Kusudama literally means medicine ball, from kusuri (medicine) and tama (ball). They are now used as gifts.

1

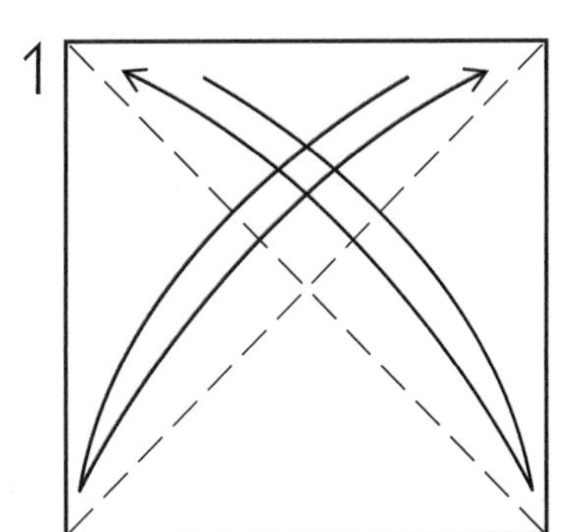

Begin white side up.
Fold and unfold diagonals.

2

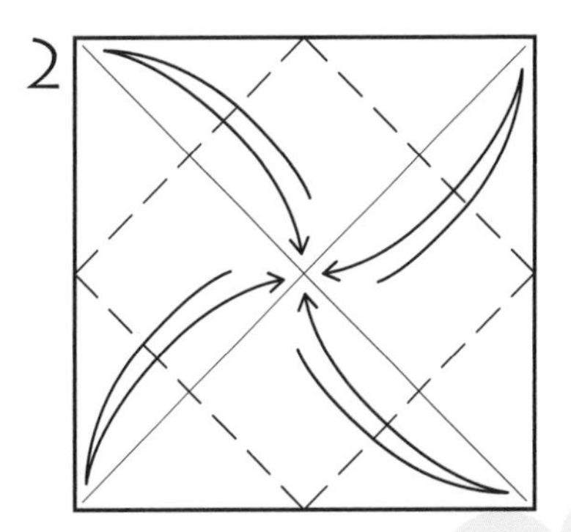

Blintz fold and unfold.

3

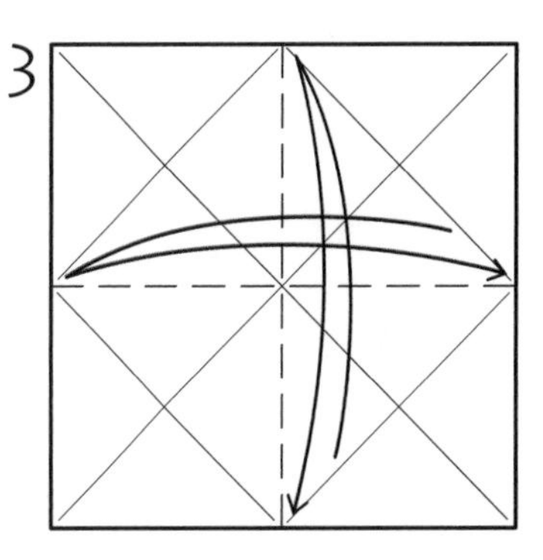

Book fold and unfold.

4

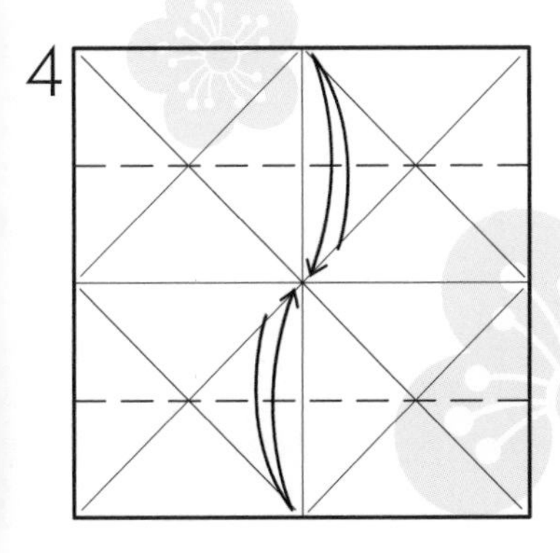

Cupboard fold and unfold.

5

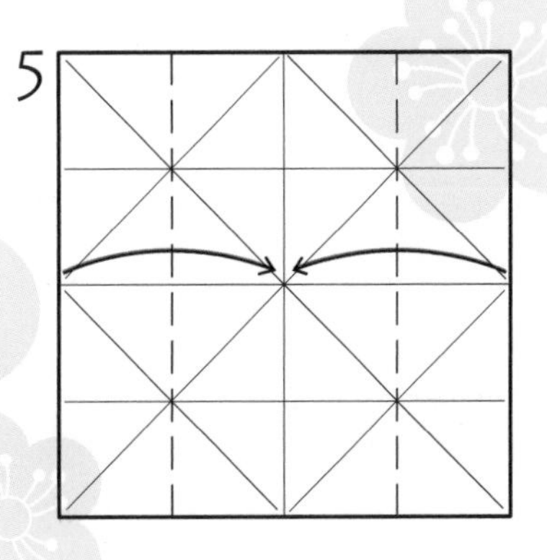

Cupboard fold.

6

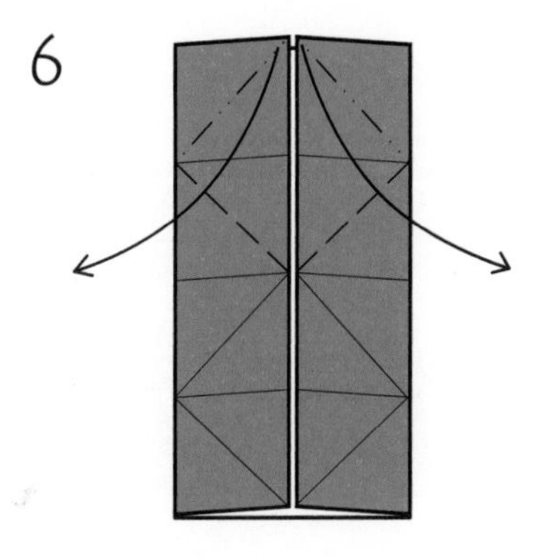

Squash fold using existing creases.

7

Repeat step 6 on the bottom.

8

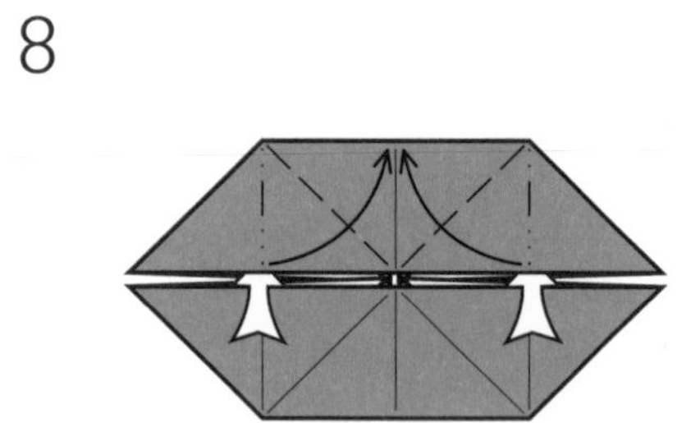

Squash fold.

9

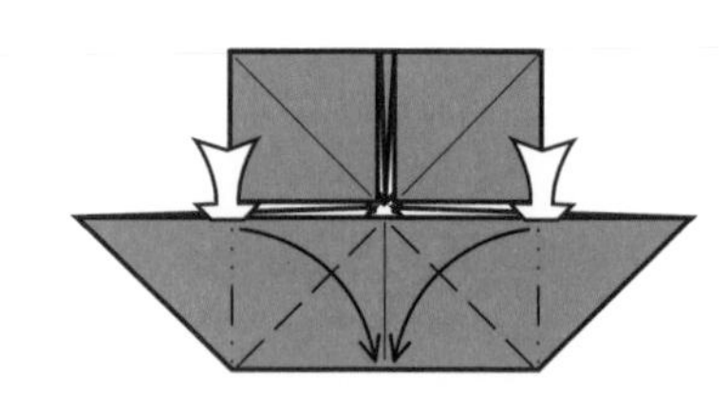

Repeat step 8 on the other side.

10

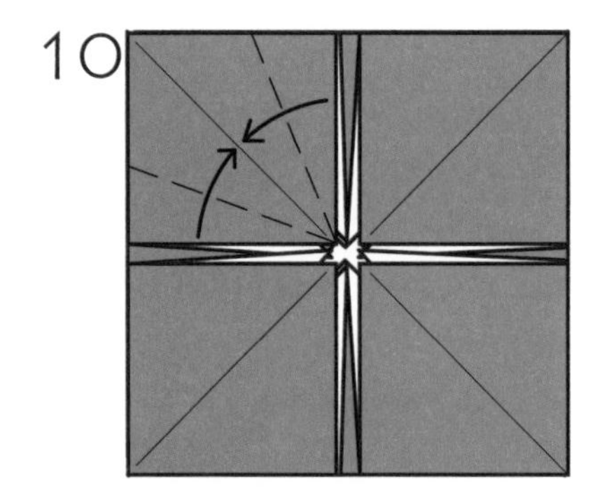

Valley fold.

11

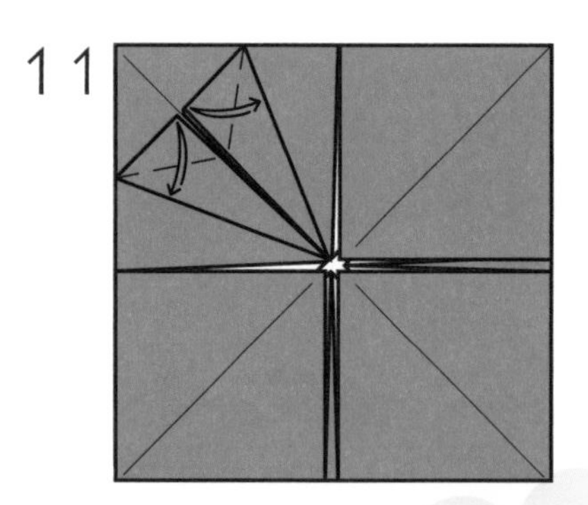

Fold and unfold.

12

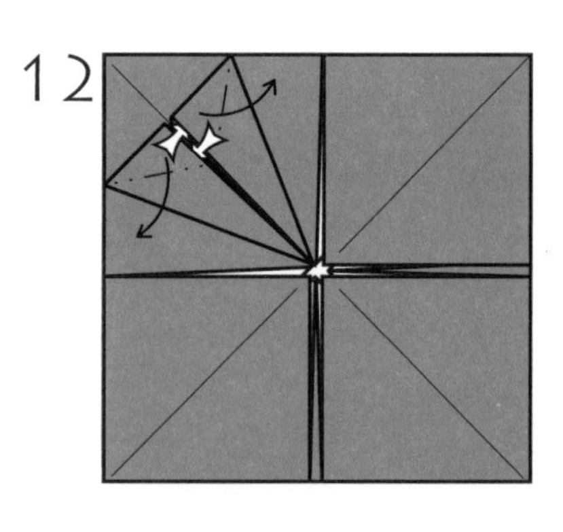

Squash fold on existing creases.

13 14

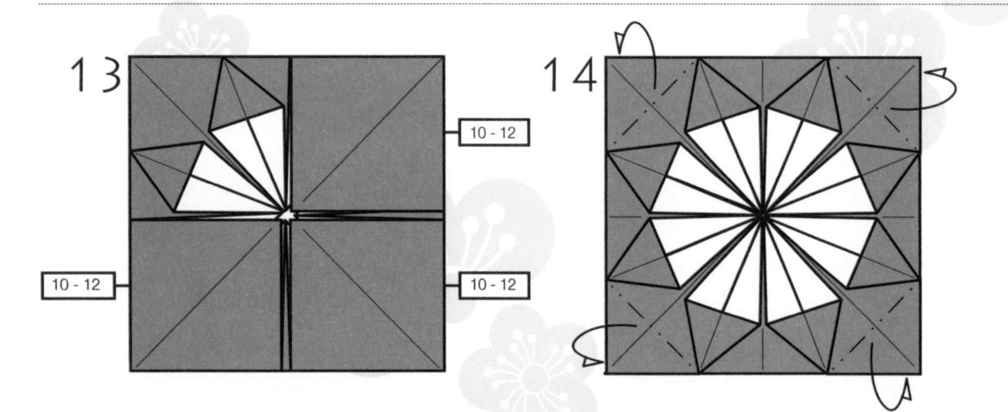

Repeat steps 10-12 on the other three sides.

Fold four corners behind.

15

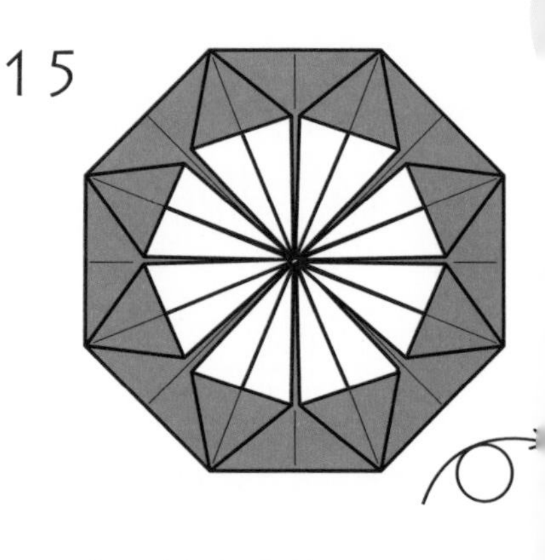

Completed unit. Turn over.

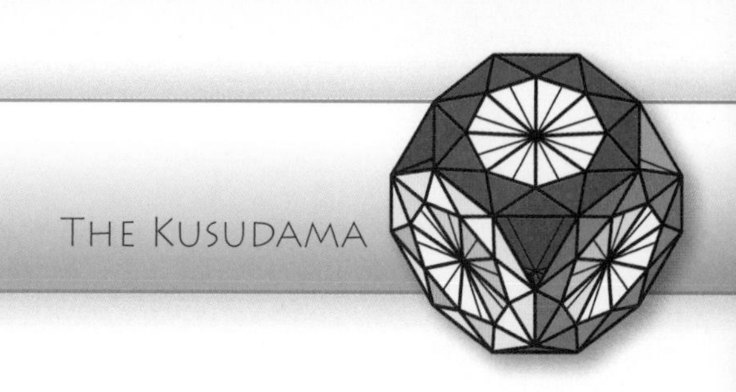

16

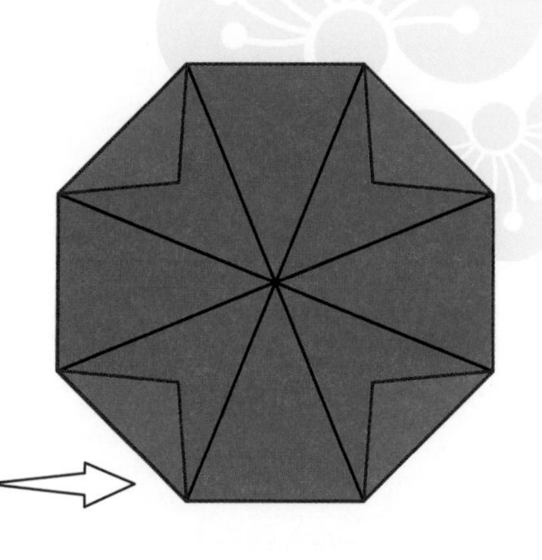

Like this.

17

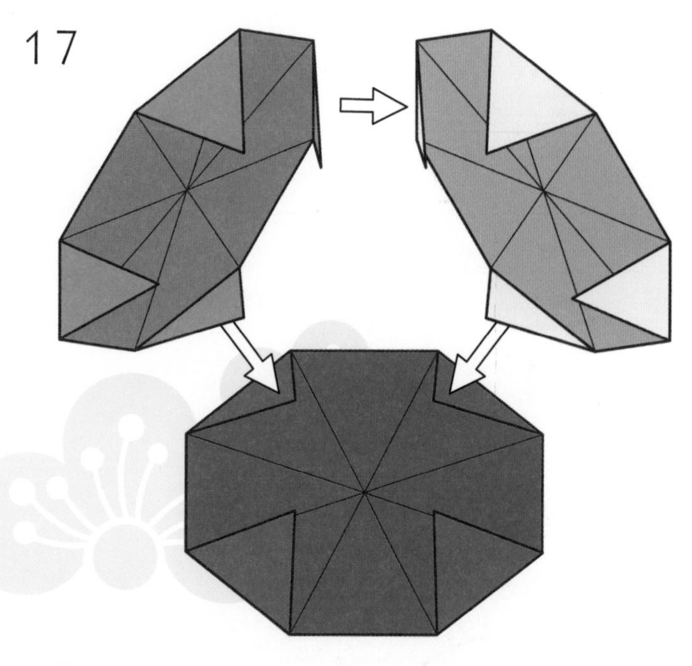

This is a 3D view. Use glue to join the units together.
Put the glue on the triangle tabs.

18

Three units joined together. Glue the last three units in the same way.

19

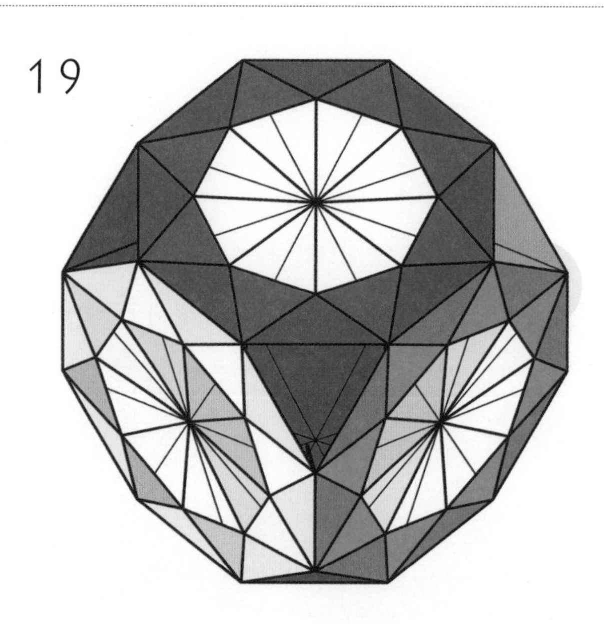

Completed kusudama.

HEART FOLD

MODEL: DARREN SCOTT
DIAGRAM: DARREN SCOTT

With a little heart on the end of each point, this flower is perfect for a handmade greeting card for someone special.

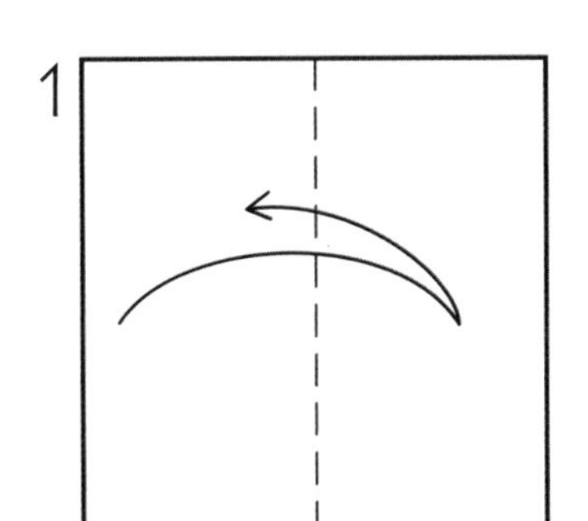

Start with paper, white side up. Book fold and unfold.

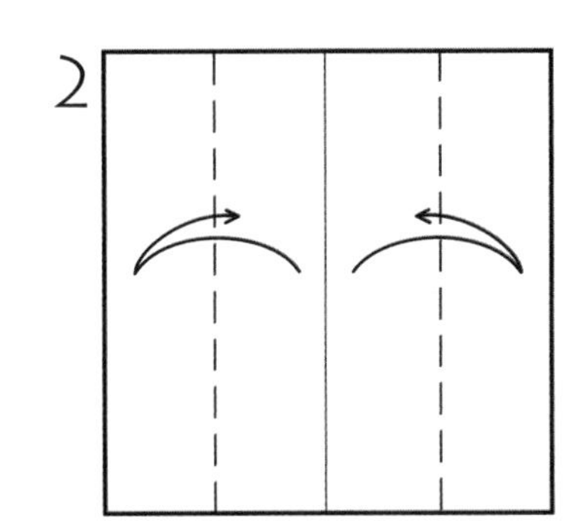

Cupboard fold and unfold.

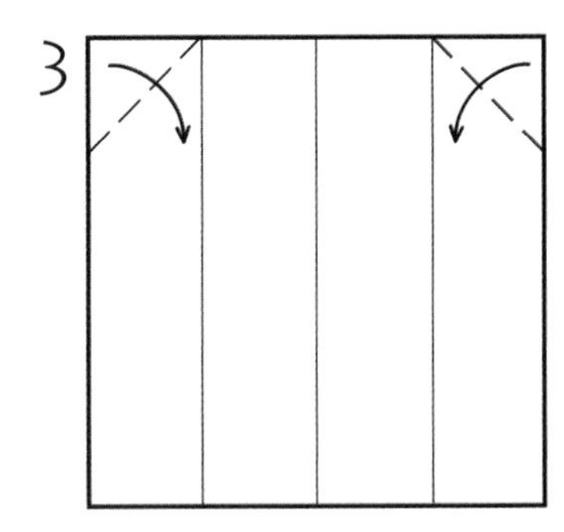

Fold the top corners so they lie along creases made in step 2.

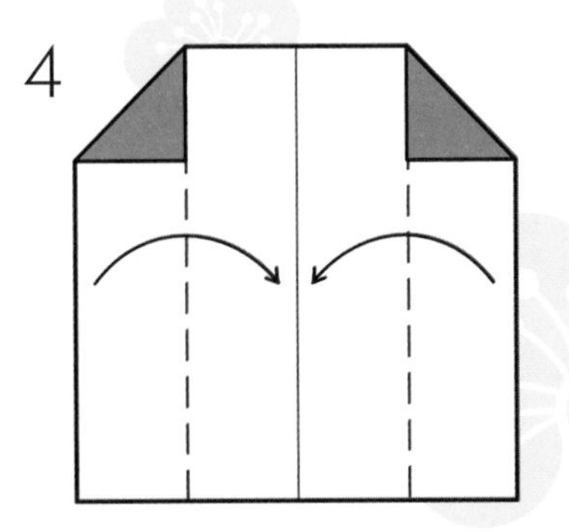

Refold creases made in step 2.

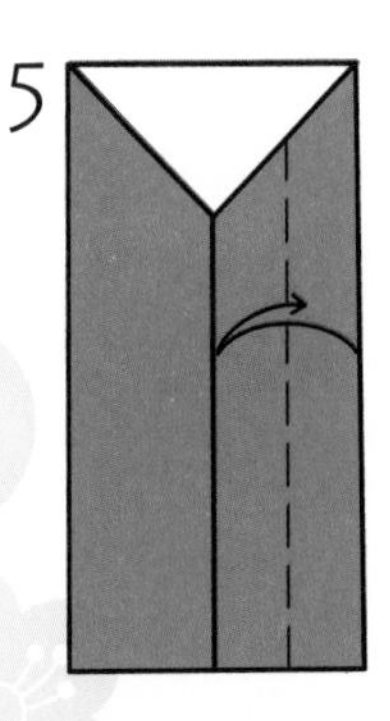

Fold the right flap in half and unfold.

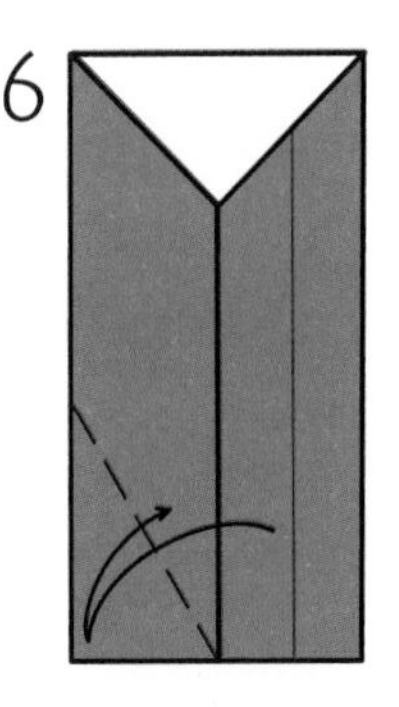

Fold the bottom left corner to meet the crease made in step 5.

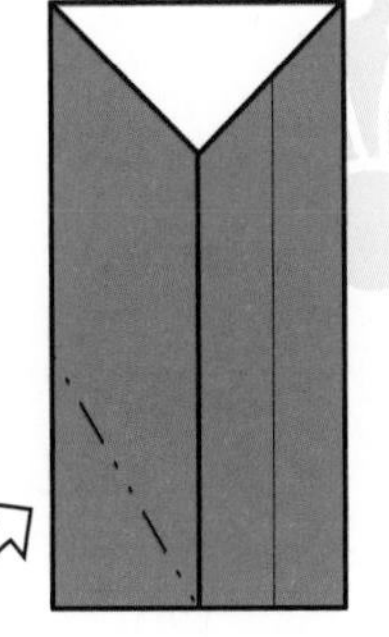

Inside reverse fold the crease made in step 6.

8

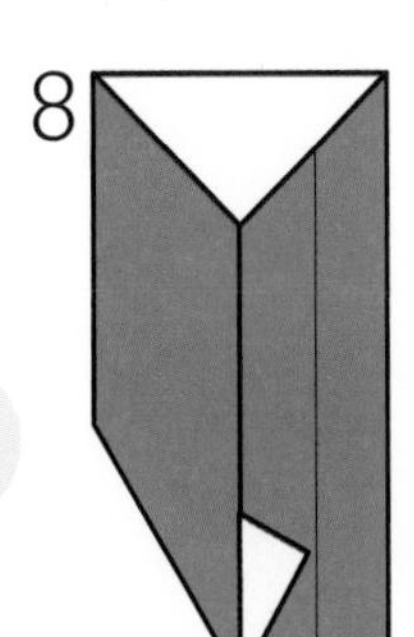

This will be the result. Turn over.

9

Fold the top two corners down to meet the centre and unfold.

10

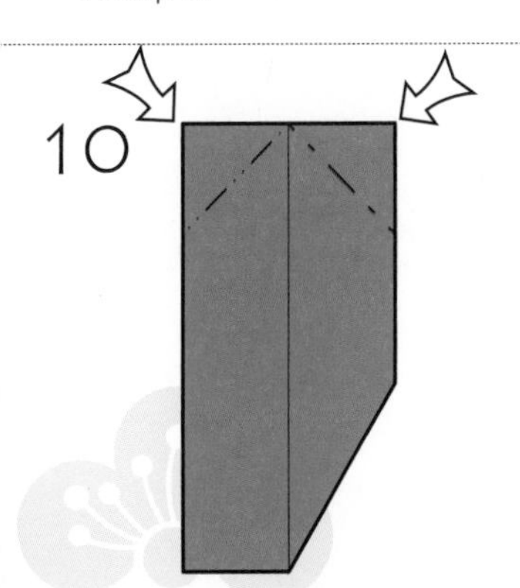

Sink the creases made in step 9.

11

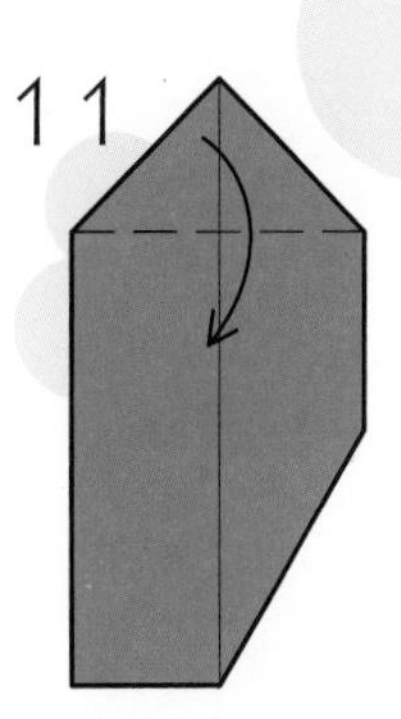

Fold the top flap downwards.

12

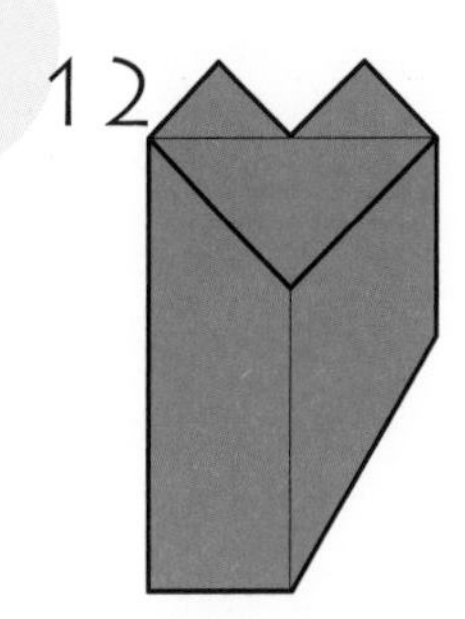

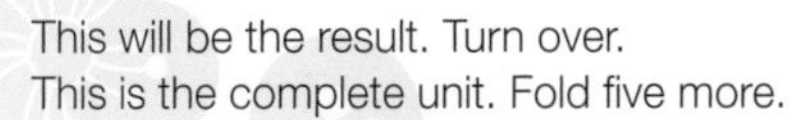

This will be the result. Turn over.
This is the complete unit. Fold five more.

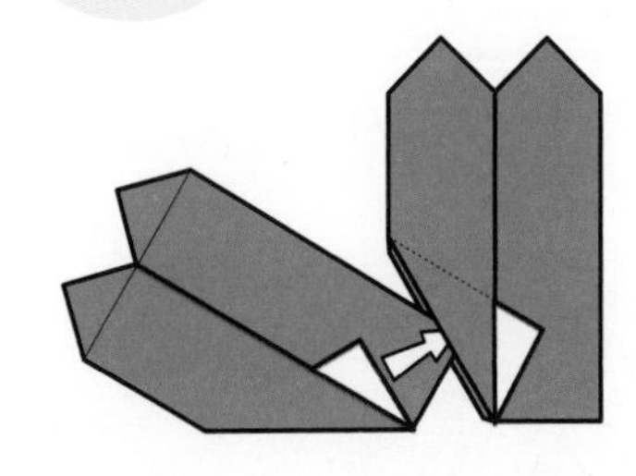

Insert one module into the next.
Repeat for the remaining units.

14

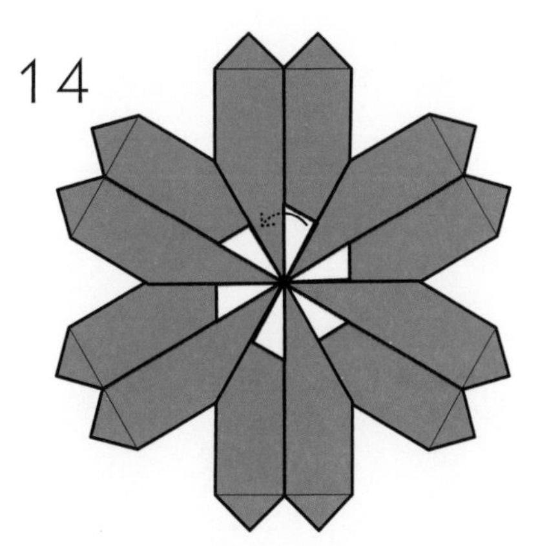

Fold the small flaps inside to lock the units in place. Repeat on remaining flaps.

15

Turn over. Completed heart fold.

Flower for Rose

MODEL: DARREN SCOTT
DIAGRAM: DARREN SCOTT

This is a variation on a traditional teabag fold. It uses origami techniques to lock the units together rather than glue, which was used in the original version.

1

Start with a square white side up. Fold and unfold diagonal.

2

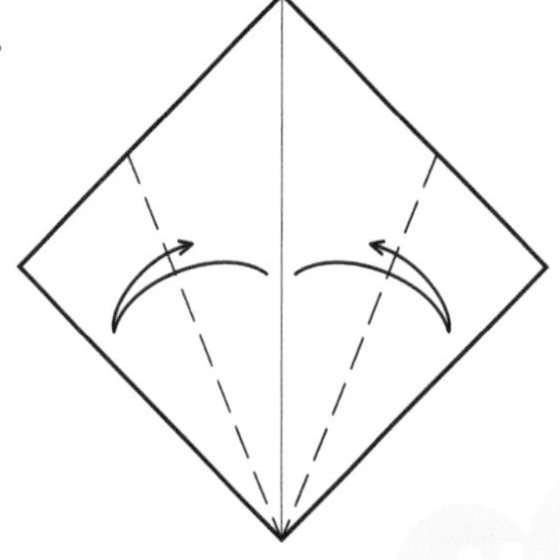

Fold the bottom two edges to the crease made in step 1 and unfold.

3

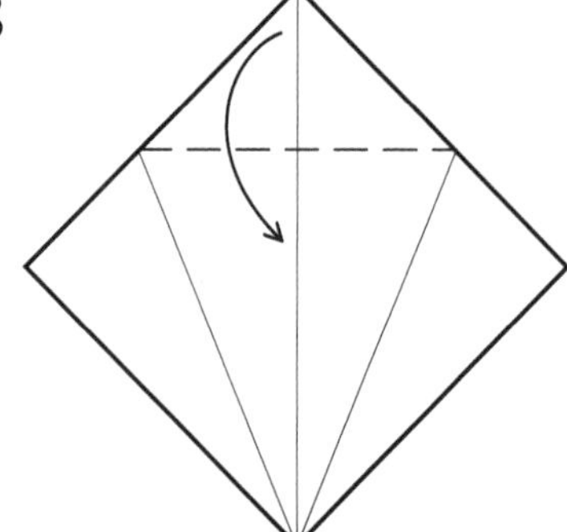

Using the the creases made in step 2 as a guide, fold the top point downwards.

4

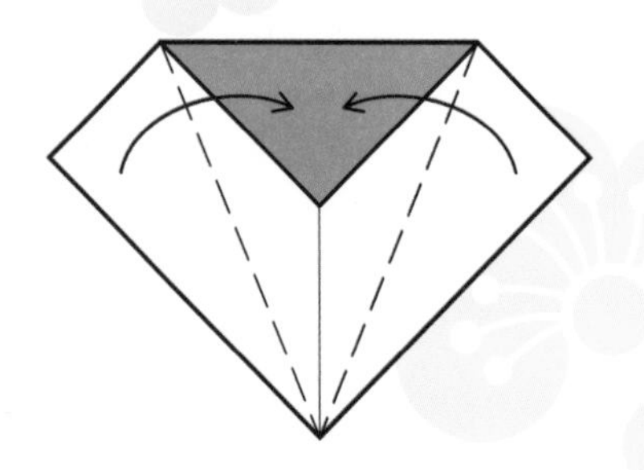

Refold the creases made in step 2.

5

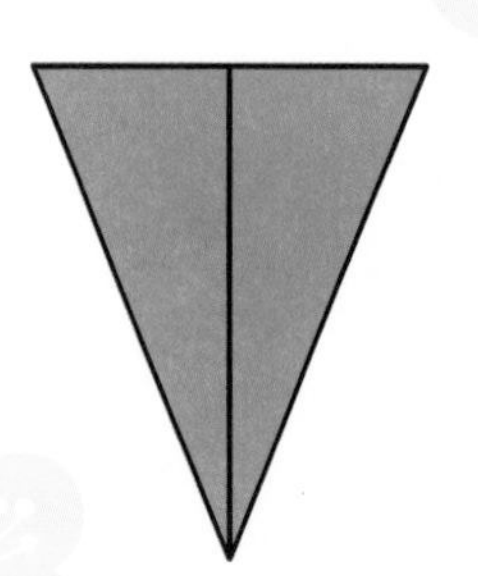

This should be the result. Turn over.

6

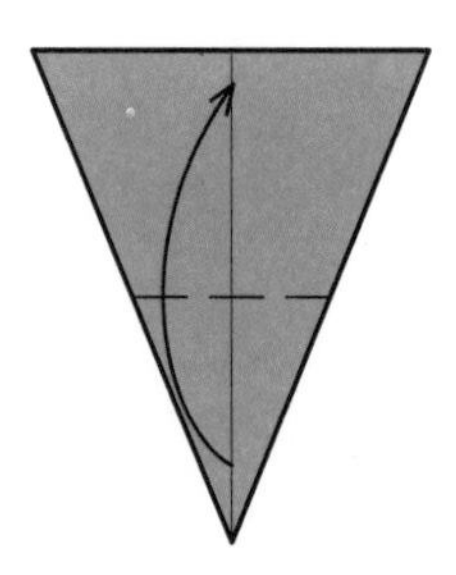

Fold the bottom point to meet the top edge.

7

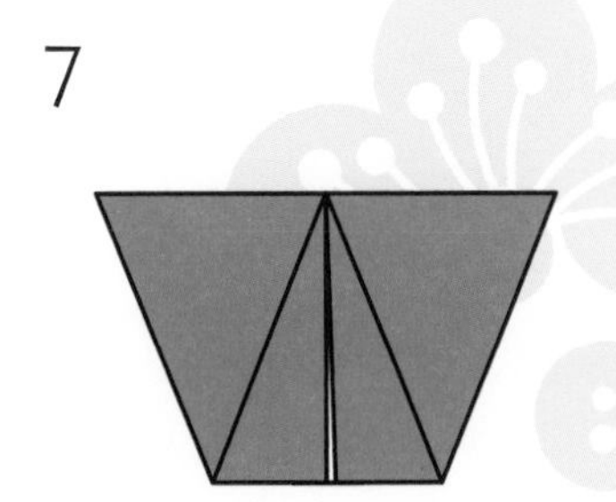

The first unit is complete.
Now fold five more.

8

Insert the bottom right corner of one unit into the next.

9

This will be the result. Turn over.

10

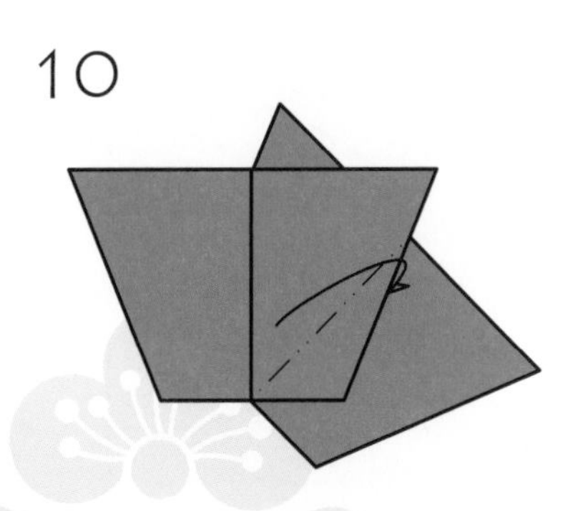

Fold the edge over to lock the units together. Fold the bottom point to meet the top edge.

11

This will be the result when the two units are locked together. Turn over.

12

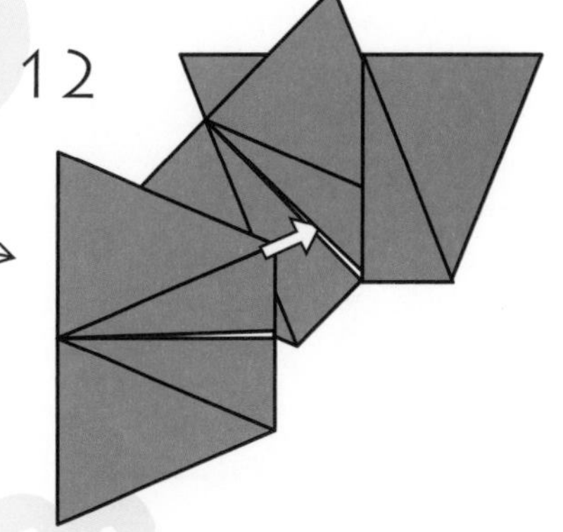

Repeat steps 8-11 on the next unit.

13

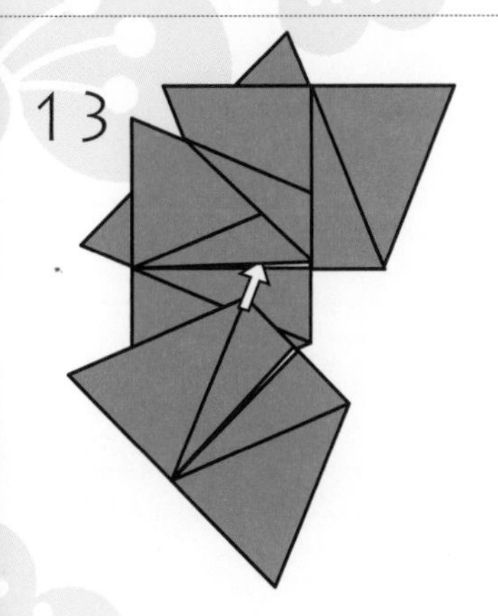

Continue with the remaining units.

14

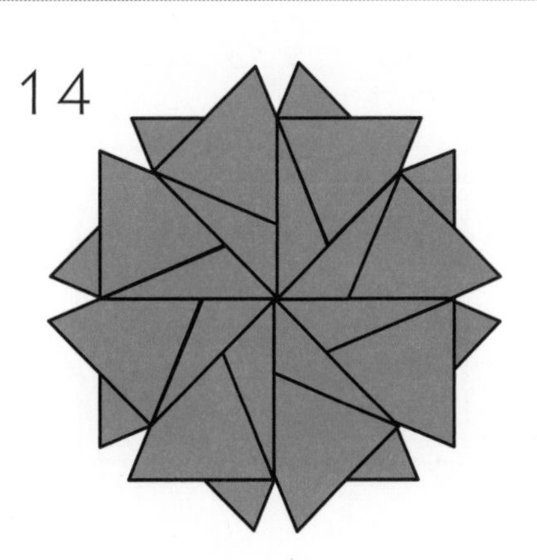

Completed flower for rose.

WREATH

MODEL: DARREN SCOTT
DIAGRAM: DARREN SCOTT

This module is unique in the way it locks each module from the front and back – it makes the lock very strong and the completed model very durable.

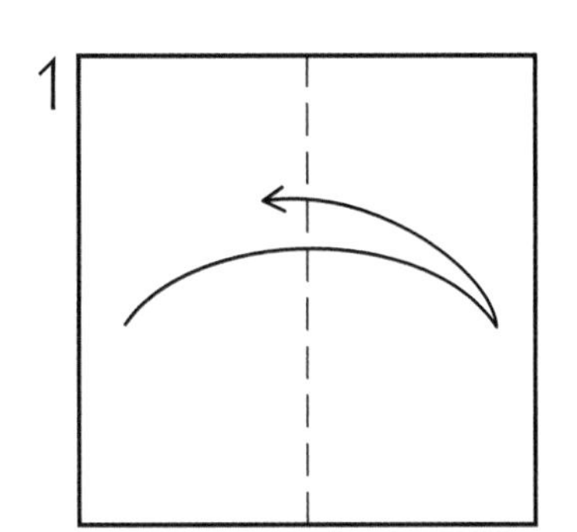

Start with a square white side up. Book fold and unfold.

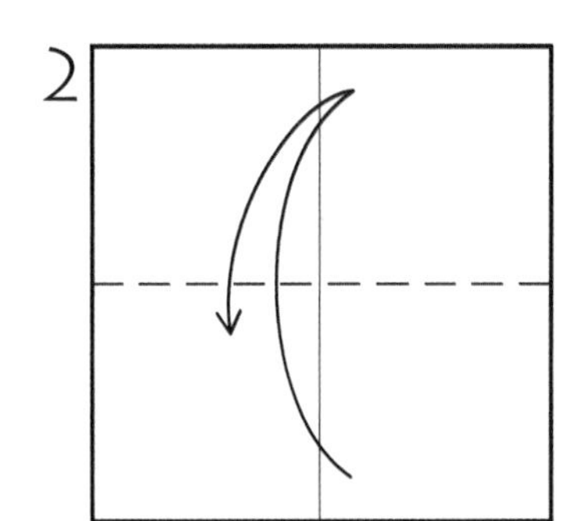

Book fold and unfold again.

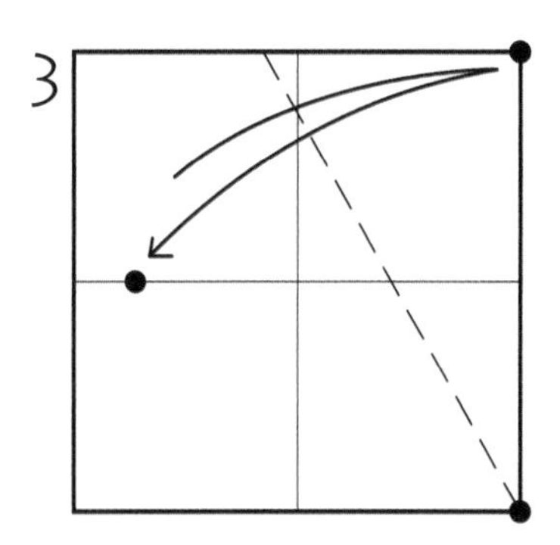

Fold the top right corner so it lies along the crease made in step 2.

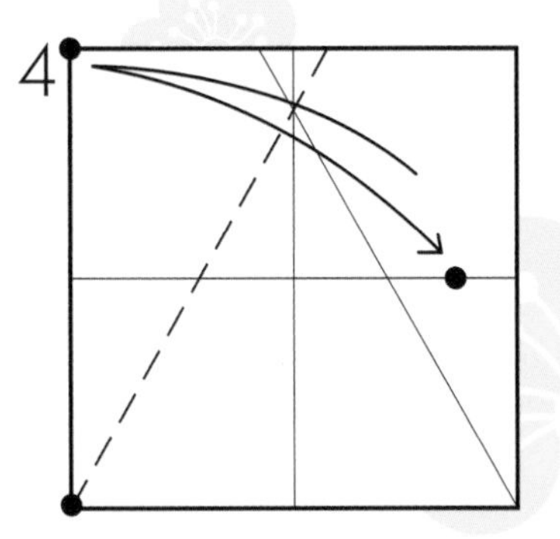

Repeat on the left corner.

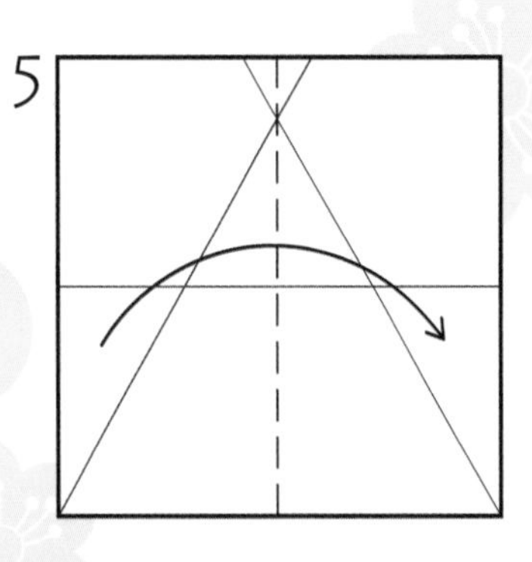

Refold along the crease in step 1.

6

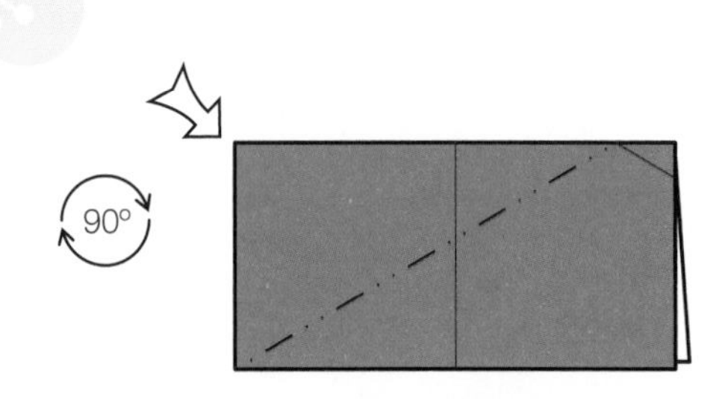

Rotate 90° clockwise. Inside reverse fold along existing creases.

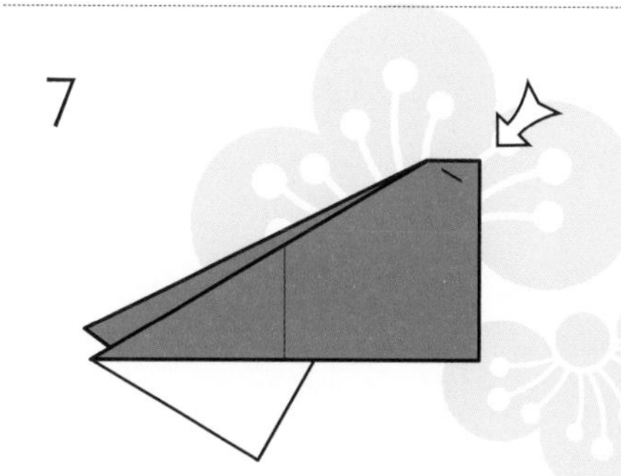

7

Inside reverse fold the top point.

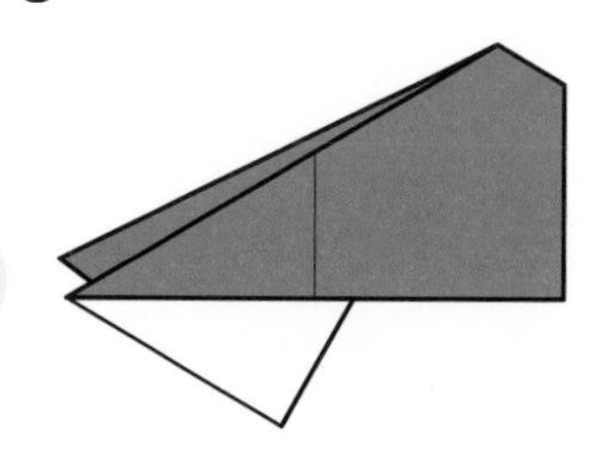

8

The first unit is complete.
Now fold five more.

9

Join the first two units together.

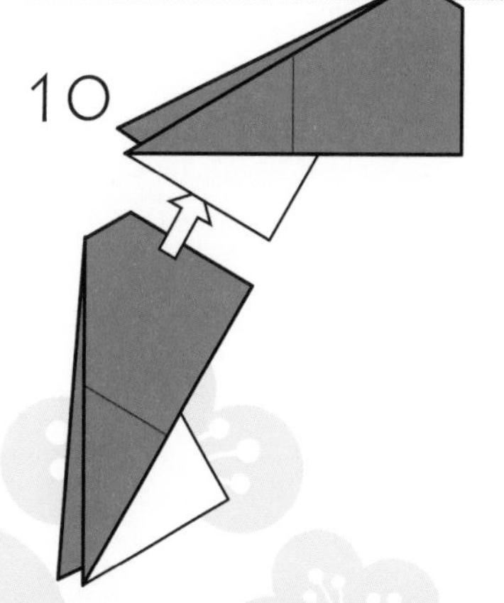

10

Fold the tips inwards to lock the units in place.

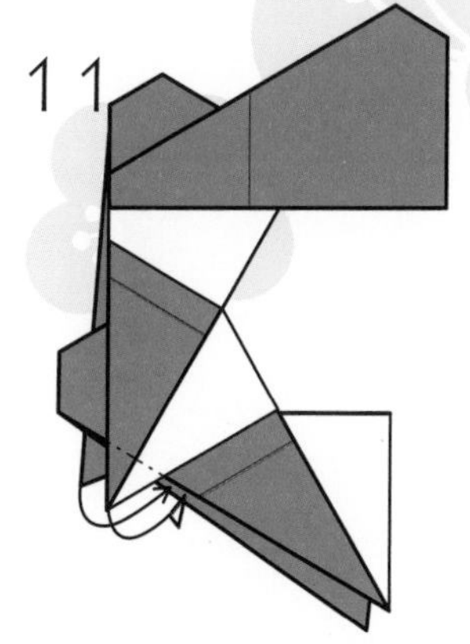

11

Add the third unit and lock it in place as in step 10.

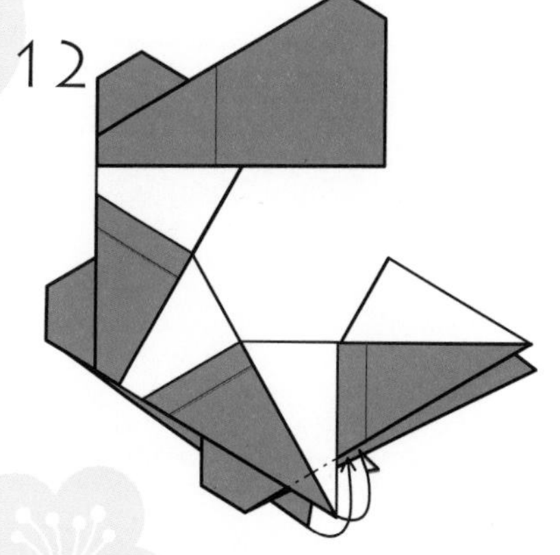

12

Add the fourth unit.

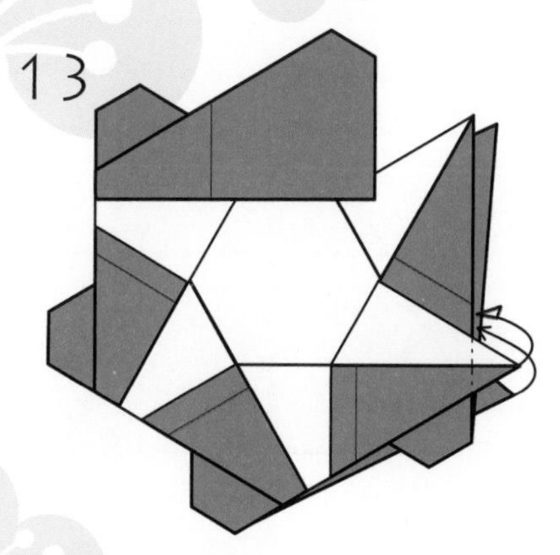

13

Add the fifth unit.

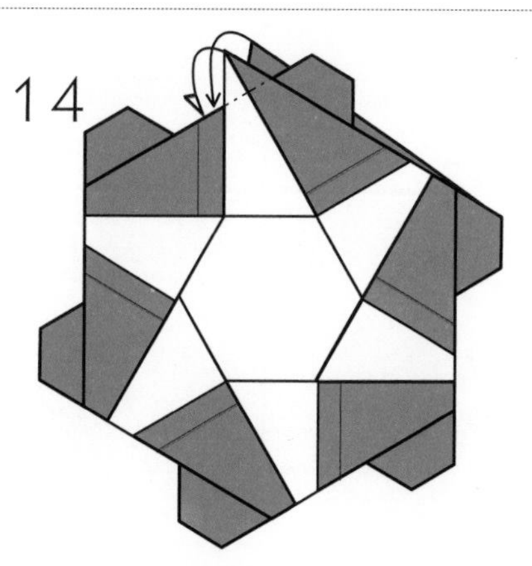

14

Add the final unit.

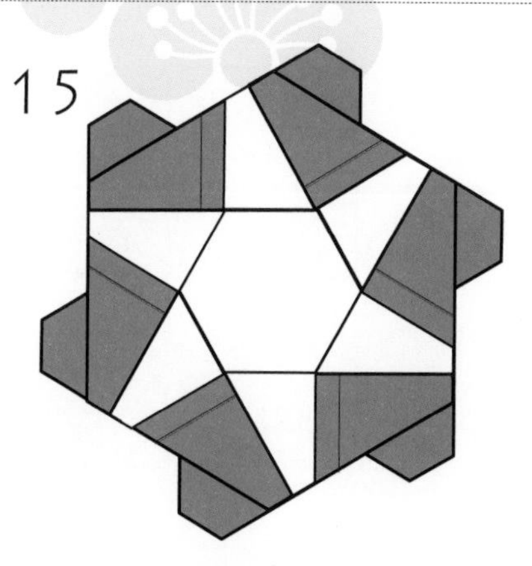

15

Completed wreath.

SIX POINT STAR

MODEL: DARREN SCOTT
DIAGRAM: DARREN SCOTT

This model locks very strongly together although it's a little tricky to assemble. However once you have it assembled, it will not come apart easily.

1

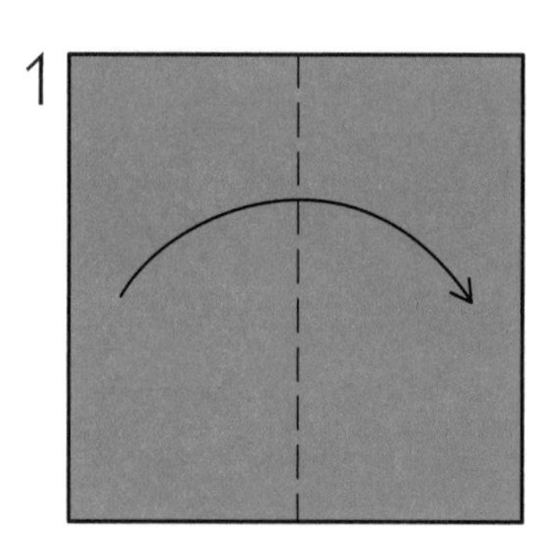

Start with the square coloured side up. Book fold.

2

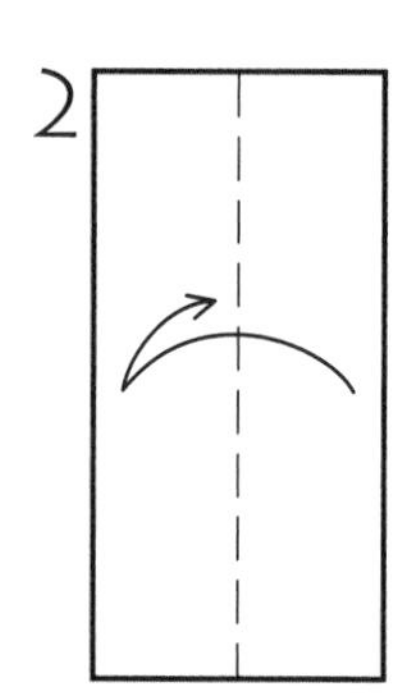

Fold the front layer in half and unfold.

3

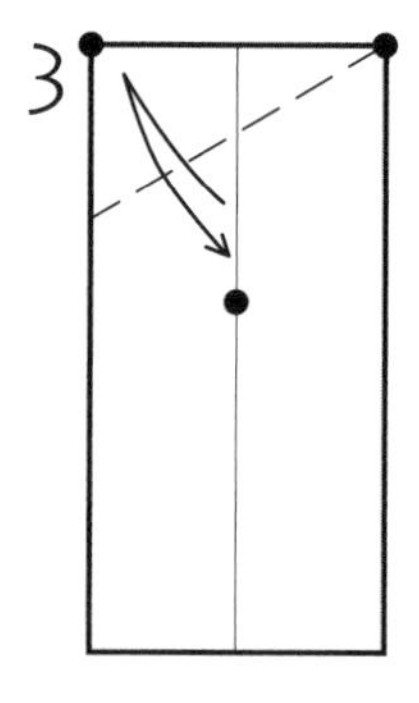

Fold the top left corner so it lies along the crease made in step 2 and unfold.

4 

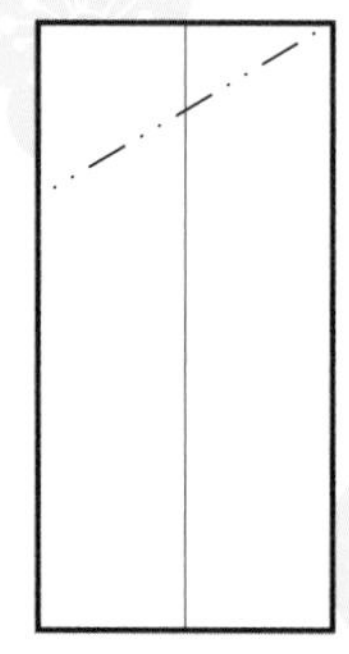

Sink the top left corner along the crease made in step 3.

5

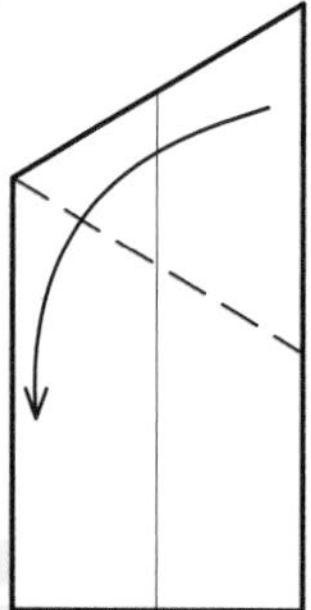

Fold the top right corner down so it lies along the left edge.

6

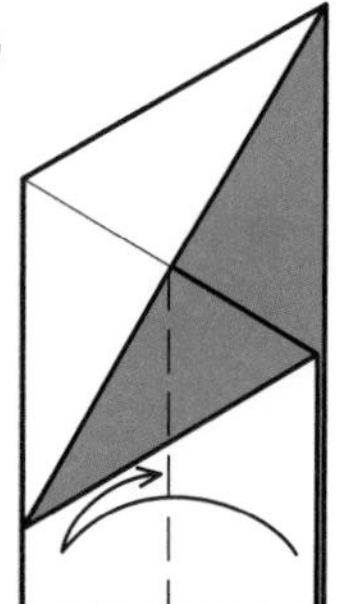

Fold the top layer to the left and unfold. This will be used to lock the units in place later.

7

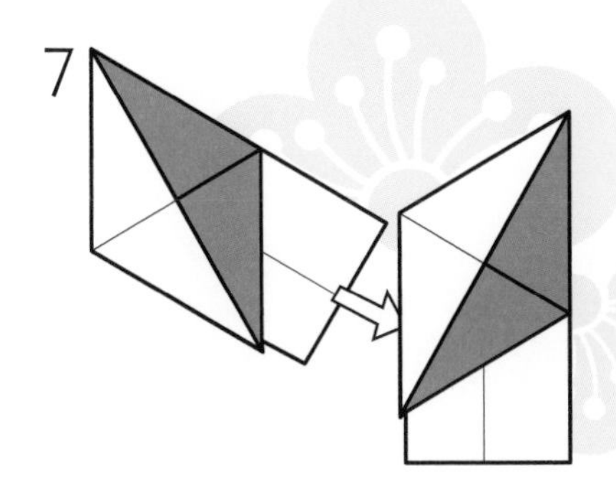

Insert two units together.

8

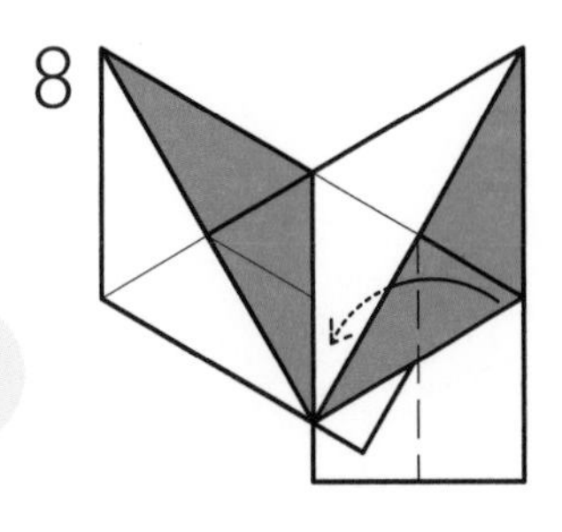

Fold to the left and tuck under flap. This locks the units together.

9

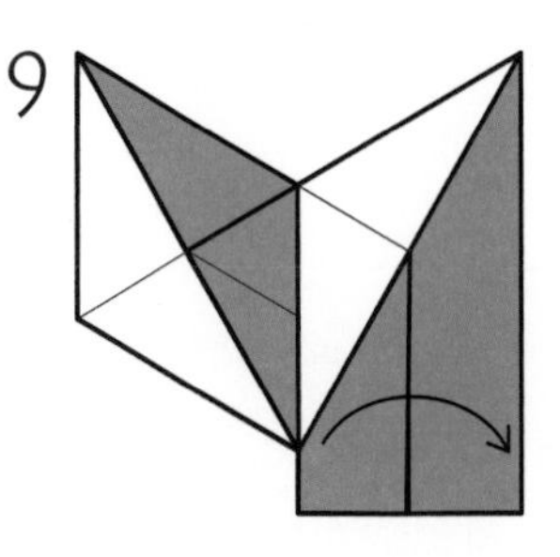

Unfold the lock. These will be refolded in steps 13 and 14.

10

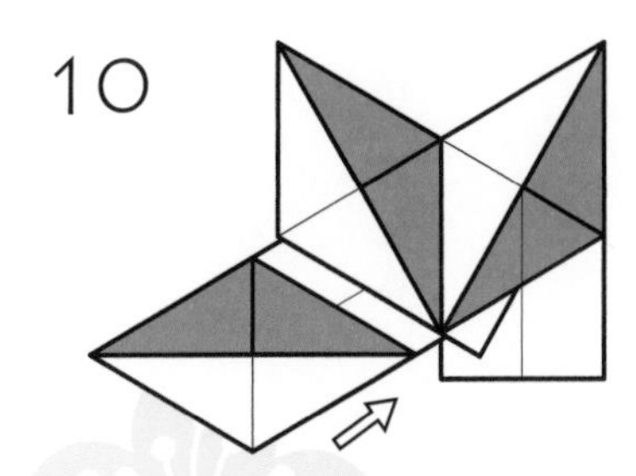

Add the third unit.

11

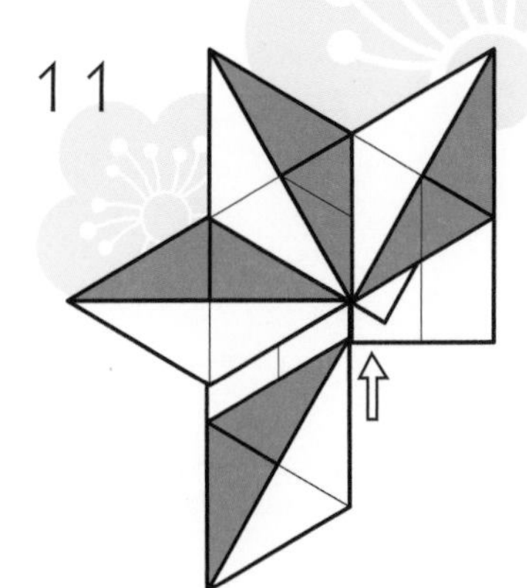

Add the remaining units.

12

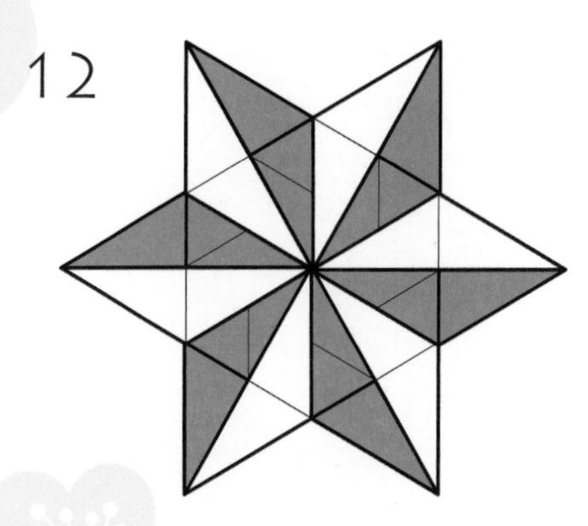

This will be the result. Now we need to lock the units in place.

13

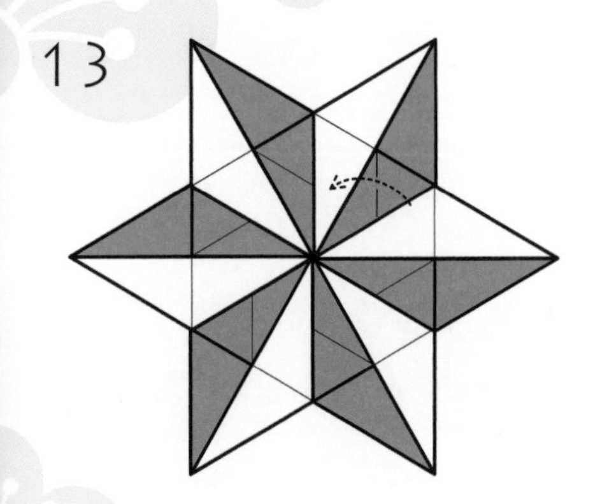

Refold the crease from step 9 to lock the units together.

14

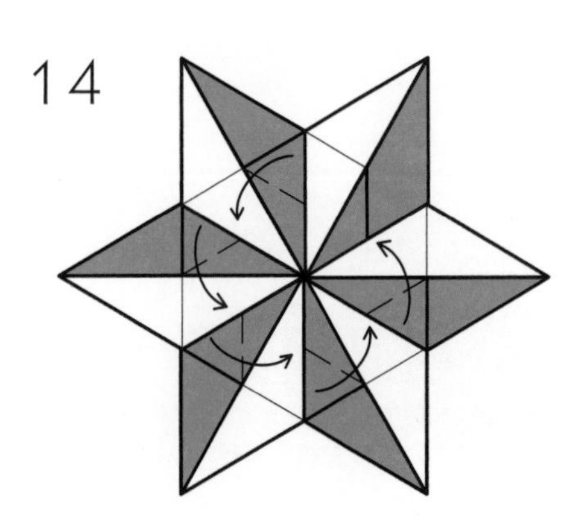

Lock the remaining units in place.

15

Completed six point star.

Platonic Solids

By: Matthew Gardiner

Platonic Solids, Polyhedra and Unit Origami

The platonic solids are named after the Greek philosopher and mathematician Plato. Platonic solids are very special shapes with the following unique properties. All faces are identical shapes with the same side length. At the vertices (corners), the angles are all the same, and the same number of sides meet at each vertex (corner).

Their Greek names come from the number of sides or faces they have. The suffix -hedron means solid form.

They are presented here as a reference for unit origami assembly. Study these forms and use the numbers of faces and edges as a reference to work out how many units you need to make a platonic solid.

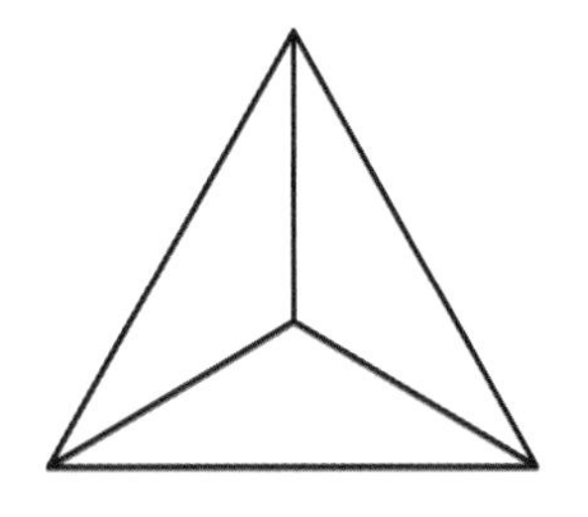

Tetrahedron

Tetra means four.

Each side is an equilateral triangle.

Tetrahedron has 4 faces, 6 edges and 4 vertices.

Hexahedron

Hex means six.

Each side is a perfect square.

Hexahedron has 6 faces, 12 sides and 8 vertices.

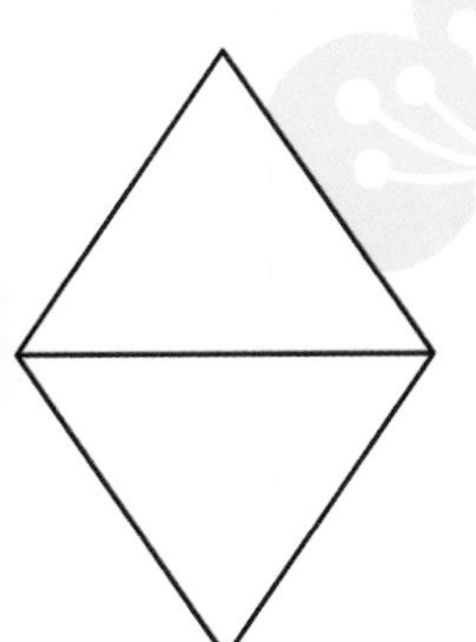

OCTAHEDRON

Octa means eight.

Each side is an equilateral triangle.

Octahedron has 8 faces, 12 edges and 6 vertices.

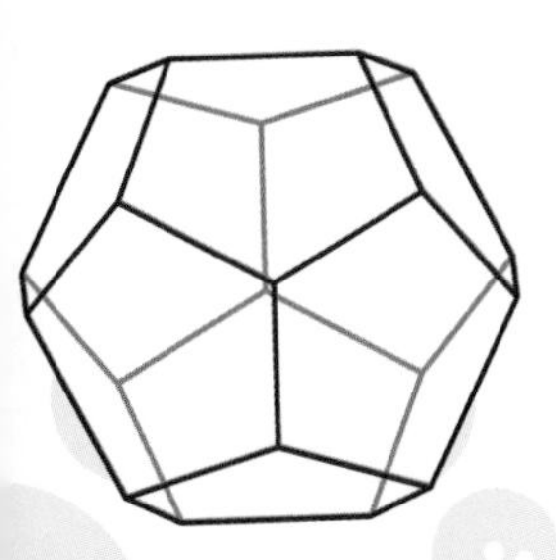

DODECAHEDRON

Dodeca means two, ten or twelve.

Each side is a perfect pentagon (5-sided shape).

Dodecahedron has 12 faces, 30 edges and 20 vertices.

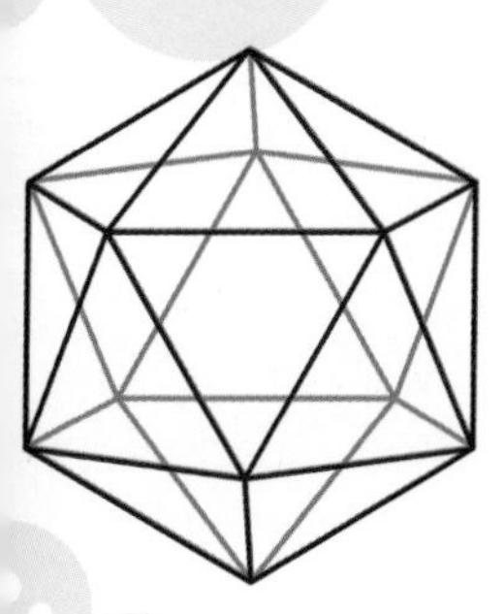

ICOSAHEDRON

Icosa means twenty.

Each side is an equilateral triangle.

Icosahedron has 20 faces, 30 edges and 12 vertices.

XYZ

MODEL: DARREN SCOTT
DIAGRAM: MATTHEW GARDINER

The XYZ is named after the cartesian planes used in mathematics. Each unit in this model is made from two halves that slot together. Each unit has a slot through which another unit can be fitted. The last unit holds the XYZ together. You will need 6 sheets of paper – three colours, two of each colour.

1

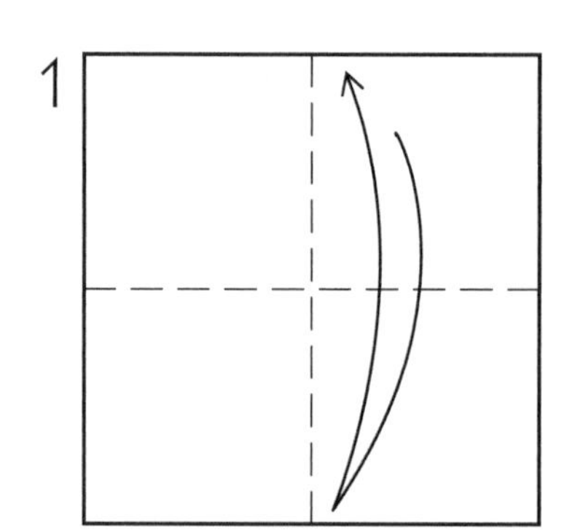

Begin white side up. Book fold and unfold.

2

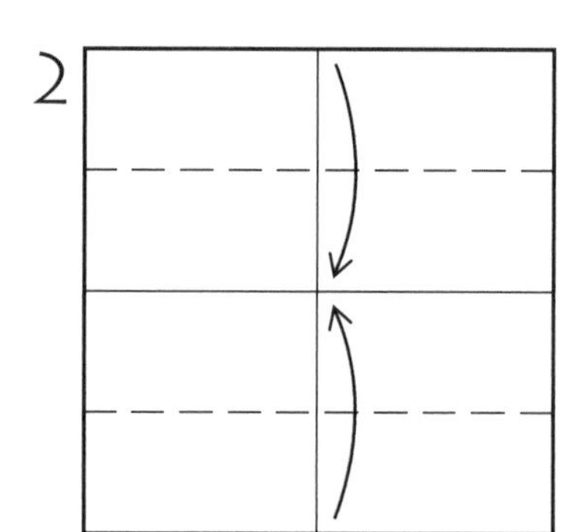

Cupboard fold.

3

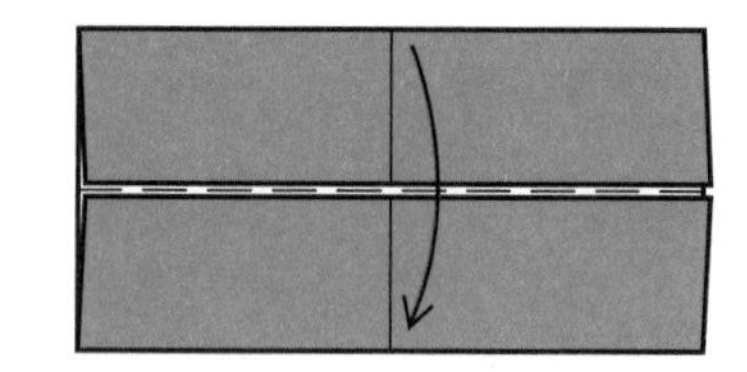

Fold the top edge to meet the bottom edge.

4

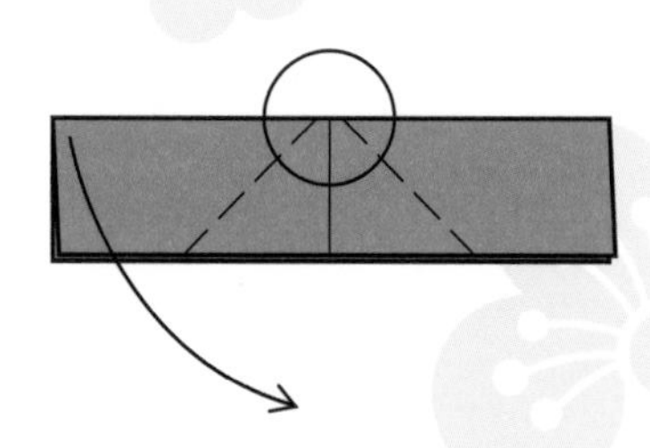

Make a diagonal crease, either side of the centre. Leave a small gap, about 2mm (1/12th of an inch), on either side.

5

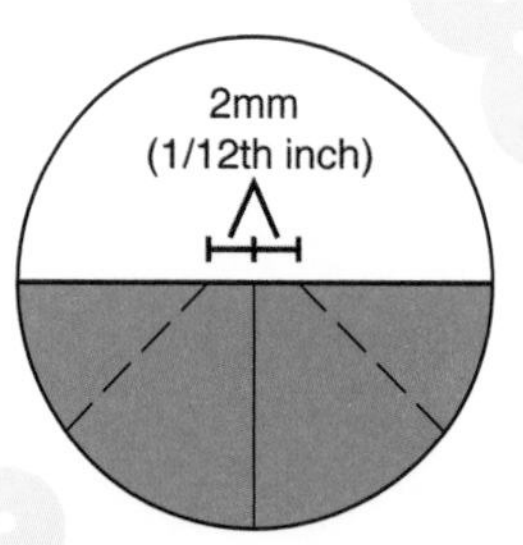

The gap is 2mm (1/12th inch) either side of the centre crease.

6

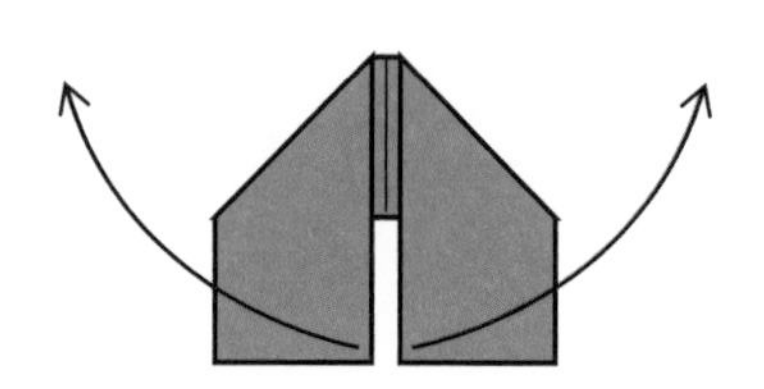

The model should look like this. Unfold back to step 4.

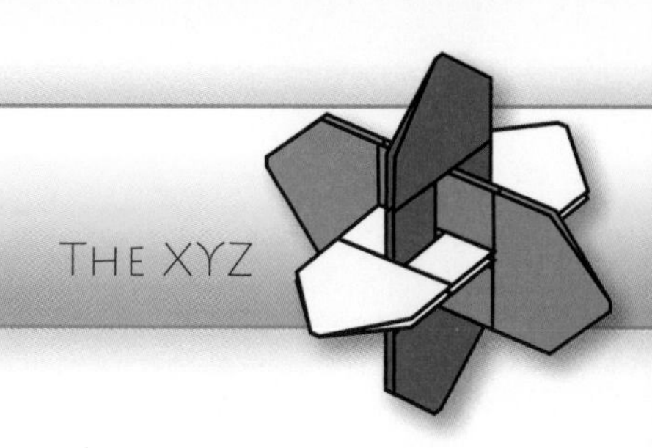

7

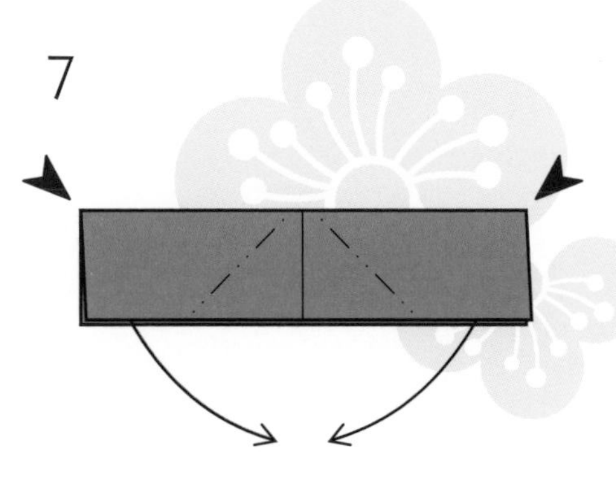

Inside reverse fold both ends on existing creases.

8

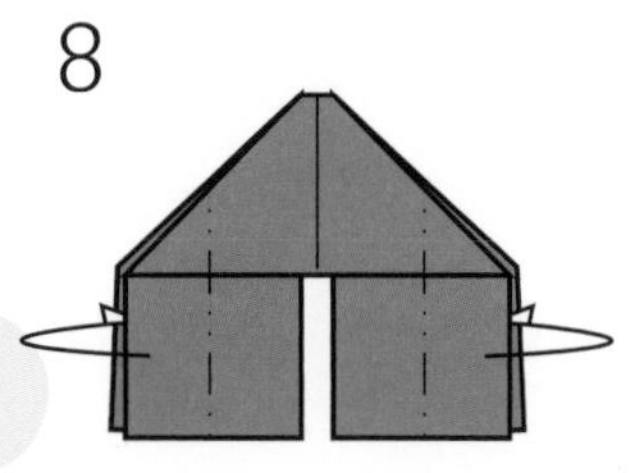

Mountain fold the front flaps in half. Repeat on the other side.

9

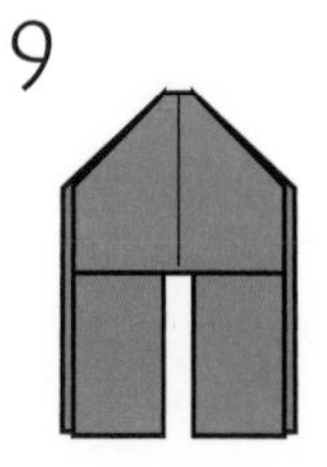

A completed half unit. You need two halves to make a unit.

10

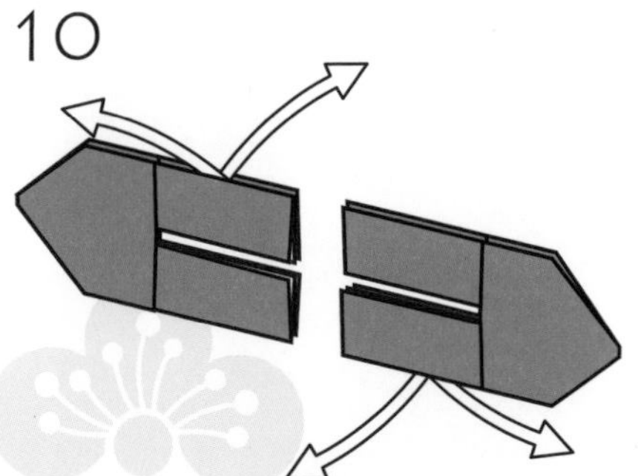

To make a unit, take two halves, and open out opposite flaps as shown.

11

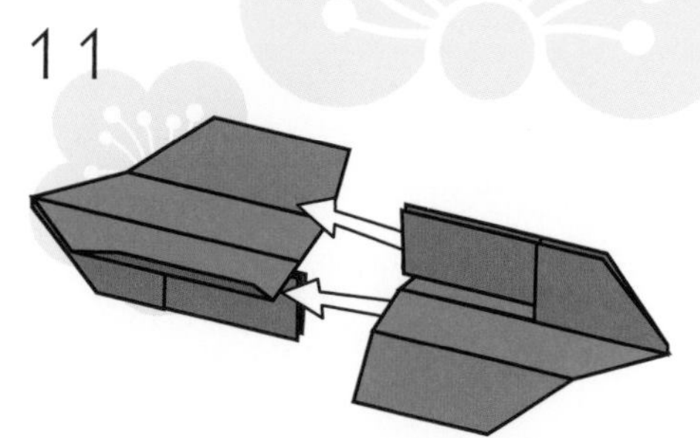

Slide the halves together.

12

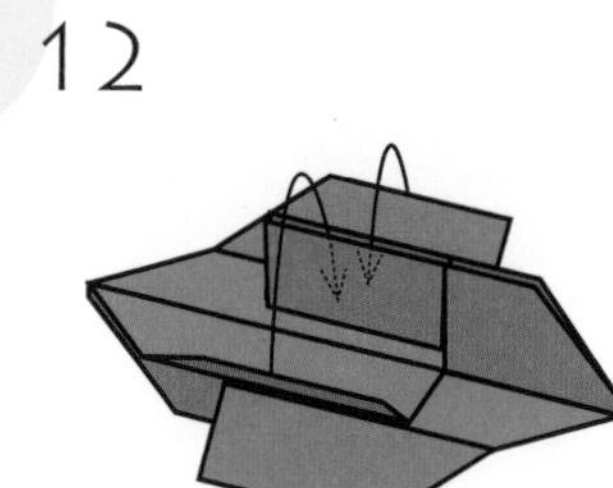

Wrap the folded flap inside the unfolded flap on both top and bottom.

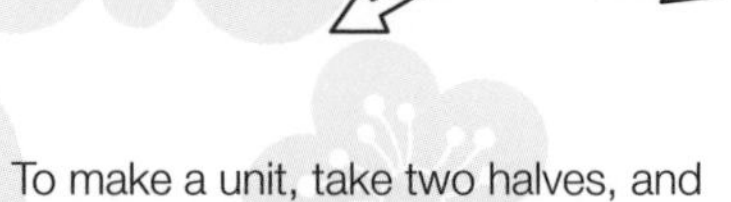

13

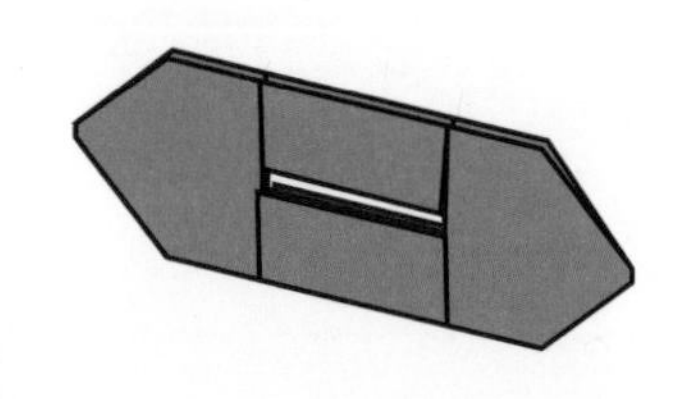

A completed unit. You need two more to make an XYZ.

14

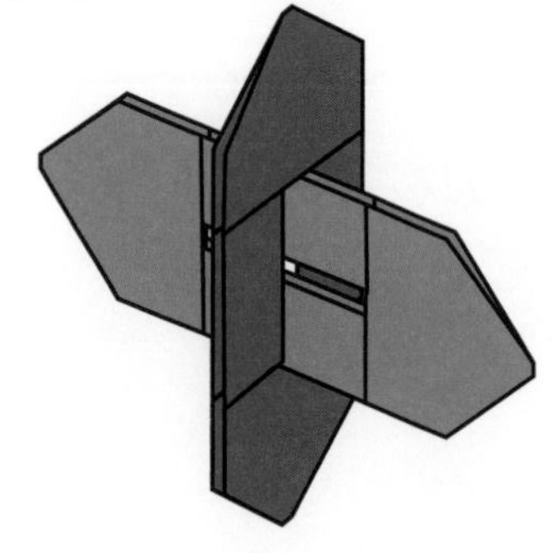

Two completed units slotted together. Slot the last unit in place.

15

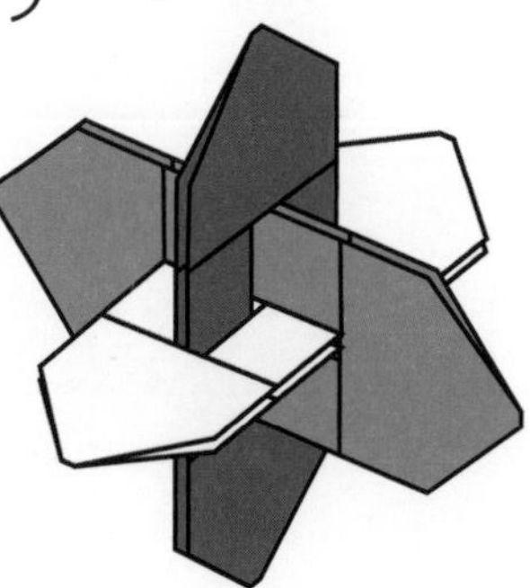

Completed XYZ.

SIXTY-FOUR

MODEL: DARREN SCOTT
DIAGRAM: MATTHEW GARDINER

The sixty-four is named after the four sixty degree triangles on each unit. The units lock together very firmly making a strong model. You will need six sheets of paper — three colours, two of each colour.

1

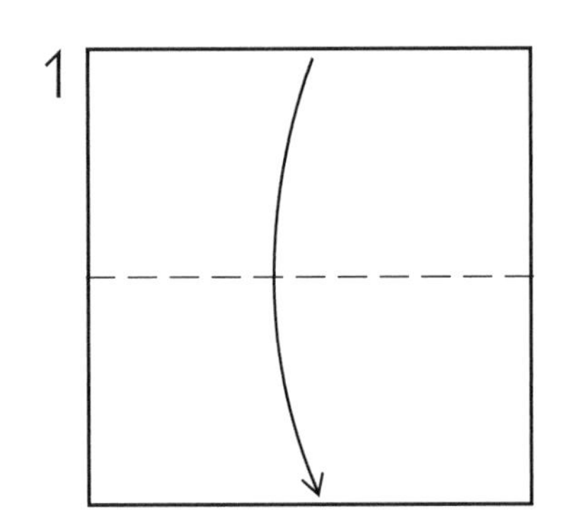

Book fold.

2

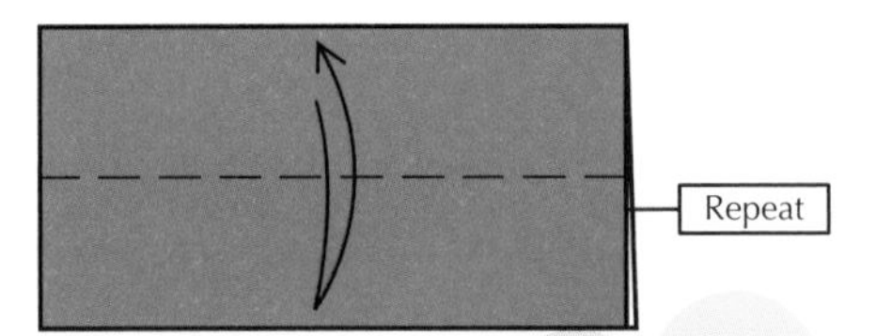

Fold bottom edge to top, and unfold. Repeat behind.

3

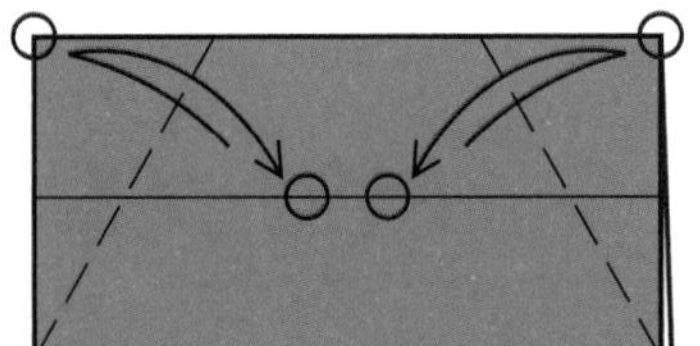

Fold corners to meet the middle crease dividing the bottom corners into two par

4

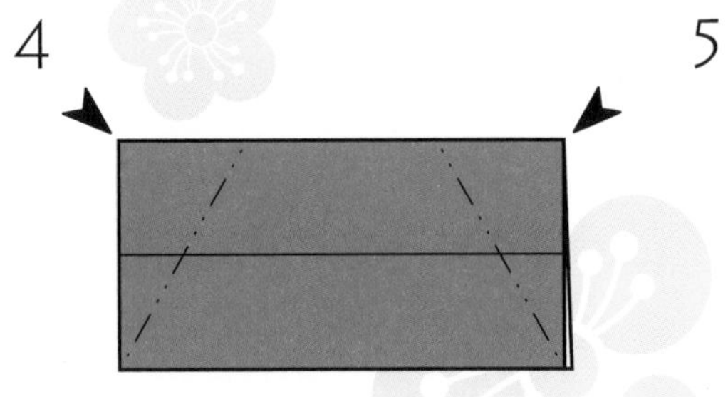

Inside reverse fold both corners.

5

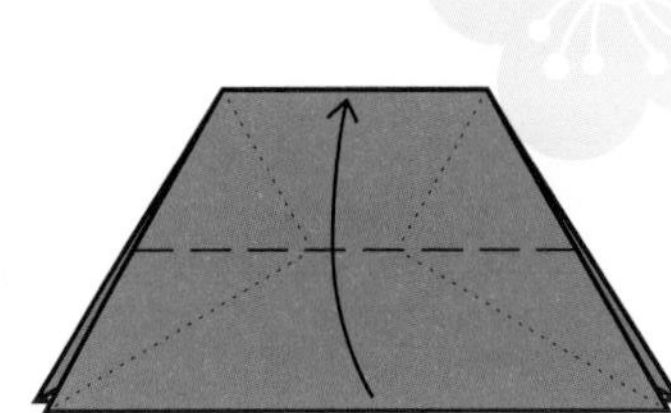

Fold bottom edge to top.

6

Repeat step 5 behind.

7

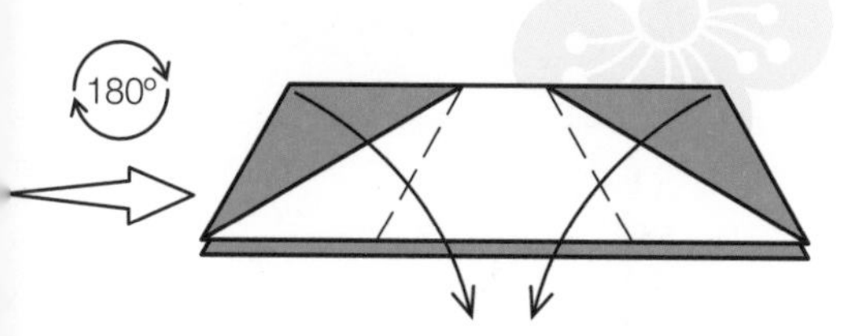

Rotate 180°. Fold both top layers over.

8

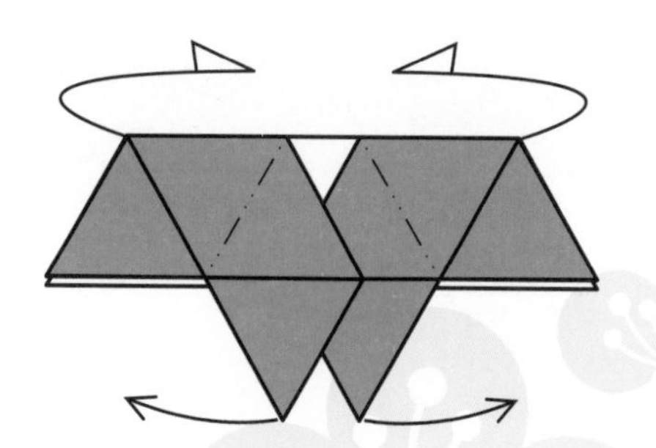

Swivel the points to 90° from the centre strip.

9

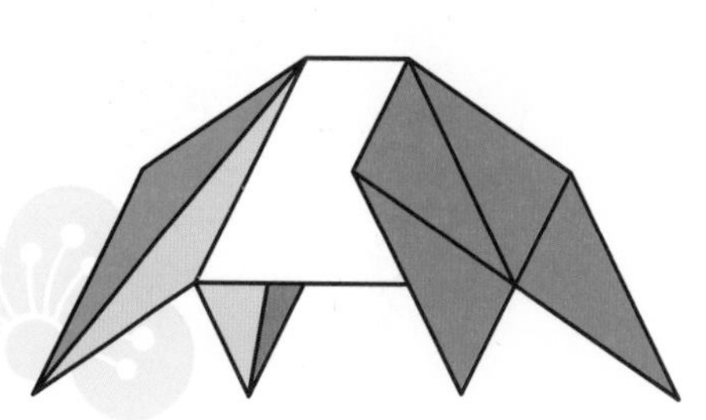

The completed sixty-four unit.

10

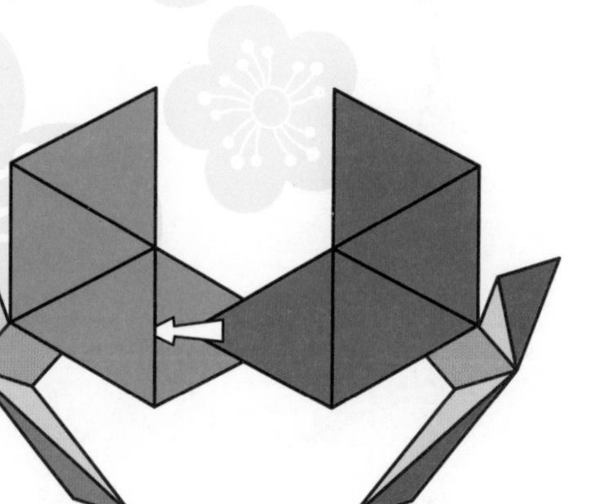

The units slot together as shown. The pointed tip of one unit slides into the pocket of another.

11

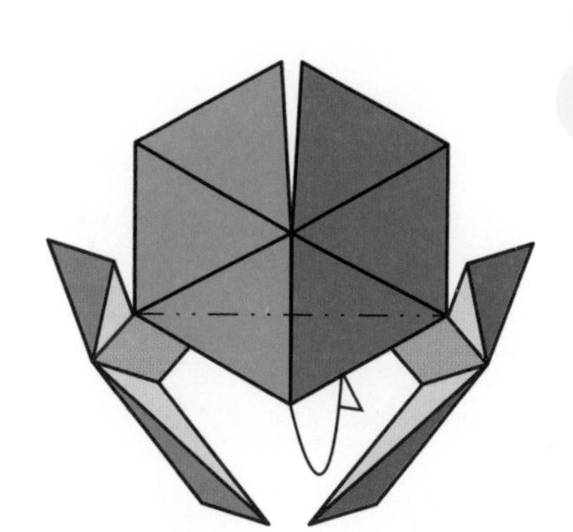

Mountain fold the joined edges to lock the unit in place.

12

A locked unit. Add a third unit to complete one side.

MODEL: DARREN SCOT
DIAGRAM: MATTHEW GARDINE

13

Mountain fold the joined edges to lock the unit in place.

14

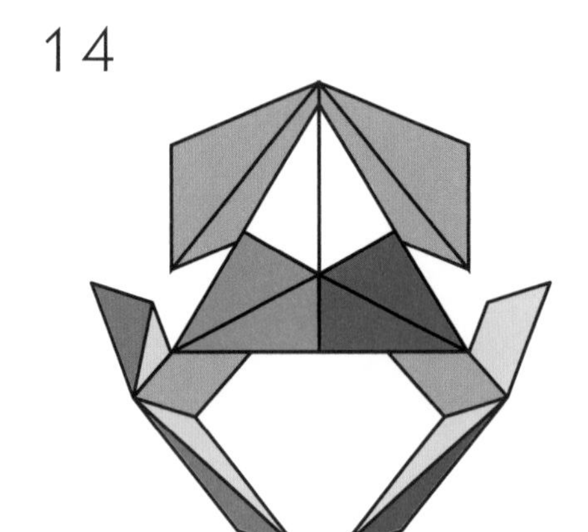

Three locked units make a completed side. Add another three units to the remaining points to complete the model.

15

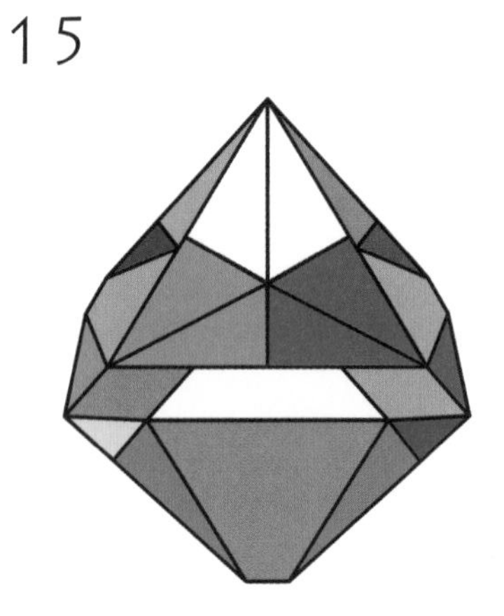

Six units assembled to make the sixty-four.

WINDMILL RODS

MODEL: DARREN SCOTT
DIAGRAM: MATTHEW GARDINER

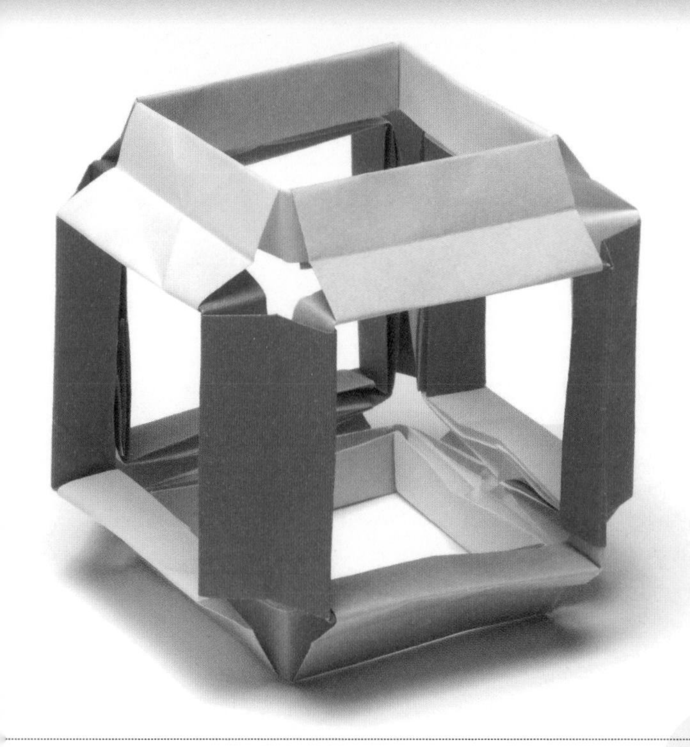

This unit is made from a windmill base, and is very versatile. With conveniently located hands and pockets, it is easy to assemble and can be made into many different geometric forms. Refer to the Platonic Solids section when attempting to build more complex geometries.

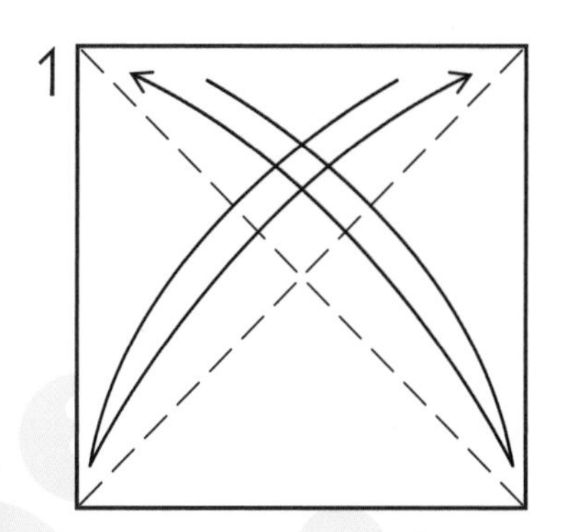

Fold and unfold diagonals.

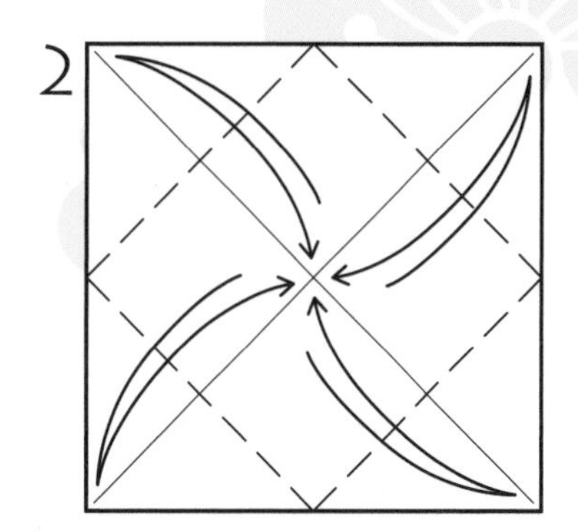

Blintz fold and unfold.

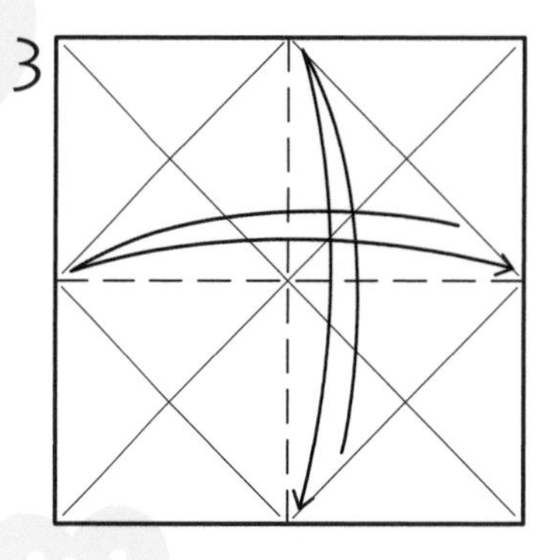

Book fold and unfold.

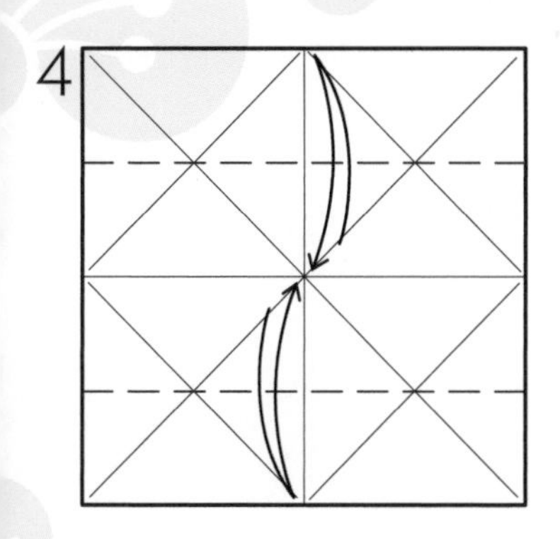

Cupboard fold and unfold.

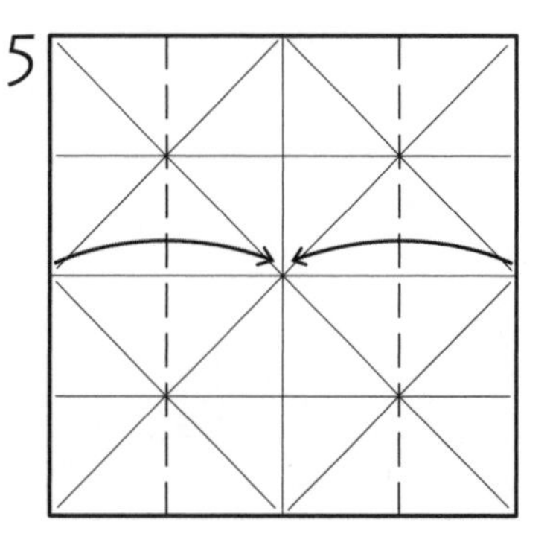

Cupboard fold.

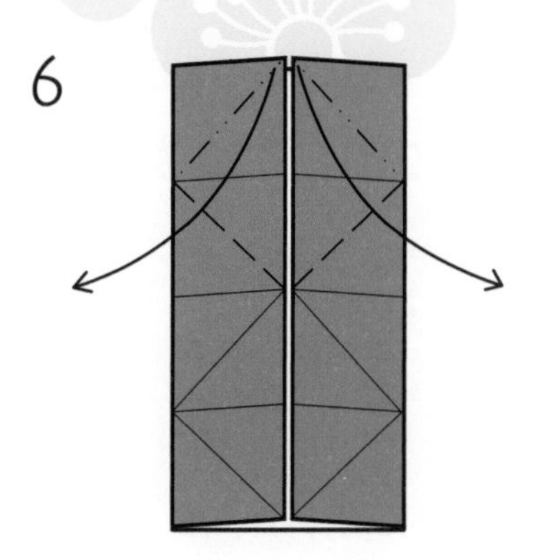

Squash fold using existing creases.

7

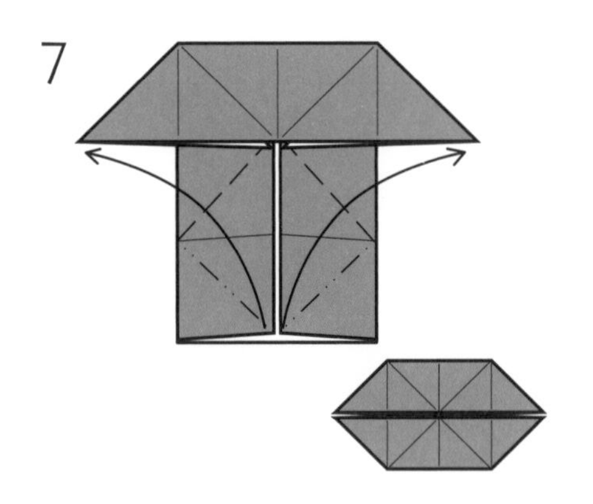

Repeat step 6 on the bottom.

8

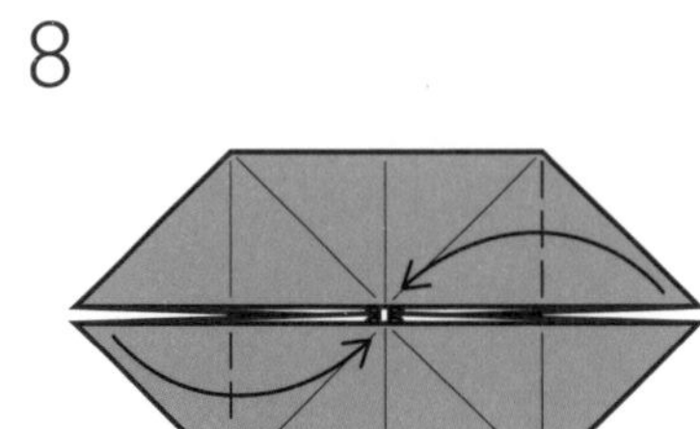

Fold two corners to the middle.

9

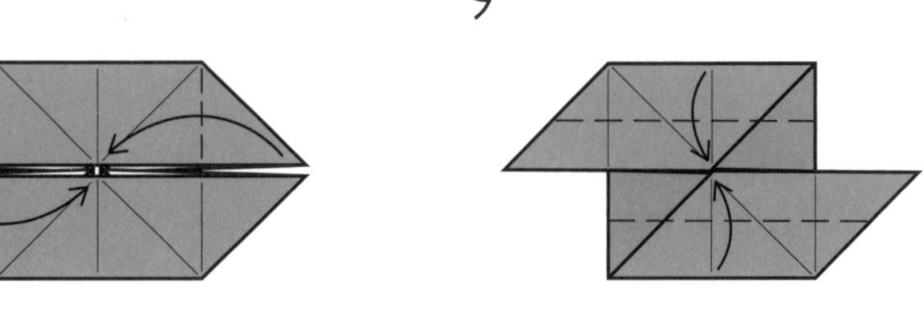

Fold edges to meet the middle.

10

11

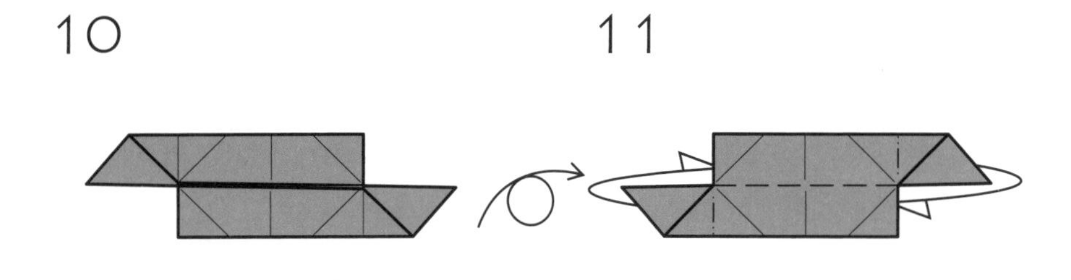

This is the bottom of the unit. Turn over.

Mountain fold the tips, and valley fold lengthways to 90º.

12

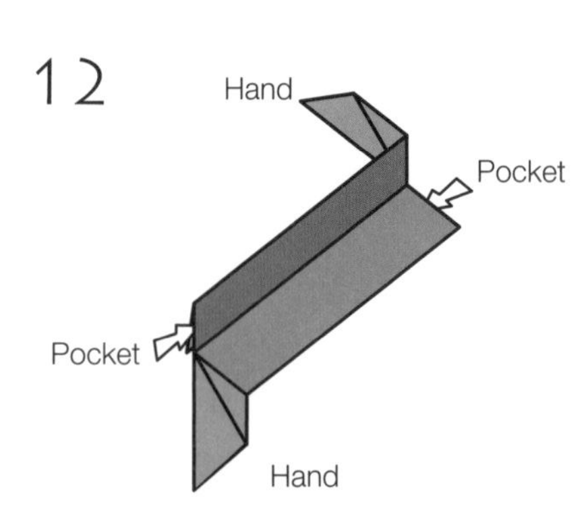

The completed unit.

13

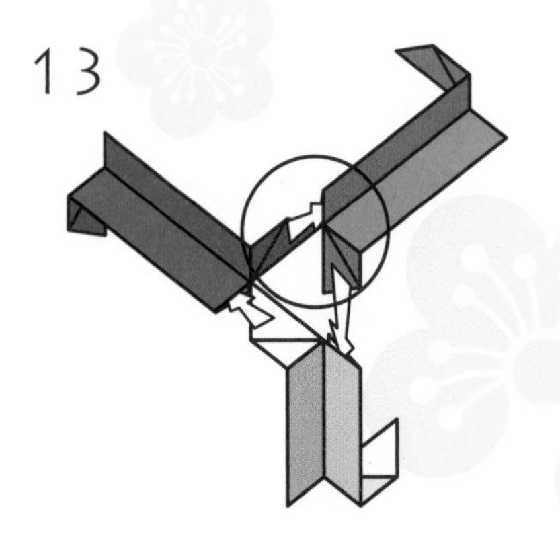

Assemble units as shown.

14

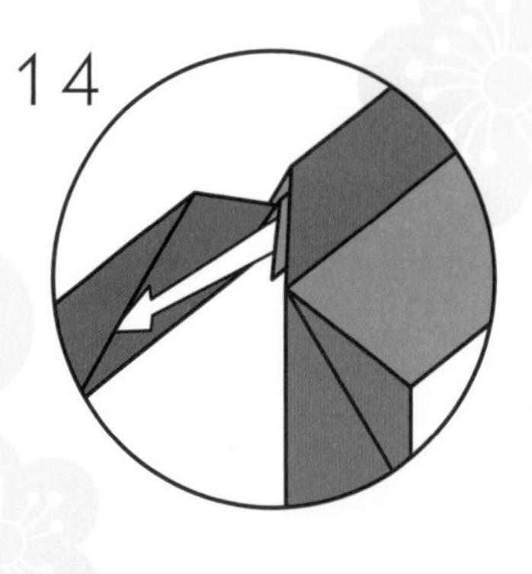

Note the way in which the units slot together. The lock is quite strong.

15

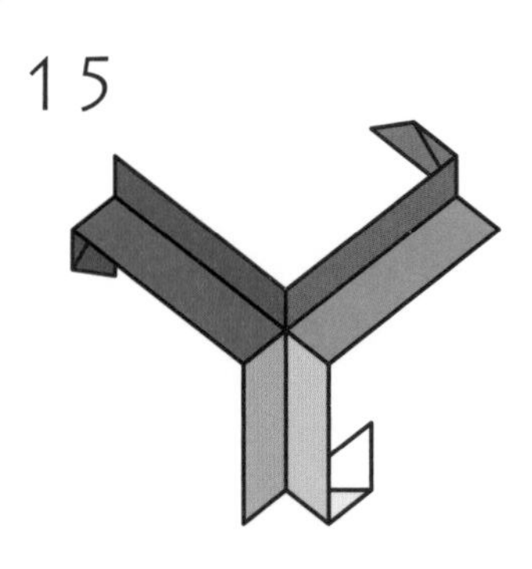

Three units assembled.

16

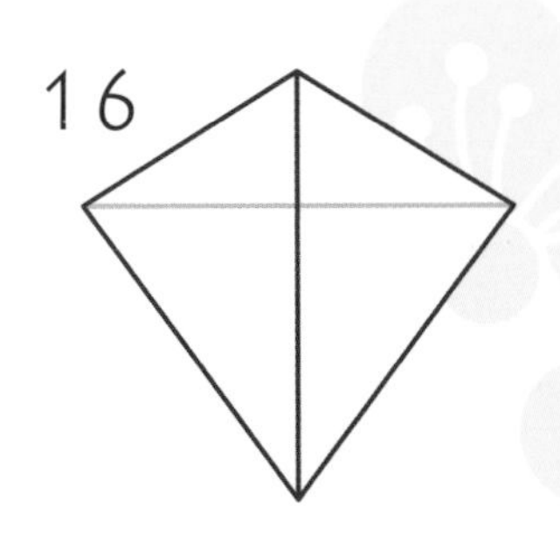

Tetrahedron

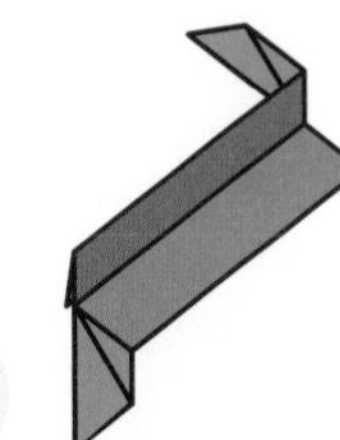

x 6

Use six units.

Completed tetrahedron.

17

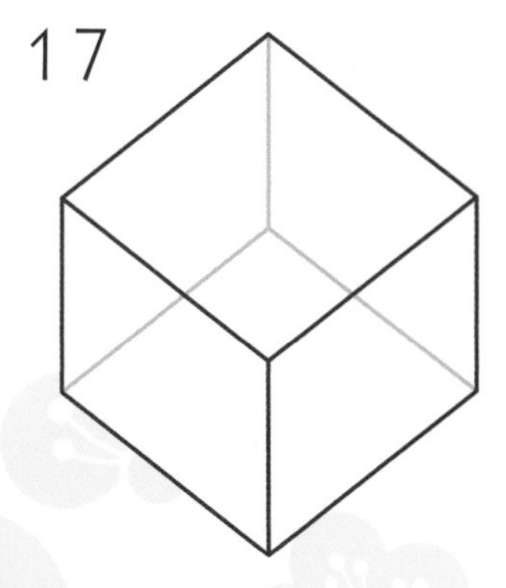

Hexahedron

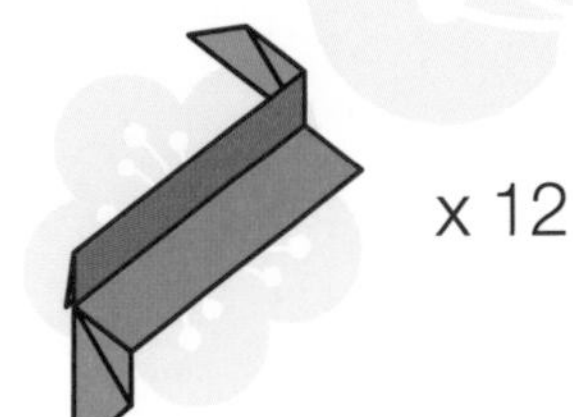

x 12

Use twelve units.

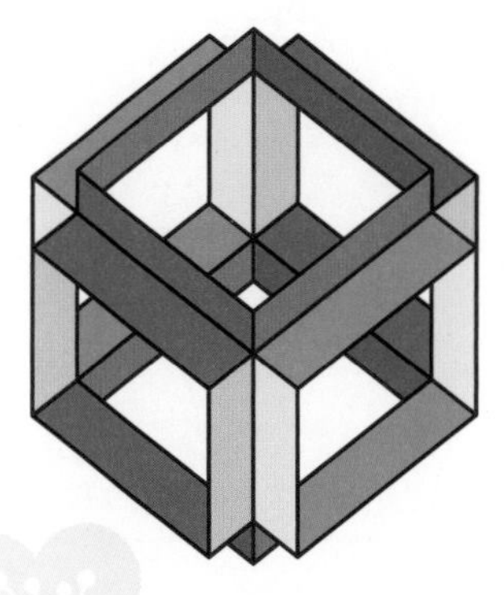

Completed hexahedron.

18

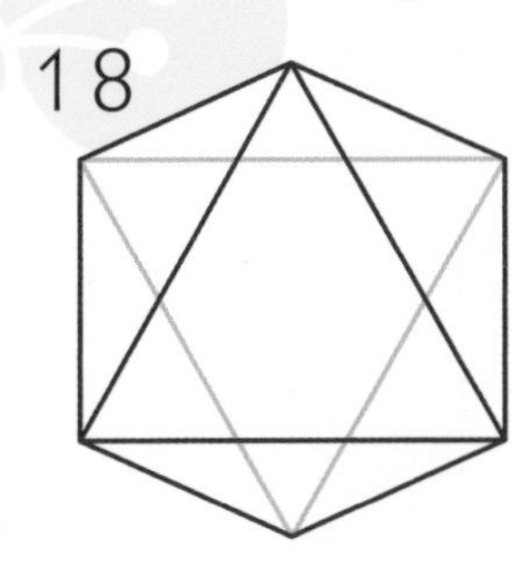

Octahedron.

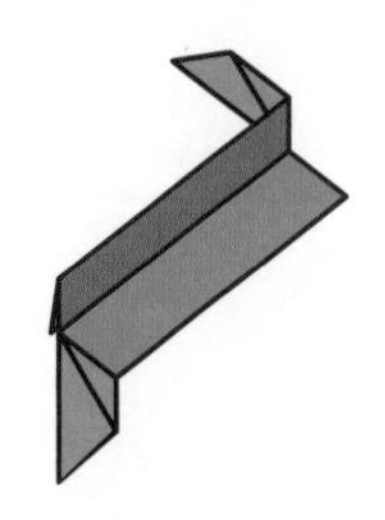

x 12

Use twelve units.

Completed octahedron.

WINGED SONOBE

MODEL: TRADITIONAL, JAPAN
DIAGRAM: MATTHEW GARDINER

This unit pays homage to a unit origami classic, the Sonobe unit by Mitsunobu Sonobe. The variation on this unit is that it has a "wing" with pockets. It can be assembled into the same range of configurations as the Sonobe unit. It's a great unit for experimenting and folding platonic solids.

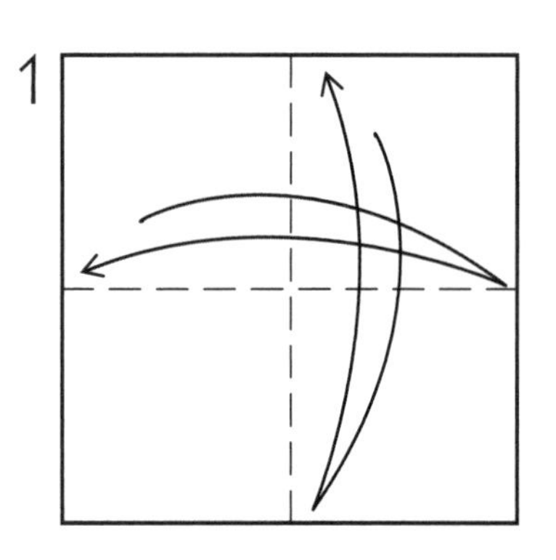

Begin white side up. Book fold and unfold.

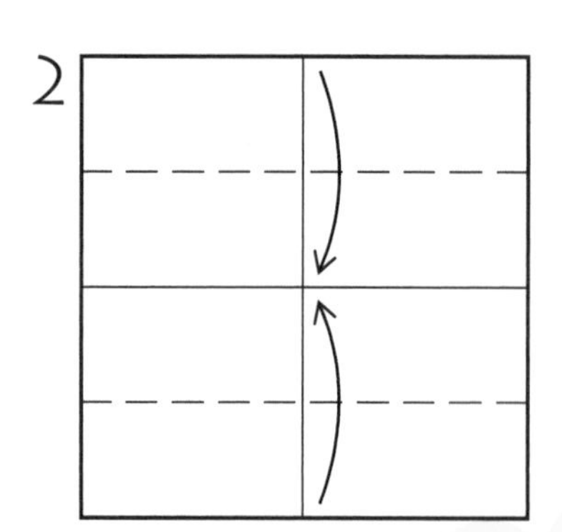

Cupboard fold.

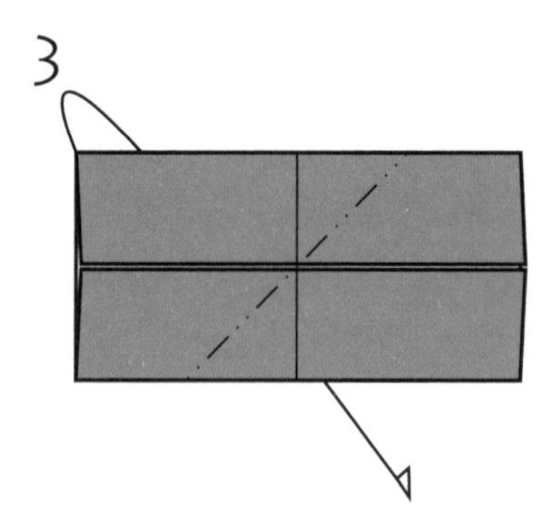

Mountain fold behind.

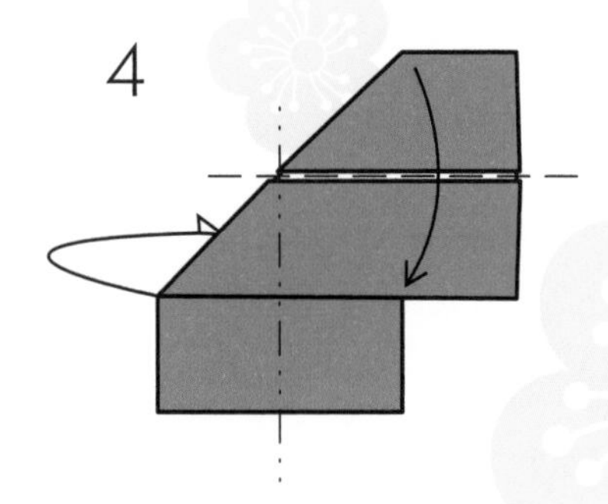

Fold flaps in half, valley fold on top, and mountain fold on the side.

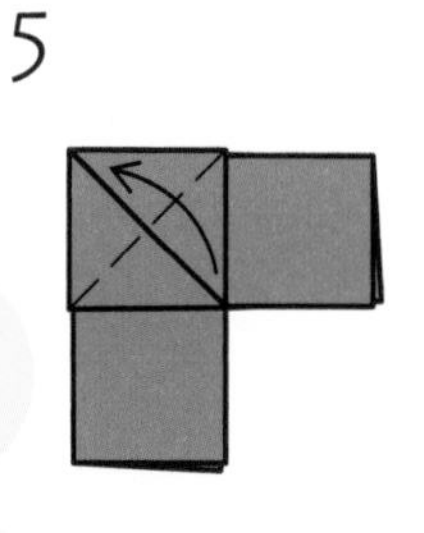

Valley fold through all layers except bottom layer.

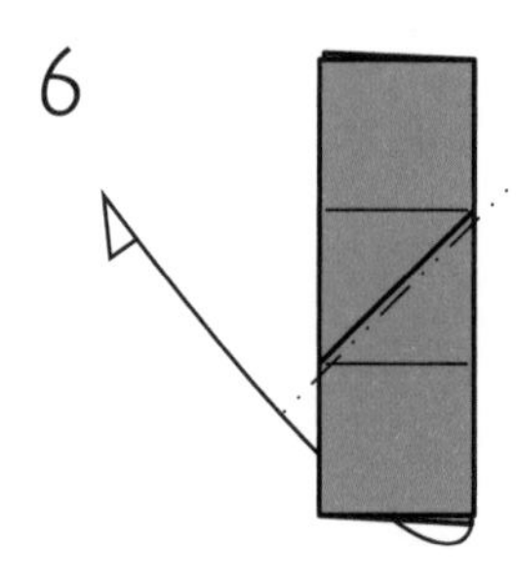

Mountain fold underneath the centre diagonal.

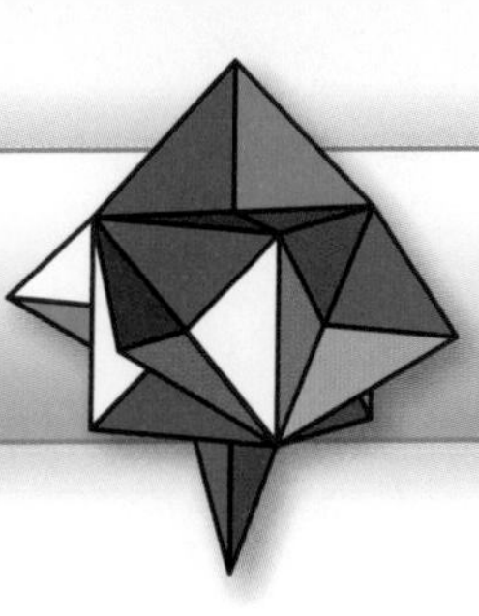

7

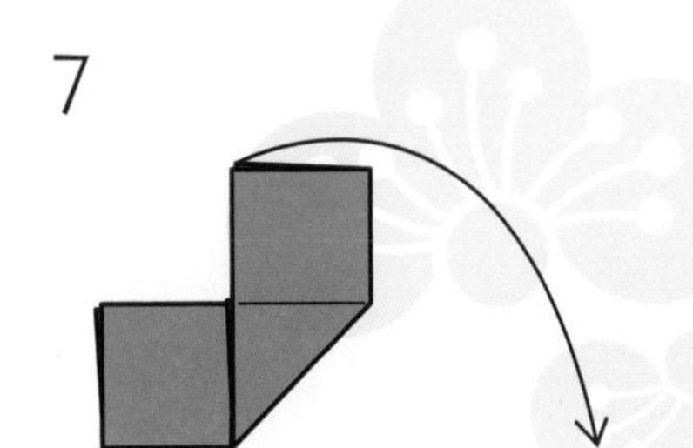

Fold the front flap down to turn it back into a strip.

8

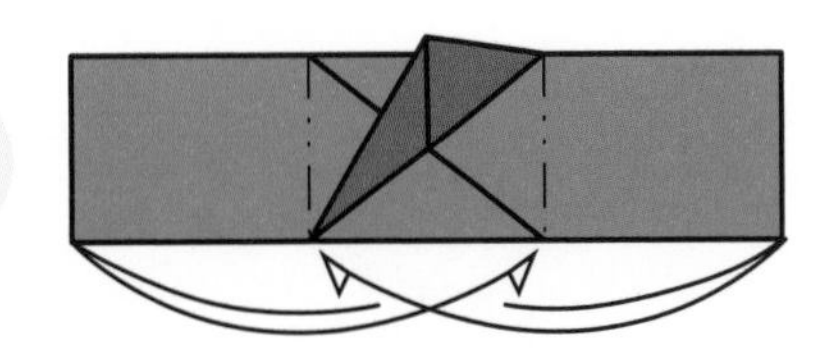

Mountain fold and unfold along the paper ridge on either side.

9

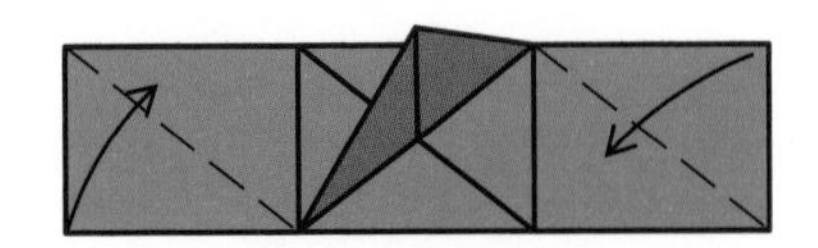

Fold the corners up to 90°.

10

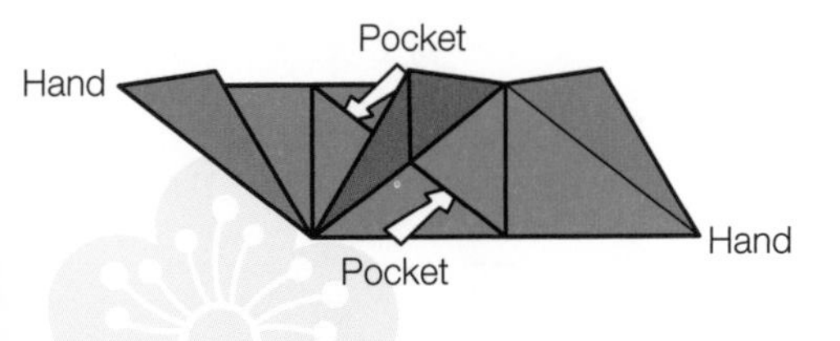

A completed unit. Note the hands and pockets on this unit.

11

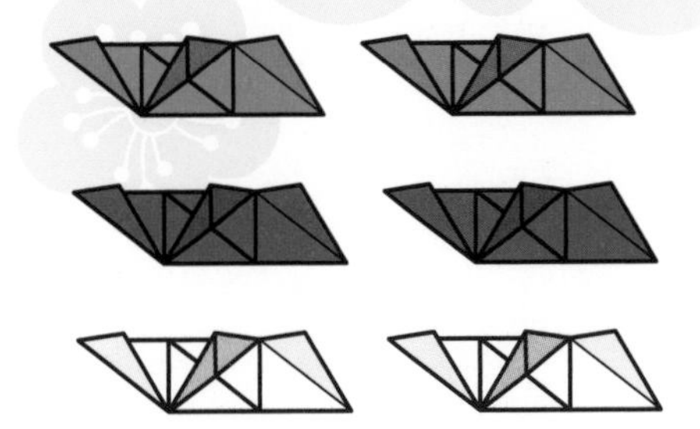

To make a cube, you need six units. Three colours look best – use two sheets of each colour.

12

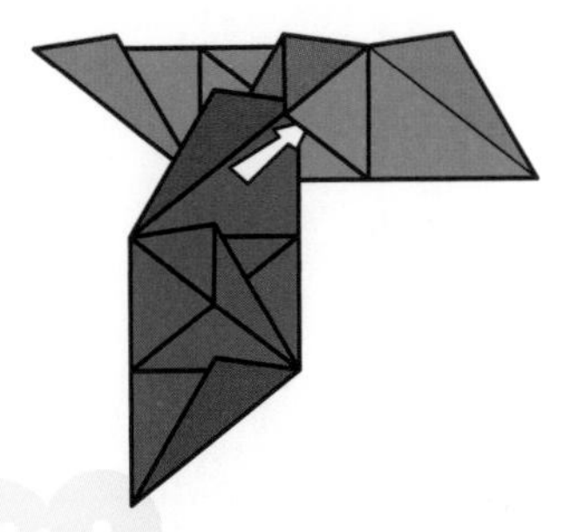

To assemble two units, insert the hand from one unit into the pocket of another.

13

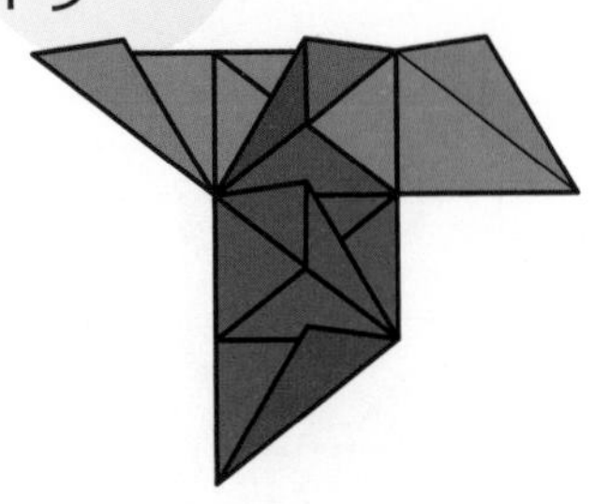

Two units assembled.

14

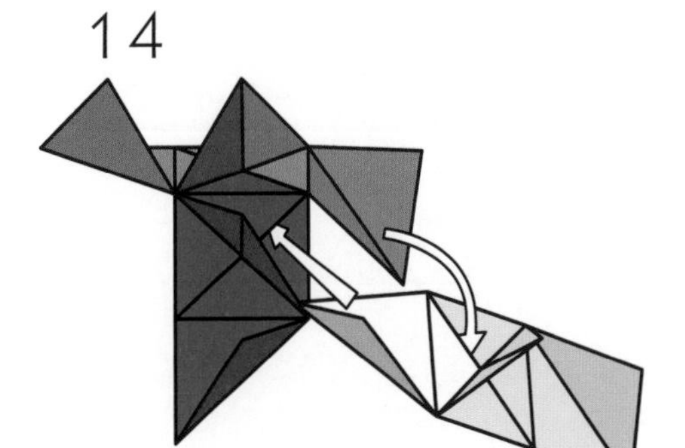

Insert the 3rd unit into the 2nd and the 1st into the 3rd to connect three units.

15

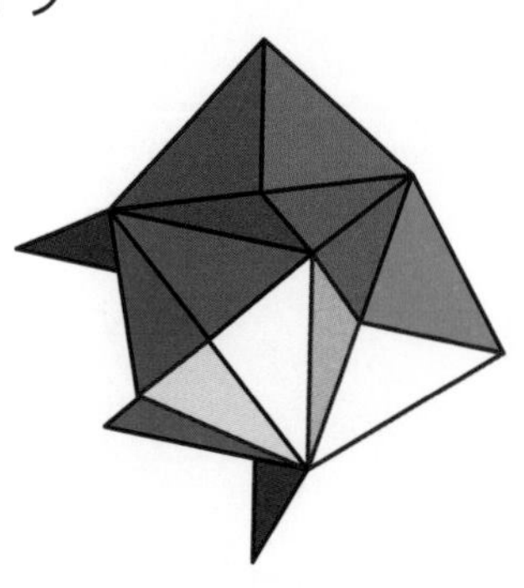

Three units connected – the joined point is the corner of a cube.

16

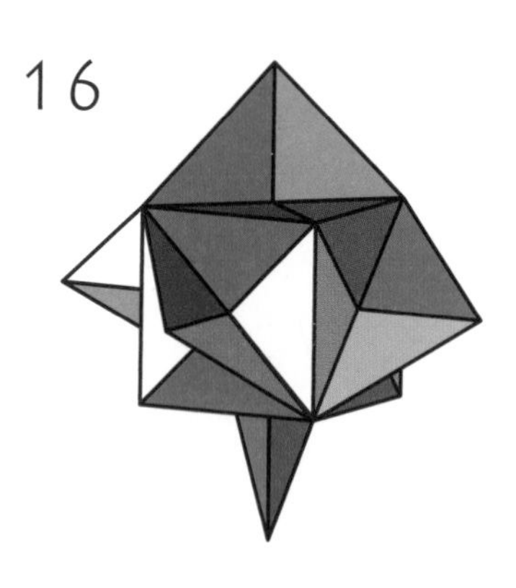

Add three more units in the same way to make a complete cube.

17

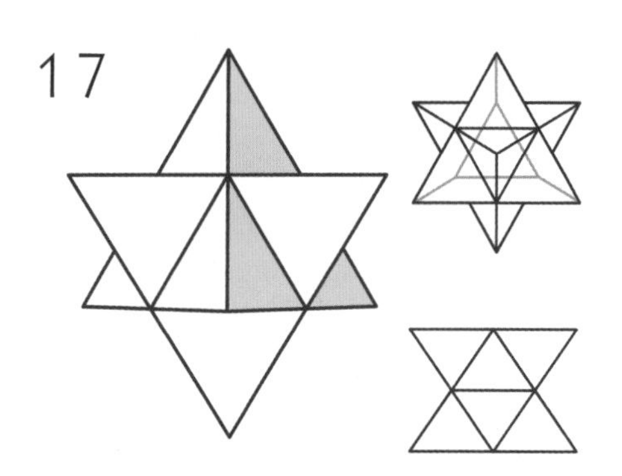

This shape is called a star tetrahedron. It's made from two tetrahedrons, one pointing up and one pointing down.

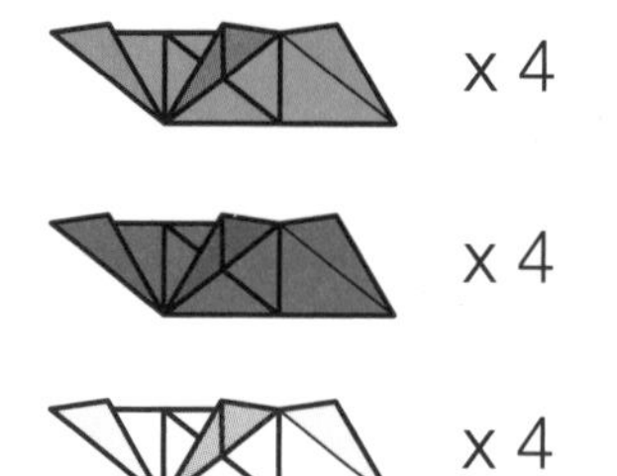

Use twelve units – three colours, four of each colour.

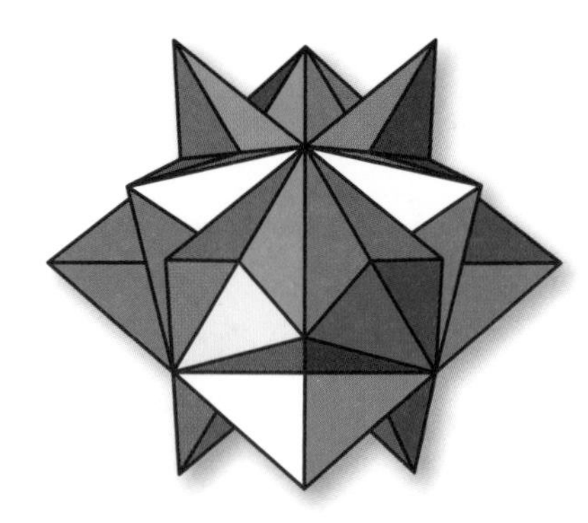

Twelve units!

18

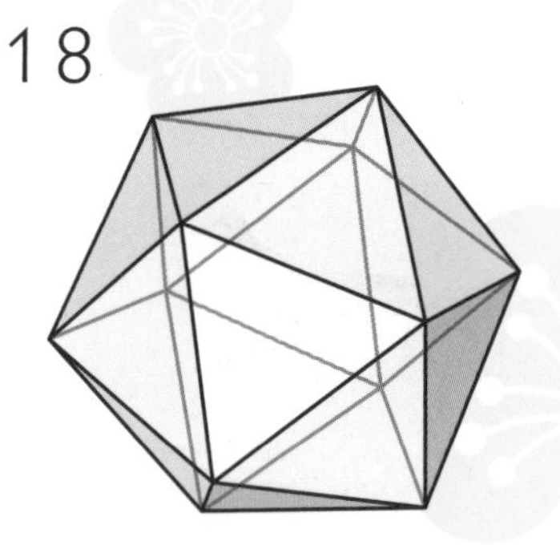

Using this icosahedron as a reference, start by assembling units around one of the pentagonal points.

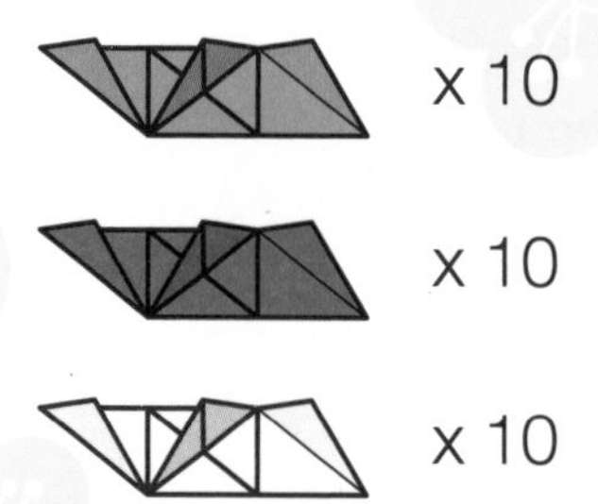

Use thirty units – three colours, ten of each colour. This takes patience.

Thirty units!